South Carolina Loyalists in the American Revolution

South Carolina in 1776
(adapted by R. S. Lambert from James Cook, 1773)

Note: Broken lines, combined with natural features (e.g. rivers) delineate boundaries of judicial districts.

South Carolina Loyalists in the American Revolution

Robert Stansbury Lambert

Second Edition

Copyright 2010 by Clemson University
ISBN 978-0-9842598-8-5

Published by Clemson University Clemson, South Carolina.

Editorial Assistants: Christina Cook, Ashley Dannelly, Steve Johnson, and Carrie Kolb

To order copies, please visit the Clemson University Press website: www.clemson.edu/press.

To Edythe and Anne

Contents

Preface	vii
Abbreviations and Acronyms	ix
Introduction: Provincial South Carolina	1

Part I: Revolution: The Isolation of the Loyalists, 1760–1780 ... 7
- 1. The Quarrel over American Rights ... 8
- 2. "The Troubles" Begin ... 22
- 3. Exile and Accommodation, 1776–1779 ... 41
- 4. The Road Back: *The Rebels at Bay*, 1779–1780 ... 55

Part II: Restoring British Authority: The Loyalist Response, 1780–1781 ... 65
- 5. Plans and Personnel ... 66
- 6. Pacifying the Interior ... 73
- 7. The "Second Revolution," Midsummer 1780 ... 89
- 8. Kings Mountain, October 1780 ... 99
- 9. Provincials, Militia, and Dragoons ... 107
- 10. Retreat from the Interior, 1781 ... 114

Part III: A War of All the People, 1780–1782 ... 131
- 11. Occupied Charlestown ... 132
- 12. Loyalists and Rebels: The Civil War ... 141
- 13. War of Attrition: Loyalist Military Action, 1782 ... 154
- 14. Displaced Persons and Pawns of War: Loyalist Refugees and Black Slaves, 1781–1782 ... 162

Part IV: The Loyalist Experience after the War ... 177
- 15. British Evacuation of South Carolina ... 178
- 16. Dispersal of the Loyalists ... 186
- 17. Retribution and Reconciliation: The Loyalists in Postwar South Carolina ... 205

Conclusion ... 220

BIBLIOGRAPHY	222
Essay on Methods and Sources	222
Other Sources Consulted	226
Manuscripts	226
Newspapers	228
Printed Primary Sources	228
Printed Secondary Sources	231
Dissertations	236
INDEX	237

List of Maps

South Carolina in 1776	Frontispiece
The World of Backcountry Loyalist Exiles, 1776–1780	47
Militia Organization: The Western Frontier	77
Militia Organization: The Northern Frontier	81

Preface

An interest in the Georgia loyalists, which I developed during a brief residence in that state, exposed me to the fact that, except for Robert W. Barnwell, "Loyalism in South Carolina, 1765–1785" (Ph.D. dissertation, Duke University, 1941), South Carolina's loyalists in the Revolution had not been studied in any comprehensive way. Although Barnwell's study showed a firm grasp of the principal groups and individuals in the province and state who dissented from the decision to seek independence, it had not been expanded to a monograph; meanwhile, much material, particularly from British sources, had become more readily accessible, and it seemed worthwhile to undertake such a study. After some preliminary investigation, my decision to begin gathering materials was made in 1963, and since then the research and writing has proceeded continuously, if sometimes at a snail's pace. An "Essay on Methods and Sources" follows the text.

Historians are fortunate to be able to work in libraries and archives served by dedicated and cooperative professionals, and I too have been helped immeasurably by them. Therefore, it is with feelings of gratitude that I express my appreciation to people who, although many now hold different positions or have retired, have been helpful to me over the years. Foremost among them are South Carolinians Wylma Wates, Archivist, Charles Lee, Director, and the staff of the South Carolina Department of Archives and History; E. L. Inabinet, former Director, and Mrs. Clara Mae Jacobs, former Manuscript Cataloguer of the South Caroliniana Library; Mrs. Mary B. Prior, Gene Waddell, and David Moltke-Hansen, successively directors of the South Carolina Historical Society; Mrs. Virginia Rugheimer of the Charleston Library Society; and colleagues George C. Rogers, Jr., David Chesnutt, and Robert Weir of the University of South Carolina; E. M. Lander, and the late Robert W. Henningson of Clemson University; and Thomas H. Pope of Newberry, Patricia Ali of Morris College, Sumter, and W. Bruce Ezell of Ninety Six. No less helpful were a number of people outside South Carolina, particularly directors J. Isaac Copeland and Caroline Daniel Wallace of the Southern Historical Collection, Chapel Hill, North Carolina; Director Mattie Russell, Manuscript Division, Perkins Library, and Professor Anne Firor Scott, Duke University; Howard Peckham, Director, and Bill Ewing of the Clements Library in Ann Arbor, Michigan; Robert W. Hill, Keeper of Manuscripts, New York Public Library; Edward T. Riley, then of the Institute of Early American History and Culture, Williamsburg, and the late Stephen Botein of the same institution; Mrs. Herbert Gambrell of the Dallas (Texas) Historical Society; and colleagues Robert A. East, Executive Director, Program for Loyalist Studies and Publications, City University of New York; Esmond Wright of the Institute of United States Studies, London; Wallace Brown and Jo-Anne Fellows of the University of New Brunswick (Canada); Clyde Ferguson, Kansas State University; Robert Davis, Jasper, Georgia; Heard Robertson, Augusta, Georgia; Geraldine Meroney, Agnes Scott College; Carole Watterson Troxler, Elon College; and J. Barton Starr, Troy State University at Fort Rucker, Alabama; and the staffs of the North Carolina Department of Archives and History; Manuscript Division, Library of Congress; State Historical Society of Wisconsin, Madison; Public Archives of Nova Scotia, Halifax; New Brunswick Museum, Saint John; and the Public Record Office, London. Comments and suggestions on the manuscript by Jerome J.

Nadelhaft of the University of Maine at Orono have been most helpful.

I am also grateful for financial support furnished by Clemson University in the form of travel money and two sabbatical leaves. A grant from the Southern Fellowships Fund in 1956 first exposed me to the question of loyalism in Georgia; another, from the American Association for State and Local History in 1963, permitted me to copy a large volume of original material so that I could continue the research when I was not free to do much traveling; and a bicentennial grant from the National Endowment for the Humanities in 1970–71, helped with support during that sabbatical year.

My interest in this period of American history was first stimulated at Chapel Hill by the late Hugh Talmadge Lefler and Albert Ray Newsome. Beyond gratitude is my debt to my wife, Edythe Rutherford Lambert, who has waited patiently for this project to reach a conclusion and who has helped with the research and reduced the number of rough spots in the manuscript.

Despite all the aid and consideration noted, I alone bear responsibility for errors of fact and interpretation that may appear in this study.

R. S. L
Clemson, SC
1987

The first edition of *South Carolina Loyalists in the American Revolution* was published shortly after I retired from Clemson University as Professor of History. The book received favorable reviews in professional journals; however, it has ceased to be in print.

Meanwhile the Clemson University Digital Press has become firmly established under the leadership of Professor Wayne K. Chapman. Because Southern readers and genealogical researchers continue to be fascinated with the Revolution in the South, it seems timely to offer a second edition of the *South Carolina Loyalists*. I am grateful to Professor Chapman and his staff for making this edition possible.

R. S. L.
Clemson, SC
2010

Abbreviations and Acronyms

AAS: American Antiquarian Society, Worcester, Massachusetts.

Accounts Audited: Accounts Audited of Revolutionary Claims Against South Carolina, SCAH.

AHR: American Historical Review

"Allaire Diary": "Diary of Lieut. Anthony Allaire of Ferguson's Corps," Lyman C. Draper, *King's Mountain and its Heroes* (New York, 1929 [orig. publ. n.p., 1891]), 484–515.

Barnwell, ed., "Exiles": Robert W. Barnwell, ed., "Reports on Loyalist Exiles from South Carolina, 1783" SCHA, *Proceedings (1937)*, 43–46..

BHP: British Headquarters (Carleton) Papers, Colonial Williamsburg, Inc., Williamsburg, Virginia.

Archibald Campbell, "Journal": "Journal of an Expedition Against the Rebels of Georgia in North America under Orders of Archibald Campbell, Esquire, Lieut. Col. of His Majesty's 71st Regiment 1778," typescript, Georgia State Library, Atlanta.

Canadian Claims: United Empire Loyalists. *Enquiry Into the Losses and Services in Consequence of Their Loyalty: Evidence in the Canadian Claims, Second Report* of the Ontario Bureau of Archives, *1904* (Toronto, 1905).

Census, 1790, S.C.:	*Heads of Families* at *the First Census of the United States Taken in the Year 1790: South Carolina* (Baltimore, Md., 1951 [orig. publ., Washington, D.C., 1908]).
CEP:	Confiscated Estates Papers, SCAH.
Chesney, "Journal":	"Journal of Alexander Chesney: A South Carolina Loyalist in the Revolution and After," ed. E. A. Jones. Ohio State University, *Bulletin* 26 (1921): 1–149.
CL:	William L. Clements Library, Ann Arbor, Michigan
Clark, ed., *Loyalists*:	Murtie June Clark, ed., *Loyalists in the Southern Campaign* of *the Revolutionary War,* 3 vols. (Baltimore, Md., 1981)
Clinton, *American Rebellion*:	*The American Rebellion: Sir Henry Clinton's Narrative of His Campaigns, 1775–1782,* ed. William B. Willcox (New Haven, Conn., 1954)
Clinton Papers:	Sir Henry Clinton Papers, CL
C.O.:	Colonial Office Papers, P.R.O.
Colls.:	Collections
"Colonel Jarvis, Loyalist":	"Colonel [Stephen] Jarvis, Loyalist: A Voice from 1776," ed. Hinton Jarvis, typescript, DUL
Conference Committee Minutes, 1784:	Rough Minutes Taken by the Committee Confiscation, &c., 1784, CEP, SCAH.
Continental Congress Papers, #51:	Papers of the Continental Congress: #51–Intercepted Letters, 1775–81, microfilm edition, LC.

Council Journal:	Journal of His Majesty's Honorable Council, 1664–1774, SCAH.
CP:	Papers of Charles, First Marquis Cornwallis, 30/11, P.R.O.
CUL:	Special Collections, Clemson University Library, Clemson, S.C.
Deeds:	Charleston County, South Carolina, Deeds, 1760–1784, SCAH.
DNB:	*Dictionary of National Biography.*
Draper Coll.:	Lyman C. Draper Collection, SHSW
Drayton, *Memoirs*:	John Drayton, *Memoirs of the American Revolution as Relating to the State of South Carolina* (Columbia, S.C., 1969 [orig. publ. Charleston, S.C., 1821]).
DUL:	Manuscripts Department, Perkins Library, Duke University, Durham, N.C.
Egerton, ed., *Royal Commission*:	H. E. Egerton, ed., *The Royal Commission on the Losses and Services of American Loyalists, 1783–1785: Being the Notes of Mr. Daniel Parker Coke, M.P., One of the Commissioners during the Period* (New York, 1971 [orig. publ. New York, 1915])
English Records:	English Records, Colonial Office Papers, 1682–1782, NCAH
Fanning, "Narrative":	"Narrative of Colo. David Fanning, Written by Himself Detailing Astonishing Events in No[rth] Ca[rolina], from 1775 to 1783," Walter L. Clark, et al., eds., *The State Records of North Carolina*, 26 vols. (Raleigh, N.C., 1886–1907), XXII, 180–239.

Fletchall, "Address":	Colonel Fletchall, et al., "Address to the King, Apr. 19, 1782," C.O. 5/82, P.R.O. KTO, Indian Affairs, Reel 10, 593–600 (microfilm)
GHQ:	Georgia Historical Quarterly
Gibbes, *Documentary History*:	Robert W. Gibbes, ed., *Documentary History of the American Revolution*, 3 vols. (Spartanburg, S.C., 1972 [orig. publ., New York, 1853–57]).
Gray, "Observations":	Colonel Robert Gray, "Observations of the Revolutionary War in North and South Carolina, and the Treatment of the Loyalists [1782]," Chalmers Collection–South Carolina, II, 151–73, NYPL.
Greene Papers:	Nathanael Greene Papers, CL, DUL, LC (microfilm), SCL
H.M.C., *Report*:	Great Britain, Historical Manuscripts Commission, *Report on American Manuscripts in the Royal Institution*, 4 vols. (London, 1904–9).

House Journal(s) *1776–1780* 1782 1783–1784 1785–1786 1787–1788 *1789–1790*:	*Journals of the General Assembly and House of Representatives, 1776–1780,* ed. W.E. Hemphill, W.A. Wares, and R.N. Olsberg (Columbia, S.C., 1970). *The Journal of the House of Representatives of South Carolina, January 8, 1782–February 26, 1782,* ed. A.S. Salley, Jr. (Columbia, S.C., 1916). *Journals of the House of Representatives* [of S.C.], *1783–1784,* ed. Theodora Thompson (Columbia, S.C., 1977). *Journals of the House of Representatives* [of S.C.], *1785–1786,* ed. Lark E. Adams (Columbia, S.C., 1979). *Journals of the House of Representatives* [of S.C.], *1787–1788,* ed. Michael E. Stevens (Columbia, S.C., 1981). *Journals of the House of Representatives* [of S.C.], *1789–1790,* ed. Michael E. Stevens (Columbia, S.C., 1984).
JAH:	Journal of American History.
JCHA:	Journals of the Commons House of Assembly, 1765–75, SCAH
Johnson, *Traditions and Reminiscences*:	Joseph Johnson, *Traditions and Reminiscences Chiefly of the American Revolution in the South* (Charleston, S.C., 1851).
Eldon Jones, "British Withdrawal":	Eldon Jones, "The British Withdrawal from the South, 1781–1785," *The Revolutionary War in the South,* ed. W. Robert Higgins (Durham, N.C., 1979, 259–85)
JSH:	Journal of Southern History
KTO:	Kraus-Thompson Organization
Laurens Papers (microfilm):	Papers of Henry Laurens (microfilm), SCL

LC:	Library of Congress, Washington, D.C
Lee, *Memoirs*:	Henry Lee, *Memoirs of the War in the Southern Department of the United States* (1812).
Leslie Letterbooks:	Alexander Leslie Letterbooks, Emmet Collection, NYPL.
LMR: .	Loyalist Muster Rolls, Military Papers, Series C, PAC (microfilm, LC)
Lockey, *East Florida*:	Joseph Byrne Lockey, *East Florida, 1783–1785: A File of Documents Assembled and Many of Them Translated by Joseph Byrne Lockey*, ed. John W. Caughey (Berkeley, Calif., 1949).
Loyalist Claims:	Great Britain, Audit Office 13, P.R.O., microfilm.
Loyalist Transcripts:	Transcripts of the Manuscript Books and Papers of the Commission of Enquiry into the Losses and Services of the American Loyalists Held under Acts of Parliament of 23, 25, 26, 28, and 29 of George III, NYPL.
McCrady, *S. C. in the Revolution, 1775–1780*:	Edward McCrady, *The History of South Carolina in the Revolution, 1775–1780* (New York, 1901)
MVHR:	Mississippi Valley Historical Review.
NBM:	New Brunswick Museum, Saint John
NCAH:	North Carolina Department of Archives and History, Raleigh.
NCHR:	North Carolina Historical Review.

NYPL:	Manuscripts Division, New York Public Library, New York City
O'Neall, "Random Recollections":	John Belton O'Neall, "Random Recollections of Revolutionary Characters and Events," *Southern Literary Journal and Monthly Magazine,* New Ser., IV, 40–47.
PAC:	Public Archives of Canada, Ottawa, Ontario.
PANS:	Public Archives of Nova Scoria, Halifax.
Plats:	Recorded Colonial Plats, 1731–75, SCAH.
Privy Council Journals 1783–1789:	Adele Stanton Edwards, ed., *Journals of the Privy Council* [of S.C.], *1783–1789* (Columbia, S.C. 1971).
P.R.O.:	Public Record Office, London.
Refugees to East Florida:	Refugees to East Florida from Carolina, C.O.5/560/816, P.R.O. (microfilm, LC).
Rogers, ed., *Laurens Papers:*	George C. Rogers, Jr., et al., eds., *The Papers of Henry Laurens,* 9 vols. to date (Columbia, S.C., 1968–)
SCAH:	South Carolina Department of Archives and History, Columbia.
SCHGM:	South Carolina Historical and Genealogical Magazine
SCHM:	*South Carolina Historical Magazine* (succeeds *SCHGM).*
SCHS:	South Carolina Historical Society, Charleston.

SCL:	South Caroliniana Library, University of South Carolina, Columbia
S.C. Records in the P.R.O.:	Records in the British Public Record Office relating to South Carolina, Sainsbury Transcripts, SCAH.
Senate Journal, 1782:	*Journal of the Senate of South Carolina, January 8, 1782–February 26, 1782*, ed. A. S. Salley, Jr. (Columbia, S.C., 1941)
SHSW:	State Historical Society of Wisconsin, Madison.
Siebert, *Loyalists in E Fla.*:	Wilbur Henry Siebert, *Loyalists in East Florida, 1774–1785* (Boston, 1972 [orig. publ. DeLand, Fla., 1929]).
Simms Coll.:	Simms Collection of Henry Laurens Papers, SCL
Spanish Census, 1784:	Spanish Census of British Subjects, 1784. East Florida Papers, LC (copy St. Augustine Historical Society).
Statutes at Large:	Thomas Cooper and David J. McCord, *Statutes at Large of South Carolina*, 10 vols. (Columbia, S.C., 1836–41).
"Sumter-Greene Correspondence":	"Official Correspondence between Brigadier General Thomas Sumter and Major General Nathanael Greene, 1780–1783," City of Charleston, *Yearbook, 1899* (Charleston, S.C., 1899), Appendix.
T50/1:	Treasury 50/1, Miscellaneous, P.R.O.
Ward, *War of the Revolution*:	Christopher Ward, *War of the Revolution*, ed. John R. Alden. 2 vols. (New York, 1952).

Wells, *Journal*:	Louisa Susannah Wells, *The Journal of a Voyage from Charlestown to London* (New York, 1968 [orig. publ. New York, 1906])
Wills:	Charleston County, S.C., Wills, 1783–1868, SCAH.
WMQ:	The William and Mary Quarterly
WPA Transcripts:	Works Progress Administration, Historical Records Survey, Transcripts of County Records, SCAH.

Introduction

Provincial South Carolina

At present there are computed to be 3000 waggons come to Charlestown in a year, loaded with deer skins, indigo, flour, bisket, hemp & tobacco, which calculation is not far from the truth, as precise accounts are taken of the number which pass over ferries.

—William Bull, June 1770

To begin the story of the South Carolina loyalists in the American Revolution—the individuals and families who served with or gave aid and comfort to the British during that conflict—it is necessary to go back to a time four decades before the outbreak of hostilities, a time when the first serious effort was made to encourage settlement beyond the coastal parishes where the original settlers and their descendants lived. In the 1730s ten townships were created in an arc 100 miles more or less from the colonial capital at Charlestown ("The "Charleston" spelling was officially adopted in 1783, at the time of incorporation. Prior to then, both "Charles-Town" and "Charlestown" were used.); and the provincial government offered bounty lands to immigrants who would settle them. Partly designed to provide a ring of settlements to protect the valuable rice-producing areas from Indian attack, the townships were also intended to increase the immigration of European Protestants to take up land in order to compensate for the heavy importation of African and West Indian blacks, an influx that had brought great prosperity to the rice planters of the tidewater but had increased fears of slave insurrection.[1]

Among the more permanent settlements established under this plan were three to which several hundred Germans and German Swiss migrated: Amelia on the south side of the lower Congaree River; Orangeburg near a sharp bend in the north fork of the Edisto River; and Saxe-Gotha just south of the junction formed by the Saluda and Congaree rivers. Among the first settlers of Orangeburg was a Lutheran clergyman whose nephew, John Giessendanner, succeeded him in that work and later took holy orders in the Church of England; there were others with German names like Linder and Rumph, but people of English origins like the Salleys also moved in during the same period. The pressure of the hundreds of other Germans and Swiss who followed the first immigrants to the area caused a movement from Saxe-Gotha across the Saluda River into the fork between that stream and the Broad River, an area that became known as the Dutch Fork.[2]

By the 1750s Moses Kirkland and Andrew Williamson, two ambitious men who were natives of America, and other settlers had begun to take up lands well beyond the original townships. Naturally acquisitive and hard-driving, Kirkland was not above selling rum to the Indians and dealing in fraudulent land warrants; he soon accumulated numerous tracts of land in the interior, built a sawmill, and ran a ferry on the lower Saluda until he had accumulated the labor of enough slaves to develop a large tract on a tributary of Stevens Creek, a branch of the Savannah. He also secured commissions as an officer in the provincial militia and as a justice of the peace. Apparently a native of South Carolina, Williamson first appeared as a cattle and hog driver for the militia posts near the Savannah and worked for a large landholder before settling at Whitehall, his plantation on Hard Labour Creek, where he raised cattle and grain. North of the Congaree, settlers began to move into the valley of the Wateree River, among them the family of the Irish Quaker, Joshua English, who settled at Pinetree Hill early in the 1750s and developed a prosperous farm tilled by slave labor. By 1760 Charlestown merchants had established a store at Pinetree Hill, later known as Camden, and engaged Joseph Kershaw to look after their interests at that place.[3]

By 1760 the townships and their environs, sometimes called the middle country, lay in an arc from the Waccamaw River on the east across the Pee Dee, Black, Wateree, and Congaree rivers to the Savannah on the west and contained a free population estimated at 9,000 souls. These settlers were all Protestants from a variety of ethnic backgrounds—the Germans, the German Swiss, and the Irish Quakers already noted, as well as transplanted Pennsylvanians of Welsh and English descent and their black slaves along the Pee Dee River. Beyond the townships lay the backcountry consisting, at the time, of settlements on Stevens and Long Cane creeks, tributaries of the Savannah; the Saluda River; the Broad River and the Enoree and Tyger rivers that flowed into it from the west; and the Waxhaw area, the region on the Catawba River then considered to be a part of North Carolina. In contrast to the settlers of the middle country, the 7,000 people of the backcountry were likely to be transplanted Americans, who came either from the older parts of South Carolina or from the northern colonies, particularly from Pennsylvania and Virginia by way of the Great Valley. The people of this last group were usually descended from the Scotch-Irish, the lowland Scots Presbyterians transplanted to northern Ireland by the British government in the seventeenth century as a part of its effort to convert the island's population to Protestantism.[4]

The development of the backcountry was interrupted in 1759 by the Cherokee War, a bitter struggle that began with tribal raids on isolated settlers who had moved beyond what the Indians understood to be the treaty boundaries of the colony. With the aid of British regulars the colony was eventually able to destroy the ability of the Cherokees to continue the fight, and agreement was obtained on a new boundary known to contemporaries as the Indian Line. Although the colony brought the war to a successful conclusion, the Indians drove some backcountry families from their homes and destroyed much property, temporarily delaying the further economic development of the area. By 1763, however, recovery was under way in preparation for the fresh wave of settlement that would sweep over the backcountry in the next decade.[5]

While the interior of South Carolina had barely reached the threshold of its potential development, the lowcountry of the province had evolved over nearly a century into a fairly stable society that had prospered from the export of staples produced by slave labor. The first settlers were whites from England and whites and blacks from the island of Barbados; they were followed by more English and by Huguenots who had fled from religious persecution in France. The development of rice as a great staple and of naval stores and indigo as lesser export commodities had provided the foundation for a society dominated by wealthy planters, the merchants who marketed these crops, and a small but increasingly important group of professional men, particularly lawyers, who handled their business and legal affairs.[6]

The hub of all this activity was Charlestown, the largest port on the south Atlantic coast of British America. The first settlers had relied on the town to handle their crops and to secure the imported goods they needed; as population spread, the coastal rivers and protected passages through the sea islands drew more produce to its wharves and enlarged its influence as the depot through which the trade of the province passed. Visited by over "three hundred top sail vessels" annually in the 1750s, Charlestown was a bustling place, and the seat of government and center of the cultural life in the province as well.[7]

The city's male population consisted of its prosperous merchants; a small but growing number of professional men; a larger group of shopkeepers, tradesmen, and artisans, and their apprentices and journeymen; and a floating population of sailors in port, Indian traders and tribesmen, and immigrants arranging the means to reach their lands in the interior. Half the people of the town were black, largely slaves, who worked for the merchants and shopkeepers or were hired out by their owners as porters and stevedores; others were fishermen and boatmen, while yet others, working on the side, provided the town with much of its garden produce. We know little of the bondsmen as individuals, but a few free blacks occasionally appear in the records of the time.[8]

The great expansion of Charlestown's export trade and the movement of population into the interior of the province offered new opportunities for the city's free population. Although the larger merchants were most important in the political and economic life of the city, there was room for young men of talent and ambition to become influential in their own right. An apprenticeship to a leading merchant could be the basis for a career in commerce, but there were other paths to positions of wealth and status. Robert Wells arrived from Scotland in the early 1750s and established himself as a bookseller and stationer; later in the decade he entered the printing business and began to publish books and tracts as well as the province's second newspaper, the *South Carolina and American General Gazette*. His wife's brother, Robert Rowand, followed in 1756 to settle as a merchant in the port. The law was an important profession in such a community, and after coming out from England in 1742, Robert Williams soon established himself as one of the leading attorneys in the city. The need for more facilities to build and repair ships grew with the expanding business of the port; following his training in a royal dockyard in Britain, John Rose, another Scot, migrated to Carolina in 1750 and soon prospered from his work on public vessels as well as through private contracts. And Rawlins Lowndes, an orphan who attracted the patronage of the provost marshal of the province, ultimately succeeded to that position and was able to turn the income from and prestige of the appointment into the foundation for a career in public service.[9]

The city's importance in the province and the empire was to a substantial extent due to the wealth generated in the lowcountry parishes where the staples were produced. A combination of hard work and luck enabled some of the early settlers to realize good returns from exploiting the fertile lands and the labor of a few slaves; then they put the profits into more land and labor and became planters. By the 1730s the demand for slaves had grown to such proportions that people of European origins made up a bare third of the total population, and in some coastal parishes it seemed, as Peter Wood has noted, "more like a Negro country." The planters built country houses befitting their status as gentry, but also devoted part of their wealth to maintaining houses in town to which their families repaired for the social season. There they conducted their business with the city's mercantile community and there many of them served in the Commons House of Assembly, the elective branch of the provincial legislature. By the 1750s the heads of some very wealthy planter families had taken up residence in England and had become absentee property owners in Carolina; other planters stayed on the scene but sought to give their sons the advantages of an education in England and Scotland, particularly as preparation for careers in law or medicine.[10]

While Charlestown remained the center of business and social activities for most lowcountry planters, two smaller port towns drew a substantial part of the trade of the areas around them. To the north, Georgetown had been established as a port in the 1730s; situated near the mouths of the Black, Pee Dee, and Waccamaw rivers, it became a depot for the rice and indigo crops of the region and for supplying the planters with imported goods. To the south on Port Royal Island, near the site of early efforts at settlement by the French and the Spanish, the town of Beaufort served the plantations in the southern corner of the province.[11]

It is not too early in our story to point out that during the American Revolution that lay ahead most South Carolina lowcountry planter families would provide at least a measure of support for the rebel cause. Nevertheless, whether because of conviction or the pressures of the war, particularly during the British occupation, some would give aid to the British. Conspicuous among the latter were several members of rice planting families north of Charlestown near the Santee River, like the Balls of St. James Santee Parish and the Gaillards of St. Stephen's; the consistently loyal Ashley River planter William Wragg; and the well-established Deveaux family, which took a leading roll for the British in the Beaufort area. The most active loyalist in the Georgetown region would be James Cassells, a Scot who came to the colony in 1758 and soon established himself as an indigo planter on the Waccamaw.[12]

By the time of the Cherokee War a unique society had developed in the South Carolina lowcountry, a society that produced a great deal of wealth but rested to a large degree on the labor of a mass of black slaves. The slaves are largely unknown to us, but a good deal has been written about the free white society for which they provided the foundation. The returns from rice and indigo planting enabled the large slaveholders to assume positions at the very top of the social, political, and economic ladder in the province. In turn, the rapid increase in the production of staples enlarged the number of merchants who earned handsome profits from marketing the planters' crops in England and southern Europe, and from importing manufactured and luxury goods demanded by the planters. Other merchants devoted their attention to the new markets that the increasing population of the interior opened to them in exchange for "country produce." The merchants and the small but growing number of professional men formed a second rung on the ladder. But the quick way to wealth and status seemed to be through planting, and members of the mercantile and professional community employed their income and influence to establish plantations in the lowcountry and to speculate in lands in the interior.[13]

Thus by 1760 there was in South Carolina an elite made up of the families of the planters and those who served them, an elite often headed by self-made men whose success was due in part to fortunate marriages into some of the earlier gentry families. Once established, the families of the elite tended to intermarry, further fastening the lines of class and status; but the elite was open to talented and ambitious young men, particularly if they caught the eye of the fathers of marriageable daughters.[14]

The gentry class also had come to dominate the local political process through its control of the Commons House of Assembly, the popular branch of the provincial legislature, a feat it accomplished by its close scrutiny of public finance. First, the Commons House gradually asserted its right to initiate tax measures, reducing the role of its sister house, the appointive Royal Council, to one of assenting to revenue proposals; more important, the Commons House established firm control over public expenditures by minutely examining accounts presented by public officials and individual citizens. Sporadically, the Royal Council attempted to defend its deteriorating position, but its prerogatives were steadily eroded. In this struggle, the royal governors could do little to help the council, with whom they tended to sympathize, because of the need to cajole appropriations from the Commons House to maintain coast defenses and protect the interior settlements against the possibility of Indian arrack. The declining influence of the Royal Council was accelerated in the 1750s as its membership was transformed from that of a group of locally prominent individuals to one dominated by "placemen," British citizens chosen by the Crown to extend its patronage in the empire. Unwittingly, British officials further damaged the local prestige of the council in 1756 by removing William Wragg, one of its most respected members, because of a quarrel with Governor Henry Lyttleton. Wragg's independent spirit will be evident again in the 1770s when he refuses to accede to rebel pressure to join in the struggle against England. In the Lyttleton controversy, however, he stood for local rights, after which the Royal Council became virtually the preserve of place men.[15]

Wragg's stand in the controversy with the royal governor illustrates the growing pride and sense of accomplishment that the South Carolina gentry felt in having transformed a wilderness into a wealthy society in less than a century. As Robert Weir has shown, their views were based on certain assumptions about human affairs that came from their familiarity with the "country ideology" developed during the eighteenth century by writers in the dissenting tradition of English political thought. As understood by the gentry, human beings were assumed to be easy prey to corruption and government influence, against which "liberty," defined as the freedom of the individual to pursue one's own destiny without interference from the state, was the only bulwark. To prevent the state from encroaching on individual freedom, it was essential that the components of government be held in balance—between legislative and executive authority as represented by Parliament and the monarchy, and within Parliament, between Commons and Lords, representing popular rule and aristocracy. The ideas derived from the "country ideology" had wide currency in colonial America in these years but, to South Carolinians, their chattel slaves were an ever present reminder of the depths to which human beings could fall if liberty were lost. In low country Carolina, where the way to success was through the accumulation of land and slaves, the best guarantee that the rights of the individual would be protected lay in controlling the Commons House.[16]

These ideas apparently were not shared by people in the interior of the province who, except in a few instances, we re not represented in the legislature and had the problems of a developing rather than a mature society.

Notes

1. Robert Lee Meriwether, *The Expansion of South Carolina, 1729–1765* (Kingsport, Tenn., 1940) 19–109.
2. Alexander S. Salley, Jr., *The History of Orangeburg County, South Carolina from Its First Settlement to the Close of the Revolutionary War* (Orangeburg, S.C., 1898), 18–90.
3. Loyalist Transcripts, LVII, 318–50; Richard Maxwell Brown, *The South Carolina Regulators* (Cambridge, Mass., 1963), 128–30; Meriwether, *Expansion of South Carolina,* 127, 106.
4. Meriwether, *Expansion of South Carolina,* 112–60.
5. Ibid., 213–40.
6. For the development of the economic base of the colony, see Converse D. Clowse, *Economic Beginnings in Colonial South Carolina, 1670–1730* (Columbia, S.C., 1971), particularly 95–138, and Clarence L. Ver Steeg, *Origins of a Southern Mosaic* (Athens, Ga., 1975), 103–32; for a view of the colony's social patterns, see M. Eugene Sirmans, *Colonial South Carolina: A Political History, 1663–1763* (Chapel Hill, N.C., 1966), 225–31.
7. George C. Rogers, Jr., *Charleston in the Age of the Pinckneys* (Norman, Okla., 1969), 3–25.
8. Richard Walsh, *Charleston's Sons of Liberty: A Study of the Artisans, 1763–1789* (Columbia, S.C., 1959), 3–25; Peter Wood, *Black Majority: Negroes in Colonial South Carolina from 1670 through the Stono Rebellion* (New York, 1974), 131–66; Loyalist Transcripts, LIII, 166–71.
9. For Robert Wells, see Wells, *Journal,* 97, and Loyalist Transcripts, LVI, 534; for the early careers of Rowand, Williams, and Rose, respectively, see Loyalist Transcripts, LIV, 297–316, 29–84, and LIII, 272–306; and for Lowndes, see Carl J. Vipperman, *The Rise of Rawlins Lowndes, 1721–1800* (Columbia, S.C., 1978), 31–58.
10. Wood, *Black Majority,* 208–36; Sirmans, *Colonial South Carolina* 226–33, 239–48.
11. George C. Rogers, Jr., *The History of Georgetown County, South Carolina* (Columbia, S.C., 1970), 30–54.
12. CEP; Loyalist Transcripts, LV, 72–86, 107–21
13. Sirmans, *Colonial South Carolina,* 226–33, 239–48.
14. Rogers, *Charleston,* 23–25
15. Jack P. Greene, *Quest for Power: The Lower Houses of Assembly in the Southern Royal Colonies, 1689–1776* (Chapel Hill, N.C., 1963), 53–67, 82–84, 85–86; Sirmans, *Colonial South Carolina* , 223–24, 247–50; M. Eugene Sirmans, "The South Carolina Royal Council, 1720–1762," *WMQ,* 3d Ser., XVIII (1961), 373–92.
16. Robert M. Weir, "'The Harmony We Are Famous For': An Interpretation of Pre-Revolutionary South Carolina Politics," *WMQ,* 3d Ser., XXVI *(1969),* 473–501, and *"A Most Important Epocha ": The Coming of the Revolution in South Carolina* (Columbia, S.C., 1970), 6.

Part I

REVOLUTION: THE ISOLATION OF THE LOYALISTS, 1760–1780

During the period after the Cherokee War, the South Carolina low-country continued to prosper and even to expand its wealth, but leaders from the region encountered problems in their colony's relations with the home government. Some problems were similar to those faced by other colonies at the time—Parliamentary taxation for imperial defense, and vigorous enforcement of hitherto neglected trade regulations—whereas others arose from circumstances unique to this province. Although the opposition to British measures centered in the Commons House of Assembly, American rights leaders increasingly resorted to extralegal methods and organizations to thwart efforts of royal officials to carry out the new program. Meanwhile, a flood of immigrants from other colonies and abroad poured into the backcountry; there some of the earlier and more prosperous settlers felt themselves neglected by provincial authorities and, in their efforts to suppress the activities of outlaw gangs who preyed on isolated settlements, brought the region to the edge of civil war.

As relations with the home government deteriorated, American rights leaders succeeded in isolating royal officials and their supporters, creating a Provincial Congress and a Council of Safety that became the effective government of the province. When they sought to secure allies for their cause in the backcountry, however, they discovered that many settlers were hostile toward or disinterested in any movement that suggested independence. When persuasion failed, the Council of Safety turned to force, sending an expedition into the backcountry that seized many leaders of the opposition and scattered most of their followers. A successful defense of the approaches to Charlestown against a British fleet and the crushing of the Cherokees in the summer of 1776 meant that for South Carolina the independence proclaimed in Philadelphia was an accomplished fact.

The new state government established itself firmly and adopted loyalty measures to force royal officials and their followers to support the new regime or leave the state. Many acquiesced, while others left for Britain or fled to the neighboring Floridas. East Florida became a refuge for loyalists from the South Carolina backcountry, and a base for harassing the rebel regimes in the southern states. Meanwhile, the entrance of France into the war forced British authorities to adopt a new strategy for prosecuting the war, that is, to concentrate on the southern provinces where the numerous loyalists awaited the necessary encouragement to recover them from the rebels.

When the new strategy was applied in 1779, British forces succeeded in recovering Georgia for the Crown and raiding to the very gates of Charlestown. In the following winter a major British expedition from New York landed on the South Carolina coast and in May forced Charlestown and its large garrison to surrender, leaving the way open for the recovery of the entire province.

Chapter One

The Quarrel over American Civil Rights

When we are censured by the Public for not inserting notices of a public nature, till they have first appeared in the General Gazette published by Mr. Robert Wells, from Glasgo,...the censure falls on us unjustly, it is not to be imputed to any negligence on our part, but to a certain influence...

—*South Carolina Gazette, April 1774*

It is well known that the period from the end of the Cherokee War until royal authority was expelled in 1775 was one of political turmoil throughout much of South Carolina. What is less readily apparent is that, despite the unrest, Charlestown and the plantation country experienced a return of economic prosperity and the further growth of its economy, while the expansion of the backcountry was resumed and accelerated.

Despite the several boycotts adopted during the quarrels with the home government, the business of Charlestown increased considerably, rice exports doubled the average quantity shipped before the Cherokee War, and those of indigo, although experiencing slower recovery, achieved new highs after 1773. Prices for both commodities were satisfactory to good for most of the period. The demand for these staples in turn stimulated the demand for slave imports, which, despite wide fluctuations because of prohibitive duties and non-importation agreements, averaged between 3,000 and 4.000 annually from 1763 to 1774.[1]

A measure of the affluence prevailing in Charlestown and its environs is found in the recent publication of more than eighty estate inventories of persons who died in 1774. Seven of the estates accounted for half the total valuation, but the inventories reveal that most of these people were substantial property owners. Indeed, as one contemporary noted, while there were few in the low country who were very rich, there were proportionately "more persons possessed of between five and ten thousand pounds sterling" than anywhere else in the colonies.[2]

The new wealth was reflected in the style of life among the gentry. One observer found much benevolence and public spirit in a society graced by good taste, although he noted that South Carolina was approaching "that state of power and opulence, when some distinctions among men necessarily take place." There was a new interest in the "polite arts" of music and dancing; the: presence of three newspapers, several book sellers, the Charlestown Library Society, the urban setting, and the new wealth made for, in Carl Bridenbaugh's words, a "surface brilliance." Apparently there was little interest in supporting serious learning among the wealthy who hired tutors for their children and sent their sons to England for a university or professional education, but all visitors remarked on the polite manners and easy hospitality they encountered among the gentry.[3]

The town's prosperity drew numerous immigrants who swelled the ranks of its commercial classes during the: 1760s. Conspicuous among them were the newcomers from Scotland who entered the community during that period as merchants, and artisans and tradesmen. Many of them attended the Scots-Presbyterian Church on Meeting Street, which their countryman, the Reverend Alexander Hewatt, served as pastor. Examples of other recent arrivals from Great Britain who settled in the low country were a master of a vessel who came out in 1763, and remained to marry an heiress and become a merchant-planter; a Scot who retired from the Royal Navy in the same year to become a planter on Goose Creek west of the city; and an English Quaker who established mercantile operations in both Charlestown and Beaufort later in the period.[4]

There were additions to the professional classes too: such lawyers as James Simpson, soon to be a member of the Royal Council, an admiralty judge, and later attorney general of the province; an Irishman, Thomas Phepoe, who would become the principal defender of persons charged with loyalism in years to come; several physicians; and Robert Cooper as rector of St. Michael's, Charlestown, and Edward 1enkins, who occupied the same position at St. Bartholomew's, southwest of the city.[5] The ranks of the city's craftsmen grew proportionately as many immigrants opened businesses during the period. Not all of these newcomers were welcomed, for many mechanics were suffering hard times in the early 1760s and did not relish the increased competition for the work available.[6]

A source of irritation to low country business and political leaders was the increasing number of Crown officials who arrived in the l760s, a constant reminder of England's attempts to extend greater administrative control over its colonies. Their offices, often obtained by lease from persons in Britain who held the actual patent from the Crown, usually entitled the holders to seats on the Royal Council. These officials resided in Charlestown, but they rook advantage of their positions to obtain grants to numerous tracts of land in the interior of the province. Thomas Skottowe, the secretary and register of the province, first came out in 1762; Egerton Leigh managed to hold the positions of judge of the vice admiralty court and attorney general simultaneously; and Thomas Knox Gordon and Edward Savage, who received appointments as chief justice of the province and vice admiralty judge, respectively, arc examples of the more important officeholders who functioned during this period. British immigrants also filled a number of positions in the customs service that were a part of the imperial patronage system, although these appointments did not entitle the holders to seats on the Royal Council.[7]

Meanwhile, the movement into the backcountry, temporarily interrupted by the Cherokee War, was resumed shortly after peace was made. The General Assembly itself stimulated the flow of immigrants by passing legislation that paid an amount toward the passage of "poor Protestants" of good character from England and Ireland who would take up lands in the interior of the province. Further encouragement came from Governor Thomas Boone, who set up two new townships of approximatcly 20,000 acres apiece on the headwaters of Long Cane and Stevens creeks, tributaries of the upper Savannah River; a third township, Hillsborough, was created in the fork of Long Cane Creek and Little River for two groups of Huguenots. Typical of the many persons who took advantage of the bounty lands were John Anderson, who came from Ireland in the early 1760s and "drew" 300 acres on a tributary of Long Cane Creek; John Phillips from County Antrim, who followed kinsmen to Carolina about 1770 and took up lands on Jackson's Creek north of the Broad River; and Robert Alexander, whose father came ashore from the

Lord Dunluce early in 1773 and soon established his family on bounty lands north of the Enoree River. Early in the 1760s John Adam Bowers and Christian Sing were among the heads of a number of German families who, having been denied lands promised to them in Nova Scotia, received grants on Hard Labour Creek, a tributary of Stevens Creek; they represented the last substantial migration of Germans to South Carolina in the colonial period. The bounty law was continued for three years in 1765, and as late as 1773 shiploads of immigrants from northern Ireland were landing at Charlestown and obtaining warrants for land in the backcountry.[8]

The expanding population in the backcountry caused Charlestown merchanrs, often Scots, to establish Stores in the interior where their interests were often represented by countrymen like John Chisholm near Nelson's Ferry on the Santee, Evan McLaurin for Joseph Curry near the junction of the Broad and Saluda, and Alexander Cheves ("Chevas" in British records) who, after a decade in the trade to the Cherokees, settled on lands he had purchased on Long Cane Creek. Meanwhile, the stream of immigrants overland from Virginia had also resumed and would continue until the outbreak of hostilities in 1775.[9]

The settlers who swarmed into the backcountry before and after the Cherokee War created a distinct society in South Carolina, a society out of touch with Charlestown, where families still worried about the danger of Indian raids and were forced to rely on their own resources to survive and prosper. The backcountry people were not all alike; not only did they spring from different nationalities, but some of the families who had first moved into the region had become well established. By the 1760s, as Rachel Klein's studies have shown, a number of the more fortunate and ambitious among the earlier backcountry pioneers had developed small plantations and had acquired slaves to work them. Acting Governor William Bull made an extensive tour of the backcountry in 1770 and found that the valleys of the numerous streams in that rolling country offered good land for farming and for mill sites. Other property records of the period show that the more prosperous planters owned substantial numbers of cattle and sheep and had developed orchards, and in some areas were raising wheat as well as corn.[10]

The immigrant families who were just settling the backcountry in the 1760s attracted less notice from contemporaries than did the more substantial planters, but one surviving description of some of these people has been left by Charles Woodmason, the itinerant Anglican rector in the huge St. Mark's Parish north of the Santee and Congaree rivers. Frustrated in his efforts to convert many back settlers in his jurisdiction to Anglicanism, Woodmason was nonetheless fascinated by them, and marveled that they could live on diets he found coarse and unappealing, and in crowded cabins far removed from the conveniences of settled communities. Most of the settlers with whom he came in contact were Presbyterians and Baptists who did not belong to organized congregations, while his own sermons were often interrupted by shiftless and sometimes drunken men who occasionally threatened his life. Yet many of these people among whom he sought to minister were anxious for a clergyman to marry them and baptize their children and, by defending him and helping him on his travels on a number of occasions, they won his grudging admiration.[11]

Woodmason's interest in backcountry life went beyond the social and religious customs he observed, for he became aware of the frustrations felt by some of the more substantial residents of the area, frustrations caused by their inability to interest the General

Assembly or officials in Charlestown in their problems. The most serious problem was the lack of law enforcement in the backcountry where, following the Cherokee War, bands of outlaws preyed on the persons and property of settlers. Virtually unrepresented in the parish-based General Assembly, a number of backcountry leaders appealed for the establishment of courts and sheriffs in the interior, and representation in the legislature for the recently settled areas. The General Assembly was not unsympathetic to their problems, passing a bill to organize courts in the interior and authorizing two companies of rangers to help in law enforcement. But the court bill was disallowed in England, and the attention of lowcountry leaders was distracted during these years by the growing struggle with the imperial and local administration over American rights; further appeals from the backcountry for help went unheeded.[12]

As the lawlessness in the backcountry became more flagrant, local leaders turned increasingly to their own resources. Organizing their neighbors, they invaded outlaw hideouts and administered their own justice against their tormentors, the storekeepers whom they suspected of dealing with the outlaws, and the more shiftless elements in the population who gave aid and comfort to them. Styling themselves Regulators, these leaders, usually small planters and justices of the peace and militia officers who had the respect of their communities, increasingly took the law into their own hands; in so doing, they sometimes acted against innocent people, who complained to authorities in Charlestown. The deputies sent by the provost marshal to serve warrants against certain Regulators for debt met armed resistance, and in one confrontation near Marr's Bluff on the Pee Dee River, the lawmen suffered casualties and were driven off by friends of the Regulators.[13]

The Marr's Bluff incident and complaints by a magistrate in the Broad-Saluda fork that he had been whipped by Regulators led Governor Lord Charles Montagu to order a bench warrant served on the perpetrators of these acts. The man authorized to make the arrests was one Joseph Coffell, who already had a bad reputation in the backcountry; true to form, Coffell deputized men suspected by Regulators of having committed crimes. As Coffell's band moved into the backcountry, it not only arrested Regulators but plundered homes along the Saluda River, and in the process succeeded in arousing the countryside to armed resistance. Before a full-scale civil war broke out, however, certain backcountry leaders convinced Montagu to rescind Coffell's authority and an uneasy peace was restored. As a result of the crisis, the General Assembly hastily passed a second court bill that met the objections that officials in England had raised to a provision on the tenure of judges in the earlier measure, and Montagu carried it to England where it was soon approved. Lieutenant Governor William Bull, who was much more sympathetic to Regulator grievances than Montagu, soon pardoned most of them and restored their commissions as magistrates and militia officers.[14]

The Circuit Court Act of 1769 divided the province into seven judicial districts, and it authorized for each the appointment of a sheriff and the erection of a courthouse and a jail. Although the Regulators would have preferred to have local courts rather than periodic sessions presided over by circuit judges, and the provisions of the law were not fully implemented for three years, a semblance of peace was restored to the backcountry. The Regulator movement did, however, put a severe strain on relations among backcountry families and neighborhoods, and the feuds that it engendered may have carried over into the civil war that raged in the backcountry during the Revolution that broke out a few years later.[15]

By 1775 population had spread over most of the province and a few settlers had encroached upon lands beyond the: Indian Line, the western boundary surveyed after the Cherokee War. There are no censuses for the period, but the best contemporary estimates of South Carolina's population on the eve of the Revolution ranged from 140,000 to 170,000, including perhaps 60,000 to 70,000 whites and 80,000 to 100,000 blacks. Most of the white population was to be found in the interior, while all but a small proportion of the slaves were in the low country parishes.[16]

The period from the treaty ending the French and Indian War to 1775 was one of intense political unrest in Britain's North American colonies. Indeed, recent studies have indicated that considerable stress had begun to develop between the imperial government in England and its provinces in America during the war with France and that the misunderstandings and suspicions that grew up during that conflict provide the foundation for the unrest that followed.

On the surface, South Carolina in the early 1760s had little reason to regret its connection with Great Britain. The colony's prosperity was based on its ability to raise and transport its great staples to British and Continental markets, and in a dangerous world the Royal Navy provided a security that seemed essential to the trade. In a colony founded by Englishmen, South Carolinians, or at least that portion of its free population that dominated the political process, were proud of their heritage and harbored no ideas of questioning their relationship with the home government. In turn, there was every indication that royal officials in England considered South Carolina to be a valuable colony that produced useful commodities and was becoming an increasingly large consumer of British goods.[17]

Despite this apparently mutual satisfaction with the imperial connection, through its control of the Commons House of Assembly the lowcountry gentry had developed defenses against royal authority as represented by the governors and the increasingly pliant Royal Council. Based upon its power to tax and to spend, the Commons House had come to think of itself as the sole legislative authority in the province and to be very sensitive to its independence from outside control. In this state of mind, it is no wonder that, when Governor Thomas Boone questioned the right of a member to his seat, the Commons House looked upon his action as an assault upon its prerogatives and reacted accordingly. The member was the wealthy merchant Christopher Gadsden whose election to a seat from St. Paul's Parish in 1762 was certified by churchwardens who had failed to take the oath required by law before acting. As a result, Boone declared the seat vacant and called for a new election to fill it. In the constitutional quarrel that ensued, the Commons House asserted its right to judge the qualifications of its members, while Boone claimed that such right derived from an election law of 1721 that also required that churchwardens take an oath before embarking on their duties. The Commons House, however, declared that its very existence rested on the natural right of freemen to be represented and demanded an apology from the governor before resuming business. It then appealed to its agent in London to bring the matter before the Board of Trade. The impasse lasted for more than a year before the board removed Boone, an act that further increased the self-esteem of the Commons House. And Christopher Gadsden became a leading figure in the ensuing struggle between Imperial authority and local rights in South Carolina.[18]

Gadsden was also deeply involved in South Carolina's resistance to the Stamp Act, a measure passed by Parliament in 1765 to raise a revenue in the colonies. With Thomas Lynch and John Rutledge, he represented the province in the Stamp Act Congress that met in New York that fall to protest against the tax and to recommend measures to force its repeal. In Charlestown the stamp masters appointed to administer the tax were intimidated into resigning by mobs in which the mechanics, calling themselves Sons of Liberty, took an important part. By early 1766, with business in the port at a standstill, the harbor crammed with ships awaiting the clearances for which stamps were required, restless crews in the taverns, and merchants anxious over the losses they were sustaining, Lieutenant Governor William Bull finally permitted ships to clear on grounds that the required stamps were not available. The tension in the port was relieved, and the arrival in May of news that the Stamp Act had been repealed caused wild rejoicing. Clearly, South Carolina had permitted violence and intimidation in defying the law, tactics that were alarming to men of conservative temper and substantial property like William Wragg and the wealthy merchant Henry Laurens.[19]

But Laurens himself ran afoul of British authority in 1767 when two of his vessels were seized by Daniel Moore, a newly arrived customs collector, on a technical violation of regulations that required all vessels to clear with his office. Egerton Leigh, Laurens's relative by marriage and judge of the vice admiralty court in Charlestown, attempted a compromise by ruling favorably on the seizure of one vessel to satisfy customs officials, and appeasing Laurens by dismissing the case against the other vessel. Laurens, angered by the arbitrary nature of the decision by a judge without jury, responded by suing George Roupell, the officer who had seized his ship; a local jury awarded Laurens a judgment for damages so large that Roupell could not pay it. Customs officials then apparently connived to seize another Laurens vessel to pressure him into dropping his suit; when Laurens refused, Judge Leigh was caught between his duty to support customs officials whom he suspected of conspiracy against Laurens, and upholding the tenet of the law. Leigh's answer to the dilemma was to dismiss the case against the seized vessel while pointing out the technical violation. Meanwhile, Laurens published documents and affidavits that exposed the abuses of both the customs officials and the vice admiralty court in Charlestown. Leigh then printed a defense of his conduct that amounted to a thinly disguised personal arrack on Laurens, who replied by publishing further documents on the matter.[20]

The publicity given to this controversy had repercussions within and beyond the province. Leigh lost his judgeship because of complaints from customs officials in South Carolina, and to some degree his tarnished personal reputation further affected local attitudes toward placemen. Laurens's experiences with the customs service tended to change his posture to one of strong criticism of British policies and officials. And, combined with revelations about John Hancock's problems with customs officials in Massachusetts in the same period, it brought Britain's commercial policy into further disrepute in America.

Meanwhile, Parliament had resumed its efforts to raise a revenue in the colonies, placing duties on tea and certain other imported goods. Massachusetts sought to have the other colonies join it in resisting enforcement of these Townshend duties, stating its views in a circular letter to them. In South Carolina, the Commons House unanimously endorsed the Massachusetts views, but citizens were less enthusiastic about resorting to nonimportation again as a means of applying pressure for the repeal of the duties. In the name of principle, import merchants would bear the load of such a sacrifice, while planters would suffer little in the short run and many mechanics might even prosper from the reduced competition with British products. After much negotiating, a large public meeting forged an agreement not to import a wide range of English goods; and a committee of thirty-nine drawn equally from planters, merchants, and mechanics was chosen to enforce the boycott. Some coercion was used to get most people to sign a non-importation agreement, which worked fairly well. Ultimately, a new ministry in England urged the repeal of the Townshend duties because they had done little to promote British trade, although the tax on tea was retained so that Parliament would not appear to give up its prerogative to raise a revenue in America. But the nonimportation agreements in the colonies collapsed in the face of this apparent concession, and in December 1770 a meeting in Charlestown rescinded the boycott on all imports except tea.[21]

Perhaps more important to the ultimate breakdown of royal authority in South Carolina was an incident that began rather innocently in 1769 when the Commons House ordered the provincial treasurer to advance £1,500 as its contribution to a fund being raised in England to defend the imprisoned radical John Wilkes. That a colonial legislative body had contributed to defend a convicted libeler of the king was bad enough; that in this instance the appropriation was made without the consent of the royal governor and his council was a startling indication that the popular branch of the General Assembly was exercising powers far beyond those that authorities in England were prepared to approve.

Instructions came swiftly to Acting Governor Bull that, upon pain of removal from office, no appropriation should be approved that did not specify the purpose for which the revenue was intended, and that treasurers who disbursed funds without the approval of the Royal Council and the governor were to be permanently excluded from office and forfeit triple the sum involved. The Commons House responded that the practice was of long standing, a view that the royal attorney general refused to countenance. Thus the stage was set in South Carolina for a renewed struggle between the Commons House, which sought by direct means and by subterfuge to raise the revenue to replace the money, borrowed for the gift to the Wilkes Fund, and the governors and the Royal Council who scrutinized all revenue measures to see if they contained the offending appropriation. All efforts to reach a compromise failed, and for three years no annual tax bill was passed.

When the general duty law, which supported the salaries of some officials and the Anglican clergy in the province, was about to expire in 1773, a majority of the Royal Council refused to assent to legislation of any kind until the Commons House would agree to extend it. Two members of the council who dissented from that decision, John and William Henry Drayton, printed a protest in the *South Carolina Gazette*, whereupon the council had printer Thomas Powell imprisoned for contempt. Powell, whose counsel argued that the council was not an upper house of the legislation and thus could not punish for contempt, sought and was granted his freedom on a habeas corpus issued by two justices of the peace, both members of the Commons House. The council then began proceedings against those justices, an effort that caused the Commons House to appeal through its agent in London for the removal of the councillors responsible.

Local attention was diverted from the dispute over these constitutional questions by the larger issues raised by the Tea Party in Boston. In 1774 the Commons House, responding to the threat of an Indian attack on the frontier of the province, issued its own bills of credit to meet outstanding obligations after local merchants and officials, even members of the Royal Council, agreed to receive them until a tax bill could be passed. Thus by resorting to powers it had used occasionally to meet emergencies in the past, the Commons House not only emerged the winner in its long dispute over the Wilkes Fund, but was in position to assume direction of what would ultimately become the Revolutionary movement in South Carolina.[22]

In 1773, in an effort to revive the sagging fortunes of the East India Company, Parliament passed legislation that gave that company an advantage in the colonial market by exempting it from the trade regulations requiring that goods destined for the colonies must first pay duty in England, When in November 1773 a cargo of East India Company tea arrived off Charlestown, the nonimportation machinery that had fallen into disuse after the repeal of the other Townshend duties was revived, and it prevented the tea from being landed and delivered to Zephaniah Kingsley, John McKenzie, and Robert Lindsay, the merchants to whom it was consigned. Lieutenant Governor Bull avoided a direct challenge to royal authority by impounding the cargo when the duty was not paid within the time prescribed by law. But when Parliament, angered by Boston's response to the Tea Act, enacted a series of punitive measures against Massachusetts, the Coercive or "Intolerable" Acts of 1774, South Carolina joined with others in support of the sister colony, now beset by what were considered to be tyrannical arracks on private property and individual and institutional liberties in America.[23]

First, in January 1774, a mass meeting in Charlestown chose a general committee to prepare for future trouble. A call was issued for a meeting to discuss a response to the act of Parliament closing the port of Boston; in July delegates from Charlestown and from other parts of the province met for several days to discuss whether to send delegates to a continental congress called by Massachusetts. On the issue of employing nonimportation as a response to the most recent acts of Parliament, the interests of planters and mechanics once again clashed with those of the more important merchants as represented by the newly organized Chamber of Commerce. The delegates chosen to attend the First Continental Congress in Philadelphia, although men of substantial property, generally were more vigorous advocates of American rights than others the Chamber of Commerce would have preferred.

At Philadelphia, South Carolina's delegation supported the Continental Association, an agreement banning the importation or consumption of British goods and the exportation of colonial staples to Britain, but only after the delegates had agreed to exempt rice from the latter prohibition.[24]

When the delegates returned to South Carolina in November, the general committee called for elections to a provincial congress to convene in Charlestown in January 1775. That body, after much debate over the terms of the Continental Association, approved the work of the delegates, and reelected them to represent the colony in the Second Continental Congress called for the following May. The congress also created a Council of Safety to act when it was not in session and a network of special and local committees of inspection to enforce the association.[25]

To this point an effort has been made to summarize South Carolina's colonial development: the characteristics of its population, its economy, its political structure and practices, and its society. Further, it has been pointed out that certain issues after 1760 had brought many of the leaders in the lowcountry to question the imperial relationship and many in the backcountry to demand greater recognition within the province. Certain ideas have been identified as fundamental to the struggle for American rights within the empire and certain local men have been cast in roles on both sides of that issue. But nowhere has it been suggested that there was substantial overt opposition to the ideas expressed by advocates of American rights or that a corps of local leaders existed who were prepared to defend the royal position in the constitutional struggles of the time.

The underlying assumption on which American rights ideas rested was that the traditional ways of operating *within the empire* must be preserved. Whether a spokesman for American rights like Christopher Gadsden really had independence in view after the Stamp Act crisis is less important than that he and more conservative advocates of the American position foreswore, in their public utterances at least, any arrangement outside the empire. The rights they went to such lengths to defend were, after all, the rights of British Americans.

If that be true, where does one begin to look for the seeds, if not the roots, of the opposition to what will become the American Revolutionary movement in South Carolina. To pose the question is, however, to open the door on the veritable wilderness that is the larger question of allegiance: Why did residents of South Carolina take one side or the other in the American Revolution? It is too early at this point to search out all the factors that might account for such positions on the part of individuals or groups. One thing is clear: the historical record for what will come to be known as the American or rebel side in the Revolution is fuller than it is for the pro-British or loyalist side, and the same is true of the use that subsequent generations, however biased, have made of the record that exists. Proud of having created a nation, the victors and their descendants have preserved both the personal records and the myths related to their great achievement; the losers appear only in surviving British records, the American records that deigned to notice them, usually in a pejorative way, and in an occasional reminiscence brought to light in Canada or in the other British possessions to which loyalists were exiled at the end of the war. Persons who at one time or another took the loyalist side but were permitted to remain in South Carolina after the war have, for obvious reasons, had virtually nothing to say about their experiences or motivation. Thus we are left with little to help us find what the "loyalist" position was before 1775 when virtually all British colonial inhabitants considered themselves to be loyal to England.

Yet it is worth probing the record for what it will reveal of clues to positive loyal acts or expressions before the outbreak of hostilities. In the lowcountry, self-interest would dictate that Crown officers, from the very nature of their positions and the sources of their authority and income, should have upheld the British view. Except for William Bull, all the Crown officers in the colony after 1760 were placemen, outsiders who, like Egerton Leigh, were caught between the imperatives of official duty and of local interest and support. Leigh, of course, was unusual among placemen because by his marriage he had established local ties that made his official position more difficult to maintain. Few others, except perhaps from a natural desire to be liked, would take the chance of alienating patrons or superiors in England by being other than faithful to the Crown in word and deed. From similar motives, men who held minor positions, especially in the customs service, also tended to support royal authority.[26]

Anglican clergymen, while not government officials, were representatives of the official church whose appointments and tenure depended to some extent on satisfying their superiors in England. Several did attempt to uphold the British position from the pulpit and were dismissed because a majority of their communicants were not in sympathy with their views. The assistant rector of St. Michael's felt called upon to preach on the "Christian duty of peaceableness" in August 1774, for which he was "through the violent outrage of the people deprived of his appointment" when a majority of the vestry urged his removal; the assistant rector at St. Philip's left in 1775 after refusing to sign the Continental Association; whereas Robert Cooper, rector of St. Michael's, by signing the Continental Association did keep his position for the time being, although in 1777 he returned to England. Nevertheless, most of the Anglican clergymen in South Carolina continued to serve their parishioners during the war and remained in the state afterward, an indication that local congregations had more influence over their ministers than did distant superiors in the Anglican hierarchy.[27]

One ethnic group that aroused fear and suspicion among advocates of American rights was the Scots, who continued and even increased their migration to South Carolina in the 1760s, where they took important places in the economic life of Charlestown. Robert Wells, who had established his bookselling and printing business and a newspaper before the Cherokee War, enlarged his activities and his income in the 1760s in several ways: serving as a vendue master selling imported goods at auction to local merchants; from an appointment as marshal of the vice admiralty court for South Carolina; and by later obtaining the position of marshal of the vice admiralty court for the Southern District of North America, established by Parliament in 1767 in an effort to crack down on violators of customs regulations. Wells invested the returns from his several enterprises in Charlestown real estate and over 3,000 acres of land in various parts of the province, and by 1770 could advertise that he had money to lend at interest. He was an active Mason and through his newspaper and bookshop a promoter of the economic and cultural elite of the city. During the Stamp Act crisis his *General Gazette* supported the American position, but as the controversy over British policy and the actions of local officials continued, Wells's defense of the ministerial position became more pronounced. Indeed, as the crisis reached the verge of hostilities, Peter Timothy, editor of the colony's original newspaper, the *South Carolina Gazette:*, and a strong exponent of American rights, complained bitterly in its columns of official favoritism toward "Mr. Robert Wells from Glasgow." But by this time, Wells himself had come to dislike the trend of political events in the province so much that in 1775 he took ship for England, leaving his son, John, in charge of the printing and bookselling enterprises. He never returned to South Carolina.[28]

Another important Scot was John Stuart from Inverness who, after participating in several trading ventures in the 1740s, came to South Carolina as a partner in a merchant house. While that particular venture ultimately failed, Stuart remained to pay off his creditors and assume such responsible positions as captain of militia and member of the Commons House. In the 1750s he became deeply involved in trade and diplomacy with the Cherokees, and in 1761, upon Governor Boone's recommendation, he was appointed to the new position of superintendent of Indian affairs for the Southern District of North America. The salary and perquisites of this position enabled Stuart to become a substantial indigo planter and slaveholder on Lady's Island near Beaufort and owner of a handsome house in Charlestown. Generally popular in the latter city, Stuart nevertheless made enemies among what his biographer has called the "anti-Scottish party," the most vocal of whom was Timothy who resented the superintendent's practice of giving information on Indian affairs exclusively to his good friend Robert Wells.[29]

The wealth and influence of Stuart and Wells, and of shipbuilder John Rose, extended through marriages into the next generation. One of Stuart's daughters married a brother of the royal lieutenant governor of Georgia, and a second became the bride of the younger Edward Fenwick, son of a prominent family in St. Bartholomew's Parish; while Rose's daughter married the successful Charlestown merchant, John Tunno, another Scot.[30]

Scots were also well represented in two important occupations in and near Charlestown. In addition to John Rose, other shipbuilders who had migrated from Scotland in the 1760s were John Imrie, James and William Begbie, and their partner Daniel Manson. Scots who were practitioners of medicine in this period included John Farquharson, James Fraser (sometimes "Frazier" or "Frazer" in British records), Alexander Garden, Peter Spence, Hugh Rose (John's son), and "Dr. John" Wells of John's Island, a brother of Robert Wells. All had lucrative practices as physicians and apothecaries. Garden owned substantial real estate in Charlestown, and Spence had a plantation near Jacksonborough and several tracts of unimproved lads in the interior.[31]

Altogether, the Scottish community numbered some thirty-five families, most of whom were merchants and artisan-shopkeepers in Charlestown. Numbered among them were several who had come out to join the growing bureaucracy in Stuart's Indian department, a clerk of the Court of Common Pleas, a collector of customs, as well as Alexander Hewatt of the Scots church. Most were members of the St. Andrew's Society, established in 1729 to celebrate St. Andrew's Day.[32]

There are few specific clues to explain individual and group motivation toward loyalism in the interior of the province before 1775. Certainly there was unrest in the backcountry, unrest that stemmed in large measure from dissatisfaction with what local leaders perceived to be indifference on the part of Crown officials and the General Assembly to the needs of frontier settlers. This dissatisfaction took the form of overt action by local leaders, the Regulators, to punish the criminal elements whose activities so disrupted peaceful development of the frontier. But the Regulator conflict in South Carolina, unlike the movement of the same name in North Carolina, was really a conflict within the backcountry, not an open rebellion against the institutions and leadership of the dominant tidewater gentry. Richard Maxwell Brown has classified some 150 men who were later pardoned for Regulator activity as "small planters and leading men," particularly those in the area later known as Camden District, but the identity of many others has been lost. After tracing the activities of pardoned Regulators in the Revolution, he finds that most whose allegiance was known were anti-British, a conclusion generally compatible with the findings of this study. But to know the identity of certain Regulators offers little help in accounting for backcountry Revolutionary allegiance, for the two questions are essentially unrelated. Whether or not one was a Regulator depended on how one's family and neighbors fared at the hands of the outlaws in the 1760s; but whether or not a backcountry man was a rebel in the Revolution might hinge on a number of factors, but primarily on the person's perception of the dangers and opportunities to come from renouncing allegiance to the Crown. And Rachel Klein has shown that once judicial and legal reforms were enacted, certain factors—the common concern for protection of property (Regulators returning escaped slaves to lowcountry masters), and the closer ties with Charlestown brought about by increased commercial activity in the backcountry—began to create a greater identity of interests between leaders in the two sections of the province.[33]

A principal reason for undertaking this study is to discern the motives that led many backcountry South Carolinians to espouse the royal cause, a choice that for some led ultimately to loss of property, exile, and even death. We do know that many backcountry men were unsympathetic to the movement for independence in 1775 and after. Many of them were relatively recent immigrants who were immersed in the problems of pioneering and who were not directly involved in the network of commercial relationships that was spreading into the interior. Except under great provocation, they were less likely to look favorably on a movement that was defying the authority from which they had obtained their lands. As the story progresses over the seven years of conflict, it will be a further purpose to explain how the shifting fortunes of war affected the allegiance of those who will be known as loyalists. At this point, however, it is worthwhile to suggest some prewar factors that may have accounted for the hostility toward the American rights movement that most observers at the time and historians subsequently have commented upon.

First, while there is no perfect correlation between Regulators and rebels, on the one hand, and moderators and loyalists, on the other, the animosities generated between individual families and neighbors in the Regulator struggle very probably carried over into the civil war that raged through the backcountry during the Revolution. Second, resentment by militia officers or justices of the peace who were temporarily deprived of their positions because of Regulator activity may have carried over to the conflict that broke out in 1775. Third, there is the possibility that disagreements, even feuds, originating on other frontiers in Pennsylvania or the valley of Virginia were brought to the Carolina frontier by migrating families. Finally, veterans of British military services in the French wars were scattered among the backcountry population and may, as one contemporary suggested, have been stimulated to spring to the defense of royal authority when it was defied by elements in the backcountry.[34]

To these possibilities must be added the normal frontier disputes over land boundaries and titles, and the theft or ownership of livestock. Depending on their perception of where the American rights side of the controversy placed them in relationship to friends, neighbors, relatives, or those with whom they had feuded in the past, there were many reasons why families and communities might choose to remain loyal to the Crown—at least until other events forced a different choice upon them.

Did the "Scottish connection" carry over into the interior? Although there were relatively few Scots who migrated to that area, several among them held influential positions. For example, Alexander Cameron, a half-pay officer from the French and Indian War and deputy to John Stuart, established Lochaber, a large farm on a branch of Long Cane Creek. His close ties with the Cherokees at a time when the memories of the recent war were still fresh aroused fears of how he would use his influence with the Indians in the event of a possible clash with royal authority. Joseph Currie, another Scot, had established a store in the fork of the Broad and Saluda rivers where, in partnership with William and James Carsan, Scottish merchants of Charlestown, he took country produce and deerskins in trade for necessary items brought from that city. Currie had aroused the ire of Moses Kirkland and other Regulators who suspected him of dealing in stolen horses and being in complicity with some of the outlaws. The partnership with the Carsans was dissolved in 1769, but William Currie took over the operation; in partnership with Evan McLaurin, fresh from Argyle, he continued the business into the Revolutionary period. John Chisholm, a storekeeper at Nelson's Ferry on the Santee River, was a veteran of the Seventy-seventh Regiment.[35]

Conclusions about the seeds of loyalism in the period before 1775 must be tentative, particularly in the backcountry, because few of the individuals who took part in the Regulator movement of the 1760s, or for the king in 1775, can be identified in the surviving records. Some leaders and participants in those movements have been identified, but whether their characteristics can be applied to the mass of their fellows or not is at best uncertain. In the lowcountry, where there was less natural sympathy for the British position, one can more confidently assess the main causes of loyalism.

Notes

1. Leila Sellers, *Charleston Business on the Eve' of the Revolution* (Chapel Hill, N.C., 1934), 134–35, 156–59, 166–68.
2. Rogers, *Charleston in the Age of the Pinckneys* (Norman, Okla., 1969), 38–41; Jones, *American Colonial Wealth: Documents and Methods*, III (New York, 1977), 1492–1619; Alexander Hewat. *An Historical Account of the Rise and Progress of the Colonies of South Carolina and Georgia* (Spartanburg, S.C., 1962 [orig. publ. London, 1779]), 294–95.
3. Carl Bridenbaugh, *Myths and Realities: Societies of the Colonial South* (Baton Rouge, La., 1952), 99–102.
4. Loyalist Transcripts, LII, 472–504; LIII, 53–81, 584–95; LV, 188–96, 293–316, 575–85; LVI, 116–52, 213–20.
5. Ibid ., LII, 568–98, LIV, 205–55, LV, 170–87, 548–55; for Phepoe, see *Canadian Claims*, 1245.
6. Loyalist Transcripts, LIII, 342–49, LVI, 26–37, 378–91, LVII, 249–59.
7. Ibid ., LIV, 411–29; LVI, 417–42; LVII, 124–33.
8. For a discussion of the movement of immigrants into the backcountry in the early 1760s, see Meriwether, *The Expansion of South Carolina*, (Kingsport, Tenn., 1940), 241–61. For Alexander's arrival in the province, see Council Journal, Jan. 6, 1773; see also Janie Revill, comp., *A Compilation of the Original Lists of Protestant Immigrants to South Carolina, 1763–1773* (Columbia, S.C., 1939); for the other individuals mentioned, see *Canadian Claims*, 674, and (George Anderson), 849; and Loyalist Transcripts, LII, 267–90; and for Bowers, see Loyalist Claims, 13/26/51, the same source as the Transcripts, but arranged differently.
9. *Canadian Claims*, 326; Loyalist Transcripts (Isabella McLaurin), LIV, 320–32; Archie Vernon Huff, Langdon Cheves of South Carolina (Columbia, S.C., 1977), 1–14.
10. Rachel Klein, "The Rise of the Planters in the South Carolina Backcountry, 1767–1808," (Ph.D. dissertation, Yale University, 1979), 32–34; Bull to the Earl of Hillsborough, June 7, 1770, S.C. Records in the P.R.O., XXXII, 278–84, SCAH.
11. Charles Woodmason, *The Carolina Backcoutry on the Eve of the Revolution: The Journal and Other Writings of Charles Woodmason, Anglican Itinerant*, ed. Richard J. Hooker (Chapel Hill, N.C., 1953), 31–43.
12. See the "Remonstrance" drawn up by Woodmason, *Carolina Backcountry*, 213–46; and the discussion in Robert M. Weir, *Colonial South Carolina : A History* (Millwood, N.Y., 1983), 275–77.
13. Richard Maxwell Brown, *South Carolina Regulators* (Cambridge, Mass., 1963), 38–54.
14. Ibid., 83–111.
15. Rachel Klein has denoted four particular groups of back country people who were targets of the wrath of the Regulators; a congregation of New Light or Separate Baptists on Fair Forest Creek who were "objects of Regulator contempt"; Indians, and whites who consorted with them; "white hunters," squatters who lived by hunting rather than from agriculture; and the outlaw gangs, particularly those who had robbed the more well-to-do Regulators, "Rise of the Planters in the S.C. Backcountry," 51 –67.
16. Evarts B. Greene and Virginia D. Harrington, *American Population before the Federal Census of 1790*

(Gloucester, Mass., 1966 [orig. publ. New York, 1932]), 176.
17. The best recent discussions of this period are those of Robert Weir, *"A Most Important Epocha": The Coming of the Revolution in South Carolina* (Columbia, S.C., 1970), and *Colonial South Carolina: A History,* particularly 275–81.
18. Jack P. Greene, "The Gadsden Election Controversy and the Revolutionary Movement in South Carolina," *MVHR,* XLVI (1959), 469–492; Weir, "A Most Important Epocha," 14. For Gadsden, see "Introduction," in Richard Walsh, ed., *The Writings of Christopher Gadsden, 1746–1805* (Columbia, S.C., 1966), xvxxxviii; for a long defense of the rights of the Commons House, see "To the Gentlemen Electors of the Parish of "St. Paul, Stono," Feb. 5, 1763 , in Walsh , *Writings of Gadsden,* 17–50.
19. Robert H. Woody, "Christopher Gadsden and the Stamp Act," SCHA, *Proceedings,* IX (1939), 3–12; Weir, *"Most Important Epocha,"* 12–24.
20. For Laurens's difficulties with customs officials in Charlestown and his controversy with Leigh, see Rogers, ed., *Laurens Papers,* V, xviii–xx, 273–76, 391–464, 722–23, 728, 737–49; VI, 287–383. For Leigh's personal acts that further embittered Laurens, see Robert M. Calhoon and Robert M. Weir, "The Scandalous History of Sir Egerton Leigh," *WMQ,* 3d Ser., XXVI (1969), 47–74; for his reputation as "Downright Placeman," see Calhoon, *The Loyalists in Revolutionary America, 1760–1781* (New York, 1973).
21. Weir, *"Most Important Epocha,"* 32–38.
22. The most thorough analysis of this controversy and its implications is Jack P. Greene, "Bridge to Revolution: The Wilkes Fund Controversy in South Carolina, 1769–1775," *JSH,* XXIX (1963), 19–52. The Powell affair may be followed in *South Carolina Gazette* (Charlestown), Jan. 13, 15, 1773.
23. John Drayton, *Memoirs of the American Revolution as Relating to the State of South Carolina* (Columbia, S.C., 1969 [orig. publ. Charleston, S.C., 1821]) I, 126–32.
24. Frank W. Ryan, "The Role of South Carolina in the First Continental Congress," *SCHM,* LX (1959), 147–53.
25. Weir, *"Most Important Epocha,"* 58–59.
26. Robert Weir, "'The Harmony We Were Famous For': An Interpretation of Pre-Revolutionary South Carolina Politics," *WMQ.,* 3d Ser. , XXVI (1969), 96n2.
27. Loyalists Transcripts, LII , 568–98; LIV, 850–92; LVII, 21–25; Edward McCrady, *The History of South Carolina under the Royal Government, 1719–1776* (New York, 1899) 752–54. .
28. Christopher Gould, "Robert Wells, Colonial Charleston Printer," *SCHM,* LXXIX (1978), 23–49. Robert Wells's daughter Louisa Susannah had clerked in his printing business and later married Alexander Aikman, one of his apprentices, Wells, *Journal,* 78–80; Loyalist Transcripts, LVI, 534–56. Timothy's complaint is in *South Carolina Gazette,* Apr. 30, 1774; a similar, if less bitter, statement by Charles Crouch, who edited the city's third newspaper, is in *South Carolina Gazette and Country Journal* (Charlestown), July 18, 1775.
29. John Richard Alden, *John Stuart and the Southern Colonial Frontier, 1754–1775* (New York, 1966 [orig. publ. Ann Arbor, Mich., 1947]), 156–75.
30. Loyalist Transcripts, LIII, 272–306; LVI, 234–59; LVII, 418–38.
31. For the shipwrights, see Loyalist Transcripts, LIII, 272–306; LV, 32–45, 293–325. The medical men are in ibid., LIII, 406–28. 566–72; LV. 170–87, 197–245, 331–43; Wells, *Journal,* 65; and biographical sketches can be found in Joseph I. Waring, *A Histoy of Medicine in South Carolina* (Columbia, S.C., 1964). I, 177–80, 185. 221–37, 266–67, 316.
32. Loyalist Transcripts, LIII, 200–222, 584–95; LVI , 213–20; J. Harold Easterby, *History of the St. Andrew's Society of Charleston South Carolina, 1729–1929* (Charleston, 1929), 49–54.
33. Brown, *S.C. Regulators,* 140, 123–24, 213n37; Klein, "Rise of the Planters in the S.C. Backcountry," 83–84.
34. See Thomas Brown to Lord William Campbell, Oct. 18, 1775, S.C. Records in the P.R.O., XXXV, 287, for the suggestion that many veterans were among the supporters of the king in 1775.
35. Loyalist Claims, LIII , 82–86, 320, 332; LV, 556–65; *South Carolina Gazette and Country Journal,* May 17, 1768; *Canadian Claims,* 326–27.

Chapter Two

"The Troubles" Begin

It is a great unhappiness to me that I cannot persuade my conscience to approve of the present measures, ... Especially since a conference with Col. Moses Kirkland, Esq. I have had no occasion to borrow a pair of Political Spectacles to detect and disown the Prime Intentions and Machinations of some of the Principle Leaders of your Party, ... they do in fact, fight against the King, desire an ultimate Separation....

—Joseph Robinson, August 1775

Generally things had gone rather well for leaders of the American rights movement in South Carolina, and their control of the lowcountry seemed as secure as was possible under the circumstances. But there remained the likelihood that efforts would be made to restore royal authority by outside help. One source of outside help might come from England, for reports were already circulating that Lord North, head of the Ministry in England, intended to send reinforcements to America. No British regulars were stationed in South Carolina early in 1775, but the presence of royal naval vessels was a constant reminder that an invasion could come at any time.

The possibility that royal troops might be sent from England was but one of the worries the Provincial Congress faced. Equally grave was the danger from the west, for if John Stuart's agents succeeded in bringing the Creeks and the Cherokees to the support of the Crown, the supporters of American rights might find themselves caught between an invasion by sea and an Indian war on the frontiers. Of course, under normal circumstances interior settlers might be counted on to defend themselves against Indian raids. But the circumstances of the winter of 1775 were hardly normal; less than fifteen years before, it had taken the strength of a virtually united colony augmented by royal troops to crush the Cherokees, and since then the Regulator uprising had shown that the rapidly increasing population of the backcountry could not easily be brought to support the interests of the lowcountry. Perhaps they could be counted on to quell an Indian uprising, but how would they respond to an attempt to restore royal authority by British arms?

The promise of courts for the backcountry had been kept, but other frontier grievances had not been met. The most obvious inequity that remained was the lack of representation for the interior settlements in the legislative bodies that decided policy. In an effort to reach out for support in the backcountry, the First Provincial Congress had allotted 55 of its 187 seats to certain districts that lay beyond the lowcountry parishes. Of course, coastal members continued to control that body, and some of the persons elected to represent backcountry areas actually resided in the tidewater. Nevertheless, the gesture did increase contact between the sections, and to the degree that interior leaders could be convinced of the justice of the American rights cause, they were valuable adherents to it.[1]

When the news that hostilities had broken out in Massachusetts reached South Carolina in the spring of 1775, the military situation in the interior of the province claimed more attention. In June the Provincial Congress voted to raise three regiments for the defense of the province, and it designated that one, a ranger or mounted unit, should defend the interior and be recruited there. When Congress selected officers for the rangers, virtually all, from Lieutenant Colonel William Thomson of Orangeburg District and Major James Mayson of Ninety Six through the junior ranks of captain and lieutenant, were drawn from the interior.[2]

Another potential source of manpower for the Provincial Congress was the provincial militia, which the General Assembly had reorganized after the Regulator controversy. Of the twelve infantry regiments authorized, seven were drawn from the districts away from the coast: two from the area between the Broad and Saluda rivers; two in Camden District from between the Broad and Catawba rivers, and including the New Acquisition; and one each from the western part of Ninety Six District between the Saluda and Savannah rivers, Orangeburg District, and the Cheraw District comprising much of the Pee Dee region northwest of Georgetown. The three ranking officers of each regiment had been chosen by the General Assembly, but the captains and lieutenants had been locally elected. Although the reorganization had brought backcountrymen into positions of leadership, the question that plagued the leaders of the congress that spring was which militia officers and units could be counted on to support the American rights cause. As the crisis deepened, the militia was further reorganized by dropping officers of doubtful allegiance and replacing them, promotion of others, and by drafts of volunteers for the enlisted ranks. By this means, it was hoped that what the militia lost in numbers it would gain from a greater degree of political commitment by those who stayed with it or enlisted later.[3]

Perhaps the most serious questions involved the response that Indians would make if white factions fought each other in South Carolina. How could a British-supported Indian invasion be thwarted? Who among the officials of the Indian department and the traders could be trusted to keep the Indians at peace, and who would have to be removed in order to keep the tribes at bay.52 Although always present in the minds of the Provincial Congress and the Council of Safety, the matter of the role that the Indians would play in the expected clash with the Crown can be deferred while the question of the allegiance of the backcountry population is examined.

The Council of Safety employed the same tactics to determine political opinion in the backcountry that had seemed to work in the tidewater—local committees of observation and inspection made up of trusted persons were to ask people to subscribe to a version of the Continental Association that the Provincial Congress had adopted early in June. Almost before the Council of Safety could begin its work, however, word had reached Charlestown that there were ominous signs of opposition to the program of the congress in one particular area of the backcountry.[4]

A particular trouble spot was that part of the Broad-Saluda fork from which the Upper Militia Regiment, commanded by Colonel Thomas Fletchall, was drawn. Fletchall came into South Carolina about 1760 and settled on Fair Forest Creek, a tributary of the Enoree River that flowed into the Broad River from the west. There he soon became a person of local importance, acquiring by grant and purchase over the next decade some 1,600 acres of land where he raised substantial quantities of grain and livestock and operated a gristmill. He received his militia commission in 1769 and also served as a magistrate and coroner in his district.⁵

On the basis of reports that Fletchall was "not a friend to liberty," the Council of Safety sent him copies of the Provincial Congress's Association and urged him to sign it and to encourage others to do likewise, hinting broadly that retention of his militia commission hung in the balance. The Council of Safety intimated that Fletchall was the victim of bad advice from "ministerial hirelings," and reminded him that positions of trust had no importance until the dispute with England was settled and the threat of invasion eliminated. Fletchall responded that, at the request of two local committeemen, he had assembled his regiment on July 13 and read the association to them, but had not pressed them to sign, and no one had. On the contrary, Fletchall declared, sentiment ran so strongly against the statement from the Provincial Congress that it was decided to compose what Lewis Jones has called a "Counter-Association" to which many men subscribed their names. This document declared that in the current controversy with the colonies King George "had not acted inconsistent with and subversive of the principles of the Constitution of the British Empire," and they saw no reason to "take up arms against him" or to renounce allegiance to him; although their opinions on the question might differ from those of their countrymen, they intended "to live in peace and true friendship" with them; further, they stood ready to defend the province against "incursions of Indians, insurrections of negroes, or any other enemy" that the lawful officers of South Carolina might require under the "statutes of Great Britain ... and the acts of the General Assembly." To this, Fletchall added the personal view that, regardless of the status of his commission, he could not agree with the Council of Safety's position, saying, "I am resolved, and do utterly refuse to take up arms against my King," until convinced that his duty required it. This ringing declaration from a prominent backcountryman is the first clear evidence of disaffection toward the congress in that area. Fletchall was really more timid than his words might indicate, but at this time he was apparently one of the "very respectable people" whom the newly appointed governor, Lord William Campbell, was privately urging to stand fast.⁶

One who had met with Governor Campbell, and who was present at the muster ground when Fletchall polled his regiment was Joseph Robinson, the author of the Counter-Association. Robinson, who held a major's commission in the militia regiment from the New Acquisition, the area recently acquired in a boundary settlement with North Carolina, had come into the South Carolina backcountry from Virginia; his property holdings on Broad River were modest, but he was a deputy surveyor and justice of the peace and owned a substantial library for a backcountryman.⁷

While the Council of Safety's efforts to convert settlers in this area were being frustrated, its cause suffered another reverse in another part of the backcountry. Acting under the council's orders, Major James Mayson at the head of two companies of the newly formed regiment of rangers seized Fort Charlotte, a vacant outpost on the Savannah River above Augusta, and removed its stock of powder and lead to the courthouse in the village of Ninety Six. Mayson's men had barely accomplished this feat when they were surrounded by 200 men from the north side of the Saluda River who arrested Mayson and Captain Moses Kirkland and, having "declared themselves entirely in favor of government," carried off the powder and lead. According to the bewildered Mayson, the raiders had been led by Joseph Robinson and the brothers Robert and Patrick Cunningham.⁸

The Cunninghams are the most interesting family of South Carolina loyalists for whom records have survived. From Pennsylvania by way of Virginia, they arrived on the Saluda River in the late 1760s. Robert almost immediately became a man of consequence in his neighborhood, obtaining commissions as a captain of militia, a deputy surveyor, and a justice of the peace. A prominent Regulator, he was stripped of his commissions by Governor Montagu, but apparently retained the respect of leaders in the backcountry. The Whig explanation for Robert's opposition is that the Provincial Congress had failed to give him a command when it reorganized the militia; Robert will, however, be consistent in his opposition to the Whig cause and undergo considerable suffering as a result. Patrick Cunningham, whose ambitions seem to have been more economic than political, acquired a number of tracts of land and a steady income from the fees he earned as a surveyor. He seems to have deferred to Robert in political matters, as did two other brothers, David and John.[9]

Shortly after the Cunningham-Robinson party took the ammunition from the rangers at Fort Charlotte, Captain Moses Kirkland resigned his commission in the rangers and immediately assumed a prominent role against the Provincial Congress. Kirkland, who has been noted as an early settler in the backcountry and was now a substantial owner of land and slaves, had been a leading figure in organizing the Regulators. Never a passive participant in political or military movements and apparently convinced that he had picked the wrong side, Kirkland was soon deeply involved in efforts to secure help from Governor Campbell.[10]

One more personality appeared in the South Carolina backcountry at this time to join the movement to thwart the designs of the Provincial Congress. Thomas Brown was not a South Carolinian but a recent Scottish immigrant to the Georgia frontier who had come with large plans for developing estates on the "Ceded Lands" above Augusta. An outspoken supporter of the Crown, he soon fell afoul of Whig committeemen in Georgia who handled him roughly when he refused to sign an association presented to him. Fleeing into South Carolina, he soon appeared in Fletchall's area where, in company with other leaders already mentioned, he helped to organize the resistance to the congress.[11]

By late July the Council of Safety was aware of strong opposition in the backcountry and resolved to try to counter it by sending several of its own leaders into the area to explain the Provincial Congress's program to the inhabitants. It was hoped that, by speaking at militia musters and to other groups gathered by local committeemen, these emissaries could persuade large numbers to sign the Provincial Congress's Association and at the same time to identify areas and leaders of opposition. Known generally as the Drayton-Tennent Mission after the indefatigable William Henry Drayton of the Council of Safety, and the Reverend William Tennent of the Independent Church in Charlestown, the group also included Oliver Hart, a Baptist clergyman; Joseph Kershaw, a prominent citizen of Camden; and Richard Richardson, the colonel of one of the infantry regiments recently raised by the congress. The work of the Drayton-Tennent Mission has been described by several of the participants, and traditional accounts have necessarily relied on these sources. The writings of Thomas Brown, fresh from his bitter experiences in Georgia, and of Moses Kirkland, sources which scholars have recently brought to light, represent the views of Nonassociators.[12]

Drayton and Tennent made their first report to the Council of Safety from the store run by the Scot Evan McLaurin below the fork of the Broad and Saluda rivers in Saxe-

Gotha Township. The inhabitants of this area of heavy German settlement immediately showed little interest in the plans of the Provincial Congress, apparently fearing that they would lose their lands if they took up arms against the king. After a week among them during which they were "harangued" several times by Drayton and led in divine services by Tennent, Drayton had to report that "the Dutch [i.e., Deutsch] are not with us."[13]

They then proceeded by separate routes to Fletchall's settlement. Tennent moved up the east side of the Broad where he first encountered much opposition at a meeting house on Jackson's Creek. After Drayton rejoined Tennent at King's Creek on the Enoree River, they were met by Robert Cunningham and Thomas Brown, who were carrying copies of Sir John Dalrymple's *Address of the People of Great Britain to the Inhabitants of America*. The *Address* emphasized three themes: that the Continental Congress offered only the alternatives of outright war, in which America could be no match for British power and wealth, or extended commercial warfare, from which the colonies would suffer more than Britain; that in denying the supremacy of Parliament the Continental Congress had revealed that its real goal was independence, which, if achieved, would make the American states prey to anarchy and foreign influence; and that "the last war was begun for the sake of English America", from which Britain incurred great burdens. According to Drayton, after the *Address* was read to the crowd and he had refuted all its main points, Brown and Cunningham had slunk away in discomfiture. But an announced election for representatives to the Provincial Congress was poorly attended because of a letter from Cunningham and Kirkland, and had to be postponed for two weeks. Close questioning of Fletchall during a private meeting revealed that the colonel had been in communication with Governor Campbell who had held out the hope that those loyal to the king would soon be supported by a royal army. They also learned that Joseph Robinson had visited the governor at Dorchester, just west of Charlestown, and had returned with blank commissions to enlist loyal officers. Most ominous was the rumor that Alexander Cameron, the deputy superintendent to the Cherokees, was preparing to send 3,000 warriors to join the loyal elements against the supporters of the Provincial Congress."[14]

Drayton had a better reception at Lawson's Fork of the Pacolet River, close to the Indian Line and the border with North Carolina, and there he organized several volunteer companies in an effort to offset the defections in Fletchall's regiment. But when the emissaries crossed to the cast side of the upper Broad River, they met a hostile reception at Bullock's Creek; after re-crossing to the west bank, they found Robinson's friends waiting in a belligerent posture at Thicketty Creek. And Drayton, upon his return to the mustering ground on the Enoree, found Fletchall completely under the control of Brown, Kirkland, Robinson, and Robert Cunningham. Kirkland openly denounced the motives of the Provincial Congress and personally insulted Drayton.[15]

The statements made by the leaders of the Nonassociators at this time demonstrate clearly that they were convinced that the Provincial Congress had independence as its goal. Fletchall had already indicated that he felt that to take the side of the congress in this dispute would mean armed resistance to the king and, during one of their confrontations on the Enoree, Brown openly charged Drayton with fomenting rebellion. Joseph Robinson responded to an attempt to persuade him of the justice of the American rights cause by denouncing the reports of "the unanimity of the colonies and their miraculous success at Boston" as "second-hand lies"; in his view, the leaders of the Provincial Congress did not wish an accommodation with England, but they "do in fact, fight against the King, desire ultimate separation, are to be Lords in these new states, to lay the Country off into manors, have taxes paid to themselves..." And, declared Robinson, the charge that he and other critics of the congress intended to "tamper with" the slaves or the Indians "against my rebellious countrymen," was false, and he understood why Kirkland, having "detected the poison" of rebellion, had joined the Nonassociators."[16]

With at best mixed results to show for their efforts in the upper district in the Broad-Saluda fork, Drayton and Tennent turned their steps across the Saluda toward the Savannah River, entering an area in which James Mayson and Andrew Williamson provided strong leadership for the Provincial Congress. Drayton now changed tactics from persuasion to a show of force to impress the wavering, placing Major Williamson of the Ninety Six militia regiment and Colonels Richardson and Thomson with about 300 men apiece at strategic locations between the Broad and the Savannah. Meanwhile, William Tennent moved toward Ninety Six, pausing near the Little River of the Saluda where Patrick Cunningham was influential. After reaching Ninety Six, Tennent made several attempts to return to the Cunningham settlements, but was thwarted by high water. He then moved on to Long Cane Creek where he received a warmer welcome from the inhabitants and was able to raise three companies of volunteers to serve under Andrew Pickens and two other trustworthy officers. From there he crossed into Georgia and moved down the Savannah on his way back to Charlestown.[17]

Left to himself, Drayton now abandoned the tactics of persuasion for the threat of force. Fearing that Moses Kirkland and others were planning to seize Fort Charlotte and possibly Augusta, Drayton issued a circular warning inhabitants that Kirkland's seditious schemes would lead his followers to "be suppressed by the sword." According to Thomas Brown, Drayton sent small groups of men to seize the principal leaders of the king's supporters, but all were forewarned and evaded capture by being "continually on the wing." Drayton also arranged for the. Council of Safety to place guards on the approaches to Charlestown to intercept wagons of Nonassociators coming from the backcountry.[18]

Because Drayton's deployment of the militia had placed Fort Charlotte beyond reach and because Thomas Fletchall had shown little enthusiasm for the venture, Moses Kirkland now undertook a mission to Governor Campbell in the hope of securing ammunition and other help for the Nonassociators. Kirkland, now thoroughly frightened at being singled out by Drayton, slipped into Charlestown accompanied by his twelve-year-old son and several men; after conferring with Governor Campbell, he succeeded in getting on board the sloop-of-war *Tamar*. Campbell was so impressed by reports of the strength of loyal sentiment in the backcountry that he decided to send Kirkland to convince General Thomas Gage, the commander in chief in Boston, that it would be advantageous to detach royal troops to assist the loyal elements in the southern backcountry. Kirkland leaped at the idea and, after stopping at St. Augustine in September, sailed for Boston, only to be taken to Philadelphia after his ship was captured by a privateer. The Continental Congress sent the documents Kirkland was carrying to Charlestown where the Provincial Congress published them, marking Kirkland for all time as an enemy to American liberty. In January 1776 Kirkland made an overture to Henry Laurens to be allowed to return to South Carolina, presumably to plead his case before the Council of Safety, but he received no encouragement. After escaping from prison, he made his way to British West Florida where from Pensacola he operated as John Stuart's deputy to the Seminole Indians. From this station he continued his efforts to convince British military planners that loyalism in the southern backcountry made those provinces ripe for recovery.[19]

Suspecting that Governor Campbell was encouraging Nonassociators from the backcountry, the Council of Safety next considered placing him under arrest. Their suspicions were confirmed through a ruse carried out by a militia officer who, by pretending to be one of Kirkland's men, was permitted to confer with the governor. The divided council was still reluctant to act, but the governor, anxious to avoid the possibility of arrest, fled to the refuge of the *Tamar*.[20]

Despite Drayton's optimistic reports of converts to the American rights cause and his aggressive measures to overawe the wavering, it soon became apparent that his opponents were still strong and active. According to Thomas Brown, Drayton's tactics had so aroused the inhabitants that Robert Cunningham was able to raise 1,200 men who were camped north of the Saluda within twenty miles of Ninety Six. Drayton now employed the stratagem of sending one order to Colonel Richardson to send a force to fall on the rear of the Cunningham camp and another to Colonel John Thomas to burn houses of Nonassociators absent from home, and then arranged to have both dispatches intercepted. He then sent a message to the leaders of the Nonassociators asking for a conference.[21]

Neither Brown nor Robert Cunningham attended this conference, suspecting that it was part of a plot to seize them. Fletchall, who had joined the party with 250 men, was so timid that some Nonassociators wanted to drum him out of camp, but they deferred to him because of his rank, and he assumed command. Brown and Cunningham tried to bind Fletchall with instructions—mutual release of prisoners, extralegal troops and rangers to be disbanded unless approved by Governor Campbell, no interference with the trade of the Nonassociators, and Fort Charlotte to be turned over to Campbell—but the timid colonel fortified himself by "such frequent recourse to the bottle" that he was incapable of carrying them out. Thus, Brown charged, Drayton was able to dictate his own terms, which representatives of both parties approved on September 16, 1775.[22]

Known in the annals of Revolutionary South Carolina as the Treaty of Ninety Six, this agreement was actually the first of two reached at that place in 1775. Under its terms, the signatories bound their followers not to take up arms in support of any British forces that might land in the colony during the "unhappy dispute" with Britain and not to "oppose the proceedings of the Congress of this colony or its authorities derived therefrom," such as the Council of Safety, by word or deed, subject to arrest and trial. The only concession made to the opponents of the Provincial Congress was the vague guarantee that they were not to be molested by Associators without the consent of congress.[23]

Needless to say, Brown, Cunningham, and other more steadfast leaders of the Nonassociators were furious when they saw the handiwork of their delegates to the conference, but they decided to await Governor Campbell's reaction before determining their course. Brown went off to Charlestown to confer with the governor but was seized and brought before the Council of Safety for questioning. Although released, he was unable to see Campbell; instead he wrote the governor a long letter in order to bring him up to date on affairs in the backcountry. He returned briefly to the interior but, learning of an order from the Council of Safety for his arrest, he fled to St. Augustine where he soon caught the attention of Governor Patrick Tonyn of the province of East Florida. Brown was soon busily engaged in defending that province against rebel raids from Georgia, aiding loyalist refugees from the southern provinces, and making contact with others who remained at home in the backcountry.[24]

Meanwhile, Drayton used the agreement of September 16 as a weapon to isolate Robert Cunningham, inquiring whether or not there was truth to the rumors that the latter did not consider himself bound by that treaty. Cunningham accepted the bait, replying that he did "not hold with that peace" because "you had all the bargain making to yourself" and had "taken advantage of men (as I believe) half scared out of their senses at the sight of liberty caps and the sound of cannon." This frank but incautious statement led to orders for Cunningham's arrest, and he was seized late in October and carried off to jail in Charlestown, an event that was to precipitate another crisis and the first bloodshed of the war in South Carolina.[25]

While these exciting events were taking place in the backcountry, the Council of Safety was necessarily concerned about the position that the Cherokee Indians would take in the event that South Carolina's quarrel with England led to open war. The council, fearful of John Stuart's influence over the Indians, had issued orders for his arrest early in June, but the superintendent was forewarned and fled, first to Savannah, and later to St. Augustine. Modern scholars have concluded that Stuart did not try to incite the Cherokees to fall on the frontier settlements in 1775; rather, his aim was to keep them loyal to the Crown but at peace with both sides. Stuart was influential with Cherokee leaders, however, for he had a long record of opposition to the encroachment of settlers beyond the Indian Line. More than that, he had tried to keep speculators from bringing pressure to bear on local chiefs to cede lands to individual speculators or traders to whom they had fallen into debt.[26]

The Council of Safety also feared that Stuart might exert his influence through Alexander Cameron, his deputy to the Cherokees, and certain traders to the Nation. Like Stuart, Cameron wanted the Cherokees to remain at peace, but he was confident that they could be brought to support British authority if war did break out, a view he expressed in a letter that fell into the hands of agents of the Council of Safety. Despite assurances from Andrew Williamson that the deputy's intentions were good, Cameron's letter and his close contact with the Cherokee Nation advanced the notion that Cherokee braves were poised to do his bidding if war came.[27]

There were other factors in this contest for the allegiance of the Indians. Would traders to the tribes take instructions from the Provincial Congress, or would they obey the superintendent? Edward Wilkinson, a longtime trader to the Cherokees, had attempted to secure a cession of land as compensation for debts owed him by tribesmen, but John Stuart, citing royal instructions against such grants, had rejected Wilkinson's application. The Council of Safety in the summer of 1775 named Wilkinson to be its agent to the Cherokees, and shortly thereafter he was chosen as one of the commissioners from the Continental Congress to the southern tribes.[28]

More important for the loyalist story, however, was Richard Pearis, a veteran of Indian trading and diplomacy in Virginia and Maryland and, more recently, the recipient through his half-breed son of a land cession twelve miles square in the valley of the upper Saluda River. Although Stuart had succeeded in getting the cession invalidated, Pearis persisted in his claim and on the basis of it ultimately received substantial compensation from the British government. In the summer of 1775, however, Pearis seems to have hoped that the Council of Safety would support his claim if he used his considerable influence with the Cherokee chiefs on its behalf, and he may even have had hopes of replacing Wilkinson as agent.[29]

Another factor in Indian diplomacy was the scarcity of powder and lead, valuable items sought by the Indians for hunting and by the Council of Safety to defend the colony against a possible British invasion. After the council had sponsored an expedition to hijack a large quantity of powder from a British vessel off St. Augustine, it was prepared to part with some of the precious commodity to secure Cherokee neutrality. William Henry Drayton had concluded his assignment in the backcountry by meeting with several Cherokee chiefs whom Richard Pearis had escorted to the conference. Drayton promised the Cherokees a quantity of powder for hunting purposes; simultaneously in a letter to Alexander Cameron he peremptorily demanded that the deputy remove himself from the Cherokee Nation. Cameron, of course, refused to comply and the Cherokees remained loyal to the British; nevertheless, the Council of Safety stood by its commitment to deliver the powder.[30]

Because Edward Wilkinson was on his way to attend a meeting of Continental Indian commissioners at Salisbury, North Carolina, the Council of Safety had no choice but to employ Richard Pearis as its agent to carry out the delicate mission. Pearis, whose reputation for straight dealing was not the best, had applied to the council for a commission as agent to the Overhill Cherokees, and at the same time had leveled certain charges against Wilkinson. Time was important, however, and the powder had been sent to the Congress where it was awaiting delivery to the Indians. The council indicated to Pearis that his application would be considered when the Provincial Congress reconvened in November; meanwhile, he was to expedite the delivery of the powder to the Cherokees at Keowee.[31]

It was at this point, just as the Second Provincial Congress was assembling for its first session on November 1, that Robert Cunningham was brought to Charlestown. Arrested on the basis of an affidavit from Captain John Caldwell of the Ninety Six Militia Regiment and presumably as a result of his letter to Drayton renouncing the September 16 treaty, Cunningham was brought before the Council of Safety on the opening day of the session. Cunningham, admitting that he had made statements similar to the one alleged by Caldwell, refused to change his view of the treaty, but simply stated that he had been living peaceably at home since the treaty was signed. Remanded to jail under a warrant authorized by the Provincial Congress, he languished there until the following summer.[32]

Robert Cunningham's arrest immediately brought his brother Patrick into the field at the head of an undetermined number of followers. Unable to recapture his brother, Patrick and his men fell upon a party of rangers near Mine Creek on November 3, and seized the ammunition they were escorting to the Cherokees under the arrangement Drayton had made in September. At the same time, to the surprise of the Council of Safety, Richard Pearis suddenly published an affidavit that charged that the gunpowder was intended to supply the Indians for use against Nonassociators in the backcountry. An odd document, the affidavit was sworn before Evan McLaurin as justice of the peace, and witnessed by such Nonassociators as Patrick Cunningham, Henry O'Neall, and Jacob Bowman. The hijacking of the powder and Pearis's assertion about its intended use precipitated another crisis in the backcountry.[33]

Major Andrew Williamson responded to the gunpowder incident by calling out his militia in order to capture Cunningham and recover the ammunition. Over 500 men from twenty-five companies mustered at Ninety Six at Williamson's order, but the response was nothing compared with that from the Nonassociators. Thomas Fletchall authorized Joseph Robinson to muster his regiment, which, augmented by volunteers, brought an estimated 1,500 to 2,000 men into the field, and on November 18 this body crossed the Saluda River and camped within five miles of Ninety Six. Williamson's militia and a party of rangers under James Mayson retreated to a hastily fortified position consisting of old fencerails connecting some outbuildings, but they were immediately surrounded by Robinson's force. A conference was held the next day at which the Nonassociators, represented by Robinson, Patrick Cunningham, and McLaurin, demanded that Williamson's force lay down its arms and disperse. When Williamson, who was playing for time in the hope that he would be reinforced, refused to surrender, a scuffle ensued and both sides commenced firing. The fighting continued sporadically until November 21, when it was agreed to reopen negotiations. The next day an agreement was drawn up and signed by Robinson, Mayson, and Williamson.[34]

On its face, the agreement of November 22 was a triumph for the Nonassociators; the militia were to march out and give up their swivel guns, destroy the fortified camp, and agree that later reinforcements were be bound by the same terms. The two sides were to have twenty days to seek instructions from their superiors, the Council of Safety and Governor Campbell, respectively, and Robinson's men were to withdraw across the Saluda pending orders from Lord William.[35]

Actually, the Nonassociators' victory was hollow. The Second Provincial Congress learned of the loss of the powder on November 6, and the next day it ordered that Patrick Cunningham and five other leaders in that escapade be brought to Charlestown for trial. At the same time, Colonel Richard Richardson was given command of a force of rangers and trusted men drafted from the six interior militia regiments (excluding Thomas Fletchall's); on November 8 Richardson was ordered to track down Patrick Cunningham and his men as violators of the September 16 Treaty of Ninety Six, to recover the lost ammunition, and to seize emissaries coming to Governor Campbell. However, as Gary Olson has shown, even before the theft of the powder was known in Charlestown, Richardson had been arresting Nonassociator militia officers and sending them to Charlestown under the authority earlier given him by Drayton. When Richard Pearis's affidavit revealed his defection and the attempt to pin the charge of inciting the Indians on the congress, that body issued a disclaimer of any intent to involve Indians in the issues that were dividing South Carolinians.[36]

Before the end of November Richardson had collected 1,500 men, and as he moved into the interior, drafts from other regiments and some units from North Carolina swelled his force to between 4,000 and 5,000 men. As his numbers grew, those of the Nonassociators seemed to dwindle; by December 22 his main body had moved nearly to the Enoree River and had taken many prisoners. On that day Richardson's advanced party surprised a remnant of the "malcontents" at the Great Cane Brake on Reedy River beyond the Cherokee line, capturing some while the others fled headlong into the woods. And then the snow came, fifteen inches and more, followed by sleet and heavy rain as his men moved "downward" toward the coast, their units being dismissed as they neared their homes.

This, the "Snow Campaign" in the annals of the Revolution in South Carolina, marked the end of organized resistance in the backcountry and meant that 1776 opened with the Provincial Congress in complete control of the province.[37]

There are two fundamental related questions to be addressed concerning the events of 1775 in the backcountry: How widespread was the opposition to the aggressive measures adopted by the Council of Safety and its agents in 1775; and how deeply committed were those who at one time or another in that year took a hostile stand against the Provincial Congress, its agents, and its military forces? Some effort must be made to answer these questions because British officials in London, acting on the basis of reports from South Carolina and neighboring colonies, would adopt a strategy for crushing the rebellion in the southern provinces. That strategy assumed the loyalists in the backcountry were so numerous that, if properly organized and supported by a minimum commitment of regular troops, they could reclaim those provinces for the Crown. A third question stems from the first two: Was that British strategy based on sound information, or were Crown officials taken in by exaggerated estimates of loyal sentiment given them by the likes of Moses Kirkland and Thomas Brown, abetted by the southern royal governors?[38]

Backcountrymen could be hostile to the Provincial Congress for more than one reason. Some, deeply loyal to the Crown on principle, were overcome by the coercive tactics of the congress; outnumbered and cut off from succor from the king's officials and armed forces, they simply waited in exile or quietly at home in the hopes that British arms would ultimately release them from Whig control and restore them to their homes and families. A second and perhaps larger group, men with no particularly deep commitment to the Crown, could have been antagonized by the coercive tactics employed by William Henry Drayton and others. Such people, swayed by the arguments of Robinson, Cunningham, Brown, and Kirkland, might resent being pressured to give lip service to a cause they but vaguely understood and whose implications for the security of their persons and property were equally unclear. These persons should perhaps be considered neutralists rather than loyalists; to them in 1775 the congress and its representatives were the aggressors who were the immediate threat to whatever tranquility they had hoped for in the hard life of their isolated farms and settlements. But the passage of time could dull their resentment; if not coerced further by committeemen and militiamen they might find a degree of security under American rule that they could live with, a security more real than the remote possibility of the restoration of a vague authority of which most had seen little evidence in the past. Under those circumstances, security would loom as the essential requirement of their lives, and security to interior settlers meant especially protection against the horrors of Indian warfare. If they could become convinced that congress had no intention of using Indians as allies against the wavering, or, more important, if the congress moved decisively to remove the threat of Indian attacks, that security would be greater than they had known for some time. Under these conditions, the restoration of British authority in the backcountry at a later date might be considerably less attractive than it had seemed in 1775.

What is the evidence for the existence of a loyalist or anticongress presence in the backcountry in 1775? First, there are the numbers reported to have turned out at Ninety Six in September to confront the force that Drayton was mobilizing in the name of the Provincial Congress, generally estimated to have been about 1,200. Second, an estimated

1,500 to 2,000 men joined Patrick Cunningham and Joseph Robinson at Ninety Six in November following the seizure of the powder and the bogus report that the congress planned to use the Indians against Nonassociators. Assuming that these estimates are accurate, who were these men who left their homes and exchanged shots with the militia and rangers led by Williamson, Mayson, Richardson, and others? When the effort is made to identify individuals actually involved in these confrontations, the evidence is scanty indeed. Those who served under Robinson, Fletchall, and the two Cunninghams were irregulars, and there are no muster rolls or pay records to supply their names, places of residence, origins, ages, or other data that could identify them more clearly. What has survived to help in this endeavor are the names of persons sought or captured by congressional leaders and military forces during the summer and fall, and a few items of testimony by confirmed loyalists in the claims they submitted to the Crown after the war. At most, they number about 175 men, some of whom like the three Cunninghams were brothers, or as in the case of the five Hambys included brothers, sons, and nephews. But it is worthwhile to analyze this small group that the congress considered to be the ringleaders of its opposition in the backcountry in order to search for clues about the nature of that opposition.[39]

The large majority of this group, 130 men, were captured by Richardson's forces in November and December, about 100 of whom were seized during his concluding sweep up the Reedy River. Considered to be inveterate enemies, some were classified by their captors according to their perceived degree of hostility—"a very bad man" or "a very active man"; anyone with Patrick Cunningham when the congress's ammunition was seized on November 3 was identified as a "powder" man. Fifteen of the group had been officers in Fletchall's or another militia regiment. Six others were referred to as "Scopholite" officers, apparently an early use of a term later applied to backcountrymen who tried to join the British army in Florida in the period when the rebels controlled the state.[40]

The largest group of the captives resided along the streams that flowed into the Saluda River from the north, particularly Little River, Beaverdam Creek, and Bush River, and their tributaries, in or near areas designated by their enemies as "Cunningham's settlement." Two smaller groups were concentrated in two other sections of Ninety Six District: the area from which Thomas Fletchall's regiment was drawn—the Tyger River and the Enoree River and its tributaries, Fair Forest Creek, and Durban's Creek; and the watershed of Stevens Creek, which fed the Savannah River above Augusta. Their origins were diverse—Germans, north Irish, and several Scots from overseas, and native Americans who had moved from Virginia or North Carolina—but virtually all shared one characteristic: they had arrived in the province since the Cherokee War. Among them could be found veterans of colonial wars and raw lads in their teens. As property owners they ranged from men who held 500 to 1,500 acres on which they raised substantial quantities of grain, indigo, and livestock, to owners of 100-acre bounty grants who lived in rough cabins and had cleared just a few acres for planting. Several owned slaves, while of the "Scopholite" captains, one was denoted as "colored" and another as "mulatto." There is no evidence that any substantial number of the men seized by Richardson in the backcountry had been Regulators during that controversy.[41]

Richardson's triumphant progress through Ninety Six District netted the largest bag of prisoners, but there is some evidence that local committeemen were at work ferreting out the other men considered to be dangerous. A trial before the Court of General Sessions at Ninety Six in November convicted nine persons of sedition and sentenced them to hang, including the five Hambys of Enoree River. Presumably the threat was sufficient to force them to agree to remain peaceably at home, for they were pardoned after independence was declared. Others who avoided capture fled into Indian country or "hid out in the woods" for awhile, but when they tried to slip back into their neighborhoods, they were confronted by committeemen who demanded that they sign statements that, if caught in arms against the Provincial Congress again, they could expect to face the hangman. Of the ringleaders, only Thomas Brown and Joseph Robinson remained out of the clutches of their enemies. After learning what his fate would be if he returned to his home, Robinson gradually worked his way through the Cherokee Nation and then the Creek lands to British West Florida, and in 1777 he found means to reach St. Augustine. Meanwhile, his family was turned out, and his property plundered and burned.[42]

So much for those "malcontents" about whom something is known, perhaps a tenth of the largest number reported to have assembled at one time in 1775. It must be remembered that the Robinson-Cunningham force that obtained the agreement of November 22 was really more of a posse than an army. Once these men withdrew across the Saluda, the desire to return to normal pursuits must have grown, a desire probably stimulated by reports of the size of the army that Richardson was bringing against them. Cut off from any real hope of succor from the governor and with winter approaching, the resolve of many probably melted away; as Richardson moved up the country he reported that large numbers of Nonassociators came in to give themselves up. All but the leaders, the "powder" men, and others considered dangerous were sent to their homes after promising to remain quietly there. Finally, only the dedicated continued to hold out, and most of them were captured or dispersed at the Cane Brake.[43]

Even most of those sent under guard to Charlestown were soon released, because, as one local editor put it, they had become "sensible of their error" and now denounced the leaders who had misled them about the "nature of the present contest." The Provincial Congress did keep about a dozen in all securely under lock and key, including the Cunningham brothers, Pearis, and Fletchall, until the threat of a British invasion had been removed during the next summer.[44]

During the winter of 1776 the Provincial Congress, having crushed the insurrection in the backcountry, was able to reorganize the processes of government in South Carolina. On March 26 it adopted a "Constitution, or Form of Government"; under its provisions, it transformed itself into a General Assembly, which subsequently chose John Rutledge as "President," the members of a Legislative Council, a Privy Council, the judiciary, and sheriffs for the judicial districts. Although the constitution was declared to be a temporary expedient until the quarrel with Great Britain was reconciled, a very long step toward independence had been taken.[45]

With the backcountry quiet it might seem that the problem of sedition would have receded, but a British fleet and army from Boston layoff the coast of the Carolinas during that winter. Under Sir Peter Parker and Sir Henry Clinton, that force, after being reinforced by troops from Britain, appeared off Charlestown at the end of May. Poor British planning and an inspired defense of Sullivan's Island caused extensive damage to the fleet, and the expedition withdrew to join a major British army then being assembled for an assault on New York. Long before the threat to South Carolina had been removed, however, the General Assembly, fearful of subversion in the face of an invasion, passed legislation to "prevent sedition and punish insurgents."

The sedition law called for the death penalty for anyone who took "up arms with a hostile intent, and by force and violence, or by words, deeds or writing" tried to persuade others to do likewise, or who communicated with the British forces or supplied them, or who incited Indians to attack or slaves to rise in support of the British government. It also provided for the sale of the property of persons convicted under the act, the proceeds to go to form a reprisal fund to compensate persons who had suffered property loss or damage in defending South Carolina against invasion. While Clinton's expedition threatened the city, royal officials were confined to their homes in Charlestown, but the rebels dealt less gently with Nonassociators in the city. John Imrie, the Scottish shipwright, detected when he attempted to reach the British fleet by boat, was imprisoned for six weeks, while John Tunno was one of several merchants sent to jail in Georgetown.[46]

But once the threat of invasion had passed, the General Assembly turned to the problem of removing causes of friction within the state; it authorized President Rutledge to proclaim pardon and amnesty for the "late insurgents," excepting certain special cases such as Fletchall, the Cunninghams, Pearis, and a few leading "powder" men. Crown officers who had been confined to Charlestown while the town was threatened were permitted to remove themselves to Great Britain or the West Indies at public expense, but only James Simpson, Justice Edward Savage, and one customs official chose to take advantage of the law. In October the merchants were released and given the choice of taking an oath of fidelity and remaining in residence or of departing for the home islands or the West Indies at public expense. Like many others, Imrie and Tunno did not take advantage of the opportunity to leave at this time, perhaps because the oath of fidelity simply required those who took it to support the March 26 constitution "until an accommodation of the differences between Britain and America" could be reached or until they were otherwise released "by the Legislative Authority of this colony." The General Assembly also postponed consideration of a bill that would have disarmed persons who were "notoriously disaffected."[47]

The end of the threat of invasion by sea permitted the release of the remaining leaders of the backcountry insurrection. Although intended as another means of reducing tensions within the state's population, its timing coincided with the long-feared Indian assault on the Carolina frontier in July. The Cherokees were apparently persuaded by such northern tribes as the Shawnee and the Delaware to participate in a general attack on the southern frontier, but fortunately for the Americans the news of the plan had leaked out and the effect was not so great as the tribes had hoped.[48]

Nevertheless, the loss of life and property inflicted by the Cherokees in their initial raids led almost immediately to demands for retaliation. Andrew Williamson responded by calling out his militia, but the panic was so general that it took over two weeks to assemble 450 men along the Indian Line. After beating off a Cherokee attack on Lindley's Fort on Rayburn's Creek, north of the Saluda, the militia counterattacked and took some prisoners, only to discover that among them were thirteen "white Indians" who were hustled off to jail at Ninety Six to await trial on charges of sedition. Indeed, it was reported that the assault force in this action consisted of 90 Indians and 120 white men and that some of the latter group were painted like Indians, a fact that proved to Whigs that the British had concocted a plan for Indian and loyalist raids on the frontier in conjunction with their expected assault on the coast. According to the Whig version, John Stuart and his agents were behind the malevolent scheme of unleashing the Indians against the frontier with the aid of the "malcontents" who had escaped Richardson's net in the Snow Campaign of the previous winter. It was even reported that where they had the opportunity to discriminate, the raiders deliberately spared the property of settlers who were known to be British sympathizers.[49]

Once again, modern historians have, in retrospect, cleared Stuart and Cameron of complicity in these attacks by the Cherokees. But the presence of white men on these raids indicates that some loyalists were desperate enough to resort to such tactics in hope of gaining a measure of revenge against Whigs who had driven them from their homes, and perhaps to contribute to the restoration of royal rule, especially if they anticipated that a British force was preparing to land on the coast.[50]

Few of the whites who cooperated with the Cherokees on these raids have been identified. Of the leaders of the Nonassociators in the 1775 campaigns only Patrick Cunningham and Joseph Robinson had evaded capture during Richardson's victorious sweep through Ninety Six District. The former was taken into custody in February, however, and joined his brother in jail in Charlestown where both languished until it was too late to have been involved in the frontier attacks. Robinson escaped capture, but no Whig or loyalist source has identified him as a participant in the raids. Hugh Brown, who resided on Reedy River, was definitely linked by the Whigs to the raids. Captured with Patrick Cunningham in February, he must have escaped while his captors were bringing him to Charlestown or he was released soon thereafter. A Captain John York, listed as a "very bad man" among the prisoners taken by Richardson's expedition, was among those whom Andrew Williamson was to escort to Charlestown, but he apparently never reached there because the Provincial Congress ordered his arrest early in February. Later in the spring Henry Stuart, who was serving his brother as a special agent to the Cherokees, received a visit from York "and some others of the loyal inhabitants of the back settlements of Carolina" to learn if help could be expected from St. Augustine or Pensacola. York then returned to keep "people in the back settlements of Carolina in spirits," but later rejoined the Indians. He must have been wanted badly by the South Carolina government because he just barely escaped capture by a party that Edward Wilkinson sent to seize him. About the same time, a report reached the Moravian settlements in piedmont North Carolina that the Indian attacks had been instigated, "not by order of the royal officers," but by about forty white men living in the Indian towns. Thomas Rogers of Tyger River was one of the prisoners sent by Richardson to Charlestown as a result of the Snow Campaign; subsequently released to his home, he was among the thirteen white men taken at Lindley's Fort, was tried for sedition at Ninety Six and sentenced to death, but was later reprieved . The young David Fanning, a resident of Rayburn's Creek and a notorious partisan leader later in the war, revealed in his memoirs that he had participated in the Cherokee raids that summer.[51]

While his militia were assembling to retaliate against the Indians, Andrew Williamson reported that on July 18 Robert Cunningham and Richard Pearis had appeared in his camp, and that the former had declared "that he came to stand or fall with us." Williamson was inclined to accept Cunningham's help, but the feeling in the ranks was so hostile to the presence of the two men because of the "behaviour of Hugh Brown" and others that it "would be improper to confer any public trust" upon him. Instead, Cunningham was advised to go home and "mind his private business." Whether Pearis also offered his services at this time is not known, but they certainly were not accepted.[52]

But Pearis must have been a special case. He later claimed that before he was released from jail he took a "test oath" as well as the oath of fidelity and was given a certificate from President Rutledge "recommending him to all good people." Upon returning to his home, Pearis discovered that much of his property had been destroyed, his livestock and slaves sold, and "the spoil distributed" among the men of the state regiment commanded by Colonel John Thomas. These charges were made in a memorial to the General Assembly, which responded by voting him £700 currency on the basis of information furnished by President Rutledge relative to the burning of Pearis's house and the sale of his property. It is not clear whether Rutledge and the legislature still feared Pearis's influence among the Indians or merely preferred not to set dangerous precedents in the handling of private property by its military forces.[53]

Any possibility of Cherokee assistance to the loyalists in the South Carolina backcountry was ended that summer when Williamson's troops burned a number of their villages among the lower towns; he then cooperated with General Griffith Rutherford's North Carolina troops in laying waste many of the middle and valley towns in that state and in Georgia. The chastened Cherokees signed a treaty in 1777 by which they gave up all claim to lands in South Carolina, and they were not to be an important facrof in the state during the rest of the war.[54]

Notes

1. *Extracts from the Journals of the Provincial Congresses Of South Carolina, 1775–1776*, ed. W. Edwin Hemphill and Wylma Anne Wates (Columbia, S.C., 1960), 3–8.
2. Ibid., 43, 45, 47–49.
3. Drayton, *Memoirs*, I, 352–53. Early in 1776 the Provincial Congress made three militia districts from the two in the Broad-Saluda fork mentioned here: a Lower District ; a Little River District that generally encompassed the upper Saluda; and an Upper, or Spartan, District that included the settlements west of the upper Broad. *Extracts from the Journals of the Provincial Congresses*, 183, 251.
4. Two excellent accounts of the events of 1775 in the backcountry are Gary D. Olson, "Loyalists and the American Revolution: Thomas Brown and the South Carolina Backcountry, 1775–1776," *SCHM*, LXVIII (1967), 201–19; LXIX (1968), 44–56; and Lewis P. Jones, *The South Carolina Civil War of 1775* (Lexington, S.C., 1975), 30–71. I have generally followed these accounts in this chapter but .have placed somewhat more emphasis on individual loyalists and their motivation.
5. For Fletchall, see Loyalist Transcripts LVII, 223–39. A description of his mill five years after these events is in the "Allaire Diary," 501.
6. Council of Safety to Fletchall , July 14, 1775, "Journal of the Council of Safety of the Province of South Carolina, 1775," *Collections of the South Carolina Historical Society* (Charleston , 1858), II, 40-42; Fletchall to Henry Laurens, July 23, 1775, Gibbes, *Documentary History*, I, 123–24; the Counter-Association is in the Simms Collection. Laurens's papers, invaluable for this period of the Revolution in South Carolina, have been found in the Simms Collection; the microfilm edition accumulated for the letterpress edition, Rogers, ed., *Laurens Papers*; and among those printed at various times in the *SCHM*.
7. *Canadian Claims*, 799–801; "Robinson, Lt. Col. Joseph, Memoir of (1797)," Rare Book Room, McLennan Library, McGill University, Montreal.
8. Mayson to Col. William Thomson, July 18, 1775, Laurens Papers (microfilm). Drayton, *Memoirs*, I,

321, says that Kirkland sent a message to Fletchall at his muster ground, which news spurred Robinson and the Cunninghams to raise the force that moved to Ninety Six and recaptured the powder. Olson, "Loyalists and the American Revolution," *SCHM* (1967), 206–17. Edward McCrady, *S.C. in the Revolution 1775–1780*, 39, has suggested that decisive action by Campbell at this time might have changed the whole course of events in the backcountry [hat summer.

9. For Robert, see Loyalist Transcripts, LIV, 317–26; *South Carolina Gazette and Country Journal* (Charlestown), Feb. 28, 1769; and Richard Maxwell Brown, *South Carolina Regulators* (Cambridge, Mass., (1963), 203, 204n. Many years after the war Andrew Pickens declared that Robert Cunningham had turned to the king's side after he failed to obtain command of one of the new regiments authorized by the Provincial Congress, Pickens to Henry Lee, Aug. 28, 1811, Thomas Sumter Papers, VV, I, 107, Draper Coll. Patrick's name appears frequently as deputy surveyor in Plats and as an applicant for land grants in JCHA.

10. Loyalist Transcripts, LVII, 318–50; Brown, *S.C. Regulators*, 128–29; grand jury presentments, Apr. 18, 1768, *South Carolina Gazette and Country Journal*, May 17, 1768, which contains Kirkland's charge that Joseph Curry had aided the criminal element. Kirkland pursued the matter further in a letter to the *South Carolina Gazette* (Charlestown), which drew Curry's caustic rejoinder that someone else must have been the author, "as he can himself, but with difficulty" write his own name," ibid., Apr. 26, 1768.

11. Olson, "Loyalists and the American Revolution," *SCHM* (1967), 201–2, 207–8.

12. Drayton to the Council of Safety, Aug. 7, 9, 16, 1775, Gibbes, *Documentary History*, I, 128–29, 134, 140–41.

13. Drayton to the Council of Safety, Aug. 17, 1775, Gibbes, *Documentary History*, I, 128–29.

14. Drayton to the Council of Safety, Aug. 7, 16, 21, and Tennent to Laurens, Aug. 20, Gibbes, *Documentary History*, I, 141–42, 145–46, 149; Dalrymple's *Address* is in Peter Force, comp., *American Archives*, 4th Ser. 6 vols. (Washington, D.C., 1837–46), I, 1413–31.

15. Drayton and Tennent to the Council of Safety, Aug. 24, 1775, Gibbes, *Documentary History*, I, 156–57.

16. Robinson to Ezekiel Polk, Aug. 21, 1775, Simms Coll.

17. Drayton to the Council of Safety, Aug. 30, 1775, Gibbes, *Documentary History*, I, 163; "A Fragment of a Journal Kept by Rev. William Tennent...," ibid., 232–39.

18. Olson, "Loyalists and the American Revolution" *SCHM* (1967), 212.

19. Drayton, *Memoirs*, I, 330. Kirkland's travels and adventures that autumn can be traced in Campbell to Gage, Sept. 20, Patrick Tonyn to Gage, Sept. 29, Frederick Mulcaster to Col. James Grant, Sept. 19, and the Earl of Dunmore to Admiral Samuel Graves, Oct. 2, Continental Congress Papers, #51; Campbell to the Earl of Dartmouth, S.C. Records in the P.R.O., XXXV, 245–52; Council of Safety to Drayton, Sept. 17, 1775, Laurens Papers (microfilm); Kirkland to Laurens, Jan. 1, 1776, Gibbes, *Documentary History*, I, 254–55; Loyalist Transcripts, LVII, 318–50.

20. Josiah Smith, Jr., to James Poyas, Sept. 21, 1775, Josiah Smith, Jr. Letterbook, SHC; John Ball to "Brother," Sept. 19, 1775, Ball Family Papers, SCHS. Baily Cheney, a young man who had accompanied Kirkland from the backcountry, was forced to participate in the ruse, Drayton, *Memoirs*, II, 3.

21. Olson, "Loyalists and the American Revolution" (1967), 213–14; Jones, *S.C. Civil War of 1775*, 62–63.

22. Brown to Campbell, Oct. 18, 1775, S.C. Records in the P.R.O., XXXV, 287, also printed as James H. O'Donnell, ed., "A Loyalist View of the Drayton-Tennent-Hart Mission to the Upcountry," *SCHM*, XLVII (1966), 15–28.

23. The treaty is in Gibbes, *Documentary History*, I, 184–86.

24. O'Donnell, ed., "A Loyalist View"; Olson, "Loyalists and the American Revolution" (1968), 22–23.

25. Drayton to Cunningham, Sept. 21, and Cunningham to Drayton, Oct. 5,1775, Gibbes, ed., *Documentary History*, I, 191–92, 200; Proceedings of the South Carolina Provincial Congress, Nov. 1, 1775, Force, comp., *American Archives*, 4th Ser., IV, 28–29.

26. James H. O'Donnell, *Southern Indians in the American Revolution* (Knoxville, Tenn., 1973), 29–33; Olson, "Loyalists and the American Revolution" (1968), 44–46; John R. Alden, *John Stuart and the Southern Colonial Frontier: A Study of Indian Relations, War, Trade, and Land Problems in the Southern Wilderness, 1754–1775* (New York, 1966 [orig. publ. Ann Arbor, Mich., 1944], 299–305; Stuart to the Committee of Intelligence, July 18, 1775, Force, comp., *American Archives*, 4th Ser., II, 168l.

27. Loyalist Transcripts, LV, 556–65; John Lewis Gervais to Alexander Cameron, June 17, 1775, Clinton Papers; Alan Cameron to Andrew Williamson, July 10, 1775, Laurens Papers (microfilm); Williamson to the Council of Safety, July 12, 1775, "Journal of the Council of Safety, 1775," *SCHS Colls.*, II, 55–56.

28. Alden, *John Stuart*, 300–301.

29. *Canadian Claims*, 190; John Bennett, "Historical Notes," *SCHGM*, XVIII (1917), 97–99; Alden, *John*

Stuart, 299–301; David H. Corkran, *The Cherokee Frontier* (Columbia, S.C., 1970), 52–56, 154, 162.

30. Council of Safety to [Drayton], Sept. 15, 16, 1775, Laurens Papers (microfilm); Laurens to Drayton, Sept. 21, Drayton to Alexander Cameron, Sept. 26, and Cameron to Drayton, Oct. 16, 1775, Gibbes, *Documentary History*, I, 192–93, 207–8.
31. Council of Safety to Wilkinson, Oct. 24, to Col. William Thomson, Oct. 25, to Pearis, Oct. 24, and to Messrs. William Arthur, et al., Oct. 24, 1775, Laurens Papers (microfilm).
32. *Extracts from the Journals of the Provincial Congresses*, 82–84.
33. Olson, "Loyalists and the American Revolution" (1967), 216: Alden, *John Stuart*, 298–300. Pearis declared in his affidavit that in a conversation during the past summer Drayton had suggested that the Provincial Congress might renegotiate Pearis's claim to the huge tract on Reedy River given him by the Cherokees, which John Stuart had invalidated, might consider delivery of the powder to the Indians as payment for the transaction, and offer him an unspecified appointment to the Cherokees. Having spurned Drayton's suggestion because it would cheat the Indians and convinced by Robert Cunningham's arrest that Drayton was engaged in double-dealing, Pearis refused to deliver the powder. Historians have usually attributed Pearis's defection to his disappointment when he learned that congress had made George Galphin its agent to the Indians, and they have, with Gary Olson, felt that Pearis's charge that congress meant to use the powder against the Indians was false.
34. Williamson to Wilkinson, Nov. 6, Mayson to William Thomson, Nov. 24, and Williamson to Drayton, Nov. 25, 1775, Gibbes, *Documentary History*, I, 209–10, 215–16, 216–19; Wilkinson to Williamson, Nov. 7, and Drayton to Pearis, Nov. 8, 1775, Simms Coll. The best account of the conflict at Ninety Six is Marvin L. Cann, "Prelude to War: The First Battle of Ninety Six, November 19–21, 1775," *SCHM* (1975), especially 205–14.
35. The Robinson-Mayson-Williamson agreement is in Gibbes, *Documentary History*, I, 214–15.
36. Olson, "Loyalists and the American Revolution" (1967), 217; Gibbes, *Documentary History*, I, 210–14, and Council of Safety to Williamson, Dec. 4,9, 1775, Laurens Papers (microfilm), for the arrest of Captain Mathew Floyd, an emissary from Robinson to Governor Campbell.
37. The progress of Richardson's force and the plight of the Nonassociators in the Snow Campaign can be followed in Richardson to Laurens, Dec. 12, 16, 22, 1775, and Jan. 2, 1776, Gibbes, *Documentary History*, I, 239–44, 246–48; Richard Richardson, Jr., to Laurens, Dec. 25, 1775, Simms Coll.; Drayton, *Memoirs*, II, 125–33; and in a few instances in the Loyalist Transcripts and *Canadian Claims*.
38. A recent statement of the idea that British strategy was based in part on the presumption of strong loyalist support in South Carolina is John Shy, "British Strategy for Pacifying the Southern Colonies, 1778–1781," *The Southern Experience in the American Revolution*, ed. Jeffrey J. Crow and Larry E. Tise (Chapel Hill, N.C., 1978), 155–73.
39. A list of those captured during Richardson's campaign is in Gibbes, *Documentary History*, I, 249–53.
40. The word "Scopholite" was adapted from a variant spelling of Joseph Coffell's name and thus would appear to denote a moderator during the Regulator conflict of the late 1760s, but one prisoner so designated was Jacob Fry, who had been a leading Regulator, Brown, *S.C. Regulators*, 204. An example of the use by the Provincial Congress of economic pressure on wavering backcountrymen is the case of Benjamin Wofford who was permitted by congress to trade with Charlestown if he took an oath of strict neutrality and agreed to adhere to the September agreement at Ninety Six, Wofford to the Council of Safety, Jan. 15, 1776, Simms Coll.
41. In addition to information in Loyalist Transcripts and *Canadian Claims* on these individuals, the following collections in SCAH have been consulted in drawing up their profiles: Plats, and JCHA on landholding; Council Journals on immigration; and for various purposes Secretary of State, Miscellaneous Records, Main Series; Deeds; Wills; and the wills and inventories that the counties began to record during and after the war, all in SCAH. About one in five of the men pardoned for Regulator activity were to perform loyal acts during the Revolutionary period; very few of the 175 men seized in the backcountry in 1775–76 had been Regulators. But even if a much higher proportion of these two groups had become loyalists, the fact that virtually all of the pardoned Regulators resided in Camden District, and that a very large majority of the Council of Safety's prisoners in 1775–76 were from Ninety Six District would make the connection dubious at best. These conclusions are drawn from the sources above; for the two groups, see Brown, *S.C. Regulators*, 144–47, and Gibbes, *Documentary History*, I, 249–53.
42. Zacharias Gibbs's statement is in Loyalist Transcripts, LII, 227–57. The young David Fanning tells of "lying out" in the woods through that winter, then returning to his Rayburn's Creek home only to be thrown into jail until someone offered to act as surety for his behavior, David Fanning, "Narrative," 180–239. For

Robinson, see *Canadian Claims*, 799.
43. Richardson to Laurens, Dec. 12, 1775, Gibbes, *Documentary History*, I, 239–41, reporting that "Captains Plummer and Smith and thirty men surrender themselves and arms." Apparently none of these captives was sent to Charlestown.
44. *South Carolina and American General Gazette*, Jan 12, 19, 1776. The sedition law is in *Statutes at Large*, IV, 343–46; Clinton, *American Rebellion*, 26–29.
45. *Extracts from the Journals of the Provincial Congresses*, 256–67; *House Journals*, 1776–1780, xi–xii.
46. *House Journals*, 1776–1780, 52, 97; Loyalist Transcripts, LV, 32–45; LVII, 418–38.
47. *House Journals*, 1776–1780, 54–55, 97; the oath is in the constitution of 1776, *Extracts from the Journals of the Provincial Congresses*, 263.
48. O'Donnell, *Southern Indians*, 40, 44–47.
49. Rev. James Cresswell to Drayton, July 27, 1776, Gibbes, *Documentary History*, II, 30–33.
50. Jack N. Sosin, " The Use of Indians in the War of the American Revolution: A Re-Assessment of Responsibility," *Canadian Historical Review*, XLVI (1965), 117.
51. Henry Stuart, John's brother and special agent to the Cherokees, reported that "a Capt. York and some others of the loyal inhabitants of the back settlements of South Carolina" had visited the Cherokees, had then returned to the settlements to bolster loyalist morale, but that later York had fled to the Cherokee Nation where Wilkinson had sought to have him kidnapped and turned over to state authorities for trial. See *State Records of N.C.*, X, 771, 776: Salem Diary, 1776, in Adelaide L. Fries, ed., *Records of the Moravians in North Carolina* (Raleigh, N.C., 1922–54), III, 1065; Williamson to Drayton, July 22,1776, Drayton, *Memoirs*, II, 367; *Canadian Claims*, 120, 241–42.
52. Williamson to Drayton, July 22, and Francis Salvador to Drayton, July 18, 1776, Drayton, *Memoirs*, II, 364, 366–7.
53. *House Journals*, 1776–1780, 62–63, 106, 109, 116, 122.
54. Drayton, *Memoirs*, II, 343–62.

Chapter Three

EXILE AND ACCOMODATION, 1776–1779

The scouting parties of our [East Florida] Rangers have conducted into this province near four hundred loyalists that have, my Lord, mostly been forced to shelter in the woods in Carolina and Georgia. Brigadier General Prevost purposes to embody them.

—*Governor Patrick Tonyn, April 1778*

The departure of the Clinton-Parker expedition for New York was followed by the momentous news that the Continental Congress had declared the colonies independent, an event celebrated in Charlestown on August 5, 1776. Almost immediately President John Rutledge summoned the General Assembly to meet in special session to take such actions as South Carolina's new status required.

An unresolved problem for the new state government was the fate of the Crown officers still residing in South Carolina. Royal officials, in the anomalous position of having to remain at their posts at a time when circumstances in South Carolina had made them completely ineffective, had been placed under house arrest in Charlestown or on their nearby plantations. There they remained so long as the Clinton-Parker expedition threatened to assault the city.

At the same time, a number of private citizens who dissented from the measures of the Provincial Congress had been hustled off to jail in the interior. The adventures of John Champneys reveal some of the tribulations suffered by loyalists during this exciting period. Champneys, a native of the province and owner of one the great wharves on the Charlestown waterfront, was one of twenty men who, while the city was under siege, were called to the State House and again offered the state oath; when they refused to take it, they were confined in nearby rooms. On hearing rumors that they were to be sent into the interior, the prisoners petitioned Rutledge to permit them to return to their homes under security for their "peaceable behaviour." While awaiting a response, a shot was fired through a window in the night; the next day six of the prisoners agreed to take the oath. Their petition was turned down, but the president and Privy Council called eight of them in for questioning; although their answers were considered to be satisfactory and some agreed to take the oath, they were required to state in writing their reasons for wishing to remain in the state. Despite their willingness to do so, six of them—Robert Rowand, James Carsan, John Tunno, and Harry Michie of the Scottish community, and the South Carolina natives Champneys and James Brisbane—were marched off to Georgetown. After several weeks in that town, Rutledge ordered Brisbane, Carson, Michie, and Champneys sent on to Cheraw District, which place they reached on August 2 after a four-day march. In October, following the death of his six-year-old son, Champneys petitioned Rutledge for permission to return to Charlestown to make business arrangements preliminary to leaving the province. Although he was permitted to return to Charlestown, in December his papers were seized and he was again placed under house arrest, and in January 1777 confined to jail. Exactly what Champneys had done to deserve so much attention from state leaders is not known, but they clearly feared that he and others like him were sources of potential subversion.[1]

In the winter of 1777 the General Assembly took steps to force people like Champneys to make a choice, passing an ordinance to "establish an oath of abjuration and allegiance." To be offered to "all the late officers of the King of Britain" and all others suspected of "holding principles injurious to the rights of this State," the oath required signers to "renounce, refuse and any allegiance or obedience" to George III, to declare their allegiance to the new state, and to defend it against all efforts by the king and his adherents to regain control of South Carolina. Those who failed to take the oath were expected to remove themselves and their families from the state within sixty days or as soon thereafter as they could settle their business affairs and secure passage; the state would pay passage to Great Britain or one of its Caribbean possessions for those who could not afford it; and they could take with them any property remaining after they paid their debts.[2]

One by one, Crown or provincial civil servants from the chief justice and the attorney general to the lowliest employee in the customs service were called in and offered the oath of abjuration. Most echoed the sentiments of Chief Justice Gordon who stated simply that he could not subscribe to an oath that was inconsistent with his opinions, principles, or allegiance, that he hoped for reconciliation between England and the colonies, and that he bore no ill feeling toward South Carolina. In addition, several who had held office at the pleasure of the General Assembly—Lieutenant Governor Bull, former Joint Treasurer Henry Peronneau, former Councillor William Wragg, and the gunner of Fort Johnson who was still receiving an allowance-refused to take the oath. The list included several natives and residents of long standing as well as less respected placemen who had come to South Carolina more recently.[3]

By spring those who had refused to take the oath were making preparations to leave the state and, through announcements in local newspapers, notified their creditors and persons obligated to them that they intended to depart as soon as shipping became available. Some who owned substantial property tried to liquidate it and, as in the case of James Simpson who bought 150 barrels of rice, to invest it in a commodity to be sold abroad. Others turned to business partners, friends, or relatives for assistance; William Bull, for example, chose to leave his Ashley River property in the care of his nephew, Stephen, a leading rebel, a decision he came to regret.[4]

These preparations made, royal officials took their departure by whatever shipping was available. Because American ports were closed to British ships, the exiles were forced to sail on American or neutral vessels bound for ports in Europe or the West Indies from which they might transfer to British vessels destined for the home islands. But American ships at sea were fair prize for British cruisers, and departing loyalists suffered long delays and consequently heavy expense as their captors took them from port to port. Thomas Irving, the receiver general, sailed for a Spanish port on a rebel vessel that was taken by a British warship in American waters. After long delays in St. Augustine and again in New York, he reached England in the summer of 1778. William Wragg paid the ultimate price for his record of unswerving loyalty to the Crown when he was drowned in a shipwreck off the Dutch coast.[5]

Although the departure of royal officials removed a potential source of subversion, a larger number of persons of uncertain loyalty to the new state government still resided in South Carolina. Certain events of the winter and spring of 1778 sparked controversy about the degree of leniency that should be shown to people who refused to declare their allegiance to the state and contribute their money and services to its support. In January Charlestown suffered one of its most devastating fires, the conflagration destroying over 250 houses in the area between Broad and Queen streets. In the aftermath of the tragedy, rumors circulated that sailors from British vessels off the coast had plotted with local loyalists to set the fire. It was in this atmosphere that the General Assembly met to take up several significant issues.[6]

One important item of business was to mark the complete separation of the state from Britain by adopting a constitution to replace the temporary measure enacted in 1776. But when the General Assembly presented its handiwork to President John Rutledge, he stunned that body, first by withholding his approval on constitutional grounds, and then by resigning his position. Despite his objections, the new constitution was approved, and the assembly proceeded to elect Rawlins Lowndes to succeed him as president until it went into effect.[7]

Of greatest importance to loyalists and neutralists in South Carolina was the passage in this session of an act to enforce "An Assurance of Allegiance and Fidelity" to the state, by far the most comprehensive loyalty measure enacted until that time. By its terms, an oath of allegiance was to be administered to males over sixteen at militia musters throughout the state, and those taking it were required to swear to defend the state against George III and all other enemies. Persons who failed to take the oath within a specified time were to be ineligible to vote, hold office, serve on juries, acquire or convey property, use the courts, or practice their trades or professions. Men who left the state to avoid taking the oath could suffer death for treason if they returned, and local magistrates were to maintain lists of signers and nonsigners.[8]

While preparations were being made to administer the oath of fidelity, word was received in Charlestown that the Continental Congress had recommended that erstwhile enemies be given new opportunities to support the American cause. When the moderate President Rawlins Lowndes attempted to implement congress's recommendation by extending amnesty to former enemies who would return and take the oath of fidelity, a crowd gathered to protest his action and to threaten harm to local editors if they printed the amnesty proclamation. Despite the unpopularity of the measure, Lowndes's proclamation and a subsequent extension of time for taking the oath had the effect of making it very difficult to enforce the law uniformly.[9]

Once the new law went into effect, local gazettes announced the imminent departure of a new group of nonsigners, principally merchants, tradesmen, and professional men from Charlestown, Beaufort, and Georgetown. As in the case of the royal officials earlier, these people resorted to various means to convert property to a form that could be sold abroad or to leave it in the hands of attorneys or friends. Circumstances had changed, however, for France was now an ally of the Continental Congress, and French ships were subject to seizure by English ships and the attendant delay while prize courts determined the disposition of cargoes. Further, more people than before were affected by the fidelity oath requirement and they had a shorter period in which to make arrangements for their property and to procure passage. Those who were fortunate enough to find buyers for their property were obliged to take local bonds and notes in payment, instruments that would be difficult to convert readily to cash in England or other parts of the empire.[10]

A few examples will suffice to show the range of difficulties that the loyalists faced in preparing for their exile. The Charlestown merchant William Creighton sold a plantation and eighty slaves for £35,000 South Carolina currency and 16,000 pounds of indigo. He took passage on the *Rebecca*, a vessel bound for Bordeaux, but she was captured by two privateers from the Isle of Guernsey and taken into Portsmouth, England, and her cargo seized. Although the prize court ordered his goods restored to him, Creighton was able to recover barely half the value of his property because of its deterioration and the change in the market while he was awaiting a decision. Among the other passengers on the *Rebecca* were Dr. John Farquharson, a Charlestown physician, and the Dorchester schoolmaster Robert Ray.[11]

The merchants Sir Edmund Head, William Hest, and George Kincaid pooled the proceeds from the sale of property to purchase 886 barrels of rice and a vessel, the *Hope*, in which they sailed for Rotterdam. Their pilot ran the ship aground on the Charlestown bar, however—deliberately, they felt—and she had to be returned to town for a period of extensive repairs. When she finally reached European waters, the *Hope* was seized and taken into Portsmouth by British revenue cutters, and her owners were able to obtain her release only after the intercession of James Simpson, the recently exiled attorney general of South Carolina.[12]

Robert Wells's daughter, Louisa, has left the most complete account of a voyage by loyalist exiles in this period. Accompanied by her uncle, Robert Rowand, and a servant, she joined several other refugees aboard the *Providence*, a ship with cargo acquired for the voyage by the loyalist shipbuilder Daniel Manson. In an effort to avoid the experience of the *Hope*, Manson hired a trusted pilot to guide them safely across the bar, but after three days at sea they were stopped by H.M.S. *Rose* and taken into New York. They were forced to wait three months before the cumbersome machinery of the vice admiralty court in that city could determine that the *Providence* was not good prize. Their party sailed in a large convoy on October 19 and did not anchor in the Downs until November 27, a full five months after leaving South Carolina.[13]

That summer representatives from perhaps fifty families left the South Carolina lowcountry because they were unwilling to pledge allegiance to the state, a group drawn primarily from the Scottish community. In addition to the British Isles, they sailed for the Bahamas, Jamaica, and East Florida among British possessions and the Dutch island of St. Eustatius. Some like Louisa Wells, a native, merchants William Currie, Thomas Inglis, and Robert Rowand, and gunsmith Walter Dick departed the state never to return.[14]

The arrival of this latest group increased the community of South Carolina exiles in the home islands to several hundred. Most were natives of Great Britain or had family connections there; if, like the small planter Thomas Harcombe of St. Paul's Parish, they had not lived abroad too long, they soon blended into familiar scenes and retained only memories of their years in America. But most of the exiles assumed that their residence in England would be temporary until the success of British arms would enable them to return to their families, property, or positions in South Carolina. Meanwhile, a way had to be found to support themselves and their families, for the long and indirect voyages had been expensive and the commodities they had with them to sell rarely brought full value. The cost of living in England was higher than they were accustomed to in America, and some were forced to turn to relatives for assistance. William Bull, for one, found London to be an expensive town and soon moved to Bristol where he could live more economically.[15]

One source of temporary relief was the British treasury, which paid temporary living allowances to many refugees. Crown officials continued to receive their salaries, and the allowances made up in part for the loss of fees they were accustomed to earn when on duty.[16]

While awaiting news of a favorable turn in the fortunes of the war, South Carolinians occasionally joined other refugees in petitioning the Crown to take particular courses of action. William Bull was among the officials from the southern provinces who urged that the Carlisle peace commission, which the North ministry sent to negotiate with the Americans in 1778, be instructed not to agree to any settlement that left the confiscation laws enacted by some of the states in place. When it learned that a British expedition was to be sent to recover Georgia, the mercantile firm of Greenwood & Higginson, a large prewar trader to South Carolina, heartily endorsed the idea and pointed out the advantages to England of removing the ban on trade with colonies in rebellion. At least a dozen South Carolinians were among those who signed a petition to the king by loyal American refugees in London in 1779.[17]

For every man who was forced to leave lowcountry South Carolina in 1778 because he would not take the oath of fidelity, an equal or greater number found reason to meet the minimum conditions imposed by the state government or the means to evade the requirement. In their own minds they could justify this action because it would be easier to manage their property and protect their families on the scene than from overseas. The Quaker merchant Zephaniah Kingsley, for example, found it sensible to affirm his allegiance to the new state and thus to retain control of his substantial property in Beaufort and Charlestown. Perhaps he found it easy to conform because he was a marked man—in 1774 committeemen had forced him to throw overboard three chests of tea consigned to him under the Tea Act. Paul Hamilton, a substantial planter in St. Bartholomew's Parish, left the province in 1775 for Bermuda; after a three-year sojourn he returned, in October 1778, and took the oath in hopes of avoiding "double-taxation" of his property. James McKeown, who signed the oath and served in the state militia, candidly told British investigators after the war that "he acted with the Americans and considered himself their subject" until the British army conquered the state. James Cassells of Georgetown District also took the oath, declaring after the war that he had felt "obliged to conform to their government."[18]

Others found the means of avoiding the oath and the penalties for failure to take it, quietly moving into the interior where they managed to avoid both oaths and militia service. Under house arrest while Sir Peter Parker's fleet lay outside the harbor in the summer of 1776, Robert McKeown, an employee in the customs service, slipped away to establish residence on a tract of land on Jackson's Creek in Camden District. There he built a mill and took advantage of the loophole in the militia regulations that exempted millers from militia duty.[19]

Medical men were especially successful at avoiding any commitment to the rebel cause while continuing to practice their profession. The widely respected Dr. Alexander Garden of Charlestown refused to serve in rebel military hospitals; however, he did take the advice of his friend Henry Laurens to certify that he "would promote the real and true interest of Carolina," thus at the same time evading the requirement that he take the oath and salving his conscience that he was not acting against his native country. James Fraser of Beaufort claimed that the oath was never tendered to him, probably because he was the only "medical man" in his community.[20]

Perhaps the classic case of a professional man who was able to carry water on both shoulders was Thomas Phepoe, the lawyer who came out from Ireland with Chief Justice Gordon in 1771. While conforming to the rebel government after hostilities broke out and even serving as a member of the House of Representatives from Charlestown, 1778-80, Phepoe made a specialty of defending persons charged with sedition against the state, and thus achieved notoriety, in the words of one witness, as the "torrie lawyer."[21]

As the year 1779 opened, the question of allegiance to the state assumed new significance because the British army had just seized the coastal areas of neighboring Georgia. Its commander, Colonel Archibald Campbell, published a proclamation urging Americans to return to their allegiance to the Crown, to which the state government responded by putting into effect a new statute that made it a crime punishable by death for South Carolinians to attempt to join the enemy. William Tweed, a Scottish shipwright who had refused to take the oath of fidelity in 1778, and one Andrew Groundwater were caught near Beaufort while carrying a message from a British prisoner of war to Colonel Campbell. Tried under the new law, Tweed and Groundwater were convicted, sentenced to hang, and on March 15 executed in Charlestown. Apparently, however, the harsh punishment meted out to the two men stemmed more from the fact that local public opinion implicated them in an attempt to set fire to a building owned by Tweed, and other acts of arson, at a time when memories of the destructive fire of the previous winter were still fresh, than because they tried to communicate with the British army.[22]

Driven into exile by the state government or forced to accept its authority, people in the lowcountry who hoped for the restoration of British rule had, before 1779, no direct evidence that British military forces were in a position to provide the relief they sought. Although vaguely aware that British arms had enjoyed some success in the northern campaigns, the news of General John Burgoyne's surrender at Saratoga and the subsequent alliance between France and the rebel government did little to encourage them. Nor had the large number of "disaffected" persons who were involved in the backcountry uprising of 1775 received any indication of encouragement in the period to follow. The decisive Richardson campaign that fall, the arrest and detention of loyalist leaders, and the crushing of the Cherokees in 1776 seemingly had deprived opponents of the Provincial Congress in the interior of the means to mount direct resistance.

Yet the ingredients were present in the backcountry, which, if properly exploited by British officials, might provide the basis for a renascence of antirebel sentiment in the interior. First, the administrative machinery of the Superintendent of Indian Affairs for the Southern Department still existed and, while John Stuart's headquarters was more remote than formerly, he and his agents still had influence among the major tribes of southeastern North America. Second, the British provinces of East and West Florida to the southward were a refuge to dissidents fleeing from rebel rule in the Carolinas and Georgia and potential bases for launching a future British campaign to recover those provinces. Finally, as effective as the Richardson campaign against loyalist leadership had been in 1775, a few of the most inveterate foes of the rebel regime had managed to escape capture and to make their way to East Florida. And preparations under way in

The World of Backcountry Loyalist Exiles, 1776–1780
(adapted by R. S. Lambert from B. Romans, 1776)

that province after 1776 permitted British sympathizers to hope that the authority of the Crown might be restored in the other southern provinces.

The men principally responsible for transforming East Florida into a base for rallying support for British recovery of Georgia and the Carolinas were Thomas Brown and Patrick Tonyn. Brown of Georgia, who, along with the Cunningham brothers and Joseph Robinson, had been so active in stirring up resistance to the Provincial Congress in the South Carolina backcountry in 1775, yearned for revenge against those who had treated him so brutally at Augusta. Tonyn, the royal governor of East Florida, worried because the rebels controlled all the neighboring states to the north, was desperate for the means to defend his exposed province.[23]

Brown's experiences in the backcountry had convinced him that loyalist sentiment was so strong there that, with the aid of friendly Indians combined with the landing of an army on the coast, British authority could be quickly restored in Georgia and the Carolinas. He proposed such a plan to Patrick Tonyn in the winter of 1776, and the governor passed it on to General Sir Henry Clinton who was lingering off the North Carolina coast. Clinton's subsequent failure to take Charlestown removed any opportunity to implement the scheme at that time, but Brown's proposal and similar ideas suggested by the royal governors of the southern colonies and by Moses Kirkland and other loyal refugees, did provide the basis for the planning that ultimately led to the recovery of Georgia and South Carolina for the Crown.[24]

Meanwhile, Brown convinced Tonyn that a volunteer unit could be raised locally whose missions would be to defend the Florida frontier against rebel incursions from the north and to conduct raids into rebel Georgia to secure cattle to feed the garrison and recruits for the cause. Commissioned by Tonyn as lieutenant colonel of the East Florida Rangers, Brown was soon actively recruiting local citizens for his regiment, and in the following months he was able to enlist refugee loyalists who made their way to Florida from the Georgia and Carolina backcountry. Brown and his command soon became a bone of contention between the civil authority, as represented by the governor, and Colonel (later Brigadier General) Augustine Prevost, the British military commander in the Floridas, who insisted that the Rangers should take orders from him. Ultimately, both men yielded sufficiently to cooperate in the defense of the province against a major American invasion from Georgia in 1778, after which Prevost grudgingly conceded that the Rangers had performed some valuable service.[25]

The first known South Carolina loyalist to reach East Florida was Evan McLaurin, the young Scottish storekeeper from the fork of the Broad and Saluda rivers. Avoiding capture by the Richardson expedition and aided by friendly Indians, he reached St. Augustine in August 1776, and was soon commissioned as major in the East Florida Rangers.[26]

Joseph Robinson, the leader of the attack on Ninety Six in November 1775, also escaped from Richardson's net. He and his brother-in-law, Moses Whitley, made the long journey through Cherokee and then Creek towns to Pensacola from whence they reached St. Augustine in 1777. How many men accompanied them is not known, but more than fifty South Carolinians were among the signers of a memorial drawn up in late 1777 to express support for Tonyn's efforts to defend East Florida.[27]

Early in 1777 Brown's Rangers made their first foray into Georgia, surprising and capturing the southernmost Whig post, Fort McIntosh on the Satilla River. As the Rangers gradually swelled in numbers from the trickle of loyal refugees who arrived from the Carolinas, Brown and Tonyn became bolder. In March 1778 the Rangers in cooperation with Creek-Seminole allies struck all the way to the Altamaha, capturing Fort Barrington and its small garrison, and destroying that installation before withdrawing into Florida.[28]

Nor were Brown's activities confined to raids along the frontier. In the summer of 1777, because of reports that Richard Pearis and others were trying to "enlist men for the King" in the South Carolina backcountry, Andrew Williamson called out some of his militia and managed to capture "eight or nine" men and to lodge them in the jail at Ninety Six. Pearis himself escaped the manhunt and with the help of friendly Indians managed to reach Pensacola the next winter. But reports persisted that the "Florida Scout" was active along the Saluda River where one James Moore recruited eighteen persons for the British service and from where a "frequent intercourse" was maintained with East Florida.[29]

The reports that the" Florida Scout" was active in the backcountry were more than mere rumors; at the same time that his Rangers were beginning to raid deep into Georgia, Brown selected a dozen of his boldest refugee recruits to communicate with pro-British inhabitants of the Broad-Saluda fork. Brown claimed that he had established contact with "Mr. Robert Cunningham," who had informed him that no fewer than 2,500 men in the Carolina backcountry were ready to rise in support of British authority. Brown's recruiters had their greatest success in the spring of 1778 when two parties estimated at 400 men assembled under Benjamin Gregory of Crim's Creek, a "powder" man of 1775, and John Murphy of Cuffeetown Creek; before the Whig militia could be turned out to pursue them, most of these men had got across the Savannah River and begun the long trek to the East Florida border. In this instance, although they lacked arms and organization, they, were able to take advantage of surprise to get away; but a more vigilant rebel militia was able to disperse other small groups that summer. John York, one of Brown's recruiters and one of the "white Indians" noted earlier, had arranged to conduct another group south that March, but he failed to reach the rendezvous at the appointed time because of increased rebel patrol activity. York slipped back into Florida to report to Brown that further operations in the Carolina backcountry would have to await more favorable opportunities.[30]

This renewed loyalist activity and information that Indians were cooperating with Brown's Rangers led to a retaliatory strike against the British base in East Florida. Under the command of a Continental officer, Brigadier General Robert Howe, a mixed force of Continental troops and about 3,000 Georgia and South Carolina militia succeeded in penetrating to the St. John's River. But a combination of summer heat and sickness, disputes between Howe and the militia commanders, and rather effective resistance by a small force of British regulars and Brown's Rangers caused the invasion to fail with little to show for the American effort except heavy losses from disease.[31]

Increased vigilance among Whig militia in South Carolina and the presence of Howe's army along the escape route to East Florida that summer stemmed the flow of loyalist recruits from the backcountry. Some loyalists went so far as to serve with the Howe expedition in hope of getting close enough to Florida to desert and join their compatriots there, a strategy that rarely worked and caused some to be tried, and a few executed, for desertion.[32]

The best evidence that Whig committees were vigilant during this period comes from the chronicle of David Fanning. Arrested and released after the Snow Campaign, he fled "into the woods," probably to the Cherokees, until he heard of the amnesty granted by the Provincial Congress, whereupon he returned to his home. His ties with the Cherokees had made him suspect, however, and he was arrested again in the summer of 1776. During the next several years he was involved in arrests and escapes, was sheltered by friends in western North Carolina, resided with the Cherokees for a period, and attempted to go to West Florida with Richard Pearis and to East Florida with John York. A marked man even during relatively calm periods, he could count on being carted off to the jail at Ninety Six if he showed his face near his home. Finally, he accepted a conditional pardon from Governor Rutledge in 1779 and returned to Rayburn's Creek for about a year until Charlestown fell to the British.[33]

It is clear from Fanning's tale that Whig committees finally wore down his resistance; presumably had the British not conquered the interior in 1780, he would have remained peacefully at home or quit the state for good. Three cases illustrate the means used by loyalists or neutralists to protect their families and property from harm. Alexander Cheves was drafted into and actually served in the rebel militia under Andrew Williamson in 1779. When his father was arrested for harboring loyalists in 1776, young Alexander Chesney joined the "Rebel Army" to save his family from "threatened ruin," and actually received promotions to the rank of lieutenant for his services. He served under Andrew Williamson in campaigns against the Cherokee Indians in 1776, "to which I had no objection," and later against the Creeks in Georgia. Chesney was only one of a number of loyalists who were willing to serve with the Americans against Indians. And for prosperous loyalists there was another means-buying their way out of trouble. William Gist, an Enoree River planter and surveyor who had been jailed in Charlestown in 1775, was charged with treason in 1777 for corresponding with the British army in East Florida. Gist claimed that he obtained the friendship of a rebel assemblyman by giving up to him a bond he held in payment for a land deal, and he then got the charges against him dismissed by advancing a large sum to the chief prosecution witness "to disappear."[34]

Perhaps as many as 600 men from the backcountry of Georgia and the Carolinas had reached East Florida by the end of 1778, and a substantial proportion of them had come from the South Carolina interior. Indeed, so many had come in that Augustine Prevost obtained permission from Sir Henry Clinton, now commander in chief of British forces in America, to create a military unit of loyalist refugees from South Carolina.[35]

Officially named the South Carolina Royalists (although often referred to in British reports as the South Carolina Regiment), this unit was classified as a provincial regiment in the British table of organization. Its origins lay in promises that Governor William Campbell had made to Nonassociator leaders in the backcountry in 1775 when he was attempting to counteract the efforts of Drayton and Tennent to claim the area for the Provincial Congress. It is known that Joseph Robinson had visited Campbell in Charlestown and returned with blank commissions to distribute among local leaders. The exact nature of Campbell's commitments or which leaders had received the commissions is not clear, but Robinson and probably Thomas Brown were able to make a good case with British authorities in East Florida for making constructive use of the refugees who had appeared there. The arrangement apparently had Prevost's blessing because these men would be under his direct command rather than Brown's, and it suited Tonyn to let the army absorb some of the expense that the refugees were costing the provincial treasury.[36]

The Royalists were authorized to enlist eight companies of up to fifty privates with the usual complement of officers and noncommissioned officers. Originally part infantry and part cavalry, it was organized under the direction of British Major James Mark Prevost, the general's brother, and command of the regiment at the rank of colonel was given to Governor Campbell's former private secretary, Alexander Innes, then on duty with the main British army in New York. Under these circumstances, recruiting for and training the regiment devolved upon Joseph Robinson as lieutenant colonel until Innes was able to assume full command in 1780. Sir Henry Clinton was not happy with the pay and conditions that Campbell had agreed to in 1775, finding them to be more generous than those granted to other provincial units in the British army, and he insisted on putting the Royalists on the same footing as the Loyal Refugees raised by John Stuart in West Florida. Except for a furlough after the British conquered South Carolina in 1780, the regiment remained on duty for the rest of the war. Efforts will be made to raise other provincial units during the British occupation of South Carolina, but only the Royalists attained anything like its authorized strength for an extended period while the war lasted.[37]

The British province of West Florida also provided a refuge for South Carolina loyalists. After Superintendent John Stuart reached St. Augustine in 1775, he determined that Pensacola would be a better base from which to control the southern Indian trade and shifted his operation to that town. His brother, Henry, was located in the Cherokee towns, where he performed the dual task of aiding loyalist refugees and preparing the Indians for cooperation with British troops when the opportunity afforded. The failure of Clinton's expedition at Charlestown and the crushing defeat imposed on the Cherokees by the Williamson foray that summer forced loyalists who had taken refuge with the Indians to move on. A number of them made their way to West Florida, which had been designated as a refuge for loyalists in 1775, and where an earlier ban on land grants to immigrants had been lifted to encourage them to settle there.[38]

One modern scholar has estimated that as many as 300 South Carolina loyalists entered West Florida in the next few years, some of whom brought slaves with them and took up lands in the Natchez District on the Mississippi River. Many of them became permanent residents and remained under British rule and some continued there even after the Spanish gained control. Conspicuous among this group was Anthony Hutchins who, driven off his plantation by Whig raiders under James Willing, led a counterattack that recovered the district for the Crown.[39]

For other South Carolinians, however, West Florida was only a way station on their way back to their homes. Richard Pearis arrived in the province in 1777 after fleeing from the backcountry and was soon involved in defending it against the rebels. As captain of a troop of light horse drawn from the refugees, he participated in the British counterattacks that recovered the post of Manchac on the Mississippi in 1778. But when East Florida was under attack that year, Pearis got permission from John Stuart to proceed to St. Augustine in company with David Holmes, another South Carolinian who was bringing a group of Indians to confer with Governor Tonyn. Pearis asked Tonyn to arrange an exchange by which his wife was allowed to join him from Charlestown where he had been forced to leave her when he fled.[40]

The hundreds of loyalists who left their homes for the Floridas were but a fraction of the number reported to have participated in the backcountry uprising against the Provincial Congress in 1775. Presumably the majority remained in their homes engaged in the routine pursuits of backcountry life, unwilling or unable to risk the exile from their families.

The experience of one group of known opponents of the Provincial Congress, the men captured and sent to Charlestown by Richardson during the Snow Campaign, is suggestive. Remarkably, a mere handful of those prisoners were among those loyalists who succeeded in reaching East Florida by 1778, although others may have attempted to do so unsuccessfully. And even though Thomas Brown had reported that his agents had made contact with Robert Cunningham, that open enemy of the rebel government and his brothers apparently did not lead or participate in the efforts to reach East Florida.

One of the most interesting developments of this period occurred when elections were held late in 1778 for seats in the General Assembly under the new state constitution adopted earlier in that year. As one would expect, most of those elected throughout the state were persons committed to independence. A startling exception to that result was the outcome of polling in the middle, or Little River, district in the Broad-Saluda fork where the voters chose Robert Cunningham as their senator, and Jacob Bowman of Reedy River and Henry O'Neall of Little River, both "powder" men of 1775, to fill two of the four seats in the House of Representatives. Apparently Cunningham and Bowman made no effort to qualify for their seats (they would have been ineligible unless they had taken the oath of fidelity), but O'Neall appeared and participated in the legislative session of September 1779. Many years after the war, one who was present during the election campaign recalled that a quarrel broke out between Cunningham and Colonel James Williams, a prominent local Whig, and an altercation ensued in which blows were struck and in which Cunningham got the better of his adversary. The success achieved by the rebels in creating and ruling the new state clearly did not extend to the Little River District, one of the centers of anticongress activity in 1775.[41]

Notes

1. *House Journals, 1776–1780*, 80, 151, 168, 173–74; *An Account of the Sufferings and Persecution of John Champneys* (Chelsea, England, 1778), 1–16; Loyalist Transcripts, LV, 373–96.
2. *Statutes at Large*, I, 135–36. There is no clue in the General Assembly journals of the period whether or not there was opposition to this act, or from whom opposition might have come.
3. The testimony of Gordon and other officials summoned to take the oath is in South Carolina Miscellany, Emmet Coll., NYPL. See also Loyalist Transcripts, LIII, 395–405; LV, 72–86; LVI, 417–42; LVII, 160–214.
4. Champneys's notice is in *South Carolina and American General Gazette* (Charlestown), Mar. 13, 1777; see also Loyalist Transcripts, LIV, 205–55; LVII, 160–214.
5. Loyalist Transcripts, LV, 72–86, 373–96; LVI, 443–82.
6. William Moultrie, *Memoirs of the American Revolution* (New York, 1968 [orig. publ. New York, 1802]), 199–201; Gabriel Manigault to his grandson Gabriel Manigault, Feb. 24, 1778, Samuel G. Stoney, ed., "The Great Fire of 1778 as Seen through Contemporary Letters," *SCHM* (1963), 23–24; Edward McCrady, *S.C. in the Revolution, 1775–1780*, 232–33. See John Wells, Jr., to Henry Laurens, Jan. 13, 1778, Simms Coll., for an excellent description of the damage caused by the fire, particularly its effects on local printers like Peter Timothy, Mrs. Charles Crouch, David Bruce, and Wells himself.
7. McCrady, *S.C. in the Revolution, 1775–1780*, 236.
8. The act is printed in *South Carolina and American General Gazette*, Apr. 2, 1778.
9. J. L. Gervais to Henry Laurens, June 6, 1778, Laurens Papers (microfilm); *South Carolina and American General Gazette*, June 11, 1778; John Wells, Jr., to Laurens, Sept. 6, 1778, Kendall Coll., SCL; Wells to

Laurens, June 10, 1778, Simms Coll. Jerome J. Nadelhaft, *The Disorders of War: The Revolution in South Carolina* (Orono, Me., 1981), 45–46, has suggested that Gervais, Wells, and Christopher Gadsden felt that the opposition to Lowndes had less to do with anti-Toryism than with concern that the recently adopted constitution of 1778 was too " radical."

10. Departures for the "West Indies," Holland, Bordeaux, and St. Eustatius were noted in Timothy's *Gazette of the State of South Carolina* (Charlestown), July 8, 15, 1778, and Wells's *South Carolina and American General Gazette,* May 15,21, and June 18, 1778.
11. Loyalist Transcripts, LIII, 566–72; LVI, 116–41, 221–26.
12. Ibid., LIII, 307–19, 539–48.
13. Wells, *Journal,* 1–70.
14. Loyalist Transcripts, LIV, 297–316; LV, 252–61; LVI, 105–15; LVII, 367–78.
15. Mary Beth Norton, *The British-Americans: The Loyalist Exiles in England,*1774–1789 (Cambridge, Mass., 1972), 37; Geraldine Meroney, "William Bull's First Exile from South Carolina, 1777–1781," *SCHM* (1979), 91–104; Loyalist Transcripts, LV, 344–51.
16. Typical annual allowances to South Carolina exiles during this period were: the Reverend Robert Cooper, rector of St. Michael's Church, £100; Robert Halliday, collector of customs at Charlestown, £240, plus his salary of £60; Angus Macaulay, who kept a boys school, £100; and John Morgridge, a waiter in the customs service, £25, plus his salary. Loyalist Transcripts, LII, 568–98; LVI, 358, 283–92, 556–59.
17. Sir James Wright, et al., to the king, Mar. 16, 1778, Benjamin F. Stevens, comp., *Facsimiles of Manuscripts in European Archives Related to America,*1775–1783, 25 vols. (Wilmington, Del., 1970), #1067; Memorial of Greenwood & Higginson, et al., to Germain, Nov. 19, 1778, BHP, #1575; Statement, to the king, of Loyal Refugees [June] 1779, English Records, Box 11, folder 5.
18. Loyalist Transcripts, LII, 472–504; LIV, 487–90; LV, 107–21; LVI, 5–20.
19. Ibid., LIV, 479–86.
20. Edmund Berkeley and Dorothy S. Berkeley, *Dr. Alexander Garden of Charlestown* (Chapel Hill, N.C., 1969), 274–75; Loyalist Transcripts, LIV, 479–86; LVI, 268–83.
21. *Canadian Claims,* 245.
22. McCrady, *S.C. in the Revolution, 1775–1780,* 323, 326–29, 336, 345–47; *Statutes at Large,* IV, 479; *Gazette of the State of South Carolina,* Mar. 17, 24, 1779; Loyalist Transcripts, LIV, 327–39.
23. For Thomas Brown in Florida, see Gary D. Olson, "Thomas Brown, the East Florida Rangers, and the Defense of East Florida," in *Eighteenth Century Florida and the Revolutionary South,* ed. Samuel Proctor (Gainesville, Fla., 1978), 15–28.
24. Ibid., 16–19; Charles L. Mowat, *East Florida as a British Province, 1763–1784* (Gainesville, Fla., 1943), 110–12.
25. Tonyn to Augustine Prevost, Dec. 24, 1777, CP, 30/11/558, IS. See also Brown to Tonyn, Feb. 19; Tonyn to Sir William Howe, Feb. 24; and Brown to Tonyn, Mar. 13, 1778, Great Britain, H.M.C., *Report,* I, 195, 197–98, 209.
26. McLaurin to Brown, Dec. 9, 1777, CP, 30/11/558, 275; Loyalist Transcripts, LIV, 320–32.
27. "Robinson, Lt. Col. Joseph, Memoir of" (1797), Rare Book Room, McLennan Library, McGill University, Montreal; *Canadian Claims,* 799; Address to Tonyn, n.d. [November-December, 1777], CP, 30/H/558, 299–301.
28. Brown to Tonyn, Mar. 13, 1778, CP, 30/11/558, 275; J. Leitch Wright, *Florida in the American Revolution* (Gainesville, Fla., 1975), 42.
29. Gervais to Laurens, Aug. 16, 1777, "Letters from John Lewis Gervais to Henry Laurens, 1777–1778," *SCHM* (1965), 23; John Wells, Jr., to Laurens, Sept. 29, 1777, Jan. 13, 1778, Simms Coll.
30. Brown to Tonyn, Feb. 19 and Apr. 10, 1778, H.M.C., *Report,* I, 227–28; deposition of Thomas Young, Ninety Six District, *South Carolina and American General Gazette,* Apr. 16, 1778. See also ibid., June 8, 1778, for a report of forty-seven "deluded people" intercepted by Colonel Andrew Williamson and sent to Charlestown; and Williamson to Bowie, Mar. 11 1778, John Bowie Papers, Manuscript Division, NYPL, for a warning that " some of the disaffected party" might try to release prisoners being held in the jail at Ninety Six.
31. Wright, *Florida in the Revolution,* 55–57. For use of the term "Scopholites" to refer to loyalist refugees fighting for the defense of East Florida, see John Faucheraud Grimke, "Journal of the Campaign to the Southward, May 9–July 14, 1778," *SCHGM* (1911), 64, 65, 130. The Whig press referred to the refugees as "about 150 of the most infamous horse thieves and other banditti" from the frontiers of Georgia and South Carolina, or as "poor, deluded, ignorant people who have been seduced or terrified" into deserting

their families for a life of plunder, *State Gazette of South Carolina,* July 15, 1778.
32. Loyalist Transcripts, LII, 291–313, 267–90; "Order Book of John Faucheraud Grimke, August, 1777 to May, 1780," *SCHGM* (1915), 44, 85 .
33. Fanning, "Narrative."
34. Susan S. Bennett, "The Cheves Family of South Carolina," *SCHGM* (1934),79–87; A. V. Huff, *Langdon Cheves of South Carolina* (Columbia, S.C.,1977) , 1–14; Chesney, " Journal," 7–8; Loyalist Transcripts, LII, 427–52.
35. The estimates come from Olson, "Thomas Brown, the East Florida Rangers... ," 19; Tonyn to Sir William Howe, Apr. 28, 1778, H.M.C., *Report,* I, 240; Grimke, "Journal of the Campaign to the Southward," 130; Siebert, *Loyalists in E. Fla.,* I, 53–54.
36. An undated memorial of George Dawkins and Edward Lane to A. Prevost [Spring 1778], H.M.C., *Report,* I, 304–5, says that Campbell reached agreement with Evan McLaurin to raise two battalions in 1775. See also Tonyn to Sir William Howe, Feb. 24, 1778, and Clinton to A. Prevost, June 3, and Sept. 30, 1778, ibid., 197–99, 274, 282; Robinson, "Memoir"; and Loyalist Transcripts, LVII, 311–17, and the *Canadian Claims,* 33, 156, 674, 799, for the statements, respectively, of Dawkins, Nicholas Crane, Christian Sing, and Robinson; Mowat, *East Florida, 112.*
37. Clinton to A. Prevost, Aug. 25, and A. Prevost to Clinton, Sept. 30, and Robinson to A. Prevost, July 20,1778, H .M.C., *Report,* I, 282, 304–5, 274.
38. Wright, *Florida in the Revolution, 32*–37; Cecil Johnson, *British West Florida, 1763–1783* (New Haven, 1942), 144–48.
39. J. Barton Starr, *Tories, Dons and Rebels: The American Revolution in British West Florida* (Gainesville, Fla., 1976), 230; Robert V. Haynes, *The Natchez District in the American Revolution* (Jackson, Miss., 1976), 31; *Royal Gazette* (New York), Jan. 27, 1779.
40. Richard Pearis, "Memorial to Sir Henry Clinton [n.d.],"Clinton Papers; returns of Pearis's troop are in BHP, VIII, 907, and Continental Congress Papers, II, 38; Stuart to Tonyn, July 18, 1778, and Tonyn to Stuart, Sept. 8, 1778, CP, 30/11/558, 227, 233; Starr, *Tories, Dons and Rebels, 103–5.*
41. J. L. Gervais to Henry Laurens, June 26, 1778, Laurens Papers (microfilm); *House Journals, 1776–1780,* 186, 322, 326; "Memoir of Colonel James Williams," Johnson, *Traditions and Reminiscences, 482*–84.

Chapter Four

THE ROAD BACK:
THE REBELS AT BAY, 1779–1780

To prevent intercourse between the enemy and the inhabitants of this state...you will offer the prisoners of war, those who are accused of sedition, now in Ninety Six gaol, to be safely conducted to [Orangeburg].

—*Governor John Rutledge, April 1779*

In the years after the Americans declared their independence it must have seemed to the loyalists of South Carolina, whether living in exile or residing uneasily within the state, that they had been forgotten by the government in whose cause they had endured so much hardship and so many indignities. Yet, at the very time that their cause seemed hopeless, civil and military authorities in England and America were reappraising war objectives, a review that was to have fateful consequences for the king's supporters in the southern provinces.

The initial plan for suppressing the rebellion in America had been to isolate New England, the area presumed to be most committed to independence, a strategy that naturally led to the concentration of offensive operations in the middle colonies. After defeating Washington's army in and around New York, Sir William Howe established that city as his headquarters and the main base for future operations. In 1777 he sallied forth on the long circuitous route by sea and land that led to the capture of Philadelphia, the rebel capital. These successes were more than offset, however, when a British force from Canada commanded by General John Burgoyne was forced to surrender at Saratoga, New York. Not only did the British army lose the services of 5,000 veteran troops, but the defeat encouraged France to enter the war openly in alliance with Britain's rebelling colonies. This development changed the whole nature of the war for the British; a vengeful France, seeking retribution for her humiliation in the Seven Years' War, now posed a direct threat to Britain's home islands and Caribbean possessions.[1]

To reallocate resources to meet these new circumstances, Britain's military planners decided to give up Philadelphia and to concentrate their armies at New York and Newport, Rhode Island. The garrisons in Nova Scotia, the Floridas, and in the Leeward Islands were to be reinforced, and some naval units were to be shifted to home waters. The new strategy was not limited altogether to defensive measures, for the North ministry was determined to salvage at least some of the rebellious colonies in America. Upon examination, the area south of the Chesapeake, although in rebel hands, seemed to offer the best prospect of success for the least expenditure of manpower.[2]

The idea of a "southern strategy," in Ira Gruber's phrase, was not completely new to the politicians in London charged with prosecuting an increasingly unpopular war. In

1777 Lord George Germain, the secretary of state for the colonies, who was directing the effort to suppress the rebellion, had suggested to General Howe that the focus of the war in America might be shifted to the southward. By the time Howe received this dispatch the disaster at Saratoga had taken place, and he was in no position to implement the idea had he cared to do so. But this bad news from America made the idea even more attractive to strategists in London because it seemed that to shift operations to the south offered England the best chance of saving some of its colonies while fending off France elsewhere.[3]

It was realized that any offensive operations on the American mainland would have to promise substantial gains with a limited and, if possible, temporary commitment of regular British land and naval forces. As early as 1776 British planners had reasoned that the mere presence of a restive slave population near the coast and hostile Indians in the interior would occupy most of the attention of the rebel governments in the southern provinces. But the key to any plan for recovering Georgia and the Carolinas was the presumption that loyalty to the Crown was widespread among their backcountry inhabitants. Now, faced with a major European foe and England's need to salvage what American colonies it could, the North ministry seized upon the plan of a southern campaign to justify continuing the war in America.[4]

If Germain needed support for selling the new strategy to Parliament, a memorial of August 1777, from the royal governors and lieutenant governors of Georgia and South Carolina, presented a detailed argument for sending regular troops to their colonies where they would be welcomed by "great numbers" of the inhabitants. These officials recommended an assault on Charlestown or, as an alternative, the capture of Savannah as a base for penetrating the interior of the two provinces. Germain forwarded their proposal to Howe who received it in December.[5]

The commander in chief could see no merit in a southern campaign that winter. His successor, Sir Henry Clinton, was more familiar with the presumption of pervasive loyalty in the southern provinces, an idea first planted in his mind by Patrick Tonyn and Thomas Brown during the unsuccessful attempt to take Charlestown in 1776. Not until Clinton had evacuated Philadelphia, conducted his army safely to New York, and waited until a French fleet had left the American coast in the fall of 1778 could he turn his attention to the possibility of a southern campaign that winter.[6]

Moses Kirkland, the South Carolina backcountry loyalist who had been in exile since 1775, now reappeared on the scene. In the winter of 1778, Kirkland, now John Stuart's deputy to the Seminole-Creeks, was directed to escort some Creek headmen to St. Augustine for talks with Augustine Prevost on how the Indians might participate in combined operations against the rebels. From there, Kirkland was given leave to go to New York "on private affairs" and to explain to the commander in chief his "project for an invasion into Georgia and [the] western frontiers of South Carolina." Prevost cautioned against undertaking such an operation in the "season when sickness and fever abound" or placing too much reliance on cooperation from the Indians, but he did not pose further objections. Kirkland was able to present his plan after Clinton had returned to New York in October.[7]

Kirkland's scheme was nothing if not comprehensive. From East Florida a combined force of British regulars, Brown's Rangers, volunteers, and Indians would invade Georgia overland with the objective of capturing forts and supplies before linking up near Savannah with a contingent of regulars coming by sea from St. Augustine. After Savannah was reduced, a detachment would be sent up the Savannah River to take Augusta, thus cutting South Carolina's trade route to the Creek Indians and establishing a base from which to make contact with the many backcountry loyalists awaiting the opportunity to rally to the king's standard. While this campaign was in progress, Stuart's deputy, Alexander Cameron, was to prepare the Cherokees to assist in liberating the Long Cane settlements where Kirkland expected that many loyalists awaited the chance to cooperate with the royal army. From Augusta messengers could be sent co the "leading men of the regulators and the Chiefs of the Scotch settlers in the lower parts of North Carolina" to prepare those loyalists to rise and organize themselves. Then, if 3,000 to 4,000 troops could be spared from New York to take Charlestown, the rebels would find themselves caught between the two forces, and the liberation of both Carolinas could swiftly follow.[8]

Kirkland's proposal was complicated and would require the close cooperation of all elements in the plan and a good deal of luck. It rested on certain assumptions, each of which remained to be demonstrated and many of which were dubious at best. First, the strength of the loyalists: backcountry South Carolina was deemed to be full of loyalists, and the mere presence of a royal army would bring them flocking in to volunteer for military service; and nor only would they rally to the cause in large numbers, bur they would come armed, organized, and equipped to serve on short notice. Second, to expect that effective communication could be established between the Scottish "chiefs" and Regulators in North Carolina and the British army around Augusta showed little understanding of the distances involved. Third, the view that the Indian allies were anxious to fight and that their participation would overawe the rebels rather than stiffen their resistance was based on a fundamental misconception of how backsettlers would react to the presence of Indians. The most dangerous assumption, however, was that all of this activity by British redcoats, Indians, and loyalists would find the rebels unprepared or unwilling to resist such an invasion. Kirkland's plan was based to a considerable degree on his personal experiences in 1775, his exposure in Florida to refugee loyalists like Richard Pearis, and his own position in the Indian department. In many respects it rested on facts that were no longer, or were only partially, accurate.

Nevertheless, encouraged by instructions from the ministry in England, Sir Henry Clinton found the idea of a southern campaign sufficiently attractive to plan to implement it in the coming winter.

The southern campaign opened when 3,000 British, Hessian, and provincial troops from New York, commanded by Colonel Archibald Campbell of the Seventy-first Regiment, arrived off Savannah in December]778. Landing below the town, Campbell's force routed the rebel militia defending the main road to Savannah and within days had secured the port and its environs. Campbell was joined at Savannah by an expedition that Augustine Prevost had led overland from Florida. a force that included Thomas Brown's Rangers and the South Carolina Royalists. By early January 1779 organized resistance in coastal Georgia had ceased with the capture of the post at Sunbury and the retreat into South Carolina of Robert Howe's Continental army.[9]

The British victory was so complete that the two commanders, having fulfilled Clinton's instructions to establish a secure base at Savannah, could move swiftly to the second phase of their campaign plan. The Prevost expedition included exiles from the southern provinces who were eager to aid in restoring British authority there; among them was a "Colonel" Boyd, who had come from New York with Campbell and was reputed to be influential in the backcountry of the Carolinas and ready to recruit loyalists there. Assuming that many backcountrymen were prepared to support British arms, Prevost and Campbell agreed to follow up the easy victory on the coast by giving the long-suffering loyalists in the interior the opportunity to show themselves. It was decided that Campbell should move up the Savannah River in order to secure Augusta as a base for opening up the Georgia backcountry and for establishing contact with loyalists in the interior of the Carolinas.[10]

Among the exiles sent into the interior to make contact with loyalists was "Colonel" Boyd, one of the shadowy figures in backcountry loyalism about whom little is known. Perhaps he was the James Boyd of Rayburn's Creek, in the heart of the Little River District where the Cunningham brothers were influential, but what he was doing in New York and how he obtained his rank and reputation for influence among the "Back Woods Men" remains a mystery.[11]

Shortly after Boyd's departure, Archibald Campbell set out for Augusta, taking Brown's Rangers, the South Carolina Royalists, and a North Carolina provincial regiment with him. Encountering little organized resistance, Campbell moved rapidly up the river and occupied Augusta on February 1. From there he dispatched mounted units from the Royalists and the North Carolinians to secure several frontier forts, to offer local settlers the oath of allegiance to the Crown, and to scout ahead for word of Boyd's party. He also authorized Evan McLaurin to recruit a second battalion of the Royalists from among the loyal inhabitants who were expected to appear in response to the news that British troops were ready to support them.[12]

Boyd and his agents succeeded in turning out about 700 to 800 loyalists in the two Carolinas. Zacharias Gibbs, a Virginian who had settled on Fair Forest Creek a few years before the war, organized one group of South Carolinians, and several parties were recruited in North Carolina by John Moore and John Spurgin. Once joined, the volunteers from the two provinces moved through Ninety Six District and crossed the Savannah River into Georgia. Their progress through the area had not gone unnoticed, however, for Colonel Andrew Pickens had called out his militia regiment, joined forces with some Georgia militia, and set out in pursuit of Boyd's party. Pickens's aim was to keep his force between Boyd and Augusta, but after he crossed the Savannah River on February 13 he found that Boyd was still ahead of him. Moving rapidly the next morning, Pickens caught up to the loyalists at Kettle Creek where they had paused to butcher some cattle. Pickens's plan for a surprise attack was given away by the eagerness of his men, and a pitched battle ensued for nearly two hours before the loyalists were put to rout. Estimates vary as to the casualties the loyalists suffered; Boyd and as many as seventy of his men were killed, and many more captured. Barely one-third of his party ever reached the British lines.[13]

Meanwhile, Archibald Campbell had become alarmed about his exposed position so far from the main base at Savannah. He was uncertain of Boyd's whereabouts, and reports had reached him that rebel forces were on the march against him; further, a detachment of Brown's Rangers had got the worst of a skirmish with Georgia rebel militia at the Burke County jail, and another scouring party was surprised by other rebels who took a number of prisoners. On February 13, not having heard from Boyd, he decided to retreat toward the coast and called in his scouring parries; on February 14, the same day that Boyd met his demise at Kettle Creek, Campbell withdrew from the town and dropped rapidly down the river until he reached Hudson's Ferry, within easy reach of the main army at Savannah.[14]

The outcome of Campbell's campaign could not have been worse for the loyalists. They had rallied to the king's standard only to suffer defeat and to find no royal army to sustain them. More ominous for the future than the defeat, however, was that, by openly attempting to reach Campbell's army, they exposed themselves to retaliation by the rebel government and its supporters.

The South Carolina General Assembly reacted quickly to the threatened British invasion, passing "An Act to Prevent Persons Withdrawing from the Defense of the State to Join Its Enemies." The measure authorized the governor to issue a proclamation allowing forty days for those who had joined the enemy to return and surrender or be liable to the death penalty and confiscation of their property. Governor John Rutledge immediately complied, and he named Thomas Heyward and John Mathews to be a special court to try all persons charged "with sedition, insurrection or Rebellion against the state."[15]

The special court proceeded to try about 150 prisoners held under guard by General Andrew Williamson. Some of these men were Kettle Creek prisoners who had been marched in chains to Augusta after the British left the town, while a group of eighty prisoners under Captain Christopher Nealey had turned themselves in after being told that they could post bond and go home. After interrogation, all were marched to Ninety Six and kept under guard. Scheduled to begin March 9, the trials ordered by Rutledge were postponed until a jury could be selected by the sheriff of Ninety Six District on the 22nd, and they were not concluded until April 12. As a result of these proceedings, about half the prisoners were released, fifty were found guilty of treason but won reprieves, and twenty-two were sentenced to death. Zacharias Gibbs, one of those condemned to die, recalled that gallows were erected and graves dug and they were required to sign their own death warrants. At this point, Rutledge ordered the condemned men moved to Orangeburg for security reasons. At that place, five were separated from the rest, marched back to Ninety Six, and hanged later in the month. Gibbs and the others were released after signing an agreement acknowledging that their sentences would be carried out if they were taken in arms against the state again.[16]

British officers were startled by these proceedings and protested vigorously that loyal subjects "endeavouring to join the royal standard" should be accorded the rights of prisoners of war just as though they had been British troops taken in battle. Archibald Campbell threatened retribution, declaring that he would hang two prisoners in his hands for each of three brothers in the Florida Rangers who had been captured and taken into South Carolina, and he actually had gallows constructed on the south bank of the Savannah River to remind rebels of his threat In response to a protest from Colonel Mark Prevost, General Williamson declared that clear distinctions were made between genuine prisoners of war and other captives who were wanted by civil authorities for crimes against the state. Among the latter were several wanted for murder and horse-stealing in the past, and others who tried to use intimidation to force law-abiding citizens to join Boyd's expedition, or who had engaged in plundering on that march.[17]

Clearly, state authorities wanted to make examples of lawbreakers like Aquilla Hall, and men like James Lindley, a reputable farmer on Rayburn's Creek, who had tried on numerous occasions to join the British. They also wished to discourage desertions from Continental and state troops. That no more of the death sentences were carried out probably stemmed from the fear that if the British invaded South Carolina, they would have ample pretext to execute rebels who fell into their hands. Nor were British officers really in a position to carry out their threats of retaliation, for they were under strict orders from Clinton in New York to do nothing that would endanger the lives of their troops held by the Americans, particularly the prisoners taken at Saratoga.[18]

Relatively few of the hundreds who participated in Boyd's uprising have been identified, but it is possible to locate the areas from which many of them came. Among Boyd's recruits were a number of men brought by Zacharias Gibbs from the area of the Enoree River, and a good many residents of Little River and other northern branches of the Saluda where the Cunninghams were influential. The Cunninghams did not participate with the latter group, who were led by Christopher Nealey. Men also came from two other pans of Ninety Six District: Stevens Creek and its tributaries, particularly Cuffeetown Creek; and from the streams that entered Saluda River from the south, areas that had earlier provided a number of recruits for Brown's Rangers and the South Carolina Royalists in East Florida. The valley of Long Cane Creek apparently was not a center of loyalist activity at this time, perhaps because many of its inhabitants were mustered to serve as militia under Andrew Pickens and had no opportunity to slip away and join Boyd had they been so inclined. Virtually all of Boyd's South Carolina recruits came from Ninety Six District, the part of the backcountry closest to Archibald Campbell's operations. However, two men from Camden District-John Fanning from the north side of Broad River, and John Harrison of distant Lynches Creek, later a notorious loyalist partisan, managed to reach Prevost's army in Savannah at the beginning of 1779 in time for Harrison to serve as one of the "spies" sent into the interior of South Carolina to recruit loyalists.[19]

As important as the battle at Kettle Creek was to the loyalists, it was just the beginning of military activity in 1779, a year in which British troops entered South Carolina for the first time and gave its residents a foretaste of the struggles that would engulf them in the years that followed.

The Continental Congress had sent Major General Benjamin Lincoln to assume command of its Southern Department. He immediately called upon governors of the southern States to send all available men to help turn back the British invasion, and by late February he had gathered perhaps 7,000 militia and Continentals in several camps in Georgia and South Carolina. It was this activity that had caused Archibald Campbell to abandon Augusta earlier in the month. One of the contingents under Lincoln's command, composed primarily of North Carolina militia commanded by Brigadier General John Ashe, had camped on Brier Creek, about forty miles above Savannah. Before Lincoln could concentrate his forces for a campaign to recover Georgia, Mark Prevost moved swiftly up the river from Savannah, surprised Ashe in his camp, and in early March thoroughly routed his troops.[20]

Despite Ashe's defeat, Lincoln was determined to attack the British in Georgia, and early in April he crossed the Savannah, leaving General William Moultrie with a small force to guard the approaches to Charlestown. In order to draw Lincoln out of Georgia, Augustine Prevost crossed the lower Savannah late in the month and moved in the direction of Charlestown. Moultrie withdrew in front of him, crossed the Ashley to Charlestown Neck, and fell back into the town; Prevost, in pursuit, followed him across the Ashley and on May 10 placed his troops on the peninsula in front of the city's defenses. Before Prevost could decide whether or not to attack, he received intelligence that Lincoln had reentered South Carolina and was marching to relieve the town. Prevost then recrossed the Ashley and withdrew his main body to Savannah by sea, but he left a strong rearguard under Colonel John Maitland at Stono Ferry to cover his retreat. Lincoln attacked Maitland's position on June 20, but was repulsed with substantial loss and Maitland was able to pull his troops back to the safety of Beaufort.[21]

There was little action during the rest of the summer, but early in September a French fleet and army commanded by the Comte d'Estaing appeared off Tybee Island and prepared to land below Savannah and to join with Lincoln's troops in a combined assault on the city. Surprised by this turn of events, Augustine Prevost called his outlying detachments in to defend the city, throwing up fortifications in which about 3,500 British regulars and Hessians, and loyalist units from Georgia, the Carolinas, and the middle colonies prepared to withstand a siege. D'Estaing did begin siege operations but lost patience with the time they consumed while his ships were vulnerable to autumn storms and to the possible arrival of a British fleet. On October 9 he ordered a full-scale assault of the British works, but it was beaten back at every point, and he withdrew his forces to the fleet as quickly as possible and sailed away. The main point of attack was the Spring Hill redoubt, a strongpoint at the northwest corner of the defense perimeter that guarded an important road into the town. A detachment of the South Carolina Royalists made up an important part of the defenders of the position; withstanding the initial assault, they enabled other troops to counterattack and inflict heavy losses on the French and Americans in the assault wave. All reports of the action praised the steadiness of the Royalists under fire, probably their finest moment as an organized unit during the war.[22]

All the marching and countermarching by the British and American forces in 1779 played further havoc with whatever posture of allegiance South Carolinians strove to maintain. During Prevost's sweep across the lowcountry to Charlestown, some property holders along his march contributed supplies to his troops and slave labor for the fortifications at Stono Ferry. Although no mass trials followed Prevost's departure from the state, those who had aided him had exposed themselves to the rebels and would suffer later in the war as a result. Paul Hamilton, a planter on James Island who had returned after three years abroad, furnished livestock and provisions to Prevost's troops; after the British withdrew, Hamilton was tried by the rebel government for not taking up arms against the invaders. On the other hand, the presence of British forces in the lowcountry enabled their sympathizers to join them. Most conspicuous among them was the younger Andrew Deveaux, a bold and dashing young man who was the scion of a wealthy planter family in Beaufort District. That Prevost's dash toward Charlestown had some effect on more distant loyalists is shown by the efforts of British sympathizers on Lynches Creek above the Santee River to reach the British in Savannah in the late summer that year. They assembled, ostensibly to hold a horse race, but with the real intention of seizing a powder magazine near Camden; their plans were discovered, however, and some were arrested and others were dispersed to their homes to await a more favorable opportunity to demonstrate their loyalty to the Crown.[23]

Although some British sympathizers were thrown into jail by local authorities while Prevost's troops hovered near Charlestown, and their families and property were exposed to private retribution by rebels after they retreated, the official reaction by the state was ambivalent. In September a bill offering pardon to persons who had declared allegiance to the king during the recent "incursion of the enemy into this state'" and others "who have joined the enemy and are willing to return their Allegiance," was debated extensively, but the two houses were unable to agree on a number of provisions in the proposal. After receiving the news that d'Estaing's fleet was off the coast, the two houses hastily extended the treason law of the previous February 20.[24]

On November 8, after the effort to retake Savannah had failed, Governor John Rutledge issued a proclamation that listed fifty-five persons who had left the state and joined the enemy, and invoked the law allowing them forty days to return to their allegiance to the state before they were declared traitors. Most of them had been with the British for some time and apparently did not take advantage of the opportunity to return, for in February 1780, fifty-one "unhappy wives" of the men listed, acting for themselves and 203 children, petitioned the General Assembly not to confiscate their property so that they could retain some means of supporting their families. The committee to whom the petition was referred, pleading insufficient information, recommended suspension of the law as it affected the petitioners; no action was taken on it, or another proposal to repeal the treason act, because of a new threat to the state: the landing below Charlestown of troops from a large British fleet that had been lying off the Georgia coast.[25]

This new invasion resulted from Sir Henry Clinton's decision to commit a substantial part of his army at New York to a winter campaign in the Carolinas. His objective was to subdue the rebellion in the two provinces and then to move against Virginia, and for this purpose he embarked about 8,500 British, German, and loyalist troops under the protection of a substantial fleet. The warships and transports were badly scattered by storms and took a month to arrive off Savannah, and it was February 11, 1780, before the first landings were made on John's Island, about thirty miles from Charlestown. The army moved by slow stages to the banks of the Ashley and crossed the stream to the Charlestown Neck on March 29, trapping Benjamin Lincoln's force on the peninsula. Further reinforced from Savannah and New York and with the city completely under the guns of the fleet, Clinton demanded the surrender of the town and its defenders. Lincoln at first refused to capitulate, then negotiated for favorable terms, and finally agreed on May 12 to surrender the town and its garrison of over 3,300 troops, largely Continentals from the southern states. A stunning and discouraging defeat, it was the largest loss of troops sustained by the Americans during the war. Overwhelming British land and naval power had been applied against an isolated American army in an untenable position, an ideal situation for the British army.[26]

In the Charlestown campaign the South Carolina Royalists, brought from Savannah with other provincial units, did routine duty in helping to seal off the city and suffered only three casualties in the entire operation. Little is known of assistance given by individual local loyalists, although British officers later revealed that some inhabitants had smuggled valuable information out of the town during the siege.[27]

Notes

1. The reappraisal of Britain's strategic position may be followed in Paul H. Smith, *Loyalists and Redcoats* (Chapel Hill, N.C., 1964), 79–84.
2. Piers Mackesy, *The War for America, 1775–1783* (Cambridge, Mass., 1965), 184–88.
3. Ira D. Gruber, "Britain's Southern Strategy," *The Revolutionary War in the South*, ed. W. Robert Higgins (Durham, N.C., 1979),217–21; Mackesy, *War for America*, 154–59.
4. Smith, *Loyalists and Redcoats*, 84–88.
5. See the memorial of Lord William Campbell, Sir James Wright, William Bull, and John Graham to Germain, Aug. 19, 1777, S.C. Records in the P.R.O., XXXVI ,76.
6. Smith, *Loyalists and Redcoats*, 91–93.
7. Stuart to Howe, Feb. 4; Tonyn to Howe, Mar. 8; and A. Prevost to Howe, Mar. 18, 1778, H .M.C., *Report*, 1, 189–90; Loyalist Transcripts, LVII, 318–50.
8. Kirkland's plan has been printed in Randall L. Miller, ed., "A Backcountry Loyalist Plan to Retake Georgia and the Carolinas," *SCHM* (1974), 207–14.
9. Smith, *Loyalists and Redcoats*, 100.
10. Archibald Campbell, "Journal"; Smith, *Loyalists and Redcoats*, 101–2.
11. Robert Scott Davis, Jr., has made the most thorough examination of the evidence relevant to Boyd, and I am grateful to him for sharing his findings on the Battle of Kettle Creek and its participants. See Davis and Kenneth H. Thomas, Jr., *Kettle Creek: The Battle of the Cane Brakes, Wilkes County, Georgia* (Atlanta, Ga., 1974), 30. They suggest, ibid., 60n, that Boyd's rank may have been a reward for having recruited more than 500 loyalists; he may have had a warrant to raise that many, for Campbell referred to Boyd as "Col." before he could have known how many men he would enlist; Archibald Campbell, " Journal," Jan. 10, 1779.
12. The march of Campbell's army and the disposition of his troops from that point may be traced in his "Journal," 77–103, particularly entries for Jan. 21, 25, 30; Feb. 3, 7, 8, 9, 1779. The authorization to McLaurin is mentioned in McLaurin to Col. Nisbet Balfour, Aug. 16, 1780, Evan McLaurin-Miscellaneous Papers, Emmer Coll., NYPL.
13. Archibald Campbell, "Journal," Jan. 21, 1779, 76; Deposition of William Millen, Jan. 28, 1779, Military Coll., War of the Revolution, Miscellaneous Papers, 1776–89, NCAH ; Plats, XIII, 528, SCAH; Davis and Thomas, *Kettle Creek*, 30–39. Siebert, *Loyalists in East Florjda*, II, 69n, places William Spurgin in North Carolina and makes him Boyd 's deputy, but there is evidence that John Spurgin is that person and that he had lived in the New Acquisition, that part of North Carolina ceded to South Carolina after the boundary between the provinces was run in 1769. Pickens's son reported many years after the war that his father had known Boyd and had spoken to the mortally wounded loyalist on the battlefield, Francis W. Pickens to Draper, Nov. 4, 1847, Draper Coll.
14. Davis and Thomas, *Kettle Creek, 20–23*; Archibald Campbell to Augustine Prevost, Mar. 2, 1779, "Journal," 121–26; Smith, *Loyalists and Redcoats*, 102.
15. *Statutes at Large*, IV, 479–80; Rutledge to Gen. Benjamin Lincoln, Feb. 28, 1779, *SCHGM*, XXV (1924), 133–35; Secretary of State, Miscellaneous Records, A, 115–16, SCAH.
16. Robert Scott Davis, Jr., "The Loyalist Trials at Ninety Six in 1779," *SCHM* (1979), 172–81. See also a list of men in confinement for "fighting in arms against this state," Apr. 10, 1779, at General Williamson's camp opposite Augusta, Matthew Singleton Papers, SCL; Williamson to Lincoln, May 1, 1779, Preston Davie Coll., SHC, for the names of forty-five prisoners sent to Ninety Six; and the petition of William Moore as sheriff of Ninety Six District seeking reimbursement for subsistence furnished prisoners escorted to Orangeburg, Accounts Audited, AA5335, SCAH.
17. Davis, "Loyalist Trials," 177; Thomas Kelly (for J. M. Prevost) to Williamson, Apr. 6, 1779, and Williamson to Prevost, n.d., *The Remembrancer. or, Impartial Repository of Public Events. For the Year 1779* (London, 1779), VIII 173–76.
18. North Carolina authorities later tried some of the Kettle Creek prisoners from that state at Salisbury, and two were executed, Davis, "Loyalist Trials," 180.
19. Loyalist Transcripts, LII, 227, 282–90; LIII, 221–28; LVII, 402–17; *Canadian Claims*, 700, 727. John Spurgin, second in command to Boyd, was killed in a skirmish in Georgia on Mar. 31, *Gazette of the State of South Carolina* (Charlestown), Apr. 7, 1779. For Harrison and John Fanning, see Loyalist Transcripts, LIV, 459–68, and *Canadian Claims*, 717.
20. McCrady, *S.C. in the Revolution*, 1775–1780, 343–44.

21. The movements of the armies that spring may be followed in Ward, *War of the Revolution*, II, 683–87; details of the Battle of Stono are in McCrady, *S.C. in the Revolution, 1775–1780*, 382–92; see also William Moultrie, *Memoirs of the American Revolution* (New York, 1968 [orig. publ. New York, 1802]), I, 291–95.
22. Ward, *War of the Revolution*, I, 688–94. For the Royalists during the siege, see A. Prevost to Lord George Germain, Nov. 1, 1779, and return of casualties, *Remembrancer*, IX, 7 l–78, 81; "South Carolina Royalists Mustered at Savannah, Dec. I, 1779," LMR.; *Royal Georgia Gazette* (Savannah), Nov. 28, 1779; and various descriptions in Franklin B. Hough, ed., *Siege of Charlestown by the British Fleet and Army under the Command of Admiral Arbuthnot and Sir Henry Clinton...* (Spartanburg, S.C., 1975 [orig. publ. Albany, N.Y., 1867]), 39, 59n, 80–81, 85, 148. The earliest surviving muster roll of the regiment, December 1779, shows nine companies composed of 263 officers and men of whom less than two-thirds were present for duty at the time, and shows that thirty-two had died during the year, seventeen had become prisoners, and the others were ill or absent. William Hanscomb, a coachmaker of Charlestown, commanded a company of black pioneers during the siege, "Return of Loyal Refugees Who Have Come into Georgia for Protection and Assistance," MS., Apr. 15, 1780, Clinton Papers; Loyalist Transcripts, LVI, 483.
23. Redmund Burke complained that Prevost's army had plundered his house near the ferry across the Combahee River, Loyalist Transcripts, LII, 5–7; and Edward Williams of the Salkehatchie River had conducted loyalists to Prevost's army in Savannah, *Canadian Claims*, 182. For the Deveaux family, see Loyalist Transcripts, LVII, 32, and Johnson, *Traditions and Reminiscences*, 175–82. John Robinson stated, Loyalist Transcripts, LII, 399–411, that one Ponder was the leader of the abortive uprising on Lynches Creek; there are references to the affair in Wade to Col. John Dunn, Nov. 13, 1779, Salisbury District, North Carolina, Superior Court Miscellaneous Papers, NCAH.
24. The progress of the two measures may be followed in *House Journals, 1776–1780*, 185–86, 190–91, 196, 199–200, 201–2, 208–10, 215, 216, 221, 228. These proceedings do not reveal the personal inclinations of individual legislators, but among the members of the committee that recommended the pardon were Thomas Phepoe, the "Tory lawyer," and the Little River District "powder" man Henry O'Neall.
25. Rutledge's proclamation is in *South Carolina and American General Gazette* (Charlestown), Nov. 24, 1779; the petition of the wives is dated Feb. 5, 1780, *House Journals, 1776–1780*, 274–75, 279–80.
26. The siege and surrender of Charlestown may be traced in Ward, *War of the Revolution*, II, 695–703.
27. For the South Carolina Royalists during the campaign, see "Anthony Allaire Orderly Book and Diary, 1780–1795," MS., Beverly Robinson Papers, NBM, entries for Feb. 13, 29, 1780, 21, 24; Bernard A. Uhlendorf, ed., *The Siege of Charleston with an Account of the Province of South Carolina: Diaries and Letters of Hessian Officers from the Von Junkenn Papers in the William L. Clements Library* (Ann Arbor, Mich., 1938), 69; Hough, ed., *Siege of Charleston*, 122; Moultrie, *Memoirs*, II, 108.

Part II

RESTORING BRITISH AUTHORITY: THE LOYALIST RESPONSE, 1780–1781

The capitulation of Charlestown and the American forces under Benjamin Lincoln opened what may be called the British Period of the Revolution in South Carolina, a time when British military forces were continuously operating in one or more parts of the state. The period lasted for thirty months and ended when the last British troops were withdrawn in December 1782, taking large numbers of loyalists and slaves with them.

The British Period passed through three fairly distinct but overlapping phases. During the nine months following Lincoln's surrender, the British army was able to exert apparent control over most of the state, forcing American Continental troops and militia to operate primarily beyond its borders. The second phase began when Nathanael Greene's Continental army reentered the state in April 1781, following its drawn battle with Lord Cornwallis's troops at Guilford Court House in North Carolina; in the ensuing six months Green's troops and state militia recovered most of the interior of the state, and the British and loyalist forces Cornwallis had left behind were pushed back into a defense perimeter around Charlestown. The last phase, comprising the last quarter of 1781 and nearly all of 1782, was confined to skirmishes between the two armies—the Americans being too weak to attempt to expel their foes from Charlestown, while the British were content to mount raids to subsist the garrison and to claim slaves belonging to loyalists and rebels alike.

Chapter Five

PLANS AND PERSONNEL

From every information I receive, and Numbers of the most violent Rebels hourly coming in to offer their Services, I have the strongest reason to believe the general Disposition of the People to be not only friendly to Government, but forward to take up Arms in its support.

—Sir Henry Clinton, May 1780

Before turning to the experiences of the loyalists in South Carolina during the British Period, it is important to recall both the objectives of the ministry in London and their commanders in America, and the assumptions on which they based the strategy to achieve those objectives. The first assumption was that there were large numbers of loyalists in the southern rebel-controlled provinces; the second was that if a British army came into South Carolina and armed and encouraged the loyalists, they were sufficiently numerous and dedicated to maintain peace and order within its borders; thus the main British force would be released to move into North Carolina where similar results could be expected. The two assumptions were intricately connected: the loyalists could not demonstrate the depth of their support for the Crown unless liberated by a British army; but only if the zeal and numbers of the loyalists were great enough would that army be free to carry the campaign of liberation to other provinces. Information coming to the North ministry from loyalist refugees and royal officials from South Carolina and Georgia formed the foundation of fact on which these assumptions rested-that large numbers of persons in the backcountry had shown themselves to be hostile to the Provincial Congress in 1775 and that thereafter hundreds had fled into exile rather than submit to the rebel government. To undertake a southern campaign on the basis of these assumptions was a calculated gamble, a risk that might yield the results hoped for if the assumptions were based on sound information.

The first step in carrying out the "southern strategy" in South Carolina had succeeded with the surrender of Charlestown and Lincoln's army, but others must follow to build on that victory. Charlestown must be made secure so that there would be no interruption in the flow of supplies to the troops, and the port must be reopened to international trade under British regulation. While American resistance was at its lowest stage, the troops must proceed into the interior to liberate and organize the loyal population to take over the duties of patrol and police throughout the backcountry. The troops not essential to carry out those duties must be moved to a position facing the border with North Carolina where, at the proper time and in coordination with an uprising of the loyalists in that province, they would be ready to take control there. This phase of the strategy also depended on the strength of loyalism in South Carolina; if less than assumed, the likelihood that a North Carolina campaign would succeed would be sharply reduced. But first, Charlestown must be made secure and plans made for the liberation of the interior.

Under the terms of the capitulation of May 12, 1780, all military personnel of the garrison were considered to be prisoners of war on parole, the Continentals until formally exchanged for British prisoners in American hands, and militia to their homes where they were to be secure in their property so long as they adhered to the terms. This stipulation, included at the insistence of Clinton and Arbuthnot, should be remembered because of the conditions those officers would later impose upon the inhabitants of the state at large. Citizens of the town were also to be considered prisoners on parole.[1]

In the last stages of the siege of the city when resistance appeared to be hopeless, a number of its inhabitants had petitioned General Lincoln to accept terms offered by the British commanders so that further loss of life and property might be prevented. Shortly after the capitulation, 207 citizens, many of whom had signed the address to Lincoln, now directed an address to Clinton and Arbuthnot congratulating them upon the success of their campaign and the restoration of English rule. These "Addressors," along with a group who later congratulated Lord Cornwallis on his victory at the Battle of Camden, became marked men and in 1782 were named in a confiscation act passed by the state government. But most of the city's residents were content to sign an oath of allegiance to the Crown by which they abjured any former allegiance to the state and placed themselves under the protection of British authorities.[2]

Nearly 1,600 men came forward to take the oath in the weeks after the surrender, an indication of substantial support for the Crown in the lowcountry. If loyalist sentiment in the backcountry proved to be as great as anticipated, the "southern strategy" offered fair promise of success. Even Clinton, a cautious man whose long experience made him skeptical of the depth of loyal sentiment among Americans, expressed pleasure at this "general disposition of the people."[3]

Yet there was also evidence that suggests that loyal sentiment might not be as deep as the number of oathtakers might indicate. James Simpson, the former royal attorney general who had accompanied the expedition from New York, had been instructed by Clinton to ascertain the sentiments of people in Charlestown immediately after the surrender. From his conversations with a number of "people of the first fortunes," he found many who were now willing to return to their allegiance, although he noted that "the Loyalists who have always adhered to the King's Government are not so numerous" as he had anticipated. A Hessian officer noted that the apparent rush to take the oath of allegiance was, in a number of instances, "on the condition that they will not be compelled to fight against their own countrymen." Clinton himself was aware that many who had taken protection had "some scruple about carrying arms against the Congress," and, with his usual caution, added that he had doubts about trusting them with arms "till they have given me more convincing proofs of their Loyalty than have appeared in so short a time."[4]

Sir Henry, anxious to return with some of his troops to his headquarters at New York, busied himself with planning for the occupation and administration of South Carolina. His most important immediate tasks were to designate an officer to carry out the conquest and pacification of the southern provinces, to define the conditions under which the inhabitants might be restored to their allegiance to the Crown, and to arrange for organizing them for civil and military service. The plans for organizing a loyal militia will be examined subsequently, but of most immediate concern were the choice of his successor and other leaders and the terms under which persons might be restored to their allegiance.

To carry out the objectives of the campaign after his departure, Clinton named Lieutenant General Charles, Earl of Cornwallis to be commander in chief in the southern provinces. Cornwallis, except for a period of leave in England, had served in America since the beginning of the war, but he had never held an independent command. Generally the two men had been on friendly terms throughout their service in America, and Clinton had asked the earl to accompany him on the southern expedition. By the time that the army was preparing to besiege Charlestown, however, circumstances had changed. In the previous year Clinton had asked his superiors in England to permit him to resign his command in America and to return home, and he had recommended Cornwallis as his successor. Seven months passed and the southern campaign was well under way before Clinton learned of the response to his request; in March 1780 he received word that the king had asked him to retain the command, and almost immediately he and the earl became estranged. Cornwallis asked for a separate command and was put in charge of a movement to secure the fords of the Cooper River above the town, and he effectively sealed off the garrison from help by land. He then sent troops in pursuit of several American units that were in hasty retreat from the province. Thus, although Cornwallis was far from headquarters when the city surrendered, he was the ranking officer and the obvious choice to be commander in chief for the southern provinces, and before departing for New York Clinton assigned that responsibility to him. Meanwhile, Cornwallis continued to lead his column toward Camden until he had actually succeeded Clinton in command, and all communications between the two men thereafter were in writing.[5]

In a proclamation of May 22, Clinton had begun the process of restoring the inhabitants to their allegiance, promising protection to faithful supporters of the Crown and threatening severe penalties for anyone who took up arms against British authority in the future. On June 1 he and Admiral Arbuthnot, acting as commissioners empowered to restore peace, offered complete pardon to those South Carolinians who would promptly profess their allegiance to the king, excepting only persons who had been responsible for executing loyal subjects during the American Period. Those receiving pardons would, when conditions permitted, be restored to the privileges of British subjects, and they were to be exempt from taxes not levied by locally chosen representatives. Thus loyal subjects would receive the benefits of British citizenship and those who remained in rebellion would be punished, but there was no requirement that persons who took protection would have to take up arms.[6]

Then on June 3, just a few days before Clinton embarked for New York, he suddenly issued another proclamation that released all persons from their paroles, except those in the Charlestown garrison at the capitulation, and required that they declare their allegiance by June 20 or be considered enemies. Writing after the war, Sir Henry justified the June 3 action as a "prudent measure" for ferreting out "inveterate rebels" in order to provide loyalists with the opportunity of "detecting and chasing from among them such dangerous neighbors." British officers who were charged with pacifying the countryside did not like this latest policy, claiming that it made their task more difficult; the diehard loyalists had learned from bitter experience who the "inveterate enemies" were and wanted them punished, not pardoned. And Lord Cornwallis and his subordinates would not be pleased with the new policy because many former rebels found it expedient to enlist in the loyal militia where they proved to be unreliable and prone to desert.[7]

Following Lincoln's surrender, British authorities established control over the city and the port. Clinton chose Brigadier General James Patterson of the Sixty-third Regiment to be military commandant of the city with the immediate duties of restoring order, taking charge of prisoners of war, and enforcing military discipline. He then created a Board of Police, which was to act as a "court of common pleas" in the settlement of civil disputes and as an advisory body to the commandant. Similar to agencies previously set up in occupied New York and Philadelphia, it consisted of loyal men known as intendants and was headed initially by James Simpson.[8]

One of the most significant appointments Clinton made at this time was that of Major Patrick Ferguson to be inspector of militia. One of the many Scots in the British officer corps, Ferguson had already become a controversial figure in the army before he came to South Carolina. He had invented a repeating rifle that his superiors in England admired but did not adopt for the army; in America he had raised one corps of picked riflemen and then had recruited the American Volunteers from loyalists serving in the middle colonies. A daring combat officer, he had lost the use of an arm at Brandywine, where he had come to Clinton's attention. Ferguson's free-wheeling style and semi-independent commands were irritating to some of his fellow officers, particularly Nisbet Balfour, who felt that he lacked "regularity" and discipline.[9]

Balfour, another Scot who had spent half his thirty-seven years in the army and had risen by 1780 to be lieutenant colonel of the Twenty-third Regiment, was chosen by Clinton to command one of the columns sent to liberate the interior. But he soon obtained a more important position when Cornwallis named him to replace the ailing Patterson as commandant of Charlestown. In that position Balfour became a kind of chief of staff in South Carolina on whom Cornwallis relied to keep supplies flowing to the troops in the interior, to interview and recommend loyalist officers for important commands, to handle communications between his army and Clinton in New York and the ministry in England, and other tasks well beyond those normally associated with the post. Although often outranked by other British officers who appeared in South Carolina from time to time, Balfour was, after Cornwallis himself, the most influential officer in the Carolinas and Georgia.[10]

Two other young officers will be highly visible during this period. Francis Lord Rawdon, eldest son of the Irish peer John Baron Rawdon, had entered the army at seventeen and seen service in America from Bunker Hill to the fall of Charlestown. In 1778 he had been named adjutant general of British forces in America, but he came to South Carolina as commander of the Volunteers of Ireland, a loyalist provincial regiment he had recruited from among the Irish population of Philadelphia and vicinity. Only twenty-six in 1780, Rawdon was soon put in charge of the important post at Camden, the key to the British position along the northern frontier of the province. He became a hero to loyalists with his brilliantly executed march to relieve the siege of Ninety Six in 1781, a reputation that did not diminish when he later approved of the execution of persons who had deserted to the Americans after having taken the British oath.[11]

But the British officer serving in South Carolina whose reputation has outlasted that of any other was Lieutenant Colonel Banastre Tarleton. He also came into the province as the field commander of a loyalist provincial regiment recruited in Pennsylvania, a mixed unit of cavalry and infantry known as the British Legion. But it was as a cavalryman that his name became infamous in South Carolina, a reputation that he established early in the campaign. Sent by Cornwallis after Charlestown capitulated to pursue some fleeing Virginia Continentals commanded by Colonel Abraham Buford, Tarleton caught up with them on May 29, 1780, put them to rout, and permitted his men to continue the slaughter while the Americans were trying to surrender. In ensuing campaigns his slashing style, lack of mercy toward enemies at bay, and pillaging of private property struck fear and loathing in the hearts of Americans. But his impetuous nature and instinct for the kill were to serve the British cause poorly in several instances, most notably at the Battle of Cowpens.[12]

These three young officers—Balfour, Rawdon, and Tarleton—along with his aide Captain Alexander Ross, became to Cornwallis an inner circle of confidants upon whom he placed greater reliance with the passage of time. Of the three, only Rawdon earned the respect of the more zealous loyalists because he seemed to appreciate their efforts and suffering in the cause. And Ferguson, who had some good things to say about some of his loyalist militia, never had Cornwallis's confidence.[13]

It was natural that British officers should play an important part in this period, but it can be too easily forgotten how much of the campaigning in South Carolina was done by loyalist regiments from the other American states and the important roles their commanding officers played during the British occupation. Most important were two New York officers: Lieutenant Colonel George Turnbull of the New York Volunteers, a Scottish officer who had settled in New York in the 1760s, would be charged with defending a vital post on the frontier with North Carolina; and Lieutenant Colonel John Harris Cruger of the First Battalion of Delancey's Brigade, the scion of a distinguished New York family, would command the western British post at Ninety Six until it was abandoned in the summer of 1781. Lieutenant Colonel Isaac Allen of the Third Battalion, New Jersey Volunteers, an attorney from that province, was Cruger's deputy and late in the occupation succeeded Balfour as commandant at Charlestown.[14]

One other matter to which Clinton devoted much attention in the weeks following Lincoln's surrender was to prescribe regulations for dealing with the inhabitants in the interior and to organize the forces that would carry out those policies. Central to his plans to help the army maintain order and to extend its control in the Carolinas was the creation of a loyal militia. To that end he appointed Patrick Ferguson as inspector of militia for the Carolinas and Georgia and instructed him to enroll young men with fewer than three children who would agree to serve six months of the next twelve in the three provinces. Recruits were to be organized into companies and battalions in which company officers were to be chosen by their men and battalion officers by British commanders; and they were to be paid when on duty at prescribed army rates, given weapons if they had none, and could be mounted if they provided their own horses. Clinton issued specific regulations that militia were not to molest civilians who remained peacefully at home or to despoil their property. Men over forty or with larger families were to be a "domestick militia" to preserve order in their settlements.[15]

Cornwallis, knowing that he would succeed to the southern command after Clinton departed for New York, drew up his own instructions for pacifying the province. In a draft of "Part of a Plan for Regulating the Province & Forming a Militia," he classified the nonloyal part of the population into three groups, stipulating that those who had held "public station" or field commissions in the militia under the rebel government, and others who had been "particularly obnoxious to Friends of Government" were to be sent to one of the sea islands as "prisoners of war on parole"; that "violent persecutors will be sent to prison"; and that the "remainder of the disaffected will be disarmed and permitted to remain at their own homes." In preparing to organize the militia, Cornwallis followed Clinton's specifications that young men would serve actively for six months out of twelve in the Carolinas and Georgia, while men over forty or with large families would keep the peace in their own neighborhoods.[16]

Reporting to Clinton at the end of June on the policies he had adopted, Cornwallis added that the militia consisted of those "of undoubted attachment" to the British cause or "whose behavior has always been moderate." The "notoriously disaffected" who had remained at home, however, had been disarmed and, instead of military service, had been asked to "furnish moderate contributions of provisions, waggons, horses, etc." As an example of how his own instructions conformed to Sir Henry's policies, Cornwallis cited the case of "two gentlemen one of whom had been in an high station & both principally concerned in the Rebellion," who came to surrender under the terms of Clinton's proclamations before the earl himself had learned of those documents. He refused their request, but when copies of the proclamations came into his hands, Cornwallis felt justified in sending the men to the islands, a military leader under the proclamation of June 3, and a civil officer under that of June 1.[17]

To secure the conquest of South Carolina and to carry the war against the rebels into North Carolina, Sir Henry detached about 4,000 troops from his invasion force. The units left in the province included six British regiments—the Seventh, Twenty-third, Thirty-third, Sixty-third, Sixty-fourth, and Seventy-first—plus a detachment of dragoons; two German regiments; and these loyalist provincial regiments or detachments: Rawdon's Volunteers of Ireland; Tarleton's British Legion; a detachment of Ferguson's American Volunteers; the New York Volunteers; the South Carolina Royalists; the North Carolina Volunteers; the Prince of Wales American Regiment; and a battalion each of the New Jersey Volunteers and Delancey's Brigade.[18]

Clinton had previously dispatched a column under Nisbet Balfour to move through the middle of the province toward Ninety Six. With Camden already occupied, and Balfour's march under way, Sir Henry joined his troops aboard the transports for New York on June 8, leaving the southern operations in Cornwallis's hands.

Notes

1. McCrady, *S.C. in the Revolution, 1775–1780*, 478–81, 495–504; the negotiations and the terms of surrender are in Franklin B. Hough ed., *Siege of Charleston by the British Fleet and Army under the Command of Admiral Arbuthnot and Sir Henry Clinton...* (Spartanburg, S.C., 1975 [orig. publ. Albany, N.Y., 1867]), 87–115.
2. Hough, *Siege of Charleston*, 148–54; *South Carolina and American General Gazette* (Charlestown), Aug. 23, 1780. The names of persons signing the oath to the Crown are in CP, 30/11/107, 1–33.
3. Ira D. Gruber, "Britain's Southern Strategy," *The Revolutionary War in the South*, ed. W. Robert Higgins (Durham, N.C., 1979), 166–67; Clinton to Cornwallis, May 29, 1780, CP, 30/11/2, 54.
4. Simpson to Clinton, May 15, in Clinton to Germain, May 16, 1780, C.O.5/99, 533; Major Wilhelm von

Wilmowsky to Von Junkenn, June 4, 1780, in Bernard A.Uhlendorf, ed., *The Siege of Charleston with an Account of the Province of South Carolina: Diaries and Letters of Hessian Officers from the Von Junkenn Papers in the William L. Clements Library* (Ann Arbor, Mich., 1938), 69; Hough, 419.

5. Franklin and Mary Wickwire, *Cornwallis: The American Adventure* (Boston, 1970), is valuable for the earl's family background and service in America; his relations with Clinton can be traced 79–133; see also the analysis of their relationship in William B. Willcox, *Portrait of a General: Sir Henry Clinton in the War for Independence* (New York, 1964), 231–33, 309–22.

6. Clinton, *American Rebellion*, 440–41.

7. Historians have generally been critical of the effects of the June 3 proclamation. Many years ago Edward McCrady pointed to Clinton's policy and the excesses of British officers like Tarleton as acts that gave life to a lost cause, *S. C. in the American Revolution, 1775–1780*, 548–51. William Willcox, a close student of the commander in chief, feels that the large numbers of South Carolinians who came in to take the oath after Charlestown fell so impressed Clinton, normally a pessimist about the strength of loyalism, that he "overreached himself," *Portrait of a General*, 320–21. Perhaps another explanation, also suggested by McCrady, is that Clinton, faced with information that many South Carolinians were reluctant to fight other Americans, feared that to allow large numbers to remain on parole would be a simple way for them not to serve at all, thus spoiling the plan by which loyalist militia would be strong enough to control the province with minimum help from British regular forces. Four more recent assessments of the effects of the proclamation on the loyalists are Paul Smith, *Loyalists and Redcoats* (Chapel Hill, N.C., 1964), 131–33; George S. McCowen, Jr., *The British Occupation of Charleston* (Columbia, S.C., 1970), 54; John Shy, "British Strategy for Pacifying the Southern Colonies, 1778–1781," in *The Southern Experience in the American Revolution*, ed. Jeffrey J. Crow and Larry E. Tise (Chapel Hill, N.C., 1978), 169; and Robert M. Calhoon, *Loyalists in Revolutionary America, 1760–1781* (New York, 1973), 485–86, all of whom find that Clinton made the task of pacification more difficult.

8. McCowen, *British Occupation of Charleston*, 13.

9. Ferguson's appointment is in Clinton to Cornwallis, June 1, 1780, CP, 30/11/61,3–6. His career may be traced in Hugh Rankin's introduction to "An Officer Out of His Time: Correspondence of Major Patrick Ferguson, 1779–1780," in Howard H. Peckham, ed., *Sources of American Independence: Selected Manuscripts from the Collections of the William L. Clements Library*, 2 vols. (Chicago, 1978), II, 287–360; see also Jonas Howe, "'Major Ferguson's Riflemen: The American Volunteers," *Acadiensis* (1906), 237–46; (1907), 30–41.

10. Henry M. Stephens, "Nisbet Balfour," *DNB*, I, 976–77.

11. George F. R. Baker, "Francis Rawdon Hastings," *DNB*, VII, 117–22.

12. The literature on Tarleton and his southern campaigns is extensive. See especially Banastre Tarleton, *A History of the Campaigns of 1780 and 1781 in the Southern Provinces of North America* (London, 1787), 85–184; and Robert D. Bass, *The Green Dragoon: The Lives of Banastre Tarleton and Mary Robinson* (New York, 1957), 73–173.

13. It is Hugh Rankin's view that Cornwallis, anxious for popularity in his new command, did not hold a tight rein on these young officers in their dealings with the civil population, and thus he was partly responsible for the later failure of the pacification process, "Charles Lord Cornwallis: A Study in Frustration," in *George Washington's Opponents*, ed. George A. Billias (New York, 1969), 104–5.

14. See Chesney, "Journal," 12n89, for Turnbull; for Cruger, see Egerton, *Royal Commission*, 376–77; and for Allen, see *Canadian Claims*, 248–51.

15. Clinton to Ferguson, May 22, 1780, CP, 30/11/2, 44–45.

16. CP, 30/11/2, 86, for the "Plan," written on an uncertain date in June 1780; see also Cornwallis to Clinton, CP, 30/11/72, 18.

17. Cornwallis to Clinton, June 30, CP, 30/11/72, 18.

18. The units left with Cornwallis and their estimated strength are taken from the discussion in Wickwire, *Cornwallis: The American Adventure*, 135–37.

Chapter Six

Pacifying the Interior

A Major Commandant…where the enemy had a field officer, a very plain man with a good character & tolerable understanding will do…all that is required of him is to have sense enough to know right from wrong & honesty enough to prefer the former to the latter.

—Lord Cornwallis, June 1780

The time had come to test the idea that large numbers of loyalists were waiting in the backcountry to help recover South Carolina for the royal cause. These British hopes were reflected in the composition of the expedition. Nisbet Balfour was leading toward Ninety Six, which included Patrick Ferguson as inspector of militia at the head of his American Volunteers, and the South Carolina Royalists, formed in East Florida from loyal refugees who were largely from the district.[1]

Balfour's men set out from Moncks Corner on May 28, 1780, moving along the west side of the Santee River until they reached the plantation of Colonel William Thomson, the commander of the Third Regiment of state troops. By then, Patrick Ferguson had reached Orangeburg, which lay in an area inhabited by second-and third-generation German families, and there had begun the process of assessing the sentiments of local people. Balfour soon concluded that "all the leading men of property have been on the rebel side"; and he was reluctant to confer any responsibility on them. Colonel Thomson apparently showed no interest in cooperating with the conquerors and, because his presence might cause trouble in such a "disaffected district," Balfour felt that he should be paroled to another place.[2]

Balfour informed the earl that he had turned instead to John Fisher of Orangeburg, a "confidential and trusty man," to form an "association nearly upon the plan you intend for the militia." Fisher had come to South Carolina from Scotland in 1760; after that, he acquired over 3,000 acres in the Orangeburg District and lots in the town , was chosen as one of the commissioners to build the courthouse and jail, and in 1773 he became the first sheriff of the district. Fisher had gone to Britain on business in 1775, but he returned to America in time to serve as a volunteer in defending Savannah against the French and the Americans. After Charlestown surrendered, Balfour had sent him ahead to assess local sentiment; in response to his report, Balfour authorized Fisher to form an association "to take up arms and keep the peace until a militia is formed." Altogether, 294 men agreed to articles for "the reestablishment of the British government in this once happy, but now distracted country," and to serve in either the six-months militia for service outside the district, or the "domestick militia" to preserve order locally.[3]

In all, twelve companies were organized in Orangeburg District for six months of service. Their officers were generally men of modest property, and two of their commanders, John Salley and Samuel Row, had actually served in the state legislature during the American Period. About 500 men enlisted in these companies, and late in June Cornwallis approved Balfour's recommendation that Fisher be given command of the district's regiment with the rank of colonel. Militia officers were instructed to make an inventory of arms in the hands of the inhabitants, take evidence of crimes committed by rebels against loyal citizens, and make a list of persons not to be trusted with arms or taken into the militia.[4]

Balfour resumed his march on June 10, leaving a detachment of 100 regulars at Orangeburg. As he approached the confluence of the Broad and Saluda rivers, Balfour divided his force, sending the South Carolina Royalists up the west bank of the Broad while, with the remainder, he planned to proceed along the north side of the Saluda toward Ninety Six. Thus the Royalists entered the "fork," the area between the rivers that was reputed to be a hotbed of loyalism, and Colonel Alexander Innes detached young Lieutenant George Dawkins, a native of the area, with a "flying party" to carry the good news of the approach of the king's troops. They were generally well received, Innes reporting that a "Capt. Cunningham" had provided "good management" in turning out the loyal inhabitants and that a Captain Henry O'Neall had also appeared at the head of a party of men.[5]

Nevertheless, Innes discerned danger signals for the long-run pacification of the area. Although he found "most violent Rebels…candid enough to allow the Game is up" and willing to accept pardons, he felt it would be necessary to remove some of the leaders from the area in order not to "disrupt the peace." He issued a proclamation announcing the restoration of British law, and he promised vigorous prosecution of disorderly persons, particularly those who engaged in the theft of horses and cattle. The area was, however, short of food and forage for the army, many people being destitute of grain because of the disruption caused by the campaigns in 1779. Still, the rather enthusiastic reception made Innes confident that a large contingent of regular troops would not be required to maintain order in this part of the province, an assessment that could only please his superiors. Having accomplished their mission of liberation, the Royalists were given long-awaited furloughs to their homes.[6]

Meanwhile, Balfour lingered near Wade Hampton's store at the Congaree area for several days, organizing voluntary associations and seeking good officers for the militia. It was while engaged in these activities that Balfour first learned that Richard Pearis, "a fellow of infamous character," was already operating around Ninety Six, "having a sett with him that must be immediately sent home, otherwise there will be much stress among the inhabitants." Before Charlestown surrendered, James Simpson, acting for Clinton, had instructed Pearis to make contact with leaders of t he areas where loyalists were known to be concentrated. He was to notify them that royal troops were coming into the backcountry, that a loyal militia would be organized and rebel leaders secured, and that horses, cattle, and grain owned by staunch rebels would be needed to supply the troops. Operating under Clinton's proclamation of May 22, Pearis and David Rees, one of the "powder" men of 1775, signed an agreement on June 10 with four representatives of "the people" south of the Saluda. By this instrument, these "people" agreed to take protection, to give up the ammunition and supplies stored in the fort at Whitehall, and to disarm and discharge its garrison. Supplies at Fort Rutledge on the Seneca River were to be relinquished, but the garrison was to occupy it as protection against Indian attack until replaced by a British force. Meanwhile, Lieutenant Colonel Thomas Brown, who had occupied Augusta, was also granting protections on similar terms, most notably to the South Carolina rebel troops commanded by Lieutenant Colonel LeRoy Hammond.[7]

Even more important than recovering arms and forts was the agency of Pearis and his followers in getting the rebel leaders Andrew Williamson and Andrew Pickens to give their paroles, a fascinating story because of the different courses that the careers of the two will take during the British occupation. According to Samuel Hammond, one of Williamson's officers, the general and Georgia rebel leaders had been planning a campaign against Savannah to relieve the pressure on Lincoln by forcing Clinton to divert men to defend the Georgia port. The news that Charlestown had fallen made such plans obsolete, and some Georgia leaders urged a retreat toward the mountains from which they might continue resistance. Williamson, who had received a copy of the capitulation terms, agreed to return to Whitehall to consult with the officers of his brigade and other local leaders on what course to follow. He still had three companies of state troops in the field and knew that Pickens had others nearby. Aware that Pearis had come into the area, Williamson on June 5 addressed a note "to the officer commanding the British troops north of the Saluda" to ask by what authority he was acting. He then assembled his officers and men to read them the capitulation terms and to offer to lead them to the mountains, but only a handful were willing to go with him. He persisted, however, and presented the same alternatives to Pickens's troops. When all but two captains and a few privates chose surrender and Pickens gave no indication of his own preference, Williamson returned to Whitehall to await the appearance of British troops, and Pickens went to his home in the Long Cane settlement. Several of Williamson's officers were among those who signed the June 10 agreement with Pearis in which "the people" agreed to end further resistance.[8]

Balfour left the Congaree area on June 15 and moved up the Saluda, crossing that stream to Ninety Six on June 22. He set to work at once to find commanders for the militia among loyal men of property and standing in the area and to work his way through the maze of conflicting paroles and proclamations that had been issued. Already suspicious of Pearis, Balfour soon found the agreement for disarming rebels to be less than satisfactory because many had turned in weapons in poor condition and kept the good ones. He also came to the conclusion that the area between the Saluda and Savannah rivers was full of "disaffected people" who, although temporarily chastened by the presence of his troops, might resume the rebellion if given the opportunity. To Balfour, "our friends" were not nearly "so numerous as expected."[9]

Under these circumstances, Balfour saw two possible courses of action: to renounce "the agreements of Pearis and Brown," exile rebel leaders to the coast, and send troops into the settlements to search systematically for arms; or, to "keep the capitulation," make rebel leaders responsible for the conduct of the people, and to incorporate moderate rebels into the militia and give that organization responsibility for defense. Balfour leaned toward the second alternative, particularly after conversations with Williamson, a man "of candour" who seemed willing to cooperate with the British so long as he was not expected to take "an active military part," and who recommended that "by degrees" local leaders like Pickens and LeRoy Hammond be given more responsibility.[10]

Balfour still found reason to complain about Pearis and Thomas Brown, fearing that by leading their men in acts of vengeance against local rebels they might upset the delicate peace prevailing in the area. Both men had close ties with Indians, but it was Brown, who had been appointed deputy superintendent for the eastern district after John Stuart's death, who was the more worrisome. In that role, he recommended that Fort Rutledge be destroyed to satisfy the Cherokees, that rebel families living on Indian lands in the Watauga area of western Virginia be evicted, and that Indians be employed to drive them out. Cornwallis consented to the destruction of Fort Rutledge, but he ordered that Indians not be employed in a military capacity at this time.[11]

The consummation of the campaign to restore British control in Ninety Six District was the organization of the loyal militia in that part of the province. As at Orangeburg, Cornwallis's concept of the nature of the militia and its commanders was put into effect: as associations of loyal citizens, they would be used for the same tasks that militia had performed before the rebellion. While Cornwallis was certainly not so naive as to believe that he might not need to call on the militia for service as field troops, he did hope to minimize civil strife until he learned the relative strength of rebel and loyal sentiment. As a result, when loyal men were considered for commissions in the militia regiments, their local standing was deemed to be more important than military talent or experience; indeed, many of the original commanders of militia regiments were designated as "conservators of the peace" as well as by military rank. As Cornwallis explained in instructions to an officer in another part of the state, the most important qualifications were honesty and good character.[12]

As a basis for organizing the loyal militia, it was decided to use the same districts that the Provincial Congress created early in the war, and when reporting on his progress, Patrick Ferguson actually identified militia districts by the names of the former rebel commanders. Although loyalist militia units were officially designated as battalions and commanded by majors, they are consistently referred to as "regiments" in British pay records. In time, their commanding officers were promoted to the ranks of lieutenant colonel and colonel.[13]

Ferguson formed seven regiments of militia in Ninety Six District. After a good deal of effort, Balfour succeeded in finding a field officer for each, remarking that they "are better than I had once hoped for." His regulations for these units were based on the instructions of his superiors and similar to those already put in effect at Orangeburg, but he added a stirring appeal that called for the enlistment of "good and trusty men" under officers who "sincerely abhor the Rebel tyranny and wish for a return to true British liberty under the King and old Constitution."[14]

The two regiments south of the Saluda were designated by the names of the tributaries of the Savannah River near which their recruits lived. The Long Cane Regiment was raised at Ninety Six and initially consisted of about 230 officers and men, most of whom lived on the Little River of the Savannah, its tributary Long Cane Creek, and their branches, the same general area from which the rebel Andrew Pickens had drawn his men. To command this unit, Balfour appointed Richard King, a native of Great Britain, who had come to South Carolina in 1763 where he farmed and raised cattle on Turkey Creek, a branch of the Saluda near Ninety Six. King had taken no known part in the war before the British returned, and few of his men had been active loyalists until then. Although King and some of his men did see hard service and suffer for their loyalty, Ferguson considered the Long Cane area to be among the less resolute in its loyalty to the Crown,

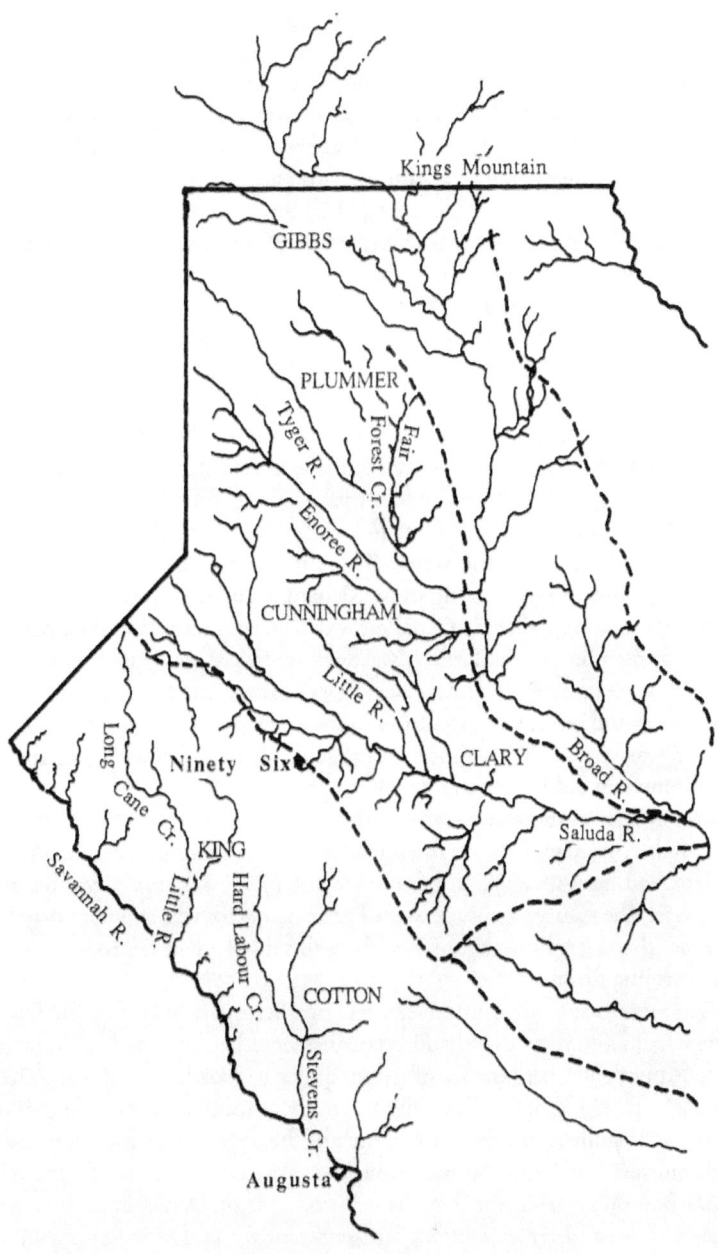

Militia Organization: The Western Frontier
(adapted by R. S. Lambert from Henry Mouzon, 1775)

despite the proximity of the British post at Ninety Six. Altogether, about fifty families, many of whom had come into the area from northern Ireland in the dozen years before the outbreak of fighting, furnished two or more recruits to the regiment.[15]

The other regiment south of the Saluda was raised along Stevens Creek and its branches, an area inhabited by Germans and, more recently, by Scotch-Irish people who had migrated from other colonies or directly from abroad. At its top strength this regiment had over 400 men and was commanded by one John Cotton about whom little is known. It included among its recruits a small group of confirmed loyalists who lived along Cuffeetown Creek, as well as veterans of the fighting around Ninety Six in 1775 and exiles to Florida in the American Period.[16]

Tory sentiment was much stronger north of the Saluda. If any single part of the backcountry deserved to be known as the center of loyalism, it was the area from which the Little River (of the Saluda) Regiment was recruited-from residents of the Little River, Beaverdam Creek, Cane and Bush creeks, and the north bank of the Saluda itself. Of the 300 men who enlisted in this unit, sixty families each furnished two or more and some as many as six men; seven families alone furnished thirty-four. This was the bailiwick of the Cunningham family where the plots to hijack the Provincial Congress's powder and to harass William Henry Drayton were hatched in 1775, and twenty-five of those who enlisted in this regiment were among those Richard Richardson had captured during the Snow Campaign and shipped off to Charlestown. The land records of the time reveal that the holdings of members of the Little River Regiment were highly concentrated and that many of them were immediate or near neighbors of the Cunninghams. With his reputation for suffering and service in opposition to the rebellion, it is little wonder that Patrick Cunningham was selected by Balfour to command this regiment with the rank of major. Robert Cunningham did not receive an appointment at this time, but bigger things were in store for him later in the year.[17]

The Dutch Fork Regiment, on the other hand, even though its commanding officer, Daniel Clary, had been involved in the uprising of 1775, was able to muster barely 100 men for service. The relatively poor record of enlistments for this regiment may have been due to the fact that a large number of men from this district had returned from exile with the South Carolina Royalists.[18]

Two regiments were raised in the extreme northern part of Ninety Six District near the North Carolina border. British officers considered it especially important to retain a secure control of this area because of its proximity to North Carolina and the need to protect the left flank of Cornwallis's army when it was ready to move into that province. The Fair Forest Regiment, named for a branch of the Tyger River, a western tributary of the Broad, mustered perhaps 150 men from the district commanded by the rebel colonel Thomas Brandon during the American Period. Major Daniel Plummer, a native of Pennsylvania who had been one of Richardson's captives in 1775, was put in charge of the regiment. Zacharias Gibbs, whom we have seen as a participant in the first battle at Ninety Six in 1775 and who had barely been reprieved from the hangman after the Battle of Kettle Creek, mustered about 150 men for his Spartan, or Upper, Regiment, some of whom probably resided across the North Carolina boundary.[19]

The command of a seventh militia regiment raised in Ninety Six District was entrusted to the ubiquitous Moses Kirkland, who had returned to South Carolina after his travels in exile and service in the Indian department in the Floridas. Reaching Savannah after the British recovered it, he served in the siege of that town before returning to South Carolina when Charlestown fell. Kirkland held the rank of lieutenant colonel and corresponded with Cornwallis and Balfour about his unit, but in the absence of the pay records that have survived for the other regiments, it is not possible to infer where his regiment was organized or who served in it.[20]

One early loyalist, Thomas Fletchall, who had been so deeply involved in the negotiations at Ninety Six in 1775, was released from jail in Charlestown in 1776 and returned to his home where he remained quietly during the American Period. Although he came forward to offer his services after the British returned to the upcountry, at fifty-five years and 280 pounds he was hardly in condition for active duty; later that year he took his family and fourteen slaves to Charlestown where he remained throughout the British Period.[21]

Perhaps 1,500 men enlisted in the seven militia regiments in Ninety Six District and saw service with them in the six-month period until December 1780, a number that confirmed the reports that this area would provide more support for the British war effort than other parts of the province. Patrick Ferguson's effort to recruit and organize the militia did not extend beyond this district, and the relatively large number who enlisted there may be attributed in part to this concentration of effort.

What the British called the northern frontier, lying east of the Broad and north of the Santee-Congaree, was to be the scene of many of the most stirring events of the Revolution in South Carolina. Physically a region of extremes, it included both tidewater and remote areas far inland, and it was laced by a number of rivers that served to link them. The people living in this vast region included all economic groups—wealthy rice and indigo planters of the tidal swamps, small indigo planters along the Pee Dee and Black rivers, and subsistence farmers on the Wateree and the upper reaches of the other principal streams. Slaveholding was more prevalent here than in the area west of the Broad, with numbers ranging from the gangs owned by some of the great tidewater planters to the extra hand or two that aspiring small farmers had acquired.

But amid this diversity a certain similarity of outlook prevailed among the people of this region, for the society of its tidewater was more recently established and perhaps more fluid than in the older areas around Charlestown. Its interior, on the other hand, composed as it was mainly of second-and third-generation Americans, many from long-established settlements in other colonies, was an older and more mature society than that found in Ninety Six District.

Before turning to their effort to organize the northern frontier, it is worth remembering that the British objective was to restore control over both Carolinas; if successful in that endeavor, perhaps the army could participate in the conquest of Virginia. With Lincoln's army removed as an immediate source of resistance, it was natural for Lord Cornwallis to concentrate a major portion of his regular force at a point from which it could readily move into North Carolina and, at the same time, maintain water communication with the port at Charlestown.

As a base for furthering such plans, however, the northern frontier of South Carolina presented a great danger and an equally great uncertainty. The danger was that if another southern Continental army were formed, it would necessarily approach from the north, and Cornwallis knew it must be destroyed before he could move toward the predominantly Scottish settlements near Cross Creek in North Carolina where pro-British sympathies were supposed to be especially strong. The uncertainty lay in the fact that there was little concrete evidence of the degree of support that could be expected from the inhabitants east of the Broad River in Camden and Cheraw districts, the areas through which Cornwallis's army would move toward North Carolina. It was assumed that elements loyal to Britain did exist in this region, but exactly where they were to be found and how deeply committed they were could only be discovered through trial and error.

The uncertainties of the British position were compounded by several other factors. One was the nature of the terrain north of the Santee where the river systems that could serve as invasion routes in the drive toward North Carolina might also act as infiltration routes for small rebel parties to disrupt the long and vital supply line from Charlestown to the main army. It would be desirable to establish a strong post at Georgetown to protect the army's eastern flank as it moved north. It was also known that certain important rebel civil and military leaders such as Governor John Rutledge, and Generals Thomas Sumter and Francis Marion were still at large and might return to arouse their partisans if given encouragement by the approach of a Continental army.

This was the situation that Lord Cornwallis faced when he reached Camden early in June at the head of about half the regular troops in South Carolina and some provincial regiments. He then dispatched several parties to establish advanced posts and to test the sentiments of the inhabitants close to the North Carolina boundary, turned the command over to Lord Rawdon, and returned to Charlestown to take care of a number of administrative matters that needed his attention.

While on his march to Camden, Cornwallis had been pleased to accept assistance from representatives of several prominent local families. According to the earl, two men in particular, Elias Ball, Sr., of Wambaw, and Theodore Gaillard, had demonstrated "ardent proofs of their loyalty." Ball, by his "zeal and activity," had "procured the intelligence which gave Lt. Col. Tarleton the opportunity of striking the decisive blow" near Lenud's Ferry on the Santee, where on May 6 Tarleton's horsemen had routed a retreating body of American cavalry. The nature of Gaillard's early aid is less clear, but from Murray's Ferry he was soon deeply involved in expediting the flow of supplies to Cornwallis's army. He and Ball were rewarded with commissions as lieutenant colonels of militia, and Ball soon set about raising the Craven and Berkeley County militia regiment for service in the area. Cornwallis was particularly elated that these men had taken an "active" role because they came from the propertied classes that British leaders counted on to pacify the general populace. Ball's son, Elias Jr., and Gaillard's brother, John, also accepted commissions at this time.[22]

While at Camden, Cornwallis set in motion plans to raise a provincial regiment in that part of the province. Provincial regiments were generally of two types: those infantry units modeled on the regular British foot regiments; and "Rangers," mixed units of infantry and cavalry that scouted and skirmished in support of regular troops, but also could be counted on to garrison outposts and maintain contact between such places and the main army. The British army in America was perennially short of cavalry, a deficiency especially felt in the extensive areas of open country in the southern provinces, and it was hoped that the mounted components of Ranger regiments would compensate for it.[21]

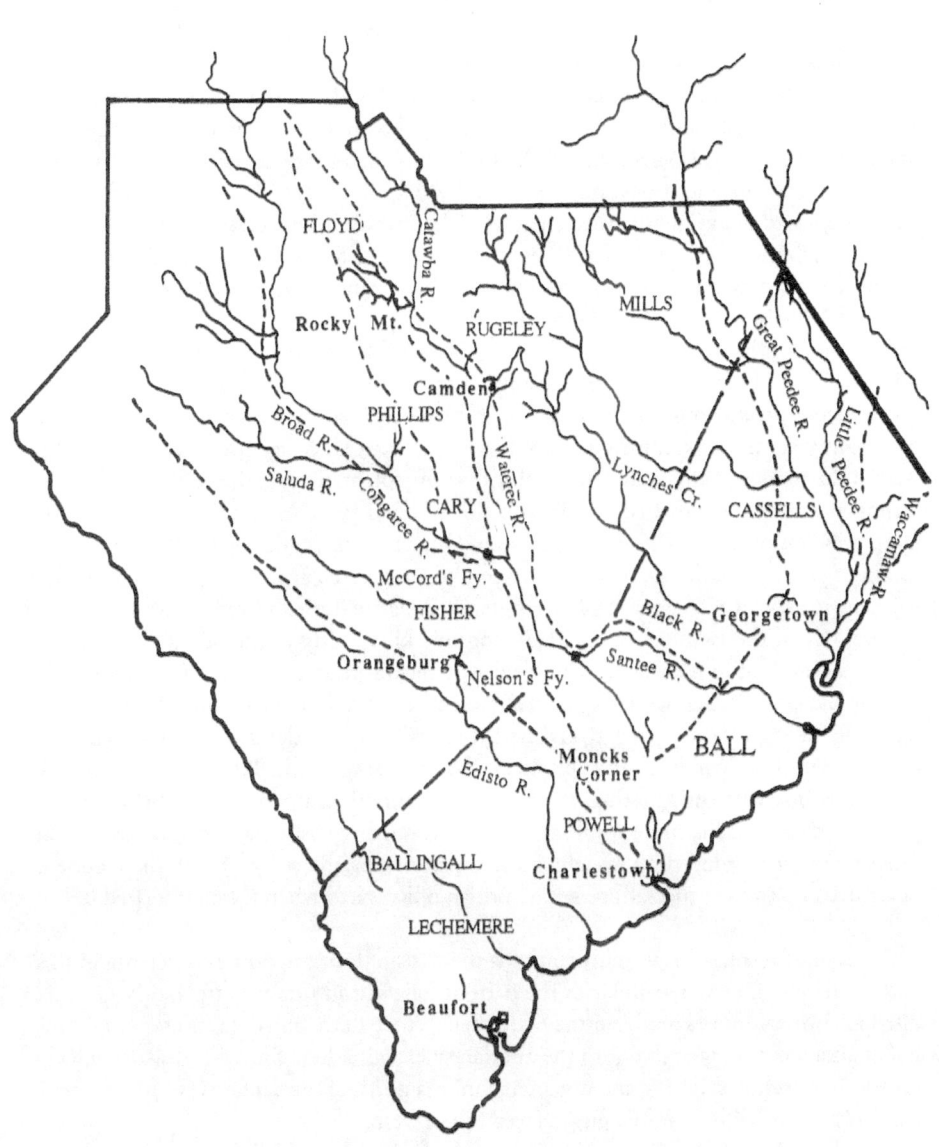

Militia Organization: The Northern Frontier
(adapted by R. S. Lambert from Mouzon, 1775)

Therefore, it could be expected that Cornwallis would seek to create additional provincial units from South Carolina, and on June 4 he commissioned one John Harrison, who resided on Sparrow Swamp above Lynches Creek, as major and authorized him to raise up to 500 men for a regiment to be called the South Carolina Rangers. Harrison, a native of Virginia, named his brothers Robert and Samuel as captains in the regiment; under the direction of Major Archibald McArthur of the Seventy-first Regiment who commanded an advanced post on the upper Pee Dee, he began recruiting other officers and the enlisted men. Despite the generous authorization he was given, Harrison's Rangers rarely numbered more than 100 men at anyone muster and usually could count on no more than sixty for actual service. Indeed, British officers were ambivalent about the value of "Harrison's Corps" to the army and among the populace, finding their actions useful and even heroic on occasion, but noting that, like militia, they were prone to "go off" when the mood seized them. A more serious criticism was that many of the Rangers seemed more anxious for "plunder" than for regular service under discipline, and the Harrisons were more than once involved in acts of vengeance against rebel partisans. In August the Rangers participated in burning over fifty plantations in the Williamsburg area during a campaign conducted by Major James Wemyss of the Sixty-third Regiment. The mere presence of the Harrison brothers seemed to spark resistance by rebels; the famous forays of partisans under Francis Marion were often directed against Harrison's men who were, in turn, in the vanguard of attempts by Banastre Tarleton and Wemyss to drive Marion out of the swamps. Robert Harrison was killed early in the fall, and two other brothers were shot in their beds by unidentified persons near Camden in December.[24]

By then, both sides had engaged in a reign of terror that scourged much of the country along the Pee Dee and Black rivers and Lynches Creek. Rawdon and Wemyss frequently used terms like "banditti" and "plunderers" in referring to the Rangers, although they did sympathize with the sufferings the Harrisons incurred in supporting the British cause. John Harrison and his more loyal followers continued to assist the army as scouts and foragers; severely reduced by casualties and desertions by the end of 1780, the regiment never lived up to the expectations senior British officers had when they authorized it.[25]

Attempts to form loyal militia units as the basis of local support and defense in this part of the province were similar to the pattern followed in Orangeburg and Ninety Six districts. British officers tendered the oath of allegiance to the inhabitants and sought influential residents to take charge of the militia. An examination of those endeavors quickly reveals, however, that raising and organizing militia north of the Santee was a more formidable task than Balfour and Ferguson faced in the west.

Archibald McArthur and two battalions of the Seventy-first Regiment reached Cheraw Hill on the upper Pee Dee on June 9 only to find that some of "Harrison's people" had preceded him to that place. McArthur then moved down the river to the Cheraw District courthouse at Long Bluff, where on June 15 he administered the oath to about 150 people and, shortly thereafter, named the officers to head the militia in that district. He estimated that "most" of the officers of the local rebel militia regiment had come in to give their paroles, and that the "country people" seemed to be anxious to join the militia as a protection against local "banditti" who plundered anything not closely guarded.[26]

McArthur's choice for colonel of the Cheraw regiment was William Henry Mills, a substantial planter who owned 2,000 acres and thirty-five slaves on or near the Pee Dee. Coming to America in 1754 as a surgeon with the Forty-sixth Regiment, Mills retired to South Carolina ten years later and began to accumulate his property. He was appointed sheriff of the newly created Cheraw District in 1773, but his strong support of the British position made him so "obnoxious" to local Whigs that he left his family and fled to the coast and then to New England. He did not return until the siege of Charlestown. To be lieutenant colonel, McArthur chose 3 (sometimes "Grey" in British records), a "Scotch gentleman," about whom little personal information has come to light except that he acquired land on the Pee Dee in 1774. Gray came to be considered a valuable officer by his superiors, and he has the distinction of writing one of the few commentaries by a loyalist on loyalism in the Carolinas. Although information on the ranking officers is meager enough, even less is known about the numbers and characteristics of the men originally recruited for Mills's regiment, whose misfortune it will be to suffer virtual destruction later in the summer.[17]

One other militia regiment was apparently organized north of the Santee about this time and the command given to a Major Samuel Tynes about whom little is known. Routed by Francis Marion in a surprise attack in the following November, the men of the unit were badly scattered and only about thirty were ever paid for their service.[28]

Four regiments were raised in Camden District. The officers chosen to command, their experiences in trying to recruit and organize their units, and the types of service they performed all reveal the difficulties the British were to face in trying to pacify the population in an area so vital to their plans.

There is no more enigmatic figure among South Carolina loyalists than Henry Rugeley, apparently a native of America who with his brother, Rowland, had opened a store in Charlestown where they dealt in general merchandise and country produce. The records of the firm show that they did business principally in Camden District, although they had customers living as far in the interior as Long Cane Creek. While engaged in their mercantile enterprise, Rowland also held the lucrative position of register of Mesne Conveyance under the provincial government, and through that appointment he managed to acquire property on Charlestown Neck and in the interior. On one tract north of Camden, Henry Rugeley constructed a small industrial village, which consisted of a sawmill, a gristmill, two bolting mills, a waterwheel , a tanyard, a store, and several log houses, where he employed the labor of twenty slaves; nearby, he built "Clermont," a dwelling described by one contemporary as "elegant." Their various enterprises indicate the range of ambitions of the brothers, but when Rowland died in 1777 their partnership was found to be badly overextended. Thereafter, Henry was constantly pressed by his creditors in Britain as well as in South Carolina, but his politics apparently were at least acceptable to the state government during the American Period. After the fall of Charlestown, however, British authorities apparently made overtures to merchants who had correspondents in the interior, and early in the occupation they became convinced that Rugeley would be a valuable ally in their efforts to restore royal rule in Camden District. Commissioned as a colonel of Camden militia, he apparently accompanied Cornwallis on the march to Camden.[29]

It was in the Waxhaw settlements near the Catawba River below Charlotte, North Carolina, that British officers first learned how difficult it might be to pacify the northern frontier. Expecting that the Volunteers of Ireland might be able to establish close ties among the large Scotch-Irish population in the Waxhaw area and Mecklenburg County, North Carolina, Cornwallis dispatched Lord Rawdon to Charlotte to prepare for the expected move into that province. But Rawdon found that the inhabitants had little interest in enlisting for service with the British, and their coolness turned to outright hostility after they learned of Tarleton's treatment of Buford's men. It was evident that many who had given their paroles were slipping away to the mountains to join the rebels. On June 10 he issued an address in which he urged them to return, promising that they could "gather crops without fear of interruption" so long as they remained peaceably at home and did not act against loyal subjects. The apparent reasonableness of the proclamation was offset, however, by its concluding statement:

> After this warning, should any person be unadvised enough to foment further disturbance in the country or to instigate his neighbors to a ruinous & unavailing show of opposition, to him alone must be charged the severities which such conduct may draw upon the District.

In hopes that an American might be more effective in quieting the area, Rawdon ordered Henry Rugeley, as an "administrator of justice," to bring his new regiment to Charlotte, while Rawdon and the Volunteers fell back to Camden where in Cornwallis's absence he assumed command of that post.[30]

Another convert to loyalism in the Camden area was James Cary, a Virginian with some education and legal training, who had been a man of local prominence in Northampton County, North Carolina, before moving to the South Carolina lowcountry in 1764. In 1770 he moved again, this time to manage the plantation of the Quaker John Milhous on the west side of the Wateree near Camden. He later purchased this and other property, and by the time the British army reached Camden owned a dozen or more slaves, had a sawmill, an orchard, and raised crops of indigo and tobacco on the Wateree tract. Cary had been a Regulator, and in 1776 the Provincial Congress chose him as a justice of the peace in Camden District, apparently the only part he took in support of the state government. Offering his services to Cornwallis, he was rewarded with a major's commission in a regiment briefly commanded by another man, then authorized to raise a regiment in the area between the Congaree and Wateree rivers and given the title of conservator of the peace.[31]

There was nothing in the background of Rugeley or Cary to indicate any strong partiality for the British cause before the fall of Charlestown, but John Phillips was a confirmed loyalist from the beginning of the conflict. Confined in irons in an Orangeburg jail in 1778 after an abortive attempt to flee to St. Augustine, he later spent four months in the Camden jail for refusing to take the oath to the state. Phillips had come to South Carolina from northern Ireland in 1770 and settled with his large family on Little River north of the Broad. When the British came to Camden, Phillips rallied his neighbors near the town of Winnsboro on Jackson's Creek and offered their services to Cornwallis. Known as the Jackson's Creek Regiment, they performed more arduous service for the British than perhaps any loyalist militia unit raised in South Carolina.[32]

A fourth regiment was raised at Rocky Mount on the Catawba between the Waxhaw area and Camden where Lieutenant Colonel George Turnbull of the New York Volunteers had been ordered to establish an advanced post. His search for a commanding officer was simplified when Mathew Floyd, an Irishman who had migrated from Pennsylvania many years before, appeared there at the head of thirty volunteers. Before the war Floyd had been a militia captain and justice of the peace living on an eastern branch of the upper Broad, but he had taken a prominent part in the uprising against the Provincial Congress in 1775 and had spent time in the Charlestown jail as a result.[33]

The four regiments thus recruited were of doubtful quality, only Phillips's men demonstrating consistent zeal for the cause. The militia records for Camden District are not complete, but there is every indication that the number of committed loyalists in the district was smaller than British officers had hoped to find.

Because of worries about the security of the eastern flank of the army and of the route along the Santee by which its supplies must come, a British naval expedition was dispatched to seize Georgetown on July 1, a move that was followed closely by the arrival by sea of Major James Wemyss and the Sixty-third Regiment. Wemyss was assigned the task of securing the port and organizing the loyal militia there before withdrawing with his regulars to Charlestown. He quickly concluded, however, that there were not enough influential loyalists there to furnish officers for three regiments, the number that the rebels had organized north and east of the Santee. Reducing the number of regiments to two, he divided the region so that one part of the rebel middle district would be included in Mills's Cheraw Regiment and the rest would be included in the Georgetown Regiment. This created a delicate situation for Wemyss, who concluded that neither John Coming Ball nor Theodore Gaillard, already commissioned as lieutenant colonels, had sufficient influence north of the Santee to be granted the command of the Georgetown Regiment. Therefore, Wemyss selected James Cassells, an indigo planter and passive supporter of the rebel government during the American Period, who began the task of recruiting for his regiment late in July.[34]

To complete the militia organization, Cornwallis authorized two regiments to be raised southwest of Charlestown: a Colleton County regiment drawn from coastal parishes bounded by Charlestown, Orangeburg District, and the Salkehatchie River; and a Granville County regiment from Beaufort District. Robert Ballingall, a substantial planter and a Scot, was commissioned to head the former, while Nicholas Lechemere, collector of customs at Beaufort before the war who had married into the prominent Deveaux family of that place, was made colonel of the Granville Regiment. Cornwallis and Balfour envisioned employing these units to replace or reinforce the militia along the northern frontier as the campaign moved into North Carolina.[35]

Thus in the two months after the fall of Charlestown, British officers had authorized eighteen militia regiments that originally mustered at least 2,500 officers and men. In addition, the South Carolina Rangers had been organized and negotiations were under way toward raising other provincial troops. Strong posts had been established at Camden and Ninety Six, and lesser ones at Rocky Mount, in the Cheraw District, and at Georgetown. Cornwallis's reports to Clinton were cautiously optimistic about the prospects for establishing a strong base from which the campaign into North Carolina might be mounted.

Cornwallis's optimism was tempered with caution because not all the signs were favorable. The response of the loyalists in certain areas of the province had been heartening, particularly in parts of Ninety Six District, but even there Balfour had found fewer loyalists south of the Saluda than had been expected. Indeed, Robert Gray estimated that barely one-third of the population was loyal, and "by no means the wealthiest" part.[36]

If British officers found the Crown's supporters to be a definite minority in the province, their own vacillating policies and excesses in action further alienated the wavering and gave heart to committed rebels. Contemporary observers and historians have found that the methods used by Tarleton's troopers at Moncks Corner and against Buford's men alienated many lukewarm rebels, while uncertainties about the terms of British protection and paroles made it difficult for the uncommitted to know what was expected of them.[37]

Another factor often overlooked in seeking to explain the British failure in South Carolina is that Cornwallis's army was seriously short of the equipment and transport necessary to supply the loyalists and to sustain itself during an extended campaign in the interior. Nearly 4,000 muskets had been lost when the cargo ship *Russia Merchant* foundered in heavy seas off the southern coast in the previous January, and another 2,000 to 3,000 were lost when a powder magazine blew up in Charlestown shortly after the capitulation. These accidents caused delays in delivering arms to loyalist militiamen, many of whom were without muskets in the early musters. The same foul weather was responsible for the decision to throw cavalry horses overboard to save other vessels. As a result, Tarleton and other dragoon commanders were forced to seek mounts after they landed. Cornwallis intended that the shortage be made up from rebel estates, but the dragoons often took horses with little regard for the political sentiments of the owners. And rebel forces outside Charlestown after the surrender of the town took care as they retreated to strip the country of wagons that would be useful in carrying supplies overland and of small boats necessary to carry them over the many rivers. Cornwallis was forced to order that the wagons with Balfour's expedition to Ninety Six be returned to him so that he would have sufficient transport to permit his army to begin its invasion of North Carolina. His own foragers were often heavy-handed when scouring the countryside for supplies, the loyalist Robert Gray noting that "the abuses of the British army in taking the peoples Horses, Cattle & provisions to make up for the shortages, in many cases without paying for them, ... disgusted the inhabitanrs."[38]

Despite these danger signals, Cornwallis's plans to complete the recovery of South Carolina for the Crown had apparently gone well. There were, however, good reasons not to move too quickly to accomplish the next goal-he did not want to commit his troops to a major campaign against organized resistance in the hottest pan of the summer, sufficient supplies and transport had to be gathered to sustain his men against whatever opposition they were to face, and there were administrative details that needed his attention. In Charlestown he turned to these tasks, including the pleasant one of notifying the ministry in England of the success achieved so far.[39]

Notes

1. Clinton to Balfour, May 20, 1780, CP, 30/11 /2, 38. Balfour's progress can be followed in the Diary of Dr. John Boudinot, Thorne Boudinot Collection, Princeton University Library (microfilm in SCAH).
2. Balfour to Cornwallis, June 6, 7, 1780, CP, 30/11/2, 96, 100.
3. "John Fisher (of Orangeburg)," Loyalist Transcripts, LV, 5–31, one of three loyalists by that name in the province; Balfour to Cornwallis, June 3, 6, Major Colin Graham to Cornwallis, June 27, and Association, June 12, CP 30/11/2, 81, 96, 129, 206.

4. Colonel John Fisher's regiment, Orangeburg Militia, 14 June–14 Dec. 1780, Pay Abstracts #23–28, 32–33, 39–40, 86, 95, 110, 120, 123, 135, 143, 149, 166, T50/1/5. These British pay records with other loyalist military and refugee records have been printed in a very useful compilation, Clark, ed., *Loyalists*, I, 197–200.
5. Innes to Cornwallis, June 7, 1780, CP, 30/11/2, 114–16.
6. Innes's proclamation of June 14, Innes to Cornwallis, June 7, and Balfour to Cornwallis, June 12, 1780, CP, 30/11/2, 114–16, 157, 185.
7. Simpson's instructions, Pearis's agreement, Brown to Cornwallis, June 18, and Pearis to Cornwallis, June 12, 1780, CP, 30/11/2, 16, 131, 134, 137.
8. " Col. Samuel Hammond's Notes," in Johnson, *Traditions and Reminiscences*, 149–52; Williamson to the Officer Commanding the British Troops North of the Saluda, June 5, CP, 30/11/2, 90. Many years after the war Pickens wrote that Williamson's failure to attack Campbell when the British briefly occupied Augusta in 1779 was evidence that he had been "corrupted," to Henry Lee, Aug. 18, 1811, Thomas Sumter Papers, Draper Coll., VV 1, 107.
9. Balfour to Cornwallis. June 24, and Cornwallis to Balfour, July 3, CP, 30/11/2, 191, and 30/11/78, 3.
10. Balfour to Cornwallis, June 24, 1780, CP, 30/11/2, 191.
11. Brown to Cornwallis, June 18, 28, 1780, CP, 30/11/2, 166–68, 208–21.
12. Cornwallis to Colonel George Turnbull, June 16, 1780, CP, 30/11/77, 11.
13. Ibid.
14. Ferguson to Baily Cheney, June 17, 1780, CP, 30/11/2, 64; Balfour to Cornwallis, July 12, 1780, CP, 30/11/1, 15–18.
15. Loyalist Transcripts, LV, 122–32; Ferguson to Cornwallis, July 24, 1780, CP, 30/11/2, 360.
16. Payroll of John Cotton's regiment, T50/1/2, #4, or Clark, ed., *Loyalists*, I, 237–52.
17. Payroll of Major Patrick Cunningham's Little River Regiment of Ninety Six Militia, T50/1/2, or Clark, ed., *Loyalists*, I, 253–68.
18. Payroll of Col. Daniel Clary's regiment of Militia in the Fork of Broad and Saluda rivers. T50/1/2, 111, or Clark, ed., *Loyalists*, I, 229–36.
19. Payroll of Major Daniel Plummer's Fair' Forest Regiment, T50/1/5, #67, 68, 94, or Clark, ed., *Loyalists*, I,323–30; for Plummer, see Drayton, *Memoirs*, II, 229; Plats, XIX, 200; Deeds, C4, 266–70; Payroll of the Spartan Regiment of Ninety Six Militia Commanded by Col. Zacharias Gibbs, T50/1/5, #63, 71, 76, or Clark, ed., *Loyalists*, I, 377–84; Loyalist Transcripts, LII, 227–57.
20. Kirkland claimed that he was commissioned as a lieutenant colonel to raise militia for nine to twelve months, Loyalist Transcripts, LVII, 318–50, but, as will be seen below, he resigned in November 1780. Partial corroboration for the existence of this unit comes from John Harris Cruger who reported the arrival at Ninety Six of "that supply for Kirkland's force" and asked for instructions about its disposition, to Cornwallis, Dec. 13, 1780, CP, 30/11/4, 136; see also Clark, ed., *Loyalists*, I, 221.
21. Loyalist Transcripts, LVII, 323–39.
22. Cornwallis to Clinton, May 26, 1780, CP, 30/11/72, 14, and to Major James Wemyss, July 30,1780, CP, 30/11/78, 61; Loyalist Transcripts, LV, 87–106. The Ball and Gaillard families were related by marriage and were owners of large rice plantations and numerous slaves in the parishes south of the Santee.
23. The best discussion of the role and characteristics of provincial forces is in Paul Smith, *Loyalists and Redcoats* (Chapel Hill, N.C., 1964), especially 32–36, 45–48, 72–78. For a ready reference to particular provincial regiments, see Philip R. N. Katcher, comp., *Encyclopedia of British, Provincial, and German Army Units, 1775–1783* (Harrisburg, Pa., 1973), 82–102.
24. A recent study of Harrison's regiment is Robert O. Bass, "A Forgotten Loyalist Regiment: The South Carolina Rangers," SCHA, *Proceedings* (1977), 64–71. See also Cornwallis to Clinton, June 30, CP, 30/11 /72, 18, Wemyss to Cornwallis, Sept. 30, CP, 30/11/64, 134, and "State of the Troops...at Camden," Aug. 13, 1780, CP, 30/11/103, 3.
25. LMR; "Roll of Officers of the British American or Loyalist Corps," New Brunswick Historical Society, *Collections* (1904), 232, 242, 252, 254–55, 267; Turnbull to Cornwallis, Oct. 14, 1780, CP, 30/11/3, 178; Rawdon to Cornwallis, Nov. 13, 21, 1780, CP, 30/11/4, 56, 87.
26. McArthur to Cornwallis, June 13, 14, 18,1780, CP, 30/11/2, 141, 155, 169.
27. Loyalist Transcripts, LVII, 80–117; Gray, "Observations," 11, 151–73; also printed as "Colonel Robert Gray's Observations on the War in Carolina," *SCHGM* (1910), 139–59, and Col. Robert Gray, "Observations," *U.N.C. Magazine* (1858).
28. Clark, *Loyalists*, I, 151.

29. Loyalist Transcripts, LVII, 379–401; two agreements executed in 1790 provide substantial evidence of Henry's acquisitions and the transactions of the partnership, Miscellaneous Records, CCC, 6–56; a description of the Clermont property dated May 16, 1782, is found in the Journals of Enos Reeves, 1780–1782, MS., DUL, VIII, 150–151; T50/1/5, #127; "State of the Troops...at Camden," Aug. 13, 1780, CP, 30/11/102, 3.
30. Rawdon to Cornwallis, June 11, 1750, and enclosed proclamation, CP, 30/11/2,123. John Shy has used the attitude of the people in the Waxhaw settlements to demonstrate the difficulties British officers faced in trying to recover the southern colonies, "American Society and Its War for Independence," in *Reconsiderations of the American Revolution,* ed. Don Higginbotham (Westport, Conn., 1978), 73–74
31. *Canadian Claims,* 187,646; R. S. Lambert, "A Loyalist Odyssey: James and Mary Cary in Exile, 1783–1804," *SCHM* (1978), 167–81.
32. Loyalist Transcripts, LII, 167–290.
33. Ibid., LIV, 469–78.
34. George C. Rogers, Jr., *History of Georgetown County, South Carolina* (Columbia, S.C., 1970), 122–23; Wemyss to Cornwallis, July 14, 22, 25, 1780,CP, 30/11/2, 290, 337, 366; Cornwallis to Wemyss, July 18, 23, 1780, 32, 40; Loyalist Transcripts, LV, 107–21.
35. Balfour to Cornwallis, Sept. 20, 1780, CP, 30/11/60, 83; Loyalist Transcripts, LIV, 360–85.
36. Robert Gray, "Observations."
37. [Charles] Stedman, *The History of the Origin, Progress, and Termination of the American War,* 2 vols. (New York, 1969 [orig. publ. London, 1794]), II, 198–99; McCrady, *S.C. in the Revolution, 1775–1780,* 559–60.
38. "Diary of Captain Johann Hinrichs," in Bernard A. Uhlendorf, ed., *The Siege of Charleston, with an Account of the Province of South Carolina...* (Ann Arbor, Mich., 1938), 223n3, 299; Robert Bass, *The Green Dragoon: The Lives of Banastre Tarleton and Mary Robinson* (New York, 1957),72; Clinton to Cornwallis, June 1, 1780, CP, 30/11/2, 68; Gray, "Observations," 151–53.
39. Cornwallis to Clinton, June 20, 1780, CP, 30/11/72, 18.

Chapter Seven

The "Second Revolution," Midsummer 1780

They have broke up the Militia...of the Upper District, [a] great part of Col. Mills officers are prisoners. It is remarkable that most of the leaders of this party, are either militia officers who were on parole or men who had taken the oath of allegiance.

—*Major James Wemyss, July, 1780*

Cornwallis was barely settled in Charlestown before he began to receive reports that the political and military situation on the apparently tranquil frontiers was anything but stable. Although he and his officers had been cautious in assessing the results of the pacification campaign so far, they were certainly unprepared for the violent resistance the rebels mounted in midsummer 1780, an uprising that British officers frequently referred to as the "Second Revolution." This revolt administered the first setback to the plans for enlarging the area of British control in the southern provinces.

On the northern frontier the revolt took place in the area between the Broad and Great Pee Dee rivers during a period of approximately two months preceding the Battle of Camden. It was characterized by direct assaults by rebel troops on fortified places manned by British and provincial units, small-scale clashes between rebel and loyalist militia, and by the worst type of civil strife—war in which rebels and loyalists alike sought vengeance for past injuries by destroying and plundering the property of the other.

More essential to the story of the loyalists in South Carolina than a detailed account of the skirmishes and battles in this period was the effect of the "Second Revolution" on them and their British sponsors. In a word, what happened to turn an apparent triumph of pacification into a campaign of open resistance that, if sustained, would certainly slow the momentum of the campaign to recover the southern provinces and perhaps jeopardize the control that British forces had established? The explanation that Americans offered then and later for this show of resistance centered upon the spirit and courage of Thomas Sumter and other officers who had refused to surrender and upon the harsh tactics of British officers like Tarleton and their Tory allies against rebel troops and civilians. British and loyalist observers and participants in these scenes also had ready explanations for the uprising, and it is worthwhile to examine their view.

First, British officers knew that some rebel leaders were still at large in the piedmont Carolinas and that they and their diehard followers offered a threat to the more advanced and isolated British posts in the interior. Second, it was soon evident that many men had joined the loyal militia out of expediency and could not be counted on to perform active service with the British until all resistance had been crushed. But the methods employed by the British in trying to crush the last resistance not only inflamed the committed rebels but others who during the American Period had been at best lukewarm toward the American cause as well.

There had been isolated skirmishes between rebel and loyalist sympathizers even before Tarleton's mauling of Buford's corps, but that event spurred further resistance, and by mid-June there were reports that certain rebel leaders were keeping "the candle of rebellion burning" in the vicinity of Colonel William Hill's ironworks on Allison's Creek. Captain Christian Huck of the British Legion was dispatched from Rocky Mount with some cavalry and militia to break up these rebel parties and to destroy the ironworks, an assignment he accomplished with apparent relish, for his troops also set the torch to other property of rebels in the area before returning to their post.¹

From the British standpoint, however, the most unfortunate event of the early summer was a premature effort by loyalists in Tryon County, North Carolina, to become actively involved before the royal army was in a position to sustain them. Colonel John Moore, an officer in the Royal North Carolina Regiment that had accompanied Cornwallis to Camden, appeared near modern Lincolnton and called local loyalists together to prepare them for the arrival of a British army in the future. Although Moore claimed that he cautioned the group that Cornwallis wanted them to remain quiet until he could assist them, other British sympathizers in the area began to gather. When local rebel leaders learned of this activity, they called out their militia and on June 20 descended on the disorganized loyalists, dispersing them in all directions. Moore himself escaped capture and made his way to Camden where he told his side of the affair to Rawdon.

Although there was little loss of life, so many loyalist sympathizers were forced to abandon their homes that the rebels were able to prevent further loyalist gatherings in that part of North Carolina.²

When the news of this incident reached Cornwallis in Charlestown, he was furious. Earlier a spontaneous effort by other North Carolina loyalists to organize under Ambrose Mills had caused the earl to dispatch one of Alexander Innes's officers to urge the group to remain quiet until the army could be ready to assist them. But an investigation of the Moore uprising revealed that another officer, Lieutenant Colonel John Hamilton of the Royal North Carolina Regiment, had also been in the area and in his zeal to recruit had precipitated the uprising. Cornwallis referred to Hamilton as "an obstinate blockhead," and called him to Charlestown for a dressing down, but the mischief was done. He also had to warn Rawdon at Charlotte that he must do nothing to give the local loyalists the impression that the army had come to stay, for if it became necessary to fall back, they would be targets for retaliation by rebels and become further discouraged.³

One effect of Moore's defeat was that many loyalists in the Yadkin Valley of North Carolina, unhappy at being drafted into the Whig militia, organized under Colonel Samuel Bryan and marched toward the British army in South Carolina. Arrangements were made for Major McArthur to send a detachment to escort Bryan's party to the post at Cheraw Hill from whence about 800 reached Camden. Charles Stedman described them as "in rags, most of them men of property," who represented the worst "horrors of civil war." Bryan's men were formed into a militia regiment and served through the Yorktown campaign.⁴

For British officers who sought to explain the continuing intransigence of the rebels, Sir Henry Clinton's June 3 proclamation seemed to supply the answer. Lord Rawdon, noting that the local people in the Waxhaw area seemed "ill disposed" toward the royal cause, felt that the "unfortunate proclamation" had forced them to make a choice. Paroled by Turnbull and himself, many of these men had not been "in arms against us"; they would have remained neutral if given the chance, but "nine out of ten of them are now embodied on the part of the Rebels." Also, in its effect on the loyalists "the proclamation wounds us," for if men who had taken the British oath were captured, it would be necessary to make examples of them; to do so would, however, expose loyalists to ill treatment if they fell into rebel hands.[5]

The proclamation aside, it is clear that British officers were disappointed in the rather free and easy manner in which Americans observed paroles and oaths of allegiance. In their own minds, anyone who had agreed to accept British sovereignty once again and then had taken up arms for the rebels was guilty of treason, a crime for which there could be only one penalty. Although in correspondence they occasionally displayed some understanding of the privations suffered by people caught up in a civil war, British and loyalist provincial officers generally showed little sympathy for those who changed sides so soon after the fall of Charlestown.

For individuals to give paroles and then switch sides was bad enough, but there was soon evidence of wholesale defections in certain of the newly recruited militia units. Learning that the rebel Colonel William Bratton was offering pardons to men who would desert the loyal militia and enlist with him, George Turnbull dispatched Captain Huck with a party of the British Legion and some militia to make a show of force in a part of modern York County. His presence aroused rebel militia under Bratton and other leaders to attack Huck's sleeping camp at Williamson's plantation on July 12, where they killed him and some of his men and dispersed the rest, gaining a measure of revenge for his earlier destruction of the ironworks and other property. Serious as Huck's defeat was, even more annoying was the defection to the rebels shortly thereafter of a large proportion of Mathew Floyd's militia regiment. John Lisle, a rebel militia officer who had been sent to the islands, gave his parole and, after returning to his home, accepted a commission in Floyd 's regiment. Shortly after Huck's demise, Lisle " had the traitorous address to carry [the regiment] off to Colonel Neale," his former commander, who was serving under Thomas Sumter on the Catawba River. Not only did Lisle take the core of Floyd's regiment with him, but he also carried off the new arms and supplies the British had provided for them. When Sumter became bold enough to assault the British post at Rocky Mount in early August, a good many of Floyd's defectors served with him. Although this attack was repulsed with considerable loss, the defection of Floyd's men exposed the families of committed loyalists to harassment by local rebels, and further shook the confidence of British officers in the steadfastness of their militia.[6]

So far, the resurgence of rebel military activity had been local and spontaneous, but their leaders were further encouraged by the formation of another Continental army in North Carolina under General Horatio Gates. When an advanced party under Baron DeKalb approached the South Carolina border, Lord Rawdon ordered Major McArthur to fall back from the post at Cheraw Hill lest he be cut off from the main base at Camden, leaving only Mills's Cheraw militia and Harrison's Rangers to operate along the Pee Dee. Because sickness had broken out among his troops, McArthur arranged that about 100 of them, escorted by a part of Mills's regiment, be sent by boat down the Pee Dee. But when the party reached Hunt's Bluff, it was suddenly attacked by North Carolina rebel militia and "some of Colonel Mills people who had just taken the oath of allegiance." Apparently acting by prearrangement, a number of Mills's men seized their officers and carried them and McArthur's sick off to captivity in North Carolina. Among those captured was the second in command, Robert Gray, and James Cassells, en route to be offered the command of the militia in the Lower, or Georgetown, District. Mills himself managed to escape to Georgetown, but, completely shaken by his experience, he soon resigned his command.[7]

To Cornwallis, this reverse was even more serious than what had happened near Rocky Mount because his supply line from Charlestown to Camden had become threatened by rebel parties, which were operating as far south as Murray's Ferry on the Santee near where the army's artillery was stored. He immediately ordered Wemyss to move to the Pee Dee and, with Mills's help, to "seize and bring off some of the most violent & dangerous people in the country." Wemyss was then to move in short stages along the Black River until he could post himself in the High Hills of Santee; on his march he was to "put a good face on things & talk big, threaten the plunderers with most severe retaliation, promise indemnification,… to our friends" out of rebel property and "try to give spirit to our cause." Cornwallis made it clear that "the severe chastisement of the traitors at Cheraws" was essential, and although it would be folly to send a force too far from its base, "we may punish the interior part of the country now, & reserve the borderers until we move on" North Carolina. Sickness had also descended on Wemyss's command, however, and except for a brief foray toward the Santee, he remained near Georgetown for the time being.[8]

Meanwhile, worried by both the deterioration of loyalist support and the threat posed by Gates's army, Cornwallis had hurried to Camden to take control of the situation on the northern frontier. On August 15 Thomas Sumter led a surprise attack on a redoubt guarding the approaches to the ferry over the Wateree River near Camden where he captured the small garrison commanded by James Cary. A few hours later he fell on a supply convoy approaching the town, capturing some much needed supplies and seventy more men, and then beat a hasty retreat from the area. While Sumter was thus engaged, the armies commanded by Cornwallis and Gates maneuvered until they met north of the town on August 16; in this action, known as the Battle of Camden, Gates's army was routed and retreated pell-mell into North Carolina, having been virtually destroyed as an effective force. In the aftermath of the battle, Cornwallis sent Tarleton in pursuit of the retreating Sumter; on August 18, the legion overran Sumter's poorly guarded camp, dispersed and killed most of his force, and released Cary and the other captives from the raids of the 15th. Sumter himself was seriously wounded (the British reported him killed) and barely escaped capture.[9]

The success of Cornwallis and Tarleton gave the British the upper hand along the northern frontier once more, effectively throwing rebel sympathizers on the defensive, and forcing Francis Marion and other partisan leaders to take refuge in North Carolina. It was Robert Gray's contention that the great victory at Camden restored tranquility to the area; had Cornwallis had more troops, he would have been able to mount a successful invasion of North Carolina while leaving South Carolina secure behind him. Cornwallis, however, had only the troops Clinton had left with him and the loyalist militia and Harrison's Rangers raised since the commander in chief's departure. The recent triumph did, however, permit him to turn his attention to two questions that had concerned him before Gates's appearance forced him to reenter the field.[10]

The first problem was to restore loyalist control along the Pee Dee where the defections in William Henry Mills's ranks had opened the frontier to the rebels and dangerously exposed the army's supply lines. Particularly exasperated by events in that area, he declared to Rawdon that "I look upon the severe chastisement of the traitors at Cheraws to be absolutely necessary." To that end he renewed his order to Wemyss to sweep through the country, punishing the turncoats as he moved toward Cheraw Hill where he was to assist Mills in reconstructing his regiment. Wemyss responded by moving to Kingstree on the Black River and then across country to the Pee Dee, pausing along the way to burn and pillage the property of more than fifty defectors and oath violators. When he called out the militia, however, the few who responded included some "doubtful characters."[11]

Robert Gray had by this time escaped from his captors in North Carolina and made his way to Georgetown. He accompanied Wemyss on his march and agreed to take command of the Cheraw Regiment from Mills, although he estimated that three-fourths of its people had taken "active parts" in the recent revolt. In Gray's view, "the only well-affected part of the district" was that between the Little Pee Dee River and the province boundary: only if the British pushed their lines toward the Cape Fear River and occupied the port of Wilmington could the loyalists there and in the Scottish settlements near Cross Creek join the king's troops. Unless this could be achieved, he saw no way to prevent strong rebel parties from infiltrating back into South Carolina.[12]

Although he was aware of the strong rebel sentiment in the Pee Dee area, Cornwallis felt that loyal militia from below the Santee could be brought up to guard the ferries and bridges and patrol the open country. His supply line thus protected, he could move into North Carolina where the presence of his army would bring loyalists there to his support. With the area of British control extended northward, he reasoned that the loyalists above the Santee would take heart and assume responsibility for the security of that area. After the poor showing by the loyalist militia in the Pee Dee, however, it is difficult to accept Cornwallis's reasoning unless he adopted Gray's idea of moving directly to the Cape Fear River in order to release the loyalists near Cross Creek.

Cornwallis had been determined to move into North Carolina even before the victory at Camden, declaring that such a drive was essential, or otherwise "we must give up both South Carolina & Georgia and retire within the walls of Charlestown." With Gates out of the way, he resumed preparations for a drive into North Carolina, but not by the route to the Cape Fear River. When planning for a move northward before the victory over Gates, he had concluded that he could most effectively employ the forces available to him by moving to Charlotte in the first stage; from there, with his left flank protected by the numerous loyalist militia in Ninety Six District, he would press forward to Salisbury where he expected loyal subjects to respond enthusiastically when he raised the royal standard. Then, and only then, would he march eastward to Cross Creek "where the Highlanders have offered to form a regiment as soon as we enter the country."[13]

The plan to enter North Carolina by way of the Catawba River to Charlotte and then to proceed to Salisbury apparently resulted from John Moore's abortive uprising and the flight of Bryan's people to the main army. Fully a month before the Battle of Camden, Cornwallis concluded that it had become "impossible long to constrain our friends" in North Carolina from taking action or "even to keep the frontiers" of South Carolina at peace unless he moved north in force. The approach of Gates's army made him realize that because matters "on the borders do not look so peaceable as they did," he would be "obliged to move very soon,...as an offensive war in the present circumstances of the country is far preferable" to assuming a defensive posture in South Carolina.[14]

These views must have continued to make sense to Cornwallis, because a few days after his great victory he ordered Innes to bring his South Carolina Royalists from Ninety Six to join the New York Volunteers as the garrison for the post at Camden. The earl then arranged to take four British regiments, Tarleton's and Rawdon's loyalists, and Hamilton's North Carolinians to Charlotte in two stages.[15]

Although the situation along the northern frontier was of greater concern to British commanders in South Carolina, the reports they were receiving from Ninety Six District were not as encouraging as they should have been. There was no Continental army nearby and the organization of loyalist militia had gone rather well, but Nisbet Balfour and his successor, John Harris Cruger, found reasons to worry about conditions there.

Most rebel leaders in the area had submitted, but several had found refuge in the Ceded Lands above Augusta in Georgia. Joining some Georgia rebels under the command of Colonel Elijah Clarke, they were able to move along the frontier of the Carolinas, obtaining information and recruits from local sympathizers and occasionally falling on isolated loyalist parties and seizing supplies intended for the principal British posts.[16]

The very size of Ninety Six District made it vulnerable to sudden incursions by rebel parties and very difficult to patrol without employing mounted troops on a regular basis. It is useful to think of the British position in the South Carolina backcountry as a whole, composed of two parts joined by a kind of hinge, with one part facing North Carolina and the other facing Georgia to the west. The analogy to a hinge is appropriate: the British expected the western part to be relatively stationary, while the northern frontier would move as Cornwallis's army penetrated North Carolina; however, the point on their line that would be most vulnerable to a sudden blow was the hinge itself—in this case where the two frontiers converged along the upper Broad River and its tributaries eastward to the Catawba. It was in this general area that in July the British suffered the three reverses already noted—the quelling by local rebels of Moore's premature uprising in North Carolina, the defections in Mathew Floyd's regiment, and Huck's defeat at Williamson's plantation in South Carolina. So long as North Carolina remained unconquered, it would be possible for rebel parties from that state, in cooperation with Elijah Clarke's followers, to slip through the breech, to hover on the western flank of Cornwallis's army, and to harass the loyalist families and their property in the undefended area.

Nisbet Balfour had early recognized the difficulty of controlling the vast open country between the major post at Ninety Six and its counterparts at Camden and Rocky Mount. Although Ferguson's efforts to recruit militia for Plummer's and Gibbs's regiments in the upper Broad-Saluda area had met a warm response, Balfour felt it essential that a fortified post be established in that area to reduce the chances of rebel infiltration and to sustain the loyalists . Detachments of militia were sent to occupy several small prewar frontier forts built to guard against Indian attacks, but Balfour was called to Charlestown before he could implement his idea, and no major base was established between Ninety Six and Camden.[17]

During July and early August a number of small-scale engagements were fought between rebel partisans from the Carolinas, Georgia, and the over-mountain settlements in the Watauga Valley against combined forces of loyalist provincials and militia. While these actions were rarely more than skirmishes and seldom resulted in heavy losses to either side, their general results tended to be encouraging to the rebels, whose hit-and-run tactics made it difficult for Patrick Ferguson to keep enough of his loyalist militia in the field to defend the area effectively. These actions were climaxed by the truly significant battle at Musgrove's Mill near the Enoree River; in this action, Alexander Innes led part of his South Carolina Royalists, just returned from furlough or recently recruited, and Daniel Clary's militia in an attack on a parry of rebels, but they were repulsed with heavy loss, Innes himself suffering a serious wound in the neck. The triumphant rebels were planning to follow their victory by mounting an assault against the base at Ninety Six, but they beat a hasty retreat when they received word of Gates's defeat. Following Camden and Tarleton's rout of Sumter, the northwestern part of the province was returned to British and loyalist control for the time being.[18]

Despite the less than satisfactory results of the engagements with local rebels, Patrick Ferguson continued to drill and maneuver his loyal militia recruits. A man of great energy, his zeal and apparent interest in his men seemed to inspire a degree of mutual respect and admiration between him and these "country people." Their chief fault, he felt, was their lack of discipline: they were "unaccustomed to military restraints & become so soon homesick" that it was impossible to keep large numbers in the field. In several instances where individuals failed to respond when called out, he took the extreme measure of cropping their hair, disarming them, and drumming them out of camp in disgrace as examples to the rest; but, he noted ruefully, his ranks "would soon become very thin" if he took this action against "every lad who left camp when the whim struck him." He then tried to meet the problem of desertion by assembling six of the regiments and having them sign a statement declaring that any man who would not assemble when called out "abandons the royal cause, & acts a treacherous part to the society in which *he* lives"; they then denounced anyone who left his unit without leave as "a worse traitor & enemy to his King and Country" than those who took up arms in violation of their paroles. But Ferguson's recruits also had admirable qualities, which "render them, when under a certain degree of discipline with a few real officers very fit for rough & irregular war, being all excellent woodsmen, unerring shots, careful to a degree to prevent waste or damage to their ammunition, patient of hunger & hardship & almost regardless of blankets, cloathing, rum & other indulgences" that regular troops required. This glowing statement could have come from the lips of a Fourth of July orator fifty years after the war in praise of the attributes of Whig fighting men.[19]

Despite his words of praise, Ferguson knew that they could not apply equally to all the regiments being raised in Ninety Six District that summer. The regiment that gave him greatest concern was that commanded by Richard King drawn from Long Cane Creek and the Little River of the Savannah, the area closest to the base at Ninety Six. Among those who signed up to serve in King's unit were a number who had served under Andrew Pickens, a development that caused Cornwallis to warn Cruger that "the absurdity of calling out those men to serve in our militia who are disarmed for being our enemies, is too glaring to need my troubling you with any instructions" on the subject. After he assumed command at Ninety Six, Cruger inspected King's unit and found " 120 men with arms and twenty odd without" and another sixty operating with Ferguson, concluding that a "great majority of the Regiment (formerly Pickens) is certainly disaffected."[20]

Before he left for Charlestown, Balfour had recommended that two steps be taken to compensate for this weakness in the Long Cane Regiment: to erect fortifications at Ninety Six to make that place secure from attack; and to make every effort to conciliate the two local rebel leaders, Andrew Williamson and Andrew Pickens. Several months would pass before the recommendation on fortifications could be carried out, but Cornwallis urged Balfour to "form if possible a close connexion with Williamson." The terms of such an agreement, if any, are not known, but Williamson did exert himself on several occasions to maintain order in the area. In turn, Cruger continued to press for good relations with the two paroled rebels. There is no evidence that Pickens agreed to any terms beyond those of his parole, although for months Cruger remained hopeful that he could be brought to accept some kind of collaborative role. Backcountry loyalist leaders like Evan McLaurin claimed to know that Pickens was in contact with Elijah Clarke and Thomas Sumter, and he reported his suspicions to Cornwallis, who relayed them to Cruger. For the time being, however, Pickens remained quietly at home and Cruger continued to hope that he could be brought around.[21]

The weakness of the British position along the Savannah River was soon demonstrated, not by a rebel attack on Ninety Six, but by a sudden assault on Augusta. From the beginning, Balfour had fumed over the presence of Thomas Brown as commander of that vital place, seeing him as a "violent" man whose thirst for revenge and official and personal ties with the Indians could only inflame local sentiment against the British. Balfour had urged Cornwallis to remove Brown's Rangers from Augusta, and mentioned the additional grievance that Major James Wright, Jr., was recruiting for his unit from the rebel prisoners in Charlestown. Young Wright was the son of Sir James Wright, Georgia's royal governor, who had returned to that province when officials in London decided to restore civil government there.[22]

Sir James, in turn, was already disturbed that Clinton had nearly stripped Georgia of royal troops for the Charlestown .campaign, leaving only the immediate vicinity of Savannah under effective British control; in his view, only the occupation of Augusta and several smaller posts in the interior of his province could demonstrate royal support of his restored government. He was further angered by the charges against his son and the suggestion that the Rangers be withdrawn from Augusta in favor of troops from Ninety Six. Brown also protested against the suggested withdrawal of his troops, stoutly defending his reputation and the record of the Rangers during the long period of exile and the campaign to recover the province. The younger Wright also tried to defend himself, claiming that a subordinate had recruited the rebel prisoners without his knowledge. The plan to replace the Rangers went forward over the protests of the Georgians until Cornwallis ordered the South Carolina Royalists to Camden; Cruger then recommended that Brown's Rangers be left at Augusta temporarily.[23]

In mid-September Augusta was suddenly assaulted by 600 men under Elijah Clarke, and Brown found himself besieged in the building where the supplies of the Indian department were kept. Brown conducted an imaginative and spirited defense of his position while awaiting help from Ninety Six: when Cruger appeared at the head of a relief expedition, Clarke raised the siege and retreated. Cruger pursued Clarke for sixty miles above Augusta before collecting some stragglers and returning to the town. Thomas Brown rook ample revenge for his ordeal by hanging a dozen rebels who fell into his hands, confirming in the minds of his superiors and rebels alike that he was indeed a "violent" man.[24]

Thus the "Second Revolution" came to an end on the western frontier, although Musgrove's Mill and Augusta were not good omens for the pacification of the district. But with Gates's army removed as an obstacle, Lord Cornwallis could proceed with his plans for carrying the war into North Carolina, and a few days after the victory at Camden he summoned Patrick Ferguson to a conference at headquarters. Ferguson learned that several provincial units under his command were to be transferred to the main army; meanwhile, he and his detachment of the American Volunteers were to lead the militia "toward Tryon County & Gilbertown" gathering more loyalists on his march and, at the same time, protecting the left flank of the army on its drive into North Carolina. In taking this step, Cornwallis reasoned that "the militia are more likely to be kept in spirits and together by the appearance of offensive operations," saying to Balfour, "if ever those people will fight it is when they attack & not when they are attacked."[25]

Notes

1. Samuel C. Williams, ed., "General Richard Winn's Notes, 1780," *SCHM* (1942), 201–12; (1943), 1–10; Turnbull to Cornwallis, June 16, 19, 1780, CP, 30/11/2, 162–71.
2. David Schenck, *North Carolina, 1780–1781: Being a History of the Invasions of the Carolinas by the British Army under Lord Cornwallis* (Spartanburg, S.C., 1967 [orig. publ. Raleigh, N.C., 1889]), 51–62; Rawdon to Cornwallis, June 22, 24, 1780, CP, 30/11/2, 179, 189.
3. Cornwallis to Innes, June 16, and to Rawdon, June 29, 1780, CP, 30/11/77,13, 20; Cornwallis to Balfour, July 3, CP, 30/11/78, 3, and to Clinton, June 30, 1780, CP, 30/11/72, 18.
4. C[harles] Stedman, *History of the Origin, Progress, and Termination of the American War*, 2 vols. (New York, 1969 [orig. publ. London, 1794]), II, 196–97; Cornwallis to Rawdon, July 6, 1780, CP, 30/11/78, 7.
5. Rawdon to Cornwallis, July 7, 1780, CP, 30/11/12, 252.
6. Clinton to Cornwallis, July 15, Aug. 6, 1780, CP, 30/11/72, 30, 36; Stedman, *American War*, II, 200–201; McCrady, *S.C. in the Revolution, 1775–1780*, 1, 619–20, 624–25.
7. Wemyss to Cornwallis, July 28, 29, CP, 30/11/2, 373, 389; Loyalist Transcripts, LV, 107–21.
8. Cornwallis to Wemyss, July 30, 1780, CP, 30/11/78, 61, and to Rawdon, Aug. 4, 1780, CP, 30/11/79, 18.
9. Sumter to Gates, Sumter Papers, Draper Coll., VV, III, 27; see Ward, *War of the Revolution*, II, 722–30, for the Battle of Camden see McCrady, *S.C. in the Revolution, 1775–1780*, I, 681–83, for Tarleton's surprise of Sumter.
10. Gray, "Observations," 153.
11. Cornwallis to Rawdon, Aug. 4, 1780, CP, 30/11/79, 8; Frederick de Peyster to Cornwallis, Sept. ?, 1780, CP, 30/11/3,16; Gray to Cornwallis, Sept. 20, and Wemyss to Cornwallis, Sept. 30, 1780, CP, 30/11/64, 133, 91.
12. Gray to Cornwallis, Oct. 7, 1780, CP, 30/11/3, 197.
13. Cornwallis to Clinton, Aug. 6, 1780, CP, 30/11/72, 36.
14. Cornwallis to Arbuthnot, July 14, 1780, CP, 30/11/78, 14.
15. Cornwallis to Cruger, Aug. 24, and to Balfour, Sept. 3, 6, 1780, CP, 30/11/79, 37, and 30/11/80, 1.
16. Cruger to Rawdon, Sept. 4, 1780, CP, 30/11/63, 13.
17. Balfour to Cornwallis, June 24,1780, CP, 30/11/2, 191 ; McLaurin to Balfour, Aug. 16, 1780, Evan McLaurin Letters, Emmet Coll., NYPL.
18. These small engagements may be traced in detail in McCrady, *S.C. in the Revolution, 1775–1780*, 587–616; Robert D. Bass, *Ninety Six* (Lexington, S.C., 1978), especially 198–221; Chesney, "Journal," 134n195; and McLaurin to Balfour, Sept. 23, 1780, Evan McLaurin Letters.
19. For Ferguson's description of his method of handling the loyal militia and his assessment of them, see his undated letter to Rawdon, CP, 30/11/63, 95.
20. Cornwallis to Cruger, Sept. 4, CP, 30/11/80, 5, and Cruger to Cornwallis, Aug. 27, 1780, CP, 30/11/63, 68.

21. Balfour to Cornwallis, June 24, CP, 30/11/2, 191; Cornwallis to Balfour, July 17, CP, 30/11/78, 20, to Cruger, Aug. 27, CP, 30/11/79, 39, and to Balfour, Sept. 27, 1780, CP, 30/11/80, 48A; and Ferguson to Capt. Alexander Ross, Aug.19, CP, 30/11/63, 48, and Balfour to Cornwallis, Sept. 20, and Williamson to Balfour, Sept. 21, CP, 30/11/64, 83, 95.
22. Alured Clarke to Cornwallis, June 23, and Balfour to Cornwallis, June 24, 1780, CP, 30/11/2, 187–88, 191.
23. Sir James Wright to Cornwallis, July 3, 9, Brown to Cornwallis, Aug. 16, CP, 30/11/2, 237, 256, 307–11, and Alured Clarke to Cornwallis, and James Wright, Jr., to Cornwallis, both Aug. 20, 1780, CP, *30/11/63*, 52, 59.
24. Brown to Cruger, Sept. 15; Cruger to Cornwallis, Sept. 15, to Balfour, Sept. 19, and to Cornwallis, Sept. 23 and 29,1780, CP, 30/11/64, 65, 67, 75,104, 116; Kenneth Coleman, *The American Revolution in Georgia, 1763–1789* (Athens, Ga., 1958), 134.
25. Cornwallis to Cruger, Aug. 27, and to Balfour, Aug. 29, CP, 30/11/79, 39,45; and Ferguson to Cornwallis, Aug. 29, 1780, CP, 30/11/63, 81.

Chapter Eight

KINGS MOUNTAIN, OCTOBER 1780

I am sorry to acquaint your Lordship that the 7th Inst. Major Ferguson was attack near King mountain by a Body of the enemy.... The action lasted an hour and five minutes...the left on seeing us broke gave way, got all in a crowd on the Hill...nothing now offered but to make a breach through the enemy;...I am sorry to say that Major Ferguson was killed before he advanced 20 yards.

—Captain Abraham de Peyster, October 1780

On September 1, 1780, Patrick Ferguson returned from his conference with Lord Cornwallis and soon thereafter led his men toward Gilbertown in Tryon County, North Carolina. Before starting out, he issued a "Declaration" to the inhabitants of Tryon County in which he denounced rebel propaganda that, by falsely depicting the British army as an agent of oppression, had "artfully excited them against their duty to God & the King," On the contrary, said Ferguson, the mission of the royal army was to restore peace and to aid in punishing those who had committed crimes, especially those "parties lately come from Georgia, Nolachucky, & some scoundrels of both sides, all of whom it is the duty & interest of every man of honest feelings to suppress & crush." Ferguson followed this bit of bombast by sending instructions to loyal subjects to wait quietly at home until the army reached them unless rebel oppression drove them to seek refuge with it; meanwhile, they should prepare to observe and provide intelligence of rebel troop movements and concentrations. He also dispatched a messenger to the over-mountain settlements along the Watauga, Holston, and Nolachucky rivers, to warn that if they persisted in rebellion that their leaders would be hanged and their property destroyed.[1]

Ferguson then began a month-long series of maneuvers, which had several objectives: to break up a body of North Carolina rebel militia commanded by a Colonel Charles McDowell; to prevent McDowell's militia and Elijah Clarke's rebels from combining into a force large enough to threaten the base at Ninety Six; and to give his own loyal militia recruits experience in the field. After a part of his force suffered some casualties in a sharp action at Cane Creek, he pursued McDowell's men deep into the hill country of North Carolina but failed to come up with them. His penetration of the area did arouse the fears of "backwater" rebel leaders who began to call out their militia to rendezvous against him. Learning of the siege of Augusta, he then fell back to Gilbertown in hope of intercepting Elijah Clarke but missed him.[2]

The forces Ferguson led on these maneuvers consisted of two parts, his own American Volunteers augmented by small detachments of New York and New Jersey provincials from the garrison at Ninety Six, numbering in all no more than 150 men; and a much larger body of militia from Ninety Six District. Ferguson's practice that summer was to draft parties of men from the militia regiments in the district for service with him and, apparently with the design of offering training to the greatest possible number, he seems to have called on several groups from the same regiment at different times. In one instance he noted that 650 "old & infirm men" were with him while the "younger classes were sent home to draw lots and prepare for the campaign." The largest contingents were drawn from Plummer's Fair Forest and Gibbs's Spartan regiments from the northwestern part of the province where he campaigned most actively. His second in command during these operations was Captain Abraham de Peyster of the King's American Regiment, a New Yorker who with others had volunteered for service with the American Volunteers for the southern campaign.[3]

After he fell back to Gilbertown, Ferguson was joined by about 500 loyal North Carolina militia from Tryon County, and he immediately threw himself into training them for service. While engaged in this activity it became more apparent that his campaign toward the mountains and his warnings to the people there had not frightened them into submission because his spies brought in reports that the "backwater men" were organizing to move against him. He therefore began a series of desultory movements in the general direction of Charlotte. On October 3 he wrote Cornwallis that he had moved twenty miles that day "toward any reinforcement your Lordship may send," but then for no apparent reason he camped for two days near Buffalo Creek. On the 6th he informed the earl that the mountain men were now "an object of some consequence," and that he had taken up his "march toward you by a road leading from Cherokee Ford [Broad River] north of King Mountain" and that "3 or 400 good soldiers part dragoons would finish the business." Cornwallis had also received intelligence that the rebels were organizing and he had become alarmed for Ferguson's safety. Seeking a means to support Ferguson, Cornwallis turned immediately to Tarleton, but the cavalryman had become ill; instead, Major McArthur was dispatched with a battalion of the Seventy-first Regiment to Arness Ford on the Catawba, and on the 5th Ferguson was ordered to meet him there. Ferguson never received this dispatch; on the 6th he broke camp and marched sixteen miles toward the Catawba, then suddenly turned from his route and moved his troops up on the commanding ridge known locally as Little Kings Mountain, but fixed forever in the annals of the Revolution as Kings Mountain. The reasons for this action are not clear, although it has been suggested that he lacked confidence in the green North Carolina militia that had recently joined him and thought that, while they awaited reinforcements, his troops would be less vulnerable on the mountaintop. But having taken this defensive position, he made no provision for throwing up obstructions or fortifications of any kind to withstand an attack. Perhaps he did not realize how close his pursuers were.[4]

They were very close. Consisting principally of three main bodies of men, North Carolinians under Colonel Benjamin Cleveland, over-mountain men under Colonel Isaac Shelby, and Virginians under Colonel William Campbell, the senior commander, they had rendezvoused at Quaker Meadows, passed through Gilbertown, and on the 6th reached the Cowpens within a few miles of Kings Mountain. Learning of Ferguson's position, the rebels set out on the 7th, moving so quietly that they were able to fire on his pickets that afternoon before he realized they were there.[5]

Thereafter, the story of the battle is a familiar one, a struggle of about an hour between two forces of Americans, Ferguson himself being the only British regular present. The rebels disposed themselves on three sides of the mountain and advanced; Ferguson sent his American Volunteers to counterattack with the bayonet three times, but each time he lost more men and the rebels pressed relentlessly on through the trees. The nearer the rebels got to the top, the more exposed the outnumbered defenders became; the raw North Carolina militia were the first to give way and pressed back on the South Carolinians and the provincials until all were a huddled mass exposed to a murderous fire. Realizing the desperation of their posit ion, Ferguson made an effort to lead his provincials in a charge to level ground; but so great was the disorder that only four men followed him, and Ferguson had advanced but a few yards before he was cut down by a hail of bullets. Abraham de Peyster then took command and, after several attempts, succeeded in convincing the rebels that he wished to surrender his command, and the shooting finally stopped.[6]

The details of the Battle of Kings Mountain became well known more than a century ago through the careful researches of the indefatigable Lyman C. Draper, who obtained a great deal of his information from the documents and traditions that had been passed on to descendants of the rebels who fought there. On the loyalist side, however, their descendants had not come forward, and the pertinent records were buried in British archives. Thus, except for Ferguson as a personality and the diary of Lieutenant Anthony Allaire, which he printed in an appendix, Draper's was essentially an American account. A good deal of mystery still surrounds the loyalist part in the battle, but British records do reveal somewhat more than has been known about who served, suffered, and died on the mountain and during the period of captivity that followed.

The occasional references to men killed at Kings Mountain in the British pay records reveal that all of the Ninety Six militia regiments were represented at the battle, a result of Ferguson's practice of drafting small contingents from those units to serve with him. It is less clear exactly how many men from each of those units fought at Kings Mountain; however, the two largest contingents were drawn from the upper Ninety Six regiments, Zacharias Gibbs declaring that about 100 men each from his own Spartan Regiment and from Daniel Plummer's Fair Forest Regiment had served in the battle. Gibbs himself was not present during the action having been ordered by Ferguson to find a place for a rendezvous in case a retreat by the main body became necessary; and there was a report that about 200 men were detached before the battle, perhaps as foragers. Alexander Chesney of Plummer's regiment declared that "some" men had "taken flight early in the action, putting white papers in their hats, by which disgraceful stratagem they got through the American lines," but it is not clear whether they were North or South Carolinians. Aside from the two local units, the largest number who have been identified were from Richard King's Long Cane Regiment, thirty-five men under Captain David Larimer who had joined Ferguson two months before. Larimer, an Irish immigrant who had settled on Cuffeetown Creek just before the rebellion broke out, and part of his men were posted as sharpshooters on one of the flanks of the defenders; they gave a good account of themselves before he was "grievously" wounded in the shoulder and they were caught up in the general confusion at the end. At one time during the previous summer sixty men from King's regiment were with Ferguson. If Gibbs's estimate is correct, and the number from the Long Cane Regiment who were engaged was typical, it seems likely that no more than 400 South Carolinians were present. The balance of Ferguson's command was made up of fewer than 100 provincials of his own detachment (Allaire says seventy), and an undetermined number of the 500 North Carolina militia who joined him shortly before the action. Thus it is probable that fewer than 1,000 men fought under him on October 7, roughly halfway between the highest rebel estimate of 1,200 and the lowest British figure of 800. Colonel Daniel Plummer, severely wounded and first reported killed, was the ranking casualty among the South Carolinians. Among other casualties were Lieutenant Thomas Cunningham of the Little River Regiment, who was wounded, made prisoner, and later escaped; and Lieutenant William Elliott of Cotton's regiment, one of the few present known to have been a veteran of the Snow Campaign in the earliest days of the war, who was killed during the action.[7]

Because of the differing estimates of numbers engaged in the battle, there is a mild disagreement on the casualties incurred by the loyalists. Rebel observers, who were in a position to make a more systematic count, report a somewhat larger number of casualties: Isaac Shelby claimed that 375 were "left weltering in their gore" after the battle; Robert Henry and David Vance counted 247 dead loyalists afterward; and Colonel Campbell reported 225 dead and 160 wounded. Allaire put the number killed and wounded at a conservative 240; the estimates by Zacharias Gibbs that about 100 men each from his own and Plummer's regiments were killed or captured are the nearest thing to a count by a South Carolina loyalist. Whatever the number of killed and wounded on the British side actually was, the scene on the field of combat after the battle was one of carnage so great that, according to one witness, "the dead lay in heaps on all sides, while the groans of the wounded were heard in every direction." The next day, a Sunday, relatives came to the battlefield in search of "husbands, fathers, and brothers"; in their haste to bury the dead "it was badly done," and bodies were simply piled into shallow pits and then covered with brush and logs. It was not long before wolves, hogs, and vultures took over the battlefield, and one witness who had helped to bury the dead returned to the scene several weeks later to find that "all parts of the human frame lay scattered in every direction."[11]

For the dead loyalists committed to the shallow graves, at least the weariness, fear, and suffering were over, but the survivors still had a long ordeal ahead of them. In the days following the action, the wounded were removed from the battlefield and distributed among the homes of local loyalist sympathizers. There they were ministered to by Dr. Uzal Johnson, the surgeon with Ferguson's detachment of provincials, to whom Colonel Campbell had given permission to remain behind for a short period before joining the other prisoners. The more seriously wounded remained in the area until early in December when Cruger arranged to send an officer of the New Jersey Volunteers with a detachment and four wagons under a flag of truce to bring them back within the British lines.[9]

The victors, fearful that reinforcements might arrive from Cornwallis's army, put their prisoners on the road the day after the battle and began the long wirhdrawa1 toward the mountains. Fortunately for them, there was to be no pursuit, for, with their own wounded and the prisoners, their progress was slow, taking five days to move the fifty miles to Biggerstaff's plantation near Gilbertown. It was not until they had arrived safely at that place that, as Allaire and other witnesses reported, it was determined to make examples of some of the prisoners. According to Allaire, "twelve field officers were chosen to try the militia prisoners-particularly those who had the most influence in the country"; thirty-nine were condemned to death by these proceedings, of whom nine were executed on the spot in full view of all the prisoners, and the rest were reprieved. John Rutledge maintained that the victims included "the most noted horsethieves and Tories" of North Carolina; but the most prominent of the victims was the influential Colonel Ambrose Mills of Green River, who also happened to be a brother-in-law to Thomas Fletchall, one of the leading figures in the 1775 backcountry uprising against the South Carolina Provincial Congress. Two South Carolinians went to the gallows, a "Captain Wilson," apparently Robert Wilson of Plummer's regiment, and an unidentified man; there might have been more executions but rumors that Tarleton was in the area caused the proceedings to be terminated.[10]

The next day the prisoners were marched thirty miles in bad weather; according to Lieutenant John Taylor of the New Jersey Volunteers, they "were so wearied that many of them were obliged to give out on the road-they then roll'd them down in the mud and many of them they left there trod to death and many of them cut to pieces." As the rebels moved deeper into North Carolina, several of their local units began to leave for their homes, and the prisoners began to find better opportunities to escape, about 100 slipping away on October 15. The remainder of the captives were marched to Quaker Meadows on the upper Catawba, moved on to Burke Court House, and then across the Yadkin to Bethebara in the Moravian settlements.[11]

A three-man commission sent by John Harris Cruger to investigate conditions among the prisoners finally caught up with them at Quaker Meadows. Andrew Pickens had agreed to head this mission, apparently at the behest of families in the Long Cane area who had men serving with Ferguson, some of whom had formerly served in Pickens's own regiment before the fall of Charlestown. The mission returned to Ninety Six on October 21 and reported that they had counted 687 prisoners but could not determine how many militiamen had been killed in the action.[11]

There were to be more escapes. On the way to Bethebara, Alexander Chesney was offered his freedom if he would drill Benjamin Cleveland's regiment for one month in "the exercise practised by Coll. Ferguson." When Chesney refused ro comply, he was threatened with death when they reached " the Moravian town," but he was able to escape and make the long way back to his home on the Pacolet River. Arriving on the 31st, he found that the rebels had left him "little" except his wife and a newborn son, "whom I named William which was all the christening he ever had." But the rebels controlled the area, and he and his cousins Hugh Cook and Charles Brandon hid in a cave to avoid their patrols while Cook's wife brought them food at night. Likewise, Anthony Allaire and Lieutenants Taylor of the New York Volunteers and William Stevenson of the New Jersey Volunteers contrived to slip away from Bethebara after Stevenson had been confined on the charge that he had stolen one of Colonel Campbell's spurs. With William Gist of Plummer's regiment, who had been Ferguson's chief scout, as their guide, they traveled by night and received help from loyalist families along the way until they reached Ninety Six. There were other reports of rough treatment of the prisoners, particularly that rebels had "knocked down our surgeon for dressing our wounded men."[13]

Rebel authorities also had complaints, declaring that by escaping, these provincial officers had violated the terms of paroles granted them. Cornwallis, who had complained about parole violations by rebels and would be severely criticized for making examples of a few of them, asked for an investigation of the conduct of Allaire and the others, threatening to turn them over to the rebels if they had broken proper paroles. The officers, however, claimed that they had signed no agreement not to try to escape and that their captors had violated the terms of paroles granted, and the matter was not pressed. Meanwhile, rebel authorities in North Carolina aroused the ire of General Gates by enlisting over 150 of the

Kings Mountain prisoners, some of them from South Carolina, in their state militia; John Rutledge reported shortly after this that thirty had immediately run away and that the rest had been released from their enlistments and thrown into jail in Salisbury. A few of the other Kings Mountain loyalists did manage to slip away after this incident, but most remained in confinement until a general exchange of prisoners was arranged during the next winter.[14]

The battle at Kings Mountain has long been recognized as an important milestone on the way to Cornwallis's surrender at Yorktown a year later; it also marked the turning point of the war in South Carolina, for before the earl actually met his unhappy fate on the Chesapeake, the rebels had regained control of most of the state. Although contemporary British and loyalist observers could not foresee the long-range result of Kings Mountain, they did feel that the defeat and Ferguson's death were severe blows from which the loyal militia—of uncertain worth before that—might not recover. The doubts that Cornwallis and his officers had always professed about the reliability of the militia and of Ferguson himself now seemed fulfilled. Further, if the militia had had any value, the heavy losses incurred in the battle and the scattering of the survivors as prisoners in North Carolina or refugees in their own neighborhoods had crippled much of its effective force and made other men more reluctant to come forward to serve in it.[15]

Circumstances also made the commanding general unable or unwilling to regain the initiative in the northwestern part of the province. At the very time when a swift blow by Tarleton might have saved Ferguson's command, the cavalryman came down with a fever and pleaded that he was unable to lead a rescue effort. Then Cornwallis himself, anxiously awaiting news from Ferguson, came down with a "feverish cold" that incapacitated him for several weeks. The news of Ferguson's demise, the presence of sickness among the troops, and the fear that the victorious rebels would move against Ninety Six all caused Rawdon, acting for Cornwallis, to order the army to pull back from Charlotte to Winnsboro, seventy miles to the south, where it would be in a position to support either of the posts at Camden or Ninety Six.[16]

This withdrawal left the remaining loyalists in the upper part of Ninety Six District out of reach of direct aid ·from the main army. As Moses Kirkland bluntly told Cornwallis, the decision to move "so low down in the Cuntry has very much disperited his Majesty's subjects and emboldens the Rebels" who now controlled all the territory north of the Enoree River. Zacharias Gibbs, away on assignment during the battle, complained that " I am fallen back to Col. Cruger and Col. Cunningham not having men to stand in my reg't"; he pleaded with Cornwallis to "consider the much distressed backwoods militia as naked & in every respect unfit for service." Gibbs closed by suggesting that "the opinion of the most experienced men is that the militia cannot hold the back country as long as Holstein's River, Nolachucky and the Western Water People remained unconquered." And it was at this time that John Harris Cruger, citing "the defenceless state of this country" and seeking some means of restoring order in the upper part of the district, commissioned Moses Kirkland to raise 400 men.[17]

The failure of the loyal militia to hold the country, while obvious at the time, was to Cornwallis and his aides a phase in a continuing experiment in how best to utilize the loyalists to maintain control of the interior of the province. Which would be received more warmly and be more effective in achieving that objective—militia, which would employ a larger part of the population; provincials, from which more service could be obtained at

Kings Mountain, October 1780   105

less expense; or, special mounted units to range over the country? To that experiment, and what it tells us about the loyalists, we shall now turn.

Notes

1. The "Declaration" and the "Instructions" are enclosed in Ferguson to Cornwallis, Sept. 14, 1780, CP, 30/11/4, 60, 63 ; and the threat to the overmountain leaders is in Hugh F. Rankin , "An Officer Out of His Time: Correspondence of Major Patrick Ferguson, 1779–1780," in Howard H. Peckham, ed., *Sources of American Independence: Selected Manuscripts from the Collections of the William L. Clements Library,* 2 vols. (Chicago, 1978), II, 294.
2. Ferguson's movements have been traced by Robert D. Bass, "The Last Campaign of Major Patrick Ferguson," SCHA, *Proceedings* (1968), 16–25; his erratic reaction to the rising of the mountaineers is in Rankin, "An Officer Out of His Time," 294–95; his dispatches in the last days are on Oct. 3, two on Oct. 6, CP, 30/11/3, 176, 189, 191, and on Oct. 5, printed in Robert D. Bass, *Ninety Six* (Lexington, S.C., 1978) 259: and Cornwallis's dispatches to him arc Oct. 1,5,6, 8, CP, 30/11/81, 3, 18, 22, 31. See also "Allaire Diary," 505–10.
3. For more than a century the standard work for the events leading up to the battle and the engagement itself has been Lyman C. Draper, *King's Mountain and Its Heroes* (New York, 1929 [orig. publ, n.p., 1891]), and I have used it extensively; another older account, David Schenck, *North Carolina, 1780–1781 (*Spartanburg, S.C., 1967 [orig. pub!. Raleigh, N.C., 1880]), 129–74, also has merit. More recently, other sources, principally British, have come to light and added to the record , and the excellent accounts of Bass and Rankin , cited above, have been based in part on the new material. See also Chesney, "Journal," 10–16, for the account of the young Irishman who was constantly in the field with Ferguson that summer.
4. Chesney, "Journal," 16–18; Ferguson's dispatches to Cornwallis of Oct. 3, CP, 30/11/3, 176, and of Oct. 5, 1780, in Bass, *Ninety Six,* 259; and Bass, "Last Campaign," 16–25.
5. Bass, *Ninety Six,* 252–63.
6. The most important personal accounts of the battle are Chesney, "Journal," 16–18; Abraham de Peyster to Cornwallis, Oct. 14, 1780, CP, 30/11/3, 210–11: [James P. Collins], *A Revolutionary Soldier,* ed. John M. Roberts (New York, 1979 [orig. publ. Clinton, La., 1859]), 51–54; and "Allaire Diary," 510. The story that loyal militiamen were killed after de Peyster sought to surrender is apparently based on Chesney, "Journal," who stated that de Peyster "gave up and sent out a flag of truce, but as the Americans resumed their fire afterwards ours was also renewed under the supposition that they would give no quarter; and a dreadful havoc took place until the flag was sent out a second time, then the work of destruction ceased," but this account was written at an undetermined date after the war. De Peyster's report made no direct reference to killing after he sought to surrender. It is always possible that British officers picked up the story from participants later, but it is worth noting that in Cornwallis's protests to Nathanael Greene about the ill treatment received by Kings Mountain prisoners he referred to the period after the battle when they were being marched into North Carolina, to Greene, Dec. 27, 1780, and Feb. 4, 1781, CP, 30/11/91, 27, 29.
7. The pay records reveal only so much. As noted elsewhere, the militia pay records in T50/1 were created in and near Charlestown in 1781 and 1782 after the British had evacuated the interior of South Carolina; unless relatives established the fact of death of a militiaman in the backcountry in order to claim the pay due him, the pay lists do not record those who died at Kings Mountain or on other battlefields; see examples in Clark, *Loyalists,* I , 221, 252, 267: see also Gibbs to Cornwallis, Oct. 12, 1780, CP, 30/11/3, 212; Loyalist Transcripts, LII , 182–90; and "Allaire Diary," 510.
8. Casualty estimates are from Isaac Shelby, "Sketch of the Revolutionary War to the Southward," enclosed with Shelby to William Hill, Aug. 26, 1814, J.G. de Roulhac Hamilton, ed. , "King's Mountain: Letters of Isaac Shelby," *JSH* (1938), 376; Robert Henry and David Vance, *Narrative* of *the Battle of Cowan's Ford, February 1st, 1781, and Narrative of the Bartle of King's Mountain* (Greensboro, N.C., 1891), 26; William Campbell to Col. Arthur Campbell, Oct. 20, 1780, Bancroft Coll., NYPL; "Allaire Diary," 510; Gibbs to Cornwallis, Oct. 12, 1780, CP, 30/11/13, 212. The battlefield after the action was described by James Collins, *A Revolutionary Soldier,* 51–54.
9. De Peyster to Cornwallis, Oct. 14, 1780, CP, 30/11/3, 210–11; Cornwallis to Cruger, Nov. 22, and Cruger to Cornwallis, Dec. 5, 1780, CP, 30/11/82, 131, and 30/11/4, 143 .
10. Statement of Lieutenant John Taylor and Lieutenant William Stevenson, Nov. 30, 1780, CP, 30/11/4, 127; Chesney, "Journal," 18–20. 11.

11. CP, *30/11/4*, 127; "Allaire Diary," 510–12.
12. Cruger to Balfour, Oct. 22, 1780, CP, 30/11/3, 261.
13. Chesney, "Journal," 18–20; "Allaire Diary," 513–15.
14. Cornwallis to Cruger, Nov. 11, CP, 30/11/82, 131, to Rawdon, Dec. 4, CP 30/11/83, 11; Statement of Taylor and Stevenson , Nov. 30, CP, 30/11/4, 127; Loyalist Transcripts, LII 427–52; Gates to the North Carolina Board of War, Nov. 16, and CO Col. Martin Armstrong, Nov. 16, 1780, Horatio Gates Letterbook, NYPL (microfilm in NCAH); John Rutledge to the Delegates to the Continental Congress from South Carolina, Nov. 20, 1780, in Joseph W. Barnwell, ed., "Letters of John Rutledge," *SCHGM* (1916), 142–46.
15. Gray, "Observations," 153–55.
16. Bass, *Ninety Six*, 269.
17. Gibbs to Cornwallis, Oct. 12, and Cruger to Balfour, Oct. 24, 1780, CP, 30/11/13, 212, 311–12: Clinton, *American Rebellion*, 228.

Chapter Nine

Provincials, Militia, and Dragoons

...[of] fifty men of my detach. that belonged to the South Carolina Royalists, thirty-five were recruits enlisted since last June, and no men could behave with greater spirit than they did in the late affair on the 19th ult.

—*Colonel Alexander Innes, September 1780*

A great deal of attention has been paid to the organization of the loyalist militia in South Carolina during the first months after Charlestown fell and to their performance in several important campaigns during that summer and early autumn. It would be premature to make a judgment on the military effectiveness of the militia at this point, but British commanders in America also expected to raise provincial corps from the loyal population in the southern provinces as they had done around Boston, New York, and Philadelphia in the first years of the war. As in the case of the militia, the effort to raise provincial corps in South Carolina is worth examining as another measure of the depth of the loyalist commitment to the cause.

Provincial troops were generally considered to be the elite among those drawn from the loyal population. They were usually established through a warrant that specified the terms and conditions under which a prominent loyalist was authorized to raise and command a unit. Although the terms of warrants varied, during the early years of the war they usually included the right to select the officers, to offer land as a bounty or incentive to enlistment for a fixed term of years or the duration of the rebellion, and to promise pay when on duty equal to that received by regular troops in America. While provincials could be considered an elite corps among loyalists, they were not eligible for allowances and perquisites equal to those received by regular troops with whom they were expected to serve, a fact that made it difficult to keep regiments up to their authorized strength. Although often exposed to the extended and arduous service expected of regulars, their officers were junior in the next lower rank to regular officers (a regular captain outranked a provincial major) and they were not entitled either to the permanent rank or to the half-pay due regular officers when their units were deactivated.[1]

Nor were British field commanders or the civil administrators in London satisfied with the results of efforts to employ provincials in America early in the war, finding them to be both ineffective and expensive. Basic to the whole idea of organizing provincials was that an "influential" person, usually someone of wealth and standing, could persuade men of local influence to serve as officers; they would, in turn, be able to recruit effectively for the ranks of their battalions and companies. In other words, gentlemen would lead and the plainer sort would become the junior officers and the rank and file, an assumption that might have produced the desired recruits except that many among the colonial gentry openly supported the rebellion. Further, regardless of their personal sentiments, the gentry often stood to risk the basis of their influence, their property, if they openly resisted local pressure to conform to the rebel side. But even if they were willing to dare the wrath of local rebels, influential loyal men did not necessarily make good field officers. As a result, while provincial units rarely reached their authorized strength in enlisted men, they often had a superfluity of officers whose relatively high compensation was a constant drain on the treasury. As the war dragged on and expenses mounted-particularly after France and Spain were drawn in—a reform of the provincial service was undertaken in hopes that recruiting for such units would be more effective and that they would be more useful as field troops.

Under these reforms, officers of provincial corps that the commander in chief could certify had strength comparable with that of regular infantry regiments were to be eligible for permanent rank and half-pay "in America"; like regulars, they were to be entitled, if maimed, to receive a year's pay in advance; and the enlisted men were to be offered a money bounty as an inducement to enlist. Sir Henry Clinton had been partly responsible for recommending the reforms, and attempts to recruit provincial units in South Carolina were based upon the new policy.[2]

Barely a month after the South Carolina Royalists had scattered to their homes and while Alexander Innes was in Charlestown, the defeat of Christian Huck forced Nisbet Balfour to take the field to restore order above the Enoree River, leaving Evan McLaurin at Ninety Six with orders to recall the Royalists from leave to garrison that post. McLaurin was generally pleased with the response by new recruits, reporting that 176 had answered his call and had removed the danger "of bringing disgrace" on the regiment. When Innes hastened from Charlestown to assume command, however, he was displeased with the turnout of the veterans of earlier campaigns, finding that many of the "Old Standers" did not wish to continue in the service, and that the "age and infirmities of many and the distresses to which their familys have been exposed during their long absence," had made them reluctant to leave home again. Further, many of the old hands were disgruntled, never having received the bounty money due them for their original enlistment and believing that their long service entitled them to a discharge. Innes recommended that these men be discharged, concluding that they might serve the cause more usefully at home if they were not forced to resume active service against their will.[3]

Cornwallis agreed that Innes should discharge the veterans among the "Blue Coat Gentry" who were not fit or willing to serve further. After Cruger succeeded Balfour as commandant at Ninety Six, he observed the Royalists as they assembled at the end of their furloughs, writing to Cornwallis that "not one hundred" of the regiment had reported "arm'd fit for duty"; several days later, he sent a strength report that showed 202 officers and men to be present, of whom twenty-six were sick, remarking that they "in point of discipline are quite militia."[4]

Although most company commanders in the Royalists returned for service when called, only fifty-one of the 188 effectives who had mustered at Savannah the previous December were to serve with the regiment in the future. Faced with the problems of inexperience and lack of discipline common to new units, the Royalists suffered substantial casualties and their commander was seriously wounded at Musgrove's Mill in mid August. When Cornwallis was preparing to move into North Carolina after his victory at Camden, he ordered the Royalists transferred to that post for garrison duty; Cruger rounded up the necessary wagons and saw them off in September, remarking caustically that the regiment made "a very sorry appearance." After recovering from his wounds, Innes returned to Charlestown, then sailed for New York where Clinton had need of his services. Although Innes remained nominally in command, the man chosen to lead the troops in the field was Major Thomas Fraser, a New Jersey loyalist whose activity and zeal had impressed Cornwallis. Joseph Robinson, no longer actively involved with the regiment, was permitted to retire from the provincial service on the half-pay of a lieutenant colonel in 1781.[5]

Cornwallis, recognizing the greenness of the recruits in the reconstituted regiment, suggested that most of it remain on routine duty near Camden. However, he did urge George Turnbull to arrange to mount "Major Frazer [sic] with 50 of the eldest soldiers" in his corps, which, joined by some of John Harrison's men and by detachments from the New York Volunteers and Robert Gray's militia, was to form a kind of roving force that could sustain the militia posts north of the Santee and near its ferries. But he was never really happy with the Royalists thereafter, bluntly ordering Rawdon to give Fraser a dressing down because of absenteeism in his regiment, saying, "I cannot allow men to be kept on the strength of this army who are acknowledged to be unfit for service by age or infirmity, or have promise of perpetual furlow..." But he soon moved into North Carolina, leaving others to employ the Royalists as they wished.[6]

The Royalists and John Harrison's corps were the only South Carolina provincial regiments that actually saw service during the war, but other attempts were made to raise such units during 1780. Of most interest in this regard was the effort made by British officers to utilize the talents and influence of the Saluda River loyalist Robert Cunningham.

When Nisbet Balfour reached Ninety Six in June 1780, Patrick Cunningham was persuaded to take command of the Little River Regiment, and brothers David and John enlisted as privates in the unit. Robert, however, had other plans, and early in July he laid before Balfour a proposal to raise a provincial regiment in the district. Balfour recommended approval to Cornwallis, pointing out that, because Robert and "his brothers are people of very considerable influence" in the area, "a great many men in this country... could be brought to inlist." Given the rank of lieutenant colonel and a warrant to recruit men for this service, Robert was apparently achieving some success when Cornwallis in mid-September called a halt to the attempt because "all the principal officers of Ninety Six are entering into it, by which means I should have been totally deprived of the use of the militia for the present," while months would pass before the new corps could be effective. Robert was disappointed at the decision, having gone to some personal expense in the attempt, and both Cornwallis and John Harris Cruger realized that something would need to be done for him, although for the time being the idea was set aside.[7]

At first the prospects for securing the backcountry by use of the militia were bright, especially in Ninety Six District, and it seemed unnecessary to go to the expense of raising and maintaining other provincial troops. However, the serious defections in Floyd's and Mills's regiments and the losses incurred by the militia at Kings Mountain seemed to confirm the views of British officers that militia could not be trusted to maintain order in the backcountry. With Cornwallis ill in Winnsboro, and Balfour far away in Charlestown, Cruger became alarmed over conditions in the district and the vulnerability of the post at Ninety Six; in the absence of directions from his superiors, he turned to Moses Kirkland, who had returned after his long exile and accepted the command of a militia battalion in the "fork." In the aftermath of the disaster at Kings Mountain, he and his men occupied a fort at Williams's plantation near Little River. Kirkland claimed that Balfour had authorized him ro raise militia for nine to twelve months' service but had failed to send his commission; further, he charged that the Cunninghams had not responded to his call for men and were making plans to move away "with their effects" in order to escape the resurgent rebels. Badly frightened because of his exposed position and with no promise of help from any quarter, Kirkland could perhaps be excused if he felt deserted on all sides. But he appears to have had little influence in an area where the Cunninghams had a substantial following, and there may have been bad blood between him and that family. Kirkland's situation suddenly improved when Banastre Tarleton dashed into the area in pursuit of Thomas Sumter and a party of Whigs from Georgia, and he soon learned the reason that Robert Cunningham had not come to his aid.[8]

After Kings Mountain, Balfour had again urged Robert Cunningham to raise a provincial regiment and had invited him to Charlestown to confer on the matter. This time Cunningham declined the offer of a commission to raise a provincial corps, but he did show interest in commanding all the militia in Ninety Six District, and Balfour sent him to Winnsboro for further discussion of the scheme with Cornwallis. About the same time, Evan McLaurin appeared in Charlestown to renew·" his offer to raise a provincial regiment; Balfour also directed him to headquarters, saying that McLaurin was a "man of sense and influence" who had "one fault....which is that he drinks some time rather hard."[9]

McLaurin's proposal was turned down once more, but on November 22 Cornwallis reported that "Cunningham was here today full of zeal. I made him a brigadr. genl. of militia with Colonel 's full pay from the 24th of last June." Thus, after five months of negotiations, Cornwallis and Balfour had obtained the services of the man they preferred to head the militia of Ninety Six District, and Robert Cunningham had the reward and recognition he expected for his services to the Crown. After Cunningham's appointment, British officers dropped any idea of raising provincial troops in Ninety Six District.[10]

For Moses Kirkland, the news of Cunningham's preferment was bitterly disappointing, perhaps as much from jealousy of his rival as from his own frustrated ambition, and in a long letter to Cornwallis late in November he resigned his commission and gave vent to his feelings. Although expressing happiness that Cunningham had finally assumed a position of leadership, Kirkland reiterated his charge that his rival had been at the point of deserting the cause and only "quit moving away" when Kirkland assumed command in the "fork"; further, he claimed that Patrick Cunningham and other officers in the district had become so disgusted with Robert's lack of spirit that they had petitioned Balfour to give Kirkland command of all the militia in the district. Balfour did indicate that Robert was "disgruntled" when he came to Charlestown to discuss his future, and Patrick and other officers did petition that a single commander be chosen for the entire district, suggesting Kirkland for the appointment, and that a strong post be established near the ironworks "to shelter the suffering loyalists."[11]

Kirkland and Robert Cunningham had been on the same side in the Regulator controversy; in 1775, however, the Cunninghams had come out forthrightly against the measures of the Provincial Congress, whereas Kirkland, who held a commission under the congress, switched to the opposition only after the Council of Safety had named James

Mayson to command the militia in their district. Although Andrew Pickens implied many years later that Cunningham too had been disappointed by Mayson's appointment, Kirkland's entire career in South Carolina seems to have been characterized by opportunism and skirting the edges of the law; before the war he was suspected of having close ties with the Indians and with harboring runaway slaves. The Cunninghams, although clearly ambitious men, apparently owed their rapid rise to positions of local leadership to talent and straight dealing.[12]

Balfour had met Cunningham when in charge at Ninety Six and was favorably impressed by him, a view that Cornwallis came to share. In contrast, Kirkland, a semi-literate and rough man, would hardly make a favorable impression on either officer, Cornwallis saying, "from the character I have always heard of him" he was "an improper person" for the command, and Balfour asserting that Kirkland had no substantial following in the district and might alienate local inhabitants if given an important role there. Cornwallis had also become impatient with Kirkland's repeated complaints about the lack of support his militia had received after Kings Mountain, remarking curtly that if those claiming to be "friends do not stir, I cannot defend every man's house from being plundered," and confiding to Cruger that he thought Kirkland was exaggerating conditions "to raise his own merit," and that he was "caballing among the militia" to serve his private interests. Kirkland's resignation did, however, make it easier to be generous, and Cornwallis warmly assured him of readiness to "bear testimony of your merit" and instructed Balfour to issue fifty guineas to him for expenses incurred during that service.[13]

Kirkland returned to the state in the following winter in hopes that Cornwallis would have another appointment for him, but by then the earl was pursuing Nathanael Greene across North Carolina and not able, had he been so inclined, to do anything for him. Kirkland then retired to Ebenezer in Georgia where he owned land; when Savannah was evacuated in 1782, he took his family to Jamaica; and in 1787, while on a voyage to England to press his claim against the Crown for compensation for his services, he was lost at sea. Thus ended the career of a man who, with Thomas Brown and certain royal officials, had been responsible for convincing the North ministry that, by encouragement to the loyalists in the Carolinas and Georgia, those provinces at least might be recovered from the Americans. Clearly, his influence outside the province was greater than within it.[14]

After he routed Gates's army at Camden, Cornwallis lost interest in further efforts to raise provincials, saying that "raising corps does not succeed in this province, Harrison has totally failed, and I don't see that Innes has 200 men fit for service." When conditions worsened after Kings Mountain, however, the earl was more receptive to proposals for raising loyalist units outside the militia system.[15]

One such proposal originated with Lord Rawdon after Francis Marion had routed a party of loyalist militia under Major Samuel Tynes on Black River, and Tynes himself had resigned his commission. This action occurred in an area where civil strife had broken out and which Major Wemyss had devastated on his march to the upper Pee Dee in September. Rawdon had induced several locally prominent men to participate in raising a "fencible" regiment to serve between the Santee and the Pee Dee for six months by having them "regard the business as opposition to a gang of freebooters; and not showing it to them in the light of a decided step in the great line of policy." He admitted that the experiment would be expensive, but that "the expense of making officers of leaders may pay for itself if they are influential enough to promote peace in the area." One Isham Moore, a planter with substantial property in the High Hills of Santee, agreed to become colonel of this regiment, and it was anticipated that representatives of the local Richbourg and Singleton families would serve as captains in it. Cornwallis reluctantly approved, saying that although he doubted Moore's success, "I am determined to let slip no occasion of trying to arm the inhabitants of that country." While these negotiations were in progress, both Moore and Henry Richbourg had their homes plundered by rebels, a development that Rawdon hoped would increase their zeal for the British cause. The two men, however, had a falling out over the new command and, despite Rawdon's attempt to hold Marion up to them as the common enemy, the whole scheme fell through and was not heard of again.[16]

Cornwallis was at first reluctant to commit his resources to raising "Provincial Troops of Dragoons," the cavalry of the day, because it would "open a door to endless applications & jobs, and cost a great deal of money & hurt the recruiting of the infantry." However, the need to maintain communication over the great distances among British posts and units helped to change his mind, and after the "Second Revolution," he did authorize several efforts to raise mounted units from among the loyalists.[17]

Several plans for raising dragoons among the loyalists were considered that fall. Daniel Clary of the lower Broad-Saluda militia regiment, with Cruger's blessing, set out to recruit two troops of forty dragoons each for service on the western frontier, but apparently because of a shortage of mounts the idea was dropped. Another officer, Captain James Dunlap of the Queen's Rangers who had come to South Carolina with Patrick Ferguson, was offered the command of a troop of dragoons that Colonel Ambrose Mills of North Carolina had agreed to raise. This idea was set aside after Dunlap was severely wounded in September and Mills was hanged at Gilbertown in the aftermath of Kings Mountain. Dunlap had caught Cornwallis's eye as a "spirited officer," however, and in November he was given a temporary commission as major and the command of a troop of dragoons that Cruger had arranged to equip with cavalry appointments brought in from Savannah. The idea of employing loyalists as mounted troops had become more attractive to Cornwallis by the end of the year, and early in 1781 he urged Balfour to see that two more dragoon units were recruited for service in Camden District.[18]

Cornwallis's reluctant commitment to the strategy of employing picked corps of loyalist dragoons was to find greater favor with his successors, Lord Rawdon and Alexander Leslie, after the earl carried his campaign into North Carolina early in the new year.

Notes

1. This summary of the characteristics of provincial regiments is based on the full discussion in Paul H. Smith, *Loyalists and Redcoats* (Chapel Hill, N.C., 1964), 62–72.
2. Ibid., 72–78.
3. McLaurin to Innes, July 30, and Innes to Cornwallis, July 24, 28, 1780, CP 30/11/2, 331, 354, 373.
4. Cornwallis to Innes, July 30, Aug. 5, 1780, CP, 30/11/78, 59; 30/11/79, 16; Cruger to Cornwallis, Aug. 23, 1780, CP, 30/11/63, 29; "Return of the Garrison of Ninety Six," Aug. 12, 1780, CP, 30/11/103, 2.
5. One company commander resigned his commission during the furlough to devote "his attention to his large family," Clark, ed., *Loyalists*, I, 8. Although Musgrove's Mill was a defeat for the Royalists, Innes was very complimentary of the steadfastness of the new recruits in that action, to Cornwallis, Sept. 5, 1780,

CP, 30/11/64, 29; the information on the turnover in personnel in the Royalists is derived by comparing the 1779 muster roll with later rolls, LMR; see also Cornwallis to Innes, Sept. 16, 1780, CP, 30/11/80,11; Cruger to Cornwallis, Aug. 23, and Sept. 7, 22, CP 30/11/63, 62, and 30/11/64, 30, 102; Clark, ed., *Loyalists*, I, 467.
6. Cornwallis to Turnbull, Sept. 27, CP, 30/11/80, 52, and Cornwallis to Rawdon, Nov. 28, 1780, CP, 30/11/82, 119.
7. Cruger to Cornwallis, Sept. 3, CP, 30/11/64, 9; Cornwallis to Cruger, Sept. 19, 1780, CP, 30/11/76, 21.
8. Except for one reference to "Lieutenant Colonel Moses Kirkland's Regiment," there are no militia pay records that indicate who served in that unit and that he commanded it, Clark, ed., *Loyalists*, I, 221; Kirkland to Cornwallis, Nov. 6, 8, 10, 12, and to McArthur, Nov. 14, 1780, CP, 30/11/4, 31, 35, 41, 54, 66.
9. Cruger to Rawdon, ace. 30, CP, 30/11/3, 324, Balfour to Cornwallis, Nov. 5, CP, 30/11/4, 15.
10. Cornwallis to Balfour, Nov. 23, 1780, CP, 30/11/82, 81.
11. Kirkland to Cornwallis, Nov. 15, and Balfour to Cornwallis, Nov. 5, and "Petition of Militia Officers of Ninety Six," Nov. 8, CP, 30/11/4, 104, 15, 36. The petition, apparently bearing the signatures of Patrick Cunningham and fourteen officers from his own and three other regiments, did recommend Kirkland; if there was bad blood between Robert Cunningham and Kirkland, the petition may have piqued the former's interest in taking such a command.
12. Pickens to Henry Lee, Aug. 28, 1811, VV, I, 107, Sumter Papers, Draper Coll.
13. Cornwallis to Cruger, Nov. 11, 16, 23, to Kirkland, Nov. 13, and to Balfour, Nov. 30, 1780, CP, 30/11/82, 24, 50, 80, 34, 133.
14. Kirkland to Cruger, Feb. 22, 1781, CP, 30/11/67, 83; Loyalist Transcripts, LVII, 318–50.
15. Cornwallis to Balfour, Sept. 3, 6, 1780, CP, 30/11/80, 1.
16. In Great Britain "fencibles" were a kind of local militia who could not be sent out of their home districts, Edward A. Curtis, *The Organization of the British Army in the American Revolution* (London, 1972 [orig. publ. New Haven, 1926]), 68, 59n. Rawdon's efforts may be followed in letters to Cornwallis, Dec. 8,9, 16, 18, CP, 30/11/4, 145, 148, 167, 176; see also Cornwallis to Balfour, Dec. 9, 1780, CP, 30/11/83, 31. Moore was apparently instrumental in inducing William Richbourg, one of Marion's officers, to seek protection, Rawdon to Cornwallis, Nov. 20, CP, 30/11/4, 85. Moore later joined Marion and was able to remain in the state, CEP.
17. Cornwallis to Balfour, July 3,1780, CP, 30/11/78, 3.
18. Cruger to Cornwallis, Nov. 1, 8, CP, 30/11/4, 1, and 30/11/63, 96; Cornwallis to Balfour, Sept. 13, 26, CP, 30/11/80, 20, 35, and Nov. 1, 4, and to Dunlap, Nov. 11, 1780, CP 30/11/82, 1,6,26, and to Balfour, Jan. 12, 1781, CP 30/11/84, 51.

Chapter Ten

RETREAT FROM THE INTERIOR, 1781

A few of the inhabitants on Long Cane have been plunderd, many more deserved it for their pusilanimous behavior, about forty to fifty rebels frightened the whole regiment,...I think I shall never again look to the militia for the least support, & I am convinced that it is the King's troops only that can hold this country.

—John Harris Cruger, November 1780

Patrick Ferguson's defeat at Kings Mountain had been a serious setback to British plans for a successful invasion of North Carolina in the fall of 1780, and Cornwallis was forced to retire to Winnsboro and a season of relative inactivity. The rebel victory and its immediate effect on British planning have to a degree diverted the attention of historians of the Revolution in South Carolina from the very serious deterioration of the British position in two areas where it would appear that they might be strongest—the vicinity of their two main interior bases at Ninety Six and Camden.

When Nisbet Balfour arrived in Ninety Six in June 1780, he found fewer loyalists near that post than had been expected, a situation that he attributed to the suspicions aroused because the unpopular Richard Pearis had been the first representative of British authority to come into the area. Balfour, therefore, decided that it might be useful to conciliate Andrew Williamson and Andrew Pickens, two men closely identified with the rebel cause in the area from the beginning of the conflict, in the hope that they might be willing to help keep the peace south of the Saluda and perhaps take a more active role in sustaining British authority there. This decision was especially important because Pickens had commanded the rebel militia regiment drawn primarily from his home area in the Long Cane settlement. When John Harris Cruger succeeded Balfour in command at Ninety Six, he assumed the essentially diplomatic task of cultivating the two men, while Balfour retained authority to specify the terms of any agreement reached with them, having been directed by Cornwallis to "employ Williamson and to give him every encouragement to take the most hearty part with us."[1]

Cruger's task was not an enviable one. There was much "disaffection" in the area, the town was not fortified to withstand a concerted attack, and it was isolated from the main British army and from the other posts except Augusta, which lay in another jurisdiction and was commanded by Thomas Brown, a person in whom British officers had little confidence. In addition, parties of rebel militia were still at large in the Georgia backcountry and posed a potential threat to the security of both Augusta and Ninety Six.[2]

Cruger was particularly disturbed that Richard King had found it necessary to accept enlistments from a number of the "disaffected in Pickens' regiment," in order to fill the ranks of the loyalist unit he had raised there. Cruger found little to please him in the Long

Cane area, saying that "the Country lads will not enlist," and that King's regiment was too easily "frightened" by the rumor that the rebels were in the neighborhood. And although he had been able to relieve Brown when he was besieged in Augusta in September, Cruger was not confident that he could expect much help if their situations were reversed. Largely on his own initiative, he "palisaded the Court House and the principal houses" nearby and brought in a stock of corn better to withstand a siege.[3]

Cruger responded enthusiastically to his instructions to consult with Williamson and Pickens and, if possible, bring them over to the British side. He soon confirmed Balfour's view that Williamson, "an honest man of friendly disposition,"was not interested in a British command, "but his grand object is a state of neutrality," adding, however, that "his neighbor the Colonl. is favorably reported." In September, when Augusta was under siege by Elijah Clarke, Williamson did perform valuable service by taking several of his paroled officers with him into the Long Cane settlement to meet Pickens and other leading inhabitants, a move that prevented any "but three or four rash young fellows" from leaving to join the rebels. From Charlestown, Balfour expressed the hope that Williamson could be persuaded to join Robert Cunningham to "make an expedition against these transmountain gentry" like Clarke and other rebels to stamp out the last resistance on that frontier.[4]

Aside from his action in keeping things quiet during the siege of Augusta, and the sale of supplies from his extensive properties in the area, there is no concrete evidence that Williamson directly took the British side. Cornwallis was certainly willing to pay Williamson or any other American who might furnish services or supplies, telling his subordinates that they might give "douceurs" for especially valuable service.[5]

There is less evidence on Pickens's relations with the British, but there is none to confirm that he cooperated with them except to serve on the commission that investigated the status of the Kings Mountain prisoners. That act, because some of his neighbors and former enlisted men were among those involved on the loyalist side in the battle, probably was to him a duty as well as an errand of mercy. Cornwallis, who had received reports from Ferguson and others that Pickens was in contact with Sumter and other rebel leaders, was never optimistic that Pickens would take an active role for the British. But Cruger continued his efforts to conciliate both Williamson and Pickens, notifying Balfour early in December that both men were prepared to accompany him to Charlestown for a conference. Cruger saw "more than a possibility" that an unnamed person (Pickens?) in the Long Cane area could be persuaded to accept a British commission; if an agreement were reached, Balfour could announce the appointment and then issue a declaration "calling on the inhabitants of the Ninety Six area to declare for the King or quit," presumably solving the problem of the "disaffected" in the militia. But before he was ready to make the trip, a raid into the Long Cane area by "forty or fifty rebels frightened the whole [of Richard King's] regiment" whose "pusillanimous behaviour" confirmed Cruger's view that militia were worthless. When things quieted down, Cruger went to Charlestown where he and Balfour conferred on conditions at Ninety Six, but neither Williamson nor Pickens made the trip with him.[6]

Cruger had barely returned to Ninety Six when a party of Georgia and South Carolina rebels, variously estimated to number from 200 to 500, raided into the Long Cane settlements again. But more than raiding was involved this time; under the cover of the excitement, Colonel Samuel Hammond led one party to Whitehall to see Williamson, and Major James McCall led another to the home of Andrew Pickens, with orders to bring the two parolees to rebel headquarters. Cruger had difficulty obtaining sound information on what was transpiring, learning only that the rebels had detained Williamson, "as our friends abandon the country." Six days later he could report more fully the purpose of the rebel raid into Long Cane; it was to cajole or threaten the inhabitants to give up paroles and rejoin the rebels on the ground that the British had violated the terms of the capitulation, and to get Williamson and Pickens and other "principal people" to lead them away. At first Cruger could report with relief that the tactics had not worked because "the gentlemen behaved like men of honor" and refused to violate their paroles. His view is confirmed by Hammond himself, who said that neither Williamson nor Pickens would comply because the British had not violated the terms of their paroles.[7]

But Cruger's joy at the response of the two men did not last. To meet the rebel incursion, he sent a mixed party of militia and provincials under Colonel Isaac Allen to pursue the raiders, and they did overtake some of the rebels, inflicting some casualties and dispersing the rest. But this minor victory proved to be a hollow one, for, as Allen reported to Cornwallis, under cover of the raid Pickens, several of his officers, and perhaps 100 men had "left the Long Cane Settlement and joined the Enemy." Williamson, who had suffered considerable losses of grain and cattle in the raid, remained at home, "distressed at the perfidious behavior of his friend Pickens."[8]

American sources have always maintained that a raid by a band of loyalist cavalry under Major James Dunlap had frightened Pickens's family and destroyed much of his property while he was absent. Convinced that the British had violated the terms of his parole, Pickens went to a small fort near his home and told the British officer in charge that he was leaving and why. British sources say nothing of this event; his action in giving up his parole is merely described as "treachery."[9]

Pickens's departure was not the only bad news, for Isaac Allen also reported that detachments of General Daniel Morgan's infantry and Colonel William Washington's cavalry had seized Williams's Fort in the upper part of the district. This information confirmed what Lord Cornwallis had already learned; a third Continental army had entered South Carolina.

There were other signs late in 1780 that the British had anything but firm control in South Carolina. For example, Wade Hampton kept a store near Friday's Ferry on the Congaree River and from time to time replenished his stock of goods from sources in Charlestown. Although one of his brothers was serving as an aide to Thomas Sumter, Hampton had been furnishing supplies to British units in the area. By November, however, Charles Stedman, Cornwallis's commissary, had become suspicious that Hampton was secretly aiding the rebels; he reported his views to the earl who, in turn, asked Rawdon to have Hampton watched because he "is said to be a good Rebel & his store entirely in their use." Late in the month another Hampton brother was reported to have "gone off to the Rebels," and when fifteen wagons arrived from Charlestown on December 4 with goods for the store, Cornwallis ordered them "to be pressed" and "detained for the public use." This move precipitated Wade Hampton's decision to flee, because he too was soon reported to have "gone off to the enemy," and Stedman took possession of his stock.[10]

So long as Cornwallis's army lay at Winnsboro the important post at Camden seemed to be secure, but the approach of a new Continental army and a serious embarrassment suffered by the local loyalist militia placed the town in jeopardy. When the British army first reached Camden, it began to use Colonel Henry Rugeley's property north of the town to store grain, and he undoubtedly ground a good deal of it at his mill. In November Cornwallis's engineer was ordered to construct fortifications on the property, and he erected a log house to protect the mill and an abatis around the barn and house. About that time Rugeley's regiment was called out to seek information about an American force reported to be operating above Charlotte. When it became apparent that a substantial Continental army—the remnants of Gates's army reorganized and reinforced and commanded by Nathanael Greene—was approaching South Carolina, Rugeley and his men were ordered to fall back to the fortifications at his mill, to scout for information, and if faced by a superior force, to retire to Camden. Rugeley reported that Daniel Morgan with 600 infantry and William Washington's cavalry had joined above his mill, but because they had no artillery he planned to defend "himself to the utmost." But on December 1 when the enemy appeared before the mill and demanded its surrender, Rugeley submitted, "without firing a shot." Rugeley's ignominious defeat became a favorite tale for historians of the Revolution in South Carolina because William Washington had employed the stratagem of pointing a fallen log in the direction of the fort, which at a distance the defenders had mistaken for artillery. Of course, Rugeley had indicated that he would hold out because the enemy had no artillery, and one bit of evidence indicates that he at first refused to comply with the summons to surrender; presumably he later became aware of the "artillery" and changed his mind. It is worth noting too that Rawdon, who had thought of trying a surprise attack on the approaching enemy, decided not to risk leaving his prepared position at Camden.[11]

Cornwallis's reaction to the Rugeley affair is interesting; "vexed" but "not surprised," he was more concerned about a reverse that would further "damp the spirits of the militia" than the "intrinsic value" of the post itself. He soon reached the conclusion, however, that Rugeley "must be a traitor" for surrendering "to cavalry only" after he could have fallen back to Camden. Actually, no charges were ever brought against Rugeley, and an exchange was arranged that released him from imprisonment in North Carolina in 1781.[12]

The Rugeley affair, coupled with the flight of Pickens, ended 1780 on a sour note for the British and their loyalist allies. More than that, however, these events illustrate the problems inherent in the task Cornwallis and his subordinates had undertaken.

The first was a military problem. Clinton and Cornwallis had destroyed two American armies, but a third had entered the state and the work had to be done all over again. By the end of the year, the British were really on the defensive, having been reduced to fortifying Ninety Six, Camden, and Georgetown and manning them with militia and provincials. The main army was concentrated at Winnsboro in preparation for the planned advance into North Carolina, bur because of Kings Mountain and Cornwallis's illness, it had remained idle since the great victory at Camden in mid-August. Actually, some reinforcements had arrived in South Carolina; Clinton had dispatched Major General Alexander Leslie and 2,000 men in to the Chesapeake to draw attention from Cornwallis's projected advance into North Carolina. Immobilized by events in South Carolina, Cornwallis had diverted that expedition to Charlestown, and by late December Leslie's troops had landed and begun their march from the port to join the main army and reinforce the base at Camden. Thus, at the end of the year, Charlestown was secure, the principal interior bases were prepared to withstand a siege, and Cornwallis was poised to drive across the border, but the rest of South Carolina lay open to a resourceful foe.

The second problem was in finding military leadership among the loyalists. Although probably not a "traitor," Henry Rugeley was representative of the type of men to whom British officers turned to lead the loyalists. Essentially a civilian who had not performed service with the Americans, he was commissioned because he was a man of some property whose role would be primarily that of a "conservator of the peace" rather than someone to lead and inspire the militia in the field. In time of military crisis, he had been found wanting; asked to do a job for which he was temperamentally unfit, he lost his nerve and surrendered abjectly as had William Henry Mills and Samuel Tynes before him. Better leaders would be found among the loyalists, but at this point they had not yet been given the opportunity to demonstrate their talents.

Finally, the loyalists themselves had turned out to be a disappointment, being neither as numerous nor as zealous as pre-capitulation estimates had indicated. Much against the wishes of Cornwallis and Balfour, men who had served with the rebels during the American Period had signed up for the militia, men whose change of allegiance did not necessarily reflect a change of heart, and who, as in the Pee Dee region and the Long Cane settlements, defected wholesale at the first opportunity. Equally serious, although perhaps not as noticeable as the defections, was the reluctance of the militia to "turn out" when called, a problem similar to that which the Americans experienced with their militia during the war. As for the provincials, the problem was not so much lack of zeal by those who signed up as unwillingness to enlist for what appeared to be unlimited duty. Faced with the fact that there were fewer loyalists than expected, Cornwallis and his officers were forced to choose between a fairly large militia of uneven quality and a smaller number of committed provincials; because they were concerned that additional provincial units would be expensive and draw too many of the better officers from the militia, it was decided to preserve the militia.

Did Clinton's proclamation of June 3 force men of dubious loyalty to sign up for the militia and thus, as Cornwallis and his officers claimed, render that branch less reliable than it might otherwise have been? That it probably had an unfortunate effect is undeniable, but it is not clear that it was crucial. The case against Clinton's proclamation assumes that everyone in the population learned of its terms at approximately the same time and that the officers responsible for carrying out policy in the various districts of the interior applied it uniformly. It also assumes that the proportion of the committed rebels, committed loyalists, and the generally uncommitted was similar throughout the state.

It is well to remember that the charges against Clinton's proclamation were two: (1) that it forced many who were neutral or were Whig sympathizers to take the oath of allegiance and sign up for militia duty; and (2) that by doing so, it blunted the zeal of the loyalists who found some of their former persecutors in equal favor with British authorities. The first charge cannot be proved or disproved; had there been no proclamation and if the American cause was as truly desperate as it appeared to be in the late spring, it would be surprising if any but the most committed rebels would fail to reach an accommodation with the restored regime by enlisting in its militia as a means of protecting families and property. There apparently was some substance to the charge that committed loyalists were disheartened by seeing former enemies and persecutors taken into the ranks with them, but if that policy bothered committed loyalists like Zacharias Gibbs, Alexander Chesney, John Phillips, and many others, it did not shake their resolve to continue their support of the cause.

The problem may lie with the assumptions on which the charges rest. The decision to honor the paroles given Williamson, Pickens, and their men is one clear instance where the conditions of the proclamation were not applied, a decision that cannot have gone unnoticed by those in Ninety Six District who had served under the two men. That the proportion of the population who were neutral or committed to one side or the other was uniform throughout South Carolina is at best a dubious assumption, for within Ninety Six District alone the proportion of committed loyalists varied widely in different locales. That there was some confusion in British policy toward former rebels when they occupied the interior and that the policy was not uniformly applied is evident, but it is doubtful that Sir Henry's proclamation of June 3 deserves the share of blame that some have attributed to it.

The presence of Nathanael Greene's Continental army just across the North Carolina line ushered in a new phase of war in South Carolina, a phase that would be fateful for the loyalists in the province.

When Greene reached Charlotte he discovered that the area around the town had been stripped of most of the means of subsistence for his troops, so he decided to divide his force in order to feed it better and to be in a position to harass Cornwallis and to respond to any move the earl made toward invading North Carolina. Therefore, he led part of the army eastward to the Pee Dee River where he took position on the east bank opposite Cheraw Hill, South Carolina, and he ordered Daniel Morgan with the remainder to operate west of the Catawba where he was to maintain contact with Cornwallis, attacking or retreating as the circumstances might dictate. While Morgan's assignment involved some risk, he had little to fear from loyalists in the area because William Washington had routed one party within fifteen miles of Ninety Six in December and another under Robert Cunningham had dispersed when Morgan entered the area. Morgan then moved west of the Broad River to a camp on the Pacolet where Andrew Pickens and the Long Cane defectors joined him.[13]

Meanwhile, Cornwallis had been waiting impatiently for Alexander Leslie to bring his reinforcements to Camden in preparation for the invasion of North Carolina. Morgan's presence west of the Broad menaced the security of Ninety Six, but Tarleton, sent to reconnoiter that area, reported that William Washington had rejoined Morgan and that Cruger's post was safe for the time being. Tarleton then asked for reinforcements so that he would be strong enough to drive Morgan across the Broad into the arms of the advancing Cornwallis. The latter agreed, and the stage was set for one of the decisive battles of the war.[14]

The story of the Battle of Cowpens has been told many times, and it serves none of the purposes of this study to give a detailed account of it here. Morgan, aware that he was threatened by a considerable force but uncertain of its location or intentions, moved rapidly up the Pacolet, then fell back toward Thicketty Creek, while Tarleton plunged forward in pursuit so as to drive Morgan into the trap that he assumed Cornwallis would be ready to spring.[15]

The goal of trapping Morgan was not achieved, a failure that was to have important consequences to the loyalists in the South Carolina backcountry. Of immediate importance was that on January 17, 1781, the impetuous Tarleton, thinking his prey at bay, charged Morgan's carefully prepared position and was utterly routed with heavy losses. Unlike Kings Mountain, local loyalists had little to do with the battle except for the few who acted as scouts with Tarleton; the battle was waged between British regulars and the provincials of the British Legion on one side, and Morgan's Continentals and rebel militia on the other.[16]

Of long-range consequence was the fact that Leslie's reinforcements had been mired down by heavy rains, forcing Cornwallis to delay his own march. Thus Morgan, who recrossed the Broad and the Catawba within two days of his great victory, was able to move his men out of reach of the other jaw of the trap that was to have been set for him. To Cornwallis, "the late affair has almost broke my heart"; stung by Tarleton's defeat and with Leslie's contingent now nearby, he set off in pursuit of Morgan, leaving South Carolina behind him for good.[17]

After Greene was apprised of the victory at Cowpens, he rode personally to join Morgan, leaving his own troops to follow as soon as possible. Eventually the two bodies were joined and on March 15 met Cornwallis's army in the important Battle of Guilford Court House in which the British repulsed Greene and held the field, but suffered such heavy losses that Cornwallis decided to move his army first to Cross Creek and then to Wilmington on the coast. After resting there, he turned his army northward to Virginia to begin the campaign that would terminate with his surrender at Yorktown in the fall. Once Greene determined that Cornwallis was going to Wilmington, he brought his own army back into South Carolina, setting up camp on Lynches Creek on April 17.[18]

Cornwallis left behind a considerable force of regulars and loyalist provincials and militia to safeguard the conquests of the year before. These troops were to be found in the principal garrisons at Charlestown, Georgetown, Camden, and Ninety Six, the three interior posts having been strengthened by the construction of defensive works. In addition a string of smaller posts had been established to support communications between Charlestown and the interior: Fort Granby, south of the Congaree just below where the Saluda and the Broad come together; Fort Motte, south of the Congaree near McCord's Ferry; Fort Watson, at Wright's Bluff on the north side of the Santee; Nelson's Ferry, south of the Santee and some forty miles from Fort Motte; and Moncks Corner, on the Cooper River thirty miles from Charlestown. Provisions and supplies from Charlestown came by water to Moncks Corner, then by wagon nearly to Nelson's Ferry where they were transferred to boats for the journey to Camden.[19]

Thomas Sumter, having recovered from his wound, returned to the field early in 1781 and soon demonstrated how much the British had been thrown on the defensive after the departure of Cornwallis and Tarleton. In late February Sumter invested three British forts, Granby, near the Congaree; Thomson's House, south of the Santee where just eight months earlier Nisbet Balfour had paused to accept paroles from the inhabitants and to organize the loyal militia of Orangeburg District; and Fort Watson, north of the Santee. Sumter's lack of artillery and the appearance of relief expeditions under Rawdon himself allowed the garrisons of regulars and loyalist militia to survive at the first two places, and a direct assault on Fort Watson was repulsed with some loss. After resting his troops briefly in the High Hills of Santee, Sumter fought a drawn engagement with the South Carolina

Royalists and militia under Thomas Fraser, then retreated toward the Waxhaw area. In a period of just three weeks, he had marched in a semicircle around the British base at Camden, captured and lost a supply convoy, and thoroughly alarmed the loyalists in the countryside. To all of this activity, Rawdon could only react, sallying forth to prevent the capture of the forts but unable to undertake a full campaign.[20]

One reason for Rawdon's caution was that he was involved in directing a campaign to the eastward against Francis Marion who, in January, had led a surprise attack on Georgetown. Although that place held out because Marion lacked artillery, the boldness of the move and his persistent threat to British supply lines had made him a marked man. Rawdon sent the Volunteers of Ireland from the north to meet a party of regulars and John Harrison's Rangers driving from the south under Colonel John Watson. Marion's supply base was destroyed, but he succeeded in drawing Watson into several traps, inflicting heavy casualties, and driving the British force to seek refuge in Georgetown. Marion then retreated into North Carolina after Watson was joined by a large body of loyalists from the Little Pee Dee under Major Micajah Gainey.[21]

Meanwhile, Andrew Pickens had been ordered by Nathanael Greene to return to the western part of the state in order to exert pressure on the British and loyalists there. Late in March some of his men serving with the Georgia partisan Elijah Clarke routed a party of ninety men from the base at Ninety Six under Major James Dunlap. Dunlap, wounded and captured during the fight, was later killed while under guard at Gilbertown, apparently as revenge for his earlier depredations.[22]

This boldness on the part of the rebels in the winter of 1781 further discouraged the fainthearted among the loyalists. Only those in the heart of Orangeburg District were relatively undisturbed by rebel activity during the period, The incursions of Sumter and Marion also served to disrupt communications with Charlestown, exposing Camden to the danger of being cut off from its source of supplies. When Nathanael Greene's troops returned in mid-April, the groundwork had been laid for a concerted campaign to recover the interior of the state in the warmer months ahead.[23]

The return of Greene's army to South Carolina began a period of about five months of intense military activities, a period characterized by two types of campaigns. First, there were three engagements that, by the scale of operations in the state, could be considered as major, and in which Greene was the commanding officer—a battle at Hobkirk's Hill near Camden in April, the siege of Ninety Six in May and June, and the last major battle in the war at Eutaw Springs in September. In each of these contests the Americans failed to achieve their objective directly, but the British subsequently abandoned the position or area they had successfully defended. Less well known, but ultimately the real cause of the failure of the British to hold their major posts in the interior, were successful assaults on minor posts, supply lines, and communications by smaller bodies of state troops under Sumter, Pickens, Marion, and other officers. In this campaigning loyalists were involved in greater or less degree in the major battles and made up the bulk of the British units in the skirmishing and defense of minor posts that went on almost continuously throughout the spring and early summer. The fact that loyalists were on the defensive or in flight during the period would have significant consequences for their future lives and those of their families and neighbors.[24]

The Battle of Hobkirk's Hill took place on April 25 when Rawdon, feeling it necessary to strike a decisive blow before Greene's approaching army and the partisan forces cooperating with it could cut him off completely from Charlestown and the smaller interior posts, learned that he might have a temporary advantage over Greene whose artillery had been sent to the rear. As Greene approached, Rawdon reported that some of the loyal militia showed "great zeal and fidelity, coming voluntarily from considerable distances to offer their services." Short of provisions for his own troops, he could only accept the services of those driven from their homes by the enemy, but he was grateful for their presence because when he marched to attack Greene, he was able to leave the militia in the fortifications, freeing his one British and four provincial regiments for the impending battle. The South Carolina Royalists, called from Ninety Six as reinforcements, slipped into the town despite rebel efforts to block their way; they formed a part of the reserve in Rawdon's plan of battle and, although not fully committed, they did suffer a few casualties and received praise in his report of the engagement.[25]

Although Rawdon succeeded in taking the American positions on the ridge that gave the battle its name, he was unable to pursue his temporary advantage because he feared to move too far from his base. Reinforced early in May by 500 men under Colonel John Watson, he set out to draw Greene into another engagement, but the latter moved out of harm's way and Rawdon returned to Camden.[26]

Despite Hobkirk's Hill, the British position was deteriorating rapidly; even as Rawdon prepared for that battle Francis Marion in cooperation with Henry Lee's legion of Greene's army captured Fort Watson north of the Santee, taking over a hundred British and loyalist prisoners. Having failed to destroy Greene's army and finding his situation no longer tenable, Rawdon decided to abandon Camden and retreat beyond the Santee. American accounts emphasize the haste with which the evacuation was carried out, the destruction of the jail, some mills and private houses, and a great deal of "baggage, stores, and even effects belonging to the inhabitants," leaving the place " little better than a heap of ruins. " Rawdon's own report says merely that he destroyed the fortifications.[27]

Rawdon did what he could to protect local loyalist families from rebel revenge, encouraging them to move with their effects from the area under escort of his troops. He noted that "we brought off not only the Militia who had been with us in Camden, but also the well affected neighbors on our route, together with the wives, children, Negroes & baggage of almost all of them." He hoped to move quickly enough to protect the smaller posts on the Congaree and Santee, but he was too late; Orangeburg surrendered to Sumter on May 11, Fort Motte fell to Marion on the 12th , and Granby was taken by Henry Lee on the 15th . Encumbered by the refugees he was escorting and with the situation deteriorating all around him, Rawdon ordered the post at Nelson's Ferry abandoned and moved on down the Santee. He reached Moncks Corner on May 24, almost exactly one year from the day on which he had accompanied Cornwallis on his march toward Camden after the fall of Charlestown. We do not know exactly who among the loyalists accompanied Rawdon on his march, but a number of loyalist men from Camden and Cheraw districts served in the militia after the interior was abandoned, and their families appear in the records as "distressed refugees" in and around Charlestown until the British left late in 1782.[28]

All of these reverses left the small British garrisons at Augusta and Ninety Six isolated and exposed to investment by overwhelming force. Even before Hobkirk's Hill, Rawdon had secured Cornwallis's permission to evacuate Camden and to consolidate the remaining British forces below the Santee to form a perimeter of defense for Charlestown and Savannah and a base for future operations. Therefore, when he decided to abandon Camden, he sent orders to John Harris Cruger to destroy the works at Ninety Six and remove his garrison across the Savannah River to join Thomas Brown at Augusta. Although Rawdon dispatched multiple copies of the order directly and through Balfour, the rebels controlled so much of the countryside around Ninety Six that all were intercepted or otherwise prevented from reaching that post. Cruger, ignorant of what the Americans already knew, continued to occupy and strengthen his fortifications until he learned that Augusta was under siege by Pickens and Lee and that Greene's army was approaching.[29]

Lee's legion and the South Carolina and Georgia militia under Pickens and Elijah Clarke first assaulted and captured the smaller of the two forts occupied by the garrison of Augusta, then summoned Thomas Brown to surrender the other. Although Brown employed every stratagem he could devise to hold out until help could arrive, he was forced to surrender on June 5. So bitter was the local feeling against Brown that he was provided with a personal American military escort until he reached the safety of the British positions above Savannah. Lee and Pickens then moved their troops to join Greene before Ninety Six where for two weeks he had been conducting a siege of that place.[30]

The month-long defense of Ninety Six against Greene's siege was the most successful military engagement fought by loyalists in South Carolina during the war. Although Greene probably erred in undertaking a prolonged investment while ignoring the garrison's dependence on a vulnerable source of water, that cannot detract from the resourcefulness and example of Cruger or the fortitude and gallantry of the men serving with him.[31]

The defenders consisted of the provincials of Cruger's own battalion of Delancey's Brigade from New York and Isaac Allen's battalion of New Jersey Volunteers, and local South Carolina loyalist militia, numbering less than 600 men in all. According to Cruger, the militia numbered about 200 men drawn primarily from Richard King's Long Cane Regiment with a scattering of others from nearby parts of the district, and there were perhaps 100 others of the "old and helpless with their families." Strong fortifications, combined with the experience and zeal of the veteran provincials and their commanders, and the desperation of the militia made for a degree of resistance disproportionate to the number of the defenders. To this point Cruger had had little good to say about the loyalists in the vicinity of his post. Indeed, he offered King's men the option of leaving the garrison while there was still opportunity to escape, but in the words of one British officer, " they nobly disdained to quit their post in the hour of danger, and turning their horses loose in the woods, determined to assist in the defense of the place, and abide by the fate of the garrison." They and some of the civilians present apparently gave a good account of themselves during the ordeal.[32]

Thaddeus Kosciuszko, Greene's engineer, directed the digging of parallels across the open ground in front of the star redoubt, an earthwork that formed the principal fortification for the post. At the end of May, Cruger reported to Rawdon that the parallels had reached within yards of the star and asked for relief. Cruger's letter, apparently the first clear information that he had not evacuated the fort, arrived just as a fleet from Ireland carrying reinforcements for Cornwallis arrived off Charlestown. Rawdon quickly took the light infantry from each of the three newly arrived British regiments, joined them with his own troops at Moncks Corner, and on June 7 set out to relieve Cruger's beleaguered garrison some 200 miles away. The relief force numbered about 1,700 men, including eighty-five loyal militia drawn from among the refugees from Camden District and commanded by John Phillips.[33]

Greene did not learn until June 11 that Rawdon had started for Ninety Six, and he then ordered Sumter to harass the relief force. By then, Lee and Pickens had arrived from Augusta, and Lee suggested that approaches be made toward a small stockade that guarded the garrison's water supply. Work on the main parallels was pressed at night to within thirty yards of the redoubt. Approaches to the spring had reached a point where the garrison would soon be deprived of water when a mounted man, who had been mingling with the rebel soldiers as country people were wont to do, suddenly made a dash for the fort waving a dispatch. Rawdon had slipped by Sumter's main force and reached Orangeburg. Learning for the first time that Augusta had fallen, he pushed his men toward Ninety Six, although many were debilitated from their long voyage and march in the heat.[34]

Greene now determined to risk a full-scale assault before Rawdon could arrive; on June 19 it was carried out from two directions-the stockade guarding the spring was taken, but the main thrust against the star redoubt was repulsed with heavy losses. Greene then raised the siege and withdrew his troops across the Saluda and then beyond Bush River out of Rawdon's reach. The siege had cost about 150 rebel casualties, while the defenders counted slightly more than half that number.[35]

Rawdon did not linger to share the joy of the garrison, but pushed on in pursuit of Greene who withdrew beyond the Enoree and Broad rivers. Rawdon then retraced his route to Ninety Six, paused there long enough to leave his light troops with Cruger, and then turned back toward Orangeburg to meet reinforcements expected from Charlestown. He met only nominal opposition, but his men suffered severely from the heat, over fifty dying from sunstroke on his march.[36]

Except for the Battle of Camden, the defense and relief of Ninety Six was the only significant British military achievement after the occupation of the backcountry a year earlier. But the victory was a hollow one for the loyalists of Ninety Six District. Rawdon, before he started on his march, had warned Cornwallis that Ninety Six could not be maintained, suggesting that only by "making the Congarees our frontier & transplanting our friends from the Back Country to the rich plantations within the boundary whose owners are in arms against us" could he "with few troops secure and command a tract that must in the end give law to the province." Therefore, when at Ninety Six, he had Cruger bring in the principal loyalists to whom he candidly disclosed the alternatives open to them: unless they were prepared to take responsibility for the defense of the area, aided only by a small force he would leave with them and the possibility of occasional relief from a post in the middle of the province, he could only offer to resettle their families on plantations in the lowcountry. The resettlement plan was more appealing, and Cruger prepared to escort the loyalist families to Orangeburg.[37]

Almost immediately loyalist families began to congregate at Ninety Six with their possessions. One of Pickens's officers slipped back into the area and quietly observed preparations for the evacuation, reporting on July 9 that loyalists were collecting horses and wagons to haul provisions, and were rounding up any livestock they could find in preparation for the journey. Others gathered along Cruger's route from Ninety Six. According to militia pay records, at least 800 men from the Ninety Six brigade were among those conducted to Orangeburg, and a number had their families with them. They reached Orangeburg safely early in July, but by then the military situation had deteriorated so much that the army soon retreated farther down, and the Ninety Six loyalists found themselves, not resettled on rebel plantations, but as refugees in or near Charlestown or on one of the sea islands.[38]

Word of the move to the lowcountry did not reach everyone, nor did all choose to take the opportunity to resettle. Seven of Richard King's men were off on a mission and returned to discover that Ninety Six had been evacuated, and it was only with great difficulty that they were able to work their way to the British lines. Pickens's informant reported on July 25 that "the tories which stay'd in this country... are giving up very fast," while others had fled to Georgia, or "into the Indian Country" from which refuge they might be expected to cause trouble. Nor were all those who decided to stay in their homes allowed to do so; ne rebel militia officer called out some of his men late that summer "to order off the families & dangerous connections of such as are now gone within the British or lies out to the British lines." Tories had stripped much of the country of anything of value before they left, but, as one rebel observer noted, there was little difference between them and the rebel families who slowly returned from exile on the frontiers of Virginia and North Carolina and who seized what was left, "either the property of friend or enemy."[39]

Thus ended the grand plans of British military strategists to recover South Carolina for the Crown. By midsummer of 1781 all of the militia commanders from the backcountry districts were refugees in the lowcountry, or, like Moses Kirkland and William Henry Mills, had left the province for good. Most of the militia officers and enlisted men and many of their families had also fled to the lowcountry with Rawdon or Cruger; others, hoping that the rebel resurgence was temporary, hid out until the country would be secure again. Of course, many could not foresee that their exile from their homes would be permanent, and their officers and the loyalist press put an optimistic face on the prospects for fresh successes for British arms.

Although the campaigning around Camden and Ninety Six and the evacuation of much of the interior by British troops and loyalist families had cost the British most of their conquests of 1780, a number of minor actions during the spring and summer of 1780 put them even more on the defensive and further discouraged the loyalists.

Early in June, as Francis Marion prepared for another attempt to take Georgetown, that small garrison was quietly withdrawn to Charlestown, and his men entered the town without opposition. On the other side of the state, rebel troops under Colonel William Harden surprised and captured Captain Edward Fenwick, commander of an independent company of loyalist dragoons, and Colonel Nicholas Lechemere of the Granville County militia regiment while they were separated from their commands. Harden then moved to Fort Balfour near the Savannah River, manned by some of Lechemere's men, and, after persuading the garrison to surrender, destroyed the installation. While Greene rested his army after the strenuous campaigns of the early summer, Thomas Sumter applied enough pressure on the post at Moncks Corner that British defenders were withdrawn toward Charlestown. Only in the Little Pee Dee where civil war had raged since Charlestown fell did the loyalists hold their own, and in June a truce was signed between Major Micajah Gainey of the loyalists and Peter Horry of Marion's corps in an effort to end the strife that had desolated the area.[40]

Indeed, much of the interior of South Carolina lay desolate in the wake of the fighting armies and the raids and foraging of the militia on both sides. Portions of the towns of Camden, Ninety Six, and Georgetown had been destroyed, livestock had been driven off, and the armies had consumed or destroyed most of the stocks of grain that farmers had gathered for their own use. One traveler, writing from Camden, noted that the town consisted of "about fourteen houses—and the ruins of several large buildings—the jail and the courthouse were among the latter." He described the area between Camden and the Waxhaw area as "destitute of inhabitants and lade waste—the British destroy'd the whigs, and the whigs retaliated on the toreys—thus none escaped the devastation." Only the departure of the British forces and their loyalist allies brought a measure of peace to those still living amid the ruins of their property, although they would not be fully secure until peace came to the entire state.[41]

The last major battle in the state between British and American troops was fought just south of the Santee at Eutaw Springs in September. At that place Greene's Continentals and state troops under Marion and Sumter attacked a force of British regulars and Cruger's provincials commanded by Colonel Alexander Stewart. After hard fighting, the Americans overran the British position and were at the point of achieving a rout when discipline broke down among Greene's troops who turned to plundering the British camp, giving Stewart a chance to rally his men and reclaim much of the field. Casualties on both sides were heavy and Stewart withdrew toward Charlestown while Greene was content to remain alert for other chances of victory that never came. The British now controlled only the environs of Charlestown, Savannah, and Wilmington in the lower south, and Cornwallis was moving toward the refuge on the Chesapeake in Virginia that became a trap from which the land and naval power of Great Britain could not extricate him.

Little remained for the British to do during the rest of the war in South Carolina bur to shore up the defenses of Charlestown and to conduct occasional raids into the interior. Greene, plagued by declining numbers because of desertions and expired enlistments, was never in a position to test those defenses and barely able to keep an army in the field.[42]

The last half of 1780 marked the high point of participation by loyalists in the British war effort in South Carolina. After that, barely one quarter of the 1,500 men who had enlisted in the seven militia battalions formed in Ninety Six District are recorded as ever serving in any type of loyalist unit during the remaining two years of the war. The proportion of men in Orangeburg District who reenlisted for service with the British is even lower. Military service is, of course, but one measure of commitment to the British cause; but this evidence, derived from interior districts where loyal sentiment was purportedly the most intense and in which the initial response had seemed to British officers to be so warm, indicates that there had been substantial erosion of the base of support on which chances for pacifying the province rested. More important, this deterioration was already evident before Cornwallis moved his army northward in pursuit of Nathanael Greene in January 1781.[43]

The apparent erosion of loyalist zeal for the British cause raises several questions about the soundness of the "southern strategy." First, had Moses Kirkland, Thomas Brown, and royal officials of the southern provinces been correct in their view that loyal sentiment was so strong in the backcountry that a British campaign there offered a good chance of recovering the Carolinas and Georgia for the Crown, Second, if those men were correct, what happened after the British gained control of South Carolina in 1780 to make the loyalists less zealous or less effective than expected?

If the estimates of the numbers of backcountry Nonassociators who turned out in 1775 to protest the policies of William Henry Drayton and the Provincial Congress were reasonably accurate, then a comparison of the numbers who enlisted in the loyal militia in the same areas in 1780 provides at least a superficial indication that there was substantial loyal sentiment there. Of course, determined action by the Council of Safety had led to the dispersal of most Nonassociators and the arrest of many of their leaders in the Snow Campaign so that sustained resistance became impossible. Nevertheless, hundreds of backcountrymen did flee to the British lines in Florida during the American Period, and many others tried to reach the British army in Georgia in 1779, another indication that loyal sentiment still existed in parts of the backcountry.

The danger in making such comparisons is that much had transpired between 1775 and 1780-conditions in the South Carolina backcountry were not the same in both periods. In the absence of British authority in the several years after 1776, the state government had provided conditions that must have seemed to many backcountry residents to be positively stable when compared to those that had prevailed in the decade preceding the outbreak of hostilities. And the threat of Indian attack had been removed by Williamson's successful campaign against the Cherokees. This quiet had been first disturbed when British troops came into the Georgia backcountry in 1779 but even more so when they reached the interior of South Carolina in the following year and demanded that loyal men enlist in their militia. Committed loyalists who had chafed under the rebel government came forward willingly, but the wholesale defections from some loyal militia units soon demonstrated that many neutralists and rebel sympathizers had signed up out of expediency. Further, among the very first loyalist exiles to appear in the backcountry after Charlestown fell were Thomas Brown and Richard Pearis, men whose close ties with Indians could not have been reassuring to many settlers.

Despite the presence of many loyalists in the backcountry and the rather swift collapse of the military and civil power of the state in 1780, why did Lord Cornwallis and his subordinates fail to employ the loyalists more effectively to establish firm control over the interior of South Carolina? Several possible contributing factors have already been noted—the tactics of Banastre Tarleton and others, the inconsistencies in the policies formulated by Sir Henry Clinton on protections and paroles, as well as the requirement of military service from nonloyal elements—all of which may have alienated people otherwise disposed to live quietly under the king's government. Another possible explanation stems from the very objectives of British planners, to subdue the southern provinces one by one using earlier successes as springboards for later conquests. Did they overreach themselves, by committing too few troops, particularly cavalry, and too little logistical support to the loyalists on whom they counted so much to maintain control over the countryside? Given the other factors mentioned, it is not clear that a greater commitment of troops, arms, and supplies would have enabled the British to recover South Carolina permanently, but there is evidence that there was a shortage of arms and horses and that, especially after Cornwallis left the state, the British and their loyalist allies were usually outnumbered by the Americans. And despite their years of campaigning in America, British officers seemed genuinely baffled by their inability to control the open country between their fortified posts, a condition that their shortage of cavalry did little to correct.

Thus the evidence suggests that in 1775 many people in the backcountry were hostile to the policies of the Provincial Congress or uncommitted, and that in 1780 loyalists were probably a majority in certain limited areas of the backcountry; by the latter date, however, a majority of people in the backcountry were either pro-rebel or uncommitted, and as British actions and policies became better known, the latter group came to lean more toward the state government.

In Cornwallis's absence, renewed actions by rebel partisans that winter made it unsafe for loyalist militia to operate in the middle of the state at any distance from the main bases at Camden and Ninety Six. These conditions and the presence of Greene's army meant that, despite his own efforts and those of the more steadfast loyalists, Rawdon had no choice but to abandon the interior to the rebels.

Notes

1. Balfour to Cornwallis, June 7, CP, 30/11/2, 100; Cornwallis to Balfour, July 3, 17, Aug. 27, 1780, CP, 30/11/78, 3, 20, and 30/11/79, 39.
2. Cruger to Cornwallis, Sept. 1, 1780, CP, 30/11/64, 15.
3. Ibid.; Cornwallis to Cruger, Sept. 4, 1780, CP, 30/11/80, 15.
4. Cruger to Cornwallis, Sept. 1, Balfour to Cornwallis, Sept. 20, and Williamson to Balfour, Sept. 21, 1780, CP, 30/11/64, 5, 83, 95.
5. Henry Lee, writing many years after the war, declared that Williamson "had been as active in supporting the royal authority since the surrender of Lincoln, as he had been firm and influential in opposing it prior to that event," Lee, *Memoirs,* 452, but Lord Rawdon responded to Lee, June 24, 1813, that Williamson "had not taken up arms against you , nor was he intermeddling in politics, but quietly residing in the neighbourhood of Charleston" when American forces attempted to get Williamson to give up his parole later in the war, Lee, *Memoirs,* 618. Indeed, most authorities admit that Williamson attempted to maintain a scrupulous neutrality after he gave his parole, although it was said that after he retired to the lowcountry he actually gave Americans information on British troop dispositions around Charlestown.
6. Ferguson to Charles Ross, Aug. 19, CP, 30/11/64, 48; Cornwallis to Balfour, Sept. 27, CP, 30/11/80, 48A; and Cruger to Cornwallis, Nov. 23, Dec. 5, 15, 1780, CP, 30/11/4, 92, 143, 166.
7. Samuel Hammond, "Expedition to Long Canes, and a Mission to Williamson and Pickens," Johnson, *Traditions and Reminiscences,* 430–532; Cruger to Cornwallis, Dec. 9, 15, 1780, CP, 30/11/4, 149, 166.
8. Allen to Cornwallis, Dec. 29, and to Henry Haldane, Dec. 20, 1780, CP, 30/11/4, 211, 213.
9. Allen to Cornwallis, Dec. 31, 1780, CP, 30/11/4, 217. See Edward McCrady, *History of South Carolina in the Revolution, 1780–1783* (New York, 1902), 18–23, for Pickens's decision to give up his parole, and Robert D. Bass, *Ninety Six* (Lexington, S.C., 1978), 291–308, for the pressures applied to the two men late in the year.
10. Cornwallis to Balfour, Nov. 17, and to Rawdon. Nov. 17, 30, CP, 30/11/82, 55,57, 138, and Rawdon, Dec. 4, CP, 30/11/83, 11, and Rawdon to Cornwallis, Dec. 5, 1780, CP, 30/11/4, 140. Franklin and Mary Wickwire, *Cornwallis: The American Adventure* (Boston, 1970), 235–39, have an extended discussion of the problems of feeding the army at Winnsboro and the zealous and often arbitrary methods by which Stedman and his department succeeded in their task.
11. Journal of Enos Reeves, 1780–1782, VIII, 150–51, DUL; Cornwallis to Rawdon, Dec. 2, 3, 4, and to Tarleton, Dec. 4, 1780, CP, 30/11/83, 3, 9, 11, 13, and Rawdon to Cornwallis, Dec. 2, 1780, CP, 30/11/4, 135.

12. Cornwallis to Balfour, Dec. 5, 1780, CP, 30/11/83, 15, and Rawdon to Cornwallis, Dec. 3, 1781, CP, 30/11/66, 25.
13. The return of the Continental forces to the state and the maneuvering that led to the battle of Cowpens can be followed in detail in McCrady, *S.C. in the Revolution, 1780–1783*, 1–16, 26–30.
14. Ward, *War of the Revolution*, 11, 62; McCrady, *S.C. in the Revolution, 1780–1783*, 30–55.
15. On the strategy of Tarleton and Cornwallis, see Henry Haldane to McArthur, Jan. 2, Cornwallis to Tarleton, Jan. 5, to Leslie, Jan. 10, to Tarleton, Jan. 14, 16, 1781, CP, 30/11/84, 5, 15, 48, 63, 76.
16. Alexander Chesney, who acted as a scout for Tarleton and was present at the battle, described the action as "a total defeat by some dreadful bad management," "Journal," 21–22.
17. Cornwallis's reaction to Tarleton's defeat is in his letter to Rawdon, Jan. 21, 1781 , CP, 30/11/84, 78.
18. The movements of the two armies can be followed in Ward, *War of the Revolution*, II, 764–800.
19. Gray, "Observations," 10–11.
20. Chesney, "Journal," 22; Loyalist Transcripts, LII, 267–90; see the petitions of Robert Phillips, who was later exchanged, of John McKeown, who was eventually exchanged at Philadelphia and reached Charlestown seventeen months later, and of Daniel Huffman, who was exchanged in Virginia and joined Lord Cornwallis there only to be captured again at Yorktown, Clark, ed., *Loyalists*, I, 157–58.
21. McCrady, *S.C. in the Revolution, 1780–1783*, 105–11; Balfour to Clinton, Feb. 24, 1781, Leslie Letterbooks, #15503; Balfour to James Cassells, Jan. 25, 1781, #15497, Leslie Letterbooks.
22. Pickens reported that Dunlap had been shot by "one Cobb an overmountain man" at Gilbertown, to Greene, Apr. 4, 1781, "Letters to General Greene and others," *SCHGM* (1915), 101–3.
23. Gray, "Observations", 11–12.
24. These campaigns may be followed in the extended discussion by McCrady, *S.C. in the Revolution, 1780–1783*, 182–331, or, briefly, in Ward, *War of the Revolution*, II, 802–34.
25. Rawdon to Cornwallis, Apr. 26, 1781, Clinton Papers. Muster rolls for the period reveal that the Royalists lost six men killed or dead from wounds and a dozen taken as prisoners; perhaps another dozen deserted in the days just before the battle, Clark, ed., *Loyalists*, I, chap. 1, rolls for April–June 1781.
26. Rawdon to Cornwallis, Apr. 26, 1781, Clinton Papers.
27. For the surrender of Fort Watson, see Gibbes, *Documentary History*, III, 58, and the petition of Robert and James Bowman, Clark, ed., *Loyalists*, I, 156. Accounts of the evacuation of Camden are Greene to Samuel Huntington, May 14, 1781, Gibbes, *Documentary History*, III, 70–71, and Rawdon to Cornwallis, May 24, 1781, Clinton Papers.
28. Lee, *Memoirs*, 348–53; see the petition of Ester Nutterville re her husband's service at Fort Granby, Clark, ed., *Loyalists*, I, 234. William Moultrie claimed that very few loyalists "attended" Rawdon on his retreat, "the greater part" preferring to stay and "trust to the mercy of their countrymen," *Memoirs of the American Revolution* (New York, 1968 [orig. publ. New York, 1802]), II, 279.
29. Balfour to Sir James Wright, May 4, 1781, CP, *30/11/109*, 31; Lee, *Memoirs*, 359–60.
30. Pickens and Lee to Brown, May 31, 1781, Preston Davie Coll., SHC, and Lee, *Memoirs*, 360–71, give Lee's account of the siege, the surrender terms to Brown, and the arrangements for his safety. Major James Grierson, who commanded the smaller fort at Augusta that bore his name, had been shot by rebels after he had surrendered the fort, an event that made Pickens and Lee particularly concerned for Brown's safety, Sir James Wright to Germain, June 12, 1781, Georgia Historical Society, *Collections*, III, 354. See also Heard Robertson, "The Second British occupation of Augusta, 1780–1781," *GHQ*, LVIII (1974), 411–46.
31. The best modern study of the siege is Marvin L. Cann, "War in the Backcountry: The Siege of Ninety Six, May 22–June 19, 1781," *SCHM* (1971), 1–14, which concludes that the failure to cut the fort off from its water supply prevented an early surrender. See also Ward, *War of the Revolution*, II, 816–22, and McCrady, *S.C. in the Revolution, 1780–1783*, 281–84, for discussions of the issue.
32. Cruger gave the strength of the garrison, to Rawdon, June 3, 1781, CP, *30/11/6*, 213; and C[harles] Stedman, *The History of the Origin, Progress, and Termination of the American War*, 2 vols. (New York, 1969 [orig. publ. London, 1794]), II, 366, tells of the determination of King's regiment, which, however, could have numbered no more than 125 at the time. Andrew Pickens noted early in May that General Robert Cunningham and some loyalist militia were camped near the fort and that the remnants of Dunlap's dragoons were nearby, but Cunningham was not present at the siege. Several men from Cotton's regiment, notably his second in command, John Hamilton, were in the garrison, *Canadian Claims*, 73, 525.
33. Cruger to Rawdon, May 31, 1781, CP, 30/11/6, 212. Phillips's command included a dozen men each from his and Henry Rugeley's regiments of 1780, but most do not seem to have served before they marched with Rawdon, Clark, ed. *Loyalists*, I, 147–48, 155–68; see also petition of Captain James Sharp, ibid.,

156. Rawdon dealt with some of the problems of his march in his letter to Henry Lee, June 24, 1813, Lee, *Memoirs*, 618.
34. Lee, *Memoirs*, 374, recounts the arrival of Rawdon's message; Cann, "War in the Backcountry," 10–11.
35. Cruger to Greene, June 19, 1781, Preston Davie Coll.; Cann, "War in the Backcountry," 11–12; Howard H. Peckham, ed., *The Toll of Independence: En*gagements & *Battle Casualties of the American Revolution* (Chicago, 1974), 87.
36. Rawdon to Cornwallis, Aug. 2, 1781, CP, 30/11/6, 347.
37. Rawdon to Cornwallis, June 5, Aug. 2, 1781, CP, 30/11/7,174, 30/11/6, 347; Chesney, "Journal," 24–25.
38. Pickens to Greene, July 10, 1781, Greene Papers, CL (Waring photostats, CUL). The figure on the number deciding to leave is drawn from the pay records for the regiments marked "Came to Orangeburg with Colonel Cruger at the Evacuation of Ninety Six," or similar heading, T50/2,5, or Clark, ed., *Loyalists*, I, 229–96, 323–30.
39. Petition of Samuel Wilson, et al., Clark, ed., *Loyalists*, I, 295; Pickens to Greene, July 25, 1781, Greene Papers, CL (Waring photostats); Robert Anderson to John McCarter, Aug. 31, 1781, Court of Common Pleas, Judgment Rolls, 1788, 290Al, SCAH. See also *Canadian Claims*, 185, for testimony that the rebels gave Henry Siteman a pass to bring his wife and six children into the British lines in August.
40. These activities may be followed in McCrady, *S.C. in the Revolution, 1780–1783*, II, 134–36, 286–87, 317–43; and Clark, ed., *Loyalists*, I, 194.
41. Journals of Enos Reeves, 1780–82, VIII, 150–151, DUL.
42. Ward, *War of the Revolution*, II, 823–37; Stewart to Cornwallis, Sept. 26, 1781, CP, 30/11/6, 399.
43. Militia pay records were compared for 1780–82. Such comparisons cannot be perfect; ninety-three of the Ninety Six militia had died in 1780 as had thirty-seven of Fisher's men; others may have actually been residents of North Carolina and served later in their militia. See Clark, ed., *Loyalists*, I, 197–342.

Part III

A WAR OF ALL THE PEOPLE, 1780–1782

The unifying theme of this part of the loyalist story is the suffering and disruption of the lives of people on both sides of the struggle, but especially those who adhered to the British cause, from 1780 until the end of the war.

Charlestown and its immediate vicinity was the one part of South Carolina over which the British retained control until they withdrew completely from the state at the end of 1782. Their control of the state as a whole was so tenuous, however, that no experiment with civil government was possible, and the commandant ran the city, assisted by an appointed Board of Police and several commissions whose members were returning loyalists or had taken the British oath. Although prices became more stable and there were profits to be made from supplying the garrison, there was much discontent among rebel sympathizers, which Nisbet Balfour attempted to quell by shipping a number of their leaders off to exile in St. Augustine.

The Revolution in South Carolina, particularly in the interior, was truly a civil war in which people of all ages and both sexes were involved. The lives of all were touched in some fashion, either through direct participation in military action or because the insatiable appetites of the contending forces for grain and livestock were a constant drain on the rural economy. The wanton disregard for life and property threatened to destroy the civilizing influences that made life worthwhile—family, home, and the few precious possessions beyond those needed for mere survival. The stage for this struggle had been set before the war by the tensions that grew up between settled planter and new immigrant, farmer and Indian trader, Regulator and moderator, or rival ethnic and religious groups. To these could be added the disputes natural to any frontier—over land titles, the ownership of cattle or ferry and mill sites, or family feuds transplanted from Virginia or Pennsylvania. After the war began, rebels had hounded some loyalists into exile, or forced them to take oaths or perform service against their wishes; then the British took control of the backcountry and tried to force residents to resume their allegiance; then they lost control, and many loyalists abandoned their homes. Under such circumstances, backcountry families might be forced as many as four or five times to make choices between the contending sides.

Although expelled from the backcountry, the loyalist men were liable for military service, and they were employed in helping to secure the defense perimeter around Charlestown, to forage for supplies, and to conduct raids to seize the slaves of rebels to compensate for their own losses. The recognized loyalist militia was better led and equipped for this kind of service and gave a good account of itself.

British withdrawal from the backcountry and the continuing civil conflict brought hundreds of loyalist men, women, and children from the interior to the sea islands near Charlestown. There they existed for nearly eighteen months on the rations and allowances provided by military authorities, and the women especially suffered severely from disease and privation, as well as the doubts and fears of an uncertain future.

Chapter Eleven

Occupied Charlestown

Buildings are rising from the ashes of that part of town burnt two years ago...ruins repaired and hasty houses for the immediate habitation and accommodation of the numerous merchants form the present prospect of the town.

—William Bull, February 1781

The Charlestown that surrendered to Sir Henry Clinton was a rebel city in which the openly loyalist or pro-British proportion of its population had been small. Under the terms of the capitulation the local people who had served in the rebel militia were paroled to their homes, and "all other persons now in town, not described [in the military articles], are notwithstanding, understood to be prisoners on parole." Thus the civilians in the city were given the same terms as the militia taken in arms; while they observed their paroles, they were nor to be "molested in their property by the British troops."[1]

Although the rebels had largely purged the city of its loyalist element, hundreds of inhabitants came forward after the capitulation to take the oath of allegiance to the king. There were good reasons for residents of the city to submit, if grudgingly, to British rule. The American cause in the Southern states was in severe straits, and there was little encouraging news from the north. The British required only that no overt aid be given by parolees to persons in rebellion, and American military forces were so far from the city as to preclude such help. And the less ardent rebels, especially business and professional men, could appreciate the reopening of the port, a return to sterling instead of rebel paper currency, and a stable and orderly climate for making money.[2]

The people who ran occupied Charlestown were drawn from two elements in the population, the loyalists and the protectionists. The protectionists were of two kinds: reluctant rebels, persons whose sympathies probably had lain with the British but who had by some means been able to remain in the state during the American Period; and reluctant Tories, persons who were rebels at heart but who figured after Lincoln's surrender that their cause was lost and the time had come to make the best terms possible. These distinctions among the protectionists, although difficult for later generations to appreciate, were very real to their rebel and loyalist contemporaries. In many cases, these perceptions will have an important bearing on the treatment accorded to protectionists by the triumphant rebels after the war.[3]

The reluctant Tories made up a substantial majority of protectionists; they had made at least nominal contributions of money and service to the rebel cause and, almost without exception, had avoided suspicion of pro-British sympathies during the American Period. Principally artisans and small merchants, they now chose to take protection from the British authorities in order to pursue their trades and businesses without interference. Having done the minimum required of them, they generally made no direct contributions to further the British cause. The merchant Aaron Loocock had contributed a good deal of money and service to the rebel cause; now after taking British protection and accepting appointment to the street commission, he sailed for England where he spent the remainder of the war. Among the more conspicuous of these protectionists were Rawlins Lowndes, the conservative revolutionary and president of the state in 1778, Colonel Charles Pinckney, Major Daniel Horry, and Arthur Middleton. The British considered these men their prize converts, but none took any overt part for the occupying authority.[4]

The reluctant rebels, a minority among the protectionists, had been suspected during the American Period of harboring British sympathies, for which they had spent time in jail or paid fines in times of crisis. Virtually all had come into the country after 1760, usually from Scotland or Ireland; although they had enjoyed some economic success, they had remained outside the circle of families and connections that had dominated the social and political life of the city. A few examples will illustrate why the reluctant rebels merited the suspicions in which they were held by the more steadfast on both sides of the conflict, but it is important to examine them because of the important roles some played during the occupation.

Among the more interesting of the protectionists who had been reluctant rebels were Robert Williams, a prominent attorney, and John Hopton, a partner in a substantial mercantile house, both of whom had left for England in 1777 in order to avoid taking the oath of abjuration. In the following year they had accompanied the Carlisle peace commission to New York and there secured permission to sail to Charlestown under a flag of truce on the grounds that they needed to look after property there. When they landed they were greeted by a hostile crowd and ordered to appear before the General Assembly where, after agreeing to take the oath of abjuration, they were granted permission to stay. Both were forced to serve in the ranks of the rebel militia while Charlestown was under siege, but both men came quickly forward to renew their allegiance to the Crown after the surrender. Williams later claimed that he was the author of the congratulatory address to Clinton and Arbuthnot.[5]

Among the reluctant rebels who did not leave the state were Jacob Valk, a Dutchman who as a merchant, broker, and auctioneer had aggressively acquired thousands of acres in the backcountry for speculation during the war; Zephaniah Kingsley, a Quaker merchant with property in Charlestown and Beaufort, who had been jailed three times before consenting to take the oath of abjuration; and Thomas Phepoe, the attorney already noted as a defender of persons charged with sedition against the state.[6]

Distinct from the protectionists, the loyalists in occupied Charlestown were those who returned in 1780 and 1781 from their various residences in exile. They also fall into rather distinct groups based, not on their degree of commitment to the British cause, but on where by chance or choice they had spent the time awaiting the recovery of the province. One group consisted of persons who had spent their period of exile in East Florida, the British West Indies, the Dutch island of St. Eustatius, or New York. After British troops conquered coastal Georgia some of these exiles sailed for Savannah while others were able to join the Clinton expedition on the South Carolina coast before Charlestown came under siege. As a result, a small number of returning loyalists were on hand when the city surrendered. First to arrive were James Simpson, the former attorney general who came with Clinton from New York; John Tunno, a merchant, and James Weir, a tavern keeper, who had gone from England to Savannah where they were joined by Alexander Wright, a son of Georgia's royal governor, and Thomas Creighton, a baker; James Begbie, a shipwright from St. Augustine; and the merchant Robert William Powell, whose travels in exile had taken him to St. Eustatius, St. Augustine, and Savannah.[7]

Months passed before the news of Charlestown's capitulation reached Great Britain and the exiles there were able to arrange their affairs and to find passage back to South Carolina. Not until September 9 did the loyalist press announce that the physician Dr. Alexander Baron, "compelled to leave this country during the late season of anarchy and misrule," had returned from England; at intervals over the next year the exiles returned more or less willingly to the province. On one day in February 1781, the papers announced that the venerable Lieutenant Governor William Bull and Sir Egerton Leigh had arrived, the first of the Crown officers to return from England. The surviving records of the returning exiles leave the reader with the sense that they came out of necessity rather than from any real enthusiasm for resuming life in Carolina. The natives like Bull, James Brisbane, John Champneys, and Henry Peronneau probably hoped to pick up the threads of their lives, but most of those whom the rebels had forced into exile were natives of Great Britain, not America. Certainly there could have been no great zeal on the part of most royal officials to come out again, but they were ordered by the Colonial Office to do so or forfeit their appointments, which most counted on as the means to higher places in the civil service, perhaps in England. Thirteen months elapsed between the fall of Charlestown and the time when Thomas Skottowe, the secretary of the province, returned to the city, and four more months passed before the vice admiralty judge Edward Savage reached his post.[8]

This explanation of the divisions within the protectionists and the loyalists has been necessary to lay the basis for examining the structure of authority during the occupation. When the Board of Police was set up, Lord Cornwallis chose its first members from the loyalists present at the capitulation—James Simpson, Robert William Powell, and Alexander Wright. When, in turn, the board chose the personnel of the commissions charged with providing services to the city, it appointed the more aggressive protectionists and a few of the early arrivals among the loyalist exiles to fill the positions. From the protectionists who had been reluctant rebels the board chose Robert Williams to be chairman of the currency commission; named John Hopton to seats on three commissions, and Zephaniah Kingsley, Robert Philp, Charles Atkins, and George Cooke to two apiece; and it filled the remaining vacancies with the more moderate protectionists. Only the three-man commission on unclaimed slaves contained a majority of loyalists. When a Charlestown militia regiment was formed, Robert William Powell was appointed colonel and Gideon Dupont, Jr., lieutenant colonel, but most of the remaining officers were drawn from the protectionists. Thus because most of the leading loyalists of the city had been expelled by the rebels and could not return until well after the capitulation, most positions of responsibility were held by protectionists and a few of the early arrivals among the loyalists. The limited opportunities for loyalists to serve would be further restricted when the refugees poured in from the backcountry during the summer of 1781, for the militia colonels who had abandoned their homes in the interior had a greater need for government maintenance than did the loyalists in the city.

An analysis of 120 persons from Charlestown and its immediate vicinity who committed loyal acts during the occupation reveals that there were slightly more protectionists than loyalists among them. The protectionists were in the majority among merchants, artisans, and small businessmen, particularly the tavern keepers, and equal to the loyalists among the planters. Royal officials made up the largest single group of loyalists, although a substantial number of merchants and professional men were included among them.

That many South Carolinians accommodated their actions to the changing political conditions during the war is clear, but no one was able to adapt his public posture to the return of British rule with the facility displayed by John Wells, Jr. Better documented than most because of his occupation as journalist and printer, the Wells case is worth examining for the light it sheds on the general question of allegiance in the Revolution.

When the British had occupied New York City and Philadelphia they had given support to local newspapers that were willing to present official news and documents. When Sir Henry Clinton's army entered Charlestown in May 1780, one of the civilians accompanying the expedition was James Robertson, a veteran editor of newspapers in New York and Connecticut who had printed the *Royal American Gazette* in New York and the short-lived *Royal Pennsylvania Gazette* in occupied Philadelphia. Within weeks of the capitulation of Charlestown the *Royal South Carolina Gazette*," printed by Robertson, McDonald and Cameron, 20 Broad St.," made its appearance and was published as a semiweekly throughout most of the rest of the occupation.[9]

Prerevolutionary Charlestown had boasted three newspapers, printed respectively by Peter Timothy, Robert Wells, and Charles Crouch. In the colony's quarrel with Britain in the 1760s, Timothy became a militant supporter of American rights in his personal as well as his journalistic contributions; a leader in the movement for independence and a vigorous supporter of the state government, he changed the name of his paper to *Gazette of the State of South Carolina*, and continued to publish it until after Clinton's army had landed on the coast; exiled to St. Augustine as a dangerous incendiary, he did not survive the war. Crouch, also a supporter of American rights, suspended the publication of his *Country Journal* in 1775 and died shortly thereafter; his widow tried to continue it as the *Charlestown Gazette* for several months during the war, but the paper ceased publication early in 1780.[10]

When Robert Wells left South Carolina in 1775, he left his oldest son, John Wells, Jr., in charge of his *American General Gazette*. But John, much to the chagrin of his family, had come to sympathize with the American rights cause and supported independence when that step was taken. He expressed his political sentiments to Henry Laurens late in 1777, declaring that

> the part I have taken in the present contest has been decided, & no future event can counteract it. I have ever thought an inconsistent and dubious character a most contemptible one, and while I have health & vigour my utmost exertions will never be wanting in the support of the cause of this my country. You know the difficulties I have had to encounter. Connected by friendship & even by blood to several who are now our public enemies, I have been frequently much embarrassed.

He resumed publication of the paper after Clinton and Parker left the coast, in 1776, and early in the following year the masthead of the paper was changed from "Printed by R. Wells & Son" to "Printed by John Wells, Jr." His younger sister, Louisa, thoroughly disgusted with his course, left with her uncle's family to join her father and mother in England the next spring. John continued to publish the *American General Gazette* until shortly before Charlestown came under siege.[11]

Soon after the British occupation began, the political sentiments of John Wells, Jr., underwent a marvelous transformation. Barely two months after the surrender of the city and just four weeks after the first appearance of Robertson's paper, the *American General Gazette* quietly resumed publication, its editor announcing that he was prepared to collect the debts due his father. Exactly what transpired during the siege and after the capitulation to enable John, Jr., to switch sides is not clear, but it would not be amiss to suspect that the returning loyalists, particularly James Simpson, may have helped to bring about the change. It will be recalled that Simpson interviewed a number of local people after the capitulation, and because of Robert Wells's long residence and close ties with the Scots community and royal officials his son may have had an opportunity to ingratiate himself with British civil and military leaders.[12]

Meanwhile, when the good news reached London that Charlestown had been recovered, Robert Wells dispatched his younger son, William Charles, to South Carolina to act as his attorney in the process of recovering his property. William Charles landed in Charlestown in mid-January 1781 prepared to find the family businesses in ruins and John, Jr., perhaps prosecuted as a rebel. Instead, he found his older brother in "good health, and an officer in a Company of Militia clothed in uniforms and well disciplined, consequently a good loyalist." Reporting also that "fathers affairs...., are in a better situation than I expected... "he soon advertised that he was prepared to accept payment of the debts due Robert Wells, "late of this place, Printer and Bookseller." The arrival of William Charles and the loyal behavior of John, Jr., apparently accounted for further changes in the family fortunes, for on February 21 the *American General Gazette* announced that after March 1 it would be known as the *Royal Gazette,* "Printed by R. Wells & Son, Printers to the King's Most Excellent Majesty" The brothers continued to publish the paper and operate the printing and stationery business until John joined his father in England in the spring of 1782, leaving to William Charles the task of closing down their enterprises and removing their press to East Florida before the British officially evacuated the province late in that year.[13]

The experience of the Wells family illustrates how some loyalists in the lowcountry were able to adapt to the changing circumstances of the war. The long record of stubborn loyalty of the father, the political resilience of the son—however sincere his zeal for independence was at the time he expressed his sentiments to Henry Laurens—and influence in high places combined to preserve the family business despite the overthrow and later restoration of British rule. Of course, the family's property and standing suffered total eclipse when the Americans reclaimed the state for good.

To the inhabitants of Charlestown the return of royal rule offered certain advantages that, given the weakness of the rebel cause at the moment, at first made the occupation somewhat more palatable than it might have been. The surrender of the town meant that an American armed camp had been replaced by a British armed camp, a circumstance that meant that there was money to be made under the restored regime. At the very least the expenditures for supplying and housing the British military forces would replace any American military expenditures on which the business community had come to rely. Further, even businessmen who were sympathetic to the rebel cause could find some solace in the fact that compensation received from British sources would be in sterling money rather than in the virtually worthless state or Continental paper currency. Thus the occupation meant an increased stimulation of wartime business for the community.

The renting and leasing of space to the troops and to the civil and military authorities provided an early and regular source of income to many of the city's residents. At one time or another during the occupation, British authorities used parts or all of over 100 commercial buildings and private residences in the town as "barracks," to quarter British and German officers and men, and in the twenty-one months after the fall of the city they disbursed over £5,500 for this purpose. In addition, leases were arranged on thirteen buildings, eight of them on the bay, by the Commissary General's Department for periods ranging from six to thirty months, and for two wharves on the bay by the Quartermaster General's Department for twelve to twenty months. The owners, who included one loyalist and a number of protectionists, were paid £955. Six buildings were leased for twenty-one months and two others for shorter periods for use as military hospitals, for which their owners received £1,118. Property used as offices and for storage by the intendant general, the engineers, the artillery, the commodore of the port, and the Commissary of Naval Prisoners was supplied by loyalists John Hopton and Alexander Rose and several protectionists. Not all the rents were paid to protectionists or loyalists; the widow of the rebel Jacob Motte received nearly £450 in rent for the use of her house at 94 King Street by Commandants Patterson and Balfour; this was an unusual case, however, for authorities preferred to lease property from loyal subjects under license. The total expended for the use of these facilities during the first twenty-one months of the occupation was £10,700.[14]

The pay of soldiers and sailors expended in the city, supplemented later in the occupation by allowances to the refugees, meant a steady source of business for the taverns and shops that purveyed certain edibles and goods, while the purchases by the Commissary and Quartermaster departments provided a further stimulus to business. Although all of this spending might have been inflationary, it is a commentary on the stability of sterling in contrast to rebel paper money that William Bull noted upon his return to the city early in 1781 that local prices had barely doubled from prewar levels—certainly an improvement over the runaway inflation experienced by residents during the American Period. During the later stages of the occupation, however, many articles became scare and prices rose sharply.[15]

The reopening of the port after the long siege was also a boon to Charlestown's business community. The city bustled with commercial activity, one resident noting that virtually all the stores and shops "thro Broad Street along King Street" were open; there was "a great plenty of all kinds of goods," although he commented further that these wares "sell cheap" at auction to the retailers who sold them "very dear" in their shops. Bull remarked that "buildings are rising from the ashes" in the area leveled by the great fire in 1778, many of them "hasty houses" to accommodate the "numerous merchants" involved in trade, that there were many commercial vessels in the harbor, and that business was "brisk and goods plenty."[16]

Although some of the benefits of a sound currency and spending by the occupying forces must have spilled over to rebel sympathizers, during the first year of the occupation British authorities adopted policies designed to restrict economic activity to those willing to declare their allegiance to the Crown. The privilege of exporting commodities was limited to those who obtained a license from the intendant general of police and who had taken the oath; likewise, the artisans of the city were led to understand that only those who returned to their allegiance might continue to practice their trades.[17]

During the weeks that Sir Henry Clinton remained in the town after the surrender he set up certain apparatus for its government. Because of Charlestown's importance as a base for supplying the army in the interior and as a center for communicating with the main base in New York and with the home islands and other British possessions, control was placed in the hands of the military authorities. Since Cornwallis was usually with the troops in the interior, the actual oversight of the town lay with the commandants, briefly with James Patterson, and then for nearly two years with the redoubtable Nisbet Balfour. As Cornwallis came to rely more and more on Balfour to supply the army and to maintain communications with interior posts and officials outside South Carolina, Balfour in turn deferred to James Simpson and the Board of Police to carry out the regulations for determining who should enjoy the commercial benefits of the port and the privilege of carrying on trades and professions.[18]

The Board of Police acted as a court of common pleas and as an advisory body to the commandant. Its principal business as a court was to adjudicate claims for debt between private citizens; it first chose arbitrators to settle the claims and then heard appeals from their decisions. Originally the board had jurisdiction only over contracts made after the capitulation of the city, but in the spring of 1781 Balfour, with Cornwallis's approval, extended its jurisdiction to matters in dispute prior to the occupation. In the early stages of its work the board met monthly to hear cases, remaining in session until its business was finished, and it then convened again later in the same month to hear the awards of the arbitrators. According to Simpson, the board heard an average of over 100 cases a month during the last half of 1780. It generally upheld the awards of its arbitrators and, although many small businessmen withheld payments of their obligations to merchants and shippers as long as they could, they rarely let suits by their creditors "proceed to an execution." The board also engaged in price-fixing in an attempt to reduce the effect of shortages of flour, salt, and other necessary commodities, and on occasion it prosecuted those who took advantage of the shortages by withholding goods to wait for higher prices.[19]

In an effort to aid the Board of Police in dealing with the problems caused by the rapid depreciation of the state's currency during the American Period, Balfour named a commission of twelve men to study the relative worth of the paper money in terms of sterling at various times since 1777. The commission secured evidence of prices charged for vital commodities in terms of gold and silver and, from this data, constructed a table of depreciation to guide the board in determining the value of sums in dispute between litigants. As in prewar times, other commissions were chosen to deal with such city problems as fire protection and care of the streets and to oversee the market.[20]

George McCowen has concluded that the men who served on the Board of Police were generally of high caliber and that their extensive legal and business experience served them well in handling its work. When Simpson was called back to New York by Clinton, he was replaced as intendant general early in 1781 by the newly returned William Bull, and John Harris Cruger later succeeded Alexander Innes as military representative. Two of the original appointees, Robert William Powell and Alexander Wright, served throughout the occupation. As the former Crown officers returned from England, the membership of the board was increased to make use of their services, but once the accumulation of cases from the American Period was settled, the board met less frequently than in the first months of the occupation.[21]

To emphasize the degree to which economic stability was restored to Charlestown, and the good qualifications of the intendants who ran the town, can obscure the difficulty British authorities faced in attempting to transform a rebel stronghold into one that calmly accepted the return of British rule. British trade and British sterling may have been attractive to commercial interests in the town, but the restrictions the authorities placed on trade were irksome at best. Despite the compensation for the use, or abuse, of their property, many of the city's residents would have preferred that troops not be quartered among them. An uneasy calm settled over the city in the first weeks after the surrender, but tension began to mount when Horatio Gates's army entered the state in midsummer. Although nothing like a "second revolution" was possible in the occupied capital, British officers felt that there had been conspiracies afoot among the paroled rebel leaders in the town that must be stamped out.

Therefore, in late August, after Cornwallis's victory at Camden, twenty-nine rebel leaders were rounded up and conveyed to a ship in the harbor that carried them off a few days later to exile in St. Augustine. Included in the group were Lieutenant Governor Christopher Gadsden and other state officials and a number of prominent rebel business and professional men whom Cornwallis charged with communicating with the enemy and with holding frequent meetings of a conspiratorial nature. Shortly thereafter, two other groups were sent to join them; altogether, sixty-five of the more prominent rebels were sent to St. Augustine where they remained until exchanged in the summer of 1781. They were not permitted to return to Charlestown, however, and many spent extended periods in Philadelphia where their wives and children, expelled from South Carolina, were reunited with them.[22]

Thus in the first year of the occupation British authorities attempted with mixed success to transform the political climate from one of scarcely veiled hostility to one of grudging acceptance of the results of the surrender of the town. Such success as these efforts achieved occurred in the first months when American military fortunes were at their worst, and because certain economic benefits could be expected from the reopening of trade. However, these apparent advantages that the British enjoyed early in the occupation were soon offset by resentment over the treatment accorded rebel leaders and the economic pressure brought to bear on local residents to conform to British policies or suffer loss of income from trades and professions. Although the policies originated with British officials, they were carried out in large measure by collaborators, the protectionists, and by enemies of long standing, the returning loyalists. And the presence of British and German troops and the British navy and the return of royal officials provided additional sources of grievance. Even though most of the state would soon be recovered by American arms, rebel sympathizers in and near Charlestown would experience further suffering as royal troops fell back into the defense perimeter and the refugee loyalists poured in from the backcountry, creating new demand for foodstuffs already in short supply, and thus driving prices higher and higher in the latter stages of the occupation.

Notes

1. The best modern study of life in occupied Charlestown is George S. McCowen, Jr., *The British Occupation of Charleston, 1780–1782* (Columbia, S.C, 1972). It is especially useful for understanding the application of British policy toward the local population, the work of the Board of Police, and the effect of the occupation on local institutions.
2. Sir Henry Clinton was correct to suspect the motives of many who took the oath at this time, for of those

who signed, fewer than one in five ever committed another "loyal" act-signed an address, accepted a position, or performed any kind of military service for the British, CP, 30/11/107, 1–33. The petition was dated May 10 and signed by about 200 persons, Leslie Letterbooks, #7626.
3. The discussion that follows is based on an analysis of persons, both loyalists and protectionists, who committed loyal acts during the period of British occupation. It is drawn from Loyalist Transcripts, CP, CEP, and the two loyalist newspapers. Specific citations will be given for the individual examples that follow.
4. Loocock contributed important service as a member of the General Committee and of the Provincial Congress in 1775–76, George C. Rogers, Jr., *Evolution of a Federalist: William Laughton Smith of Charleston* (Columbia, S.C., 1962), 101–2; Carl Vipperman, *The Rise of Rawlins Lowndes, 1721–1800* (Columbia, S.C., 1978). 227–30; petitions of various dates, September-December 1780, in James Simpson to William Knox, Dec. 31, 1780, Bancroft Coll., NYPL.
5. Loyalist Transcripts, LN, 29–84, 509–30; *South Carolina and American General Gazette* (Charlestown), Aug. 23, Sept. 27, 1780; and Charleston, *City Directory*. 1782 (Charleston, n.d.).
6. For Phepoe, see *Canadian Claims*, 1245; Loyalist Transcripts, LIII, 5–31; Chesney, " Journal," 61; *House Journals, 1776–1780*, 186, 216, 248, 250, 281; and *House Journals, 1787–1788*, 93; Valk's numerous property transactions may be traced in CEP, Deeds, and Plats, particularly for 1773–75, and *Gazette of the State of South Carolina* (Charlestown), Sept. 16, 1778, and July 9, 1779; and Kingsley is found in Loyalist Transcripts, LII, 472–504, CEP, and *South Carolina and American General Gazette*, Sept. 27, 1780.
7. Loyalist Transcripts, LIV, 205–55; LV, 526–33, 539–47; LVI, 284–93, 360–77; LVII, 418–38; *South Carolina and American General Gazette*, Sept. 9, 1780, Feb. 7, 1781.
8. *Royal Gazette* (Charlestown), June 6, Oct. 17, 1781.
9. Little is known about the printers of the *Royal South Carolina Gazette*. Robertson made brief mention of commanding a militia company in Charlestown, Egerton, ed., *Royal Commission*, 165–66; his association with other newspapers is in Clarence S. Brigham, comp., *History and Bibliography* of *American Newspapers, 1690–1820*, 2 vols. (Worcester, Mass., 1947), II, 1035–36, who has found no other press connections for Robertson's partners (who are listed as Alexander Cameron and Donald McDonald). There are large gaps in the extant files of the *Royal South Carolina* Gazette.
10. Hennig Cohen, *The South Carolina Gazette, 1732–1775* (Columbia, S.C., 1953), 3–12; McCowen, *British Occupation, 153.*
11. *South Carolina and American General Gazette*, Nov. 20, 1777; John Wells, Jr., to Laurens, Nov. 28, 1777, Simms Coll.
12. Charlestown artisans Patrick Hinds and Thomas Elfe testified in 1783 that they had signed the loyal addresses to Clinton and to Cornwallis only because they were "severely threatened" by John Wells, Jr., *House Journals*, 1783–1784, 16, 46; Simpson to Clinton, May 15, 1780, "James Simpson's Reports on the Carolina Loyalists, 1779–1780," ed. Alan S. Brown, *JSH, XXI* (1955), 513–19.
13. William Charles Wells to James Currie, Mar. 18, 1781, *SCHGM, XXVI* (1925), 41–44; *South Carolina and American General Gazette*, Feb. 21, 1781; *Royal Gazette*, Mar. 10, 1781, May 4, 1782; Loyalist Transcripts, LVII, 351–66; Wells, *Journal,* 84–96.
14. BHP, #9970.
15. William Burrows to an unnamed correspondent, Feb. 21, 1781, CP, 30/11/105, 4; Bull to Hillsborough, Feb. 16, 1781, S.C. Records in the P.R.O., XXXVI, 104.
16. William Burrows to an unnamed correspondent, Feb. 21, 1781, CP, 30/11/105, 4.
17. See McCowen, *British Occupation*, 86–90, for a discussion of British trade regulations; Richard Walsh, *Charleston's Sons of Liberty: A Study of the Artisans, 1763–1789* (Columbia, S.C., 1959), 93–94, 97–98.
18. Unless otherwise noted, material in this chapter on the commandants and the Board of Police is based on the discussion in McCowen, *British Occupation*, 13–42.
19. Simpson to William Knox, Dec. 31, 1780, Bancroft Coll., NYPL. Based on a complaint filed by the Commissioners of the Market, one Richard Ellis was convicted by the Board of Police of "forestalling cattle driven to the Charlestown market," and sentenced to two months in jail and forfeiture of the profits of the transaction, *Royal Gazette*, May 12, 1781.
20. McCowen, *British Occupation*, 16–23.
21. The work of the Commission on Depreciated Currency can be followed in CP, 30/11/108, 1–34. One severe problem faced by the returning loyalists was that the rebel government had permitted persons indebted to absentees (the exiles) to repay the obligations by depositing state currency in the state treasury, often at a fraction of their sterling value; at the same time the loyalists' creditors in Britain were pressing for payment of their obligations in sterling. See the petition of 150 inhabitants, Feb. 5, 1781, Clinton Papers.
22. McCrady, *S.C. in the Revolution, 1775–1780,* 715–26; McCowen, *British Occupation,* 58–63.

Chapter Twelve

Loyalists and Rebels: the Civil War

The Whigs and Tories pursue one another with the most relentless fury, killing and destroying each other wherever they meet;... The great bodies of militia chat have been in service this year employed against the enemy, and in quelling the Tories have almost laid waste the country.

—Nathanael Greene, December 1780

In the decades before 1780 people living in the interior of South Carolina had suffered in greater or less degree through a series of experiences that frequently strained the basis for social order. First came the struggle to develop homes in the wilderness, the terrors of Indian war, the raids of bandit gangs, and the retaliatory campaigns and crude justice meted out by the Regulators. Then, in the relative calm that followed the easing of Regulator tensions, came the strangers from the lowcountry in 1775 with their pleas to resist the unwise policies of the English ministry, and once again parts of the frontier were in turmoil, this time between the advocates of American rights and those who stood for the Crown or wished to be left alone. The triumph of the Whigs and the crushing of the Cherokees in 1776 brought a measure of stability to the state, a period of quiet created in part by purging the lowcountry of royal officials and sympathizers and the backcountry of some of its more committed loyalists. Into this period of quiet came the British army, briefly in 1779 as detachments that occupied Augusta and swept to the gates of Charlestown, but which in the following year returned in full force, capturing the city, eliminating the Continental army, and spreading over the state. Once more a brief period of calm settled over the area as rebel leaders gave up or fled into neighboring states.

The civil war in South Carolina began after the fall of Charlestown and broke into full flame during the year in which the British held all or most of the backcountry; it was reduced in scope if not in intensity during the year or more that they held onto Charlestown and its environs; and it nearly flickered out when they finally left the state at the end of 1782, although a few sparks flared up briefly after the war. With the peace came the first writings about what today are known as "atrocities" committed by the British and their loyalist minions against the patriots—of "bloody Tarleton," "Bloody Bill" Cunningham, and the execution of Isaac Hayne; this writing was drawn from American sources by American authors in the flush of the triumph of the American cause. No amount of fresh writing can erase the stain of Tarleton or Cunningham or the martyrdom of Hayne; but British and loyalist sources do provide the materials for a more balanced view of the civil strife of the period, showing that the outrages against life and property were not instigated by one side alone, and that loyalists suffered indignities, injury, and death at the hands of rebels.

When Nathanael Greene first entered South Carolina as the newly appointed commander of the southern Continental army, he faced the difficult problems of reorganizing a beaten army and of acquainting himself with unfamiliar people and surroundings. What struck him most was the devastation of the people and the countryside by the civil war then raging in the state. Six months later, having campaigned across North Carolina and into Virginia, fought a battle against Cornwallis at Guilford Court House and another against Rawdon in South Carolina, he found himself before Ninety Six facing complaints from local civilians that a part of Colonel LeRoy Hammond's regiment under his command " plunders without mercy and murders the defenseless people just on private peak [sic], prejudice, or personal resentment."[1]

These selections from Greene's many comments serve as an introduction to the nature of the civil war in South Carolina, a war that observers from both armies described most frequently by the adjective "savage." Greene's observations also point up the fact that both sides carried on the war in "savage" fashion, and that although more prevalent in certain areas, the condition was general throughout the interior and occasionally was carried to the gates of Charlestown itself.

The methods employed by certain British and loyalist officers in handling the conquest of the interior and suppressing the "Second Revolution"—Tarleton's massacre of Buford's troops, the burning of Hill's ironworks and other private property by Christian Huck, the hanging of several individuals who had rejoined the Americans after serving in the loyal militia, and the vengeance exacted by Thomas Brown on his prisoners at Augusta—fixed the character of the war in the state. It is not certain how much direct information Whig officers and men had about each of these events, but the British reputation for pillaging, giving no quarter in battle, and for mistreating prisoners was well established by the end of the summer of 1780.

Except for a few isolated incidents, the rebels could not be charged with pillaging Tory property or mistreating prisoners during this period because they were in no position to do so. Kings Mountain changed all that, although it took awhile for the reports of the loyalists who participated in the battle and the subsequent march as prisoners to North Carolina to filter back to Cornwallis's headquarters. The hanging of Ambrose Mills and others at Gilbertown, and the mistreatment of prisoners along the route of march infuriated Cornwallis and Balfour, and they used these incidents as part of the rationale for transferring some of the Continental prisoners to prison ships in Charlestown harbor in the following spring.[2]

Other incidents occurred that fall in the area between Camden and Georgetown. In December Whigs gained a measure of revenge for the depredations of John Harrison's provincials by breaking into a house where two of his brothers were recuperating from smallpox and shooting them in their beds. They also engaged in pillaging civilians, one of Rawdon's patrols finding a house recently visited by a rebel party "stripped of everything that could be carried off," the woman of the house "left standing in her shift,...; her four children stripped stark naked." These and similar activities made it difficult for Cornwallis to obtain intelligence because rebel parties "have so terrified my people, that I can get nobody to venture far enough out to ascertain anything."[3]

Although the incidents noted were frightening to the persons involved, they were minor compared to the degree of Whig vengeance against the Tories in the winter and spring of 1781. After Cornwallis's army left the state, the military situation became much more fluid as rebel militia operated freely between the British posts in which loyalists served or took refuge. As these forts were threatened or brought under siege, then abandoned or surrendered to troops under Marion, Sumter, or Pickens, some loyalists were se t aside and hanged or shot individually or in small groups. In some cases, the action was taken in revenge for past loyalist involvement in injuring or pillaging Whig neighbors, friends, or relatives, but in others the victims seemed to be chosen at random. There is no evidence that Whig commanding officers were directly implicated in the executions, and in several instances Marion and Pickens tried to exert some measure of control over their men by offering rewards for the apprehension of the perpetrators of specific killings.

The reports of such incidents, like those that described British and loyalist atrocities, came from persons who claimed to have been eyewitnesses. A principal source for such reports in the middle of the stare was one Levi Smith, who kept a "back store" north of the Congaree, and who served in the garrison of Fort Motte. When that post surrendered he saw Lieutenant George Fulker and a John Jackson hanged for having in the past caused the death of a woman and one of Sumter's men; another was then killed, and Smith himself was about to be hanged when Marion intervened and turned him over to General Greene as a prisoner. Smith also charged, in an incident never verified from an American source, that Colonel Wade Hampton had arranged to have one Burke from North Carolina kill the father of Lieutenant George Dawkins of the South Carolina Royalists and a James McWhorter, and that Greene had Burke arrested for the crime. Smith also related the story of one Joseph Cooper, a militiaman in Fisher's regiment who, although presumed dead, survived the shooting of fourteen of the prisoners being escorted to Greene's camp after Sumter captured Orangeburg. Captain Samuel Row and sixteen other men survived, joined the rebels temporarily, but deserted to the British when Rawdon was on his way to relieve Ninety Six. Smith himself later escaped and returned to the lowcountry with Rawdon's army.[4]

Other accounts were generated by loyalists themselves or by Whigs in their reminiscences after the war. One rebel bragged that "around [Adam] Steedham's neck I fastened the rope, as a reward for his cruelties," referring to a Fair Forest loyalist who had provided information t hat led a Whig party into an ambush in which the hangman's brother was killed. James Sloan, who had served with his brothers Andrew and John in Richard King's regiment, received the pay due them after they were "murdered" in separate incidents in March and April near Ninety Six. The Sloans may have been victims of vengeance exacted about the time that Major James Dunlap and his provincials were forced to surrender after suffering heavy casualties during a skirmish at Beattie's Mill. Dunlap and the survivors were marched as prisoners toward Virginia, but, Pickens reported, at Gilbertown "an inhuman action occurred against Major Dunlap" by a "'set of men" who "forced the guard and shot him." Pickens offered a $1,000 reward for the capture of one of the party who had been identified, but in a letter of apology to Cruger he cited the killing of a Whig captain traveling under a British flag of truce as a possible reason for Dunlap's murder.[5]

Other incidents took place in the vicinity of Camden. Major William Downes, a former officer in the Royal Irish Artillery who had settled as a blacksmith nearby, held a commission in the loyal militia. Just before the battle at Hobkirk's Hill, a large party of Whigs surrounded his home and demanded that he surrender; he and his overseer defended the house, killing several of the attackers with firearms loaded by his wife and children; after surrendering, his wife later testified, they "fired nine balls into him." While on a reconnaissance for Lord Rawdon during the same period, Lieutenant Samuel Bradley of the loyal militia was captured and hanged on Hobkirk's Hill by a party of Whigs, ostensibly because Bradley's brother had captured a man who was later hanged for deserting to Gates after holding a commission in the loyal militia. The victim's brother was in the party that killed Samuel, apparently the first Bradley to fall into their hands.[6]

Revenge for past injury was the reason most frequently given by Whigs for killing Tories, but other loyalists were apparently victims of random acts of violence. One man was shot by a party of rebels at his home because he shut an open door in the face of demands that he turn over someone suspected of being in the house. One of Greene's dispatch riders told of the "horrid murders" of two men on the road from Granby to Ninety Six, reportedly killed by nine men whom witnesses did not recognize. An escaped rebel officer was robbed of his horse and clothing and insulted by a loyalist who "was despatched" as soon as a group of Whigs could gather to track the offender down. And in July Colonel Henry Hampton, one of Sumter's officers, led cavalry on a daring raid all the way to the Quarter House on Charlestown Neck where they dispersed a party of loyalist dragoons, killed their commander, David Waugh, and carried off a number of prisoners. The British claimed that Waugh was shot after he surrendered.[7]

Between Camden and Georgetown the civil war raged in all its fury that winter, and British and American officers exchanged threats of retaliation for crimes committed by partisans on the other side. Lord Rawdon charged that, after Sumter offered pardons to Tories who enlisted with him by February 23, threatening death to those who continued to resist, several persons "were inhumanly murdered, tho unarmed & remaining peaceably at their own houses." Colonel John Watson accused Sumter's men of killing seven militiamen after they surrendered after an attack on a supply train in March, and said that unarmed civilians "taking side with neither contending party," had been killed in their homes. To Marion's complaint that rebel prisoners were hanged as deserters, Watson replied "that if your followers are composed of our people (for all people upon parole to us I call ours) who have broken their paroles, then they must expect to suffer from taking up arms" against the king.[8]

Indeed, as Edward McCrady wrote many years ago, the rebels were turning the tables on the British, using various means to force loyalists to desert just as in the previous summer the British had sought to exact allegiance from Whigs and the wavering. It was a part of the contest to force the uncommitted, the vacillating, and the less confirmed Whigs and loyalists, by fair means or foul, to choose sides. For their part, Whig militiamen rarely used violence against British regulars, preferring to act against loyalists as individuals or in small groups. A writer in the *Royal Gazette* complained that Whig militiamen preferred to deal directly with their Tory prisoners as traitors while considering the British to be foreign enemies, but captured rebels were turned over to British officers who respected the conventions of organized warfare. As the rebels regained more of the country, these tactics became more effective.[9]

British officers retaliated for the mistreatment of the loyalists by imprisoning and threatening to execute prominent Americans who fell into their hands. When Captain John Postell came to Georgetown under a flag of truce, Captain John Saunders of the

Queen's Rangers, who commanded the post at the time, detained him because he had been a prisoner on parole under the capitulation of Charlestown. Balfour commended Saunders and ordered him to send Postell to Charlestown under heavy guard, saying, "I have his parole which he has broke." At the same time, Balfour had two rebel officers on parole, Colonel John F. Grimke of South Carolina, and Major James Habersham of Georgia, imprisoned on the grounds that they had been corresponding with the rebels in violation of the terms of the capitulation."[10]

As a part of his campaign to retaliate for rebel mistreatment of loyalist militia and civilians, Balfour ordered the transfer of a number of the remaining Continental prisoners to prison ships in the harbor. Shortly thereafter, Lord Charles Montagu, a former royal governor of the province, arrived in Charlestown bearing a warrant to raise a British regiment for service in the West Indies, and he was authorized to recruit Continental prisoners for that purpose. He even entered into correspondence with Brigadier General William Moultrie, the ranking Continental officer among the prisoners, offering to serve under Moultrie if he would consent to command the unit. Moultrie spurned the offer in a celebrated letter that spoke of "my duty to my country," but, by promising that they would never have to serve against their countrymen, Montagu's recruiters induced over 500 prisoners to enlist in what became known as the Duke of Cumberland's Regiment. It is a commentary on the conditions under which the prisoners lived in Charlestown and on the prison ships as well as the nature of the war itself that so many of the best rebel troops could be persuaded to accept foreign service with the British. Henry Rugeley, the Camden loyalist, accepted a lieutenant's commission in the new regiment, but his case was exceptional.[11]

For some time representatives of Lord Cornwallis and General Greene had been attempting to work out a comprehensive exchange of the prisoners held by the two armies, but negotiations had broken down on the British demand that certain parole violators in their hands be excepted from the terms of an agreement. Balfour's order to transfer Continentals on shore to the prison ships may have stimulated rebel negotiators to come to terms, but a counterthreat by Greene's negotiators to require that British prisoners on parole in Charlestown return to American custody probably had equal effect. By the terms of the cartel all prisoners taken by the two armies by June 15, 1781, were to be "immediately exchanged," but while it was being carried out, several events caused its implementation to be suspended. Most important in this regard was the execution of the rebel Colonel Isaac Hayne on August 4, 1781.[12]

The hanging of Hayne caused one of the celebrated controversies of the Revolution, not only in South Carolina, but throughout America and in England, a controversy that has been analyzed in state histories and Revolutionary studies ever since the event. Hayne, a planter in St. Bartholomew's Parish in the lowcountry, held a commission in the state militia and had served during the siege of Charlestown, but was not in the garrison when it surrendered. When his wife and children became ill, he went to the city for medical assistance, but British authorities refused him permission to return unless he took the oath of allegiance. Hayne acquiesced, claiming that he did it only out of necessity, that he accepted protection only while the British effectively controlled the area in which he lived, and that he had been assured that he would not have to perform military service for them. He continued to reside at home until the spring of 1781 when, after the Whig troops of Colonel William Hardin had regained control of his part of the state, he accepted a colonel's commission and assumed active command of the militia of his district. In one of their campaigns, Hayne's men seized General Andrew Williamson, who was living under British protection in the lowcountry; Balfour responded by dispatching Major Thomas Fraser and a strong detachment of the South Carolina Royalists to the rescue. Fraser came upon Hayne's camp by surprise, dispersed his men, rescued Williamson, and carried Hayne off to Charlestown where he was confined in the basement of the Exchange.[13]

British commanders, sorely pressed by the resurgence of rebel strength in the interior and the low morale of loyalist militiamen who were deserting in substantial numbers, now had an opportunity to demonstrate their willingness to carry out Cornwallis's earlier orders and their own threats to execute persons who took the British oath and then joined the rebels. In this case, they had custody of a man of some rank and prominence, and both Rawdon, who had just returned from his exhausting expedition to relieve Ninety Six, and Balfour felt they had no alternative but to order Hayne's execution. The two officers placed the matter before a court of inquiry at which Hayne was not present or able to present witnesses or have counsel; although they did grant him a brief reprieve at the request of William Bull and other loyalists, their intentions were clear and the execution was carried out as ordered. When writing about the matter thirty years later Rawdon showed no remorse over Hayne's death, feeling that Hayne should have known the consequences of rejoining the rebels; he also pointed out that the Americans had used a court of inquiry in determining the guilt and sentence of John André, the British spy implicated in Benedict Arnold's treason. Further, Rawdon made it clear that, after the abduction of Williamson, it was essential that the loyalists understand that there was no weakening of British resolve to defend their interests.[14]

General Greene threatened retaliation against British officers in reprisal for Hayne's death, but a combination of his own repugnance for the idea and a series of unusual circumstances prevented any action, although Cornwallis was in American custody after Yorktown, and Rawdon himself fell into French hands on his voyage home. The need to assure that the St. Augustine exiles would be exchanged under the cartel, the capture by the British of Colonel William Washington, a Continental officer, at Eutaw Springs, the gradual realization after Yorktown that peace might soon come—all militated against any direct action to avenge Hayne.[15]

Amid the violence and threats of retaliation an agreement was worked out during the summer of 1781 to suspend hostilities in one of the most devastated and bitterly contested areas of the state. The region in question was the valley, of the Pee Dee River where Francis Marion had gained his reputation as a partisan leader and where neither the armies of Cornwallis and Rawdon at Camden, the British post at Georgetown, nor the raiding of Tarleton and Wemyss had been able to quell the spirit of rebellion. Although the rebels had prevented the British from controlling this country, the area of the Little Pee Dee River close to the North Carolina border was a Tory stronghold. Supplied at first from the post at Georgetown and later from Wilmington, it offered what Robert Gray estimated to be as many as 500 fighting men who had been armed by Major McArthur, and who, Gray maintained, were the only loyalists "who did not run to the Rebels" when Horatio Gates approached South Carolina in 1780. From this stronghold loyalists sallied forth to carry on a "predatory war" against the rebels, breaking up their musters, and, by threatening their homes, prevented them from leaving to campaign with Marion. Gray contended that when the British evacuated Georgetown in June 1781, "the loyalists on the Little Peedee...entered into a truce for three months with Marion who gladly embraced the opportunity of disarming a hardy and intrepid race of men whom he had never been able to crush."[16]

Although Gray perhaps exaggerated the strength of the Little Pee Dee Tories, the agreement was to the advantage of both sides and was later extended for nine months. The terms worked out between Colonel Peter Harry for Marion and Major Micajah Gainey for the loyalists required a cessation of hostilities, free trade in the region, and the adjudication of disputes by tribunals chosen from the two sides. The extension three months later was more in the nature of a surrender on the part of the loyalists who agreed to take oaths to the state and obey its laws, and to imprison or expel inhabitants of North Carolina who had taken refuge with them. The truce did not work perfectly, and from time to time disputes flared up because of continued intercourse between the inhabitants of the Little Pee Dee and loyalists in North Carolina. Even after the British left Wilmington in November, Colonel David Fanning's raiders passed through that area on their way to and from North Carolina, much to the chagrin of Marion and other Whig officers. But despite the violations, compared to the ravages visited upon the region in the year after the British captured Charlestown, the Marion-Gainey truce was an improvement.[17]

If "Bloody Tarleton" stood for all that was hated and feared by rebels about British tactics against American troops in Revolutionary South Carolina, "Bloody Bill" Cunningham became the symbol of Tory vengeance in the civil war that was carried on simultaneously with the more traditional conflict between the two armies. In many respects "Bloody Bill's" reputation was only in the process of being formed when the war ended.

Although reputed to be a cousin of the Saluda River Cunninghams, William claimed Ireland as his birthplace. He was granted 200 acres on the Saluda River in 1766, but he purchased other lands near Dorchester just west of Charlestown where he apparently retained a tenant family and a few slaves. When the war broke out in 1775, he was once again in the backcountry, taking the Whig side and participating in the attack on Fort Charlotte and in Williamson's expedition against the Cherokees. At the time when Robert, Patrick, and David Cunningham were being jailed in Charlestown by the Provincial Congress for resisting its measures in the backcountry, there was apparently no question among rebels of where William's sympathies lay.[18]

William Cunningham did become disenchanted with the Whigs because of a disagreement over the terms of his enlistment; later he tracked down and killed a Whig who had killed his brother and abused his father. But there is no evidence that his disaffection for the Whig cause propelled him toward the British side while the Americans controlled the state, although hundreds of backcountrymen succeeded in joining the British in Georgia and Florida, and many others made the attempt.[19]

When the British army gained control of the backcountry in 1780, William Cunningham enlisted as a private in Patrick Cunningham's regiment, and there is some evidence that he served at Kings Mountain. The circumstances under which he received a commission and a field command are not readily apparent. Although he was listed as a private in Patrick's regiment when Cruger escorted the loyalists to Orangeburg in July 1781, the first notice of activities beyond those of an ordinary militiaman came when Wells's *Royal*

Gazette announced in September that a Captain William Cunningham, "who had retired to Cane Creek, a branch of the Seneca," before Ninety Six was evacuated, had managed to collect about sixty loyalists between the Enoree and the Saluda. Subsequently the paper reported that he and his men had captured several rebel blockhouses along the Reedy River, then dispersed a party of rebels south of the Saluda. British records show him to have been in Charlestown by October 23 when he received pay for his militia service in 1780.[20]

Early in November, now a major, William Cunningham took command of a regiment of militia in Charlestown that numbered eighty-four officers and men and set out on the expedition that made his name infamous in the Revolutionary annals of South Carolina. However, his did not begin as a separate command but as a part of a militia force of about 500 men commanded by General Robert Cunningham that included Hezekiah Williams's regiment and other units. Involved in a skirmish near Orangeburg with a detachment from Sumter's army, the loyalists split up when rebel reinforcements appeared, William Cunningham moving toward the Saluda, Williams toward the Savannah, and the remainder falling back toward the coast. Cunningham's and Williams's units thus became raiding parties operating on their own far from the British lines.[21]

Whether Bill Cunningham's foray had a military objective is uncertain, but his men were going into an area that was generally familiar to them. Half of his men and all of his officers had served in Patrick Cunningham's regiment in 1780, and about half of the rest had served in the other Ninety Six regiments raised at that time. Virtually all had been driven from their homes or had preferred to come with Cruger in the exodus from the backcountry that summer. Probably a dozen had served with Patrick Ferguson and at least one besides Cunningham himself had been at Kings Mountain. Fourteen families contributed two or more men each and accounted for nearly 40 percent of Cunningham's command. Returning to familiar scenes could not have been a pleasant experience for these men, for it is likely that in some cases they found that Whig families had taken over their homes and other property.[22]

Two particular bloodlettings took place during this raid, the first on Cloud's Creek, a tributary of the Little Saluda that flowed into the parent stream from the south. There on November 7 Cunningham's men came up with a party of twenty-four rebels who were badly outnumbered and sought to surrender. Terms might have been granted but for the presence of one Butler, a young rebel who had been involved in killing a Tory whom Cunningham knew. James Butler attempted to surrender in his son's place, but the young man forced the issue by firing a shot that killed one of Cunningham's men. Then, according to American accounts, Cunningham and some of his men slew all the rebels but two who escaped to tell what had happened. After Cunningham returned to Charlestown, the *Royal Gazette* reported the affair as a successful attack on a Whig detachment by loyal militia who inflicted heavy casualties with but slight loss to themselves. The second event took place north of the Saluda a few days later when John Hood, one of Cunningham's officers, came upon a small party of Whigs at Hayes Station, the residence of Colonel Joseph Hayes, and demanded its surrender. When Hayes refused and a Whig shot one of Hood's men, Cunningham appeared on the scene and ordered an assault on the house. After a siege of several hours during which a number of casualties were suffered, the loyalists succeeded in setting fire to the house and Hayes asked for quarter. He and all of his men were cut down and left for dead.[23]

It seems clear that Cunningham and at least some of his men were anxious to take revenge for their own sufferings and the hardships experienced by their families. It is said that Cunningham personally hanged Hayes and another man, charging Hayes with cruelty to women and children because he forced Tory families from their homes under the instructions from returning Governor John Rutledge as reprisal for British expulsion of the families of the Whigs deported to St. Augustine. Cunningham's other victim was charged with the murder of one Thomas Ellison who had served with Patrick Cunningham and whose widow and three children were then in Charlestown. Bill Cunningham then turned his men loose on the other Whigs, all fourteen of whom were killed. It is not known which of his men engaged in the slaughter, but of the fourteen families who had two or more members present in his unit, six were represented among those killed and wounded on this expedition, and six others had lost members killed at earlier times in the war. It is also likely that the slaughter was the work of a relatively small part of his regiment, for some persons who served with him on this expedition were able to return to their homes after the British left the state.[24]

Cunningham burned a number of mills and storehouses in the area, bypassed Sumter's force near Orangeburg, and slipped back into Charlestown early in December. Hezekiah Williams also returned safely after having moved all the way up to Whitehall, where he forced the surrender of a small garrison.[25]

The atrocities committed by William Cunningham and his men defy explanation except as acts of vengeance. In the light of their importance in the folklore of the Revolution in South Carolina, however, they do raise certain questions about the nature of the struggle between rebels and Tories that might otherwise be passed over. Aside from the obvious enormity of the massacres at Cloud's Creek and Hayes Station, why were "Bloody Bill's" name and exploits so greatly reviled by later generations? In the absence of a Whig press to publicize charges of brutality, such stories would necessarily be spread by word of mouth, a process that could be expected to take a good deal of time to become general knowledge. It is likely, therefore, that Cunningham's misdeeds became a matter of record quickly because they happened shortly before the General Assembly met at Jacksonborough, where such upcountry members as General Andrew Pickens, Colonel LeRoy Hammond, and Patrick Calhoun could exchange such information with their colleagues. It is perhaps significant that the first published account of Bill Cunningham's exploits appeared just three years later in *The History of the Revolution of South Carolina* by Dr. David Ramsay, one of the St. Augustine exiles, who was also present at Jacksonborough. It does not require much imagination to see Ramsay, whose associations were essentially with lowcountry people, soaking up the stories of Tory depredations in the backcountry. And there is little wonder that the future historian, having from his own knowledge found lowcountry Tories to be "gentlemen of honour, principle and humanity." could characterize the "great proportion" of back country loyalists as "ignorant, unprincipled banditti" whose violence was "instigated by love of plunder."[26]

Another reason that so few of the atrocities committed by loyalists became known during the war was that they really had fewer opportunities to commit them than did the Whigs. Atrocities against civilian populations are usually committed by those in power, either permanently or locally for brief periods who, for reasons of revenge or to crush dissent, take advantage of their power in abnormal ways. Atrocities against military personnel were committed because of temporary advantages gained over defeated foes such as Tarleton achieved over Buford , or as reprisals for past injuries in the obvious case of Thomas Brown at Augusta. In fact, the rebels held power in most parts of the state for between four and five years until Charlestown fell, and it was they who jailed many and hanged a few who dared to try to join the British. The acts of Tarleton and Brown occurred when the British controlled the areas in which they were operating, whereas Bill Cunningham had a brief and local advantage that he exploited to the full. But after the evacuation of Camden and Ninety Six, the Whigs soon regained control everywhere except in the coastal enclaves to which the British army had retreated, and with that advantage were able to exact reprisals against the loyalists and their families who remained behind.[27]

On the other hand, while the British still held Charlestown the only newspapers in the state were in the British interest, and it was possible for them, especially Wells's *Royal Gazette,* to publicize at least some of the tales that were circulating about the ferocity shown by the rebels in dealing with loyalists and their families. In order to show loyalists what they could expect at the hands of their new masters if independence from Britain were finally achieved, the catalogue of horrors already experienced by loyalists was set before them at every opportunity. Thus "Lucullus" described a hypothetical trial of someone charged with Toryism after the beneficial laws and traditions of Great Britain had been set aside for the illusory bliss of independence; the evidence presented for the defense was the number of loyalist militiamen who had been killed after surrendering at Fort Motte and Orangeburg, and the fate of Lieutenant Fulker and George Dawkins's father. Wells did not limit his concern to the actions of South Carolina rebels, warning the loyalists of North Carolina that their steadfast compatriots who refused to join the rebels had "with an affectation of candour," been. released only to be followed and killed by their erstwhile captors. All of the publicity was, of course, designed to persuade loyalists within the lines not to trade their security for the illusion that by accepting amnesty from the rebels they could return peacefully to their former homes.[28]

The charges in the loyalist press were clearly intended to stiffen the spines of the Tory refugees, but a pair of documents not publicized in South Carolina at the time give weight to the contention that many loyalists were killed by rebels, not through direct action in organized combat, but when residing at home as noncombatants. The first of these papers was a petition to the king dated April 18, 1782, that described the efforts of the Duke of Richmond in the House of Lords to make it appear that when Lord Rawdon and Nisbet Balfour ordered the execution of Isaac Hayne for treason, local loyalists "did not hesitate to denominate his execution" to be murder "of the foulest complexion." This charge the petitioners refuted, declaring that Hayne's fate was "a proper example and just reward for his treason and infidelity, and [we] are heartily sorry the same mode of correcting rebels was so long deferred through laudable but we conceive mistaken motives." In calling Hayne's execution murder, the petitioners declared that Richmond must have been unaware that "the usurpers in this province have murdered three hundred men, some after and some without pretense of trials, "simply because they were suspected of "being attached to Your Majesty's government."[29]

The eleven men who signed the petition were officers in the loyal militia of Ninety Six and Camden districts, including such regimental commanders as Zacharias Gibbs, Daniel Plummer, Daniel Clary, John Phillips, and William Ballentine, as well as Joseph

Robinson and Evan McLaurin, two high-ranking officers with long service in the South Carolina Royalists. These men then presented a second document as evidence to support the petition, a list of persons " massacred in this province" by the rebels. Although the list was limited to specific victims in Ninety Six District, parts of Camden and Orangeburg districts, and five men from Charlestown the total number "butchered and hanged they declared", was fully "thrice that number." The "massacred" list itself consisted simply of names ordered by the letters of the alphabet that were, in a few cases, accompanied by simple but eloquent comments such as "James Moore of Camden, and his four sons," and "John Donnahoe, aged 75." Some of the names had been made known in the columns of the *Royal Gazette,* such as Fulker and the senior Dawkins, or, like John Groundwater, have been noted during the American Period, or have come to light from other sources. Over half the names, however, had not appeared in any available record of loyalist activity before this; in many cases the less common surnames are familiar, indicating that the men on the list were related to persons who have been identified as loyalists.[30]

The existence of the petition naturally raises questions about its origin. Was the idea for it hatched by a British official, Nisbet Balfour or William Bull perhaps, or had it sprung spontaneously from the minds of several of the officers who signed it? One can almost visualize several of these men who had committed their lives and property to a cause whose future must have seemed bleak, indignantly setting out to prepare a case to refute Richmond's contention that they considered Hayne's execution to have been murder. What of the names on the list; were the signers in a position to know that these men had actually been "butchered and hanged"? Certainly all of the signers could not have known of all of these cases firsthand, but all could contribute to the list—particularly Robinson and McLaurin from their days as exiles in Florida; Gibbs, who had been at Kettle Creek and then spent many anxious days before rebels spared him the fate of five others he had witnessed; Plummer, left lot dead at Kings Mountain; and Phillips, who had lost a son and been a prisoner himself. Further, if all the names were not derived from observation by the signers, a number of them as "inspectors" from their home districts were in position to pick up in the refugee camps the experiences of the refugees themselves. That more than half the men on the "massacred" list are not recorded on the numerous British muster rolls and pay records that are available, and that some were of advanced age strongly suggests that the victims met death at their homes at the hands of Whig militiamen or sympathizers.

The "massacred" list also raises a tantalizing question about what responsibility, if any, the misdeeds of Bill Cunningham and his men may have had in generating some of the names on it. Rebel sources indicate that Cunningham deliberately exacted vengeance on Whigs who had killed or injured loyalists and their families in the past, and that he allowed his men to do the same. Does the fact that family names of men serving with him appear on the "massacred" list mean that they took revenge on Whigs who had murdered their kinsmen before Cunningham's bloody raid, or are they listed there because Whigs took revenge on some of the families of men who served with him at Cloud's Creek and Hayes Station in the five months that passed between his raid and the creation of the list in April 1782?

Of course, the real significance of the "massacred" list is that if the men named there were actually murdered by rebels, then more loyalists or their male sympathizers died from causes unrelated to military action than died from all causes while serving in the organized provincial and militia units from 1778 until the end of the war in 1782.[31]

Notes

1. Greene to General Robert Howe, Dec. 21, "Revolutionary Letters," *SCHGM*, XXXVIII (1937), 16; to President of Congress, Dec. 28, 1780, Letterbook, Oct. 16, 1780–April 8, 1782, Greene Papers, LC (microfilm); and to Pickens, June 6, 1781, Greene Papers, DUL.
2. Balfour to Cornwallis, May 21, 1781, CP, 30/11/6, 93; *South Carolina and American General Gazette* (Charlestown), Dec. 20, 1780.
3. Rawdon to Cornwallis, Dec. 5, Cornwallis to Rawdon, Dec. 11, and Samuel Mathis to Henry Haldane, Nov. 21, 1780, CP, 30/11/14, 140, 30/11/183,38, and 30/11/71, 9.
4. Smith's account appeared in the columns of the *Royal Gazette* (Charlestown), Apr. 17, 1782, nearly a year after the events he described. All the individuals Smith said the rebels had killed are among those listed by loyalist militia officers as having been "massacred" by the rebels, in Fletchall, "Address." I am grateful to Wylma Wates, SCAH, for calling this document to my attention, one more instance of my indebtedness to her for help in the research for this study. For Smith himself, see Loyalist Transcripts, LVII, 257–90. The pay records in T50/1, 5, and Clark, ed., *Loyalists*, I, 205, list thirty-two members of Fisher's regiment "killed" or "dead" during the period, and Fulker and Syfritt as " hanged by the Rebels."
5. One such incident occurred after Dunlap led a party of provincials and loyal militia into an ambush near Cedar Spring on Fair Forest Creek. Samuel Hill, a loyalist serving with a detachment of mounted militia of the Long Cane Regiment, while lying wounded and presumed dead, watched as his nephew, William Conway, and two other men were shot after they surrendered, Loyalist Transcripts, LJV, 287–97. For Steedham, see Johnson, *Traditions and Reminiscences*, 446–47; for the Sloans, Clark, ed., *Loyalists*, I, 287,288; and for Dunlap's murder, Pickens to Greene, Apr. 8, 1781, Greene Papers, DUL. This was actually the second attempt to assassinate Dunlap, who had been wounded and left for dead at Gilbertown in the fall of 1780 by the enraged fiancé of a young woman who had died after being abducted by Dunlap. Dunlap had a history of unrestrained violence as a cavalry officer in the northern campaigns, Lyman C. Draper, *King's Mountain and Its Heroes* (New York, 1929 [orig. publ. n.p., 1891]), 156–64.
6. Loyalist Transcripts, LII, 365–85, for the description by his widow of the affair at Downes's house; *Royal Gazette*, Feb. 27, 1782.
7. William Harden to Greene, Nov. 11, 1781, Greene Papers, SCL; Johnson, *Traditions and Reminiscences*, 496; Wade Hampton to Greene, June 10, 1781, Preston Davie Coil., SHC; McCrady, *S.C. in the Revolution, 1780–1783*, 328.
8. Balfour complained to Moultrie of "the treatment our militia received" as prisoners by Marion's troops, March [?], 1781, William Moultrie, *Memoirs of the American Revolution*, 2 vols. (New York, 1802), II, 172; Watson to Marion, Mar. 9, and Balfour to Saunders, Mar. 12, 1781, Gibbes, *Documentary History*, III, 30, 35.
9. "Lucullus" in *Royal Gazette*, Sept. 29, 1781.
10. Marion to Balfour, to Watson, and to Saunders, Mar. 7, 1781, Watson to Marion, Mar. 9, Balfour to Saunders, Mar. 12, 1781, and Postell 's parole, May 19, 1780, Gibbes, *Documentary History*, III, 29–30, 33–36: McCrady, *S.C. in the Revolution, 1780–1783*, 354–55.
11. Clark, ed., *Loyalists*, I, 471–79; Montagu to Moultrie, Mar. 11, and Moultrie to Montagu, Mar. 12, 1781, Moultrie, *Memoirs*, II, 166–71; McCrady, *S.C. in the Revolution, 1780–1783*, 350–56.
12. McCrady, *S.C. in the Revolution, 1780–1783*, 358–60.
13. A recent study of the Hayne affair is David K. Bowden, *The Execution of Isaac Hayne* (Lexington, S.C., 1977), although it has nor supplanted the discussion in McCrady, *S.C. in the Revolution, 1780–1783*, 130–32, 318–21, 382–98.
14. *Royal Gazette*, July 11, 1781. Correspondence related to Hayne's execution and petitions in his behalf are in Gibbes, *Documentary History*, III, 108–14; Earl of Moira (Rawdon) to Henry Lee, June 24, 1813, Lee, *Memoirs*, 613–20.
15. See the excellent discussion of the implications, to both sides, of Hayne's execution and of possible reprisals for it, in Bowden, *Execution of Isaac Hayne*, 47–66.
16. Gray, "Observations," 12–14, 36–40.
17. Gibbes, *Documentary History*, III, 98–99: Robert O. DeMond, *The Loyalists in North Carolina during the Revolution* (Hamden, Conn., 1964 [orig. publ. Durham, N.C., 1940]), 152.
18. Loyalist Transcripts, XXVI, 42. The Royal Commission set up after the war to examine the claims of loyalists for losses because of their loyalty refused, in William Cunningham's case, to make an award, declaring his claim to be fraudulent, ibid., XXXII, 243; Siebert, *Loyalists in E. Fla.*, 1774–1785, II, 314–15.

Loyalists and Rebels: The Civil War   153

O'Neall, "Random Recollections," 40–47, claimed that William Cunningham was a native of South Carolina.
19. McCrady, *S.C. in the Revolution, 1780–1783*, 467–70. O'Neall, "Random Recollections," 42, says that Cunningham came all the way from East Florida to avenge his brother's death; McCrady says he came from Savannah.
20. Two William Cunninghams appear in the militia pay records for 1780, one serving in Patrick Cunningham's regiment, the other in Daniel Plummer's, Clark, ed., *Loyalists*, I, 260, 262, 264, 330, 541; *Royal Gazette*, Sept. 12,29, 1781.
21. Clark, ed., *Loyalists*, I, 269–75; Sumter to Greene, Nov. 14, 17, 1781, "Sumter-Greene Correspondence," 55–57.
22. Clark, ed., *Loyalists*, I. 253–75.
23. A contemporary account of these massacres is LeRoy Hammond to Greene, Dec. 2 [1781] (dated 1782, but clearly in error), Greene Papers, DUL. See also McCrady, *S.C. in the Revolution, 1780–1783*, 470–76; David Ramsay, *History of the Revolution of South Carolina from a British Province to an Independent State*, 2 vols. (Trenton, N.J., 1785), II, 272–73; *Royal Gazette*, Dec. 8, 1781.
24. Information on the fourteen families is drawn from military records in Clark, ed., *Loyalists*, I, 269–75, and several death lists. Sec also O'Neall, "Random Recollections," 40–47, and Ramsay, *History of the Revolution of South Carolina,*II, 272–73 .
25. Clark, ed., *Loyalists*, I, 268, 270; Sumter to Greene, Nov. 23, Dec. 17, 1781, "Sumter-Greene Correspondence," 57–58, 61.
26. Ramsay, *History of the Revolution of South Carolina*, II, 275–76.
27. There were numerous protests by Moultrie about conditions on the British prison ships, and by Greene and others about Hayne's execution. In turn, Balfour protested the killing of Lieutenant Fulker and Majors Dunlap and Grierson; Greene replied that he had never heard of the Fulker matter and that spontaneous retaliation by "an enraged people" was more understandable than "deliberate executions," Greene to Balfour, Sept. 19, 1781, Gibbes, *Documentary History*, III, 168–70; Leslie drafted a protest to Greene over the confinement in irons of Captain Christian House of Fisher's regiment and two other militiamen, but it was never sent, Leslie Letterbooks, #15547.
28. *Royal Gazette*, Feb. 16, 20, 1782. The issue of Jan. 30 charged that while he lay ill on Daufusky Island, Captain Philip Martinangel of Lechemere's regiment had been shot by a group of "banditti" called the "Blood Legion" from Hilton Head.
29. Fletchall, "Address," was received in London on June 6, 1782.
30. Ibid., comparing it with other death lists.
31. Ibid., comparing it with military deaths reported in pay records and muster rolls in Clark, ed., *Loyalists*, I, 1–48, 87–344, and in other death lists.

Chapter Thirteen

WAR OF ATTRITION: LOYALIST MILITARY ACTION, 1782

Gen. Sumter is posted at Orangeburg and Four Holes to cut off the Tories from communication with the British army. The Tories are coming in in great numbers daily

—Francis Marion, December, 1781

The concentration near Charlestown of the refugees and surviving militia from the interior, and all of the regular and provincial troops formerly located at some distance from the city, inevitably meant that by the end of 1781 the people living within the British defense perimeter were suffering severe shortages of provisions with commensurate price increases for the necessities of life. Much of the duty of British and loyalists troops in the last year of the war was essentially foraging, securing stocks of food and driving cattle from plantations in the lowcountry into the defense perimeter for the use of the garrison.

Although not so numerous as in 1780, the loyalist provincials and militia actually improved their performance in this period because they were better led and equipped for the kinds of duty they were asked to perform; with their families secure behind the lines, the chance to plunder and torment the rebels provided an incentive not present during the earlier campaigns. The civil war continued, although in this phase it was loyalists who had been displaced from their homes in the interior and were hiding out who annoyed state troops by attaching small parties and stealing cattle and supplies. Military activity gradually slackened in 1782, and some loyalists took the first step toward reconciliation and obtained pardons from the state government by enlisting for a term in the state troops.

Major General Alexander Leslie, who had brought reinforcements to Cornwallis just before the earl moved into North Carolina in pursuit of Nathanael Greene, was recalled from that campaign to take command of His Majesty's forces south of Virginia, a post he held until the end of the war.[1]

Once all British forces had been concentrated in the lowcountry, most loyalist military units were thoroughly reorganized. Most important was the organization of some loyalists as light dragoons or cavalry in an attempt to overcome the deficiency in mounted troops that was especially noticeable after Tarleton left the state with Cornwallis. Part of John Harrison's South Carolina Rangers had acted as dragoons in their campaigns north of the Santee, bur otherwise the earlier efforts to raise cavalry among the backcountry loyalists had failed. Early in 1781, however, young Edward Fenwick, son of a prominent planter who had resided in England for a number of years, raised a troop of forty light dragoons who served in the lowcountry without distinction during the rest of the year. As a unit it disappeared from the records after that, and Fenwick himself apparently had a change of heart because he began to send information secretly to the Americans.[2]

Fenwick's experiment was not an outstanding success, but the need for cavalry was as great as ever; from time to time, young men were authorized to raise troops of dragoons or simply to transform existing companies into mounted militia. Several of these units were led by officers who had commanded companies in Robert Ballingall's Colleton County regiment, but most of the men were recruited from the swelling numbers of refugees from the backcountry. Thus Joseph Rhem, who had commanded a company drawn from the Buckhead area, recruited men from Jackson's Creek and other locales in the interior for a troop of light horse that served in 1781, while Captain Benjamin Smith Legge of the Ashley River company enlisted a number of back country refugees for three months' service in another troop. Altogether, a half dozen of these "independent" units were employed for three months or more in 1781 on scouting and patrol duty and occasionally on campaigns with regular and provincial troops.[3]

The South Carolina Royalists had seen hard service around Ninety Six in 1780; after being transferred to Camden they fought at Hobkirk's Hill and retreated with Rawdon to the vicinity of Charlestown. There, through the generosity of a number of the "principal inhabitants of this town," a subscription of nearly 3,000 guineas was raised to equip "a corps of dragoons." Rawdon, finding that such a corps could be raised only by drafting from the regular infantry regiments, decided to retain the connection between the gift and the province by ordering that "the South Carolina Regiment be converted into cavalry," and the necessary mounts and appointments for their new kind of service were found in June 1781.[4]

Few of the officers in the original Royalists continued to serve with the regiment throughout the British period. Thomas Fraser continued to command the regiment with John Coffin, a Massachusetts loyalist who had come south with the New York Volunteers, placed in charge of the cavalry. Evan McLaurin, who had failed in his efforts to raise a second battalion for the regiment, continued to receive an allowance as a militia officer, as did Robert Pearis, one of the original commanders who also died during that year. Martin Livingston was killed in action in June 1781, about the time the regiment was converted to cavalry.[5]

Under Fraser's command the regiment had a peak strength of just under 300 officers and men, divided about equally between three troops of cavalry and three companies of infantry. As in the case of George Dawkins, who was a lieutenant when the regiment was formed, some new company commanders achieved their rank by promotion for past service. In other cases—Stephen Jarvis of Connecticut from the Queen's Rangers became a company commander, and Charles Allicocke of New York, a lieutenant—officers were drawn from outside the province, although the enlisted men continued to be primarily from South Carolina. In 1782 the remnant of John Harrison's South Carolina Rangers was incorporated in the Royalists as a company and continued with it until it was disbanded after the war.[6]

The Royalists were actively engaged in the lowcountry, especially around Moncks Corner in June, and a detachment went with Rawdon to Ninety Six. Isaac Hayne was captured and Andrew Williamson rescued by Fraser's dragoons, who also suffered a few casualties at Eutaw Springs, and they were involved in raiding the interior for cattle and slaves in 1782. Desertions were numerous after Hobkirk's Hill, but after the regiment was reorganized its morale improved, it generally performed well, desertions were rare, and it was able to recruit replacements for its casualties.[7]

Once the backcountry had been abandoned there was a major reorganization of the militia. Fewer men would be employed in fewer units, since many men originally recruited had not made the trek with Rawdon or Cruger because they were hiding out, had not returned from captivity in distant places, or had made their peace with the rebels. Most noticeable was the change in leadership; of the commanders of the eighteen regiments formed in 1780, only three continued in that capacity after leaving the interior, and two of them acted only for brief periods in 1782.

Obviously, fewer regiments would require fewer colonels to command them, but a more reasonable explanation is that the original commanders had outlived their usefulness. Chosen originally on the basis of their presumed local influence and their capacity to act as conservators of the peace rather than for their military talents, few had demonstrated any real ability to command in the field. Because it was expected that the reorganized militia would necessarily be employed in field service, particularly the mounted units, younger men who had demonstrated qualities of combat leadership were chosen to command the new regiments.

Five regiments were formed from Ninety Six District. Thomas Pearson, a young Virginian who had served as a captain in Patrick Cunningham's regiment and participated in the exciting events of 1775, was made colonel of a new Little River regiment that mustered just under 200 veterans of the original unit and new recruits. Hezekiah Williams from Stevens Creek, a captain in Cotton's regiment, became colonel of a regiment drawn primarily from residents south of the Saluda. William Young of Tyger Creek, a veteran of 1775, who had fought in Georgia, and as a captain in Zacharias Gibbs's regiment had been captured at Kings Mountain, took command of a mounted regiment that saw much service in 1782. Baily Cheney, a mere stripling when he had accompanied Moses Kirkland to the rendezvous with Lord William Campbell in 1775, was given a separate command for about seven months in 1782. The best known of all the new leaders was William Cunningham, who has already been introduced. On his return from the Saluda campaign, he raised a new troop of dragoons whose enlisted personnel was essentially new, although his senior officers stayed with him throughout the period. Among the more faithful were Captain William Helms who held land south of the Saluda, Captain William Parker, a very active officer who commanded an independent company for a period; Captain Richard Long from Stevens Creek; Captain John Hood; and Ensign Daniel Cargill of the large family of that name living on Little River. With their reputations linked firmly with his, they accompanied him to East Florida after the war.[8]

Men of the loyalist families escorted by Lord Rawdon on the retreat from Camden or whom the rebels had driven out of Orangeburg District were recruited for two regiments that served primarily as infantry. Of the regiments originally organized in Camden and Cheraw districts, only that from Jackson's Creek had survived beyond 1780, and a part of it under John Phillips had participated in the relief of Ninety Six. Although John Fisher's regiment had mustered 400 men in 1780, many had deserted or abandoned their homes when Orangeburg was overrun by the rebels. The new units were called the First and Second Camden regiments; the First numbered about 150 men who had served with

Phillips, Samuel Tynes. James Cary, or Henry Rugeley, and was commanded by Robert English. The Second had recruited loyalists, many of whom had no prior service for the British, from Orangeburg and the Dutch Fork as well as Camden District, and it was led by William Ballentine of Orangeburg, formerly an officer in Daniel Clary's regiment.[9]

Probably 750 mustered with these regiments in the fall of 1781. Apparently they were better led and equipped than their counterparts of 1780, and, as exiles, they did not suffer from the usual internal conflicts of militiamen—whether to defend their homes by serving in the militia, or, by remaining at home, provide their own defense for families and property. There was the added incentive of a soldier's pay, a means to subsist in a strange country, which, with refugee allowances, might offset some of the loss incurred when their farms could no longer provide for their families.[10]

Although the mounted militia engaged in some spectacular raiding, most service involved the routine of guarding prisoners and supplies on James Island or performing patrol duty. Operating from their small enclave, however, gave them advantages they had not enjoyed in the interior: the close support of regular troops, plentiful arms and ammunition, a secure base, and opportunities to strike unexpectedly at isolated rebel installations and bodies of troops. Rebel militia, on the other hand, suffered after Eutaw Springs from desertions and low morale, and state regiments had trouble filling their ranks and were chronically short of ammunition to the point that they retired from skirmishes because they could not keep up sustained firing.[11]

These were tactical advantages, however, and life for loyal militiamen was not easy as the heat and fevers took their toll and some yielded to the state's offer to change sides. By mid-1782 Cheney's and Williams's regiments had been absorbed into Pearson's, and English's into Ballentine's; they, with the remnants of Fisher's and King's old regiments on James Island and the mounted troops of Young and Bill Cunningham, amounted to about 450 men who were still serving in the militia when campaigning ceased in preparation for the evacuation of the province.[12]

Through most of 1782 British forces were content to conduct occasional raids into the surrounding areas or to respond to probing by the rebels outside the city. The most spectacular raids were conducted by Benjamin Thompson, a Massachusetts loyalist, who landed at Charlestown on his return from England where he had become undersecretary of state and engaged in the scientific and literary pursuits that would earn him a knighthood as Count Rumford after the war. Commanding a mixed force of regulars and militia, including Young's and William Cunningham's mounted troops, Thompson swept north to the Santee and twice inflicted heavy casualties on Marion's men. Thompson then sailed for New York, but in March Fraser's Royalist dragoons and Young's militia again raided to the Santee, while on another foray Cunningham raided as far as Daniel Horry's plantation where he captured and paroled Thomas Pinckney and returned with 150 slaves rounded up in the area.[13]

In addition to his exploits in the lowcountry, in May Cunningham appeared once more in the Saluda River area, but without the sanguinary results of his earlier campaign. According to American sources, this time a measure of revenge was taken for his earlier misdeeds when his small party was surprised and routed by a larger body of Whigs commanded by Captain William Butler, brother of one and son of another of the victims of Cloud's Creek. Cunningham himself barely escaped because of the superior speed of his horse. Cunningham continued to command a troop of mounted militia until the end of the war, but this was his last active engagement in South Carolina. Hezekiah Williams conducted the last "excursion into the country" in June with unknown results, then resigned his commission in order to go to Florida. The short lived *Parker's Ferry Gazette*, a Whig paper, reported that a party of Tories raiding out of the "Indian Ground" was successfully repulsed with the loss of several men killed, although its leader, a "Col. Black," was able to escape.[14]

The South Carolina Royalists engaged in raiding from their base at the Quarter House on Charlestown Neck. In January the regiment participated under Major John Coffin in a surprise attack on a larger Whig force at Smith's plantation in St. Thomas's Parish, routing them with considerable loss, although Archibald Campbell, one of its company commanders, was killed, and another, Alexander Campbell, was wounded. Its last action occurred in August when Thomas Fraser, hoping for a surprise, impetuously attacked a rebel force that had been warned of his approach and was prepared to receive him. His dragoons suffered considerable loss, and Captain George Dawkins was severely wounded.[15]

There was little direct conflict between the two sides in the last six months of the war. British foraging parties occasionally made contact with American troops, but having the advantage of surprise and mobility, they usually returned to their base unscathed. They also used their command of coastal waters to land foraging parties to collect rice from outlying plantations. One such foray in late August resulted in the last skirmish of the War when Henry Laurens's son, John, who had got up from a sickbed in anticipation of a fight with the British, was killed when he rashly charged a fixed British position when fired upon. Laurens had many admirers on both sides of the conflict, and the *Royal Gazette* mourned the loss of such a promising young man.[16]

Not all the loyalists had been forced into Charlestown or had given up and returned to their homes after the backcountry was abandoned, for all rebel commanders had become aware of "outlyers," a term they used to describe Tories of all ages and both sexes who had taken to the woods or swamps for fear the rebels would drive them completely from their homes. From these hideouts, loyalists could steal cattle, horses, and grain to supply their own needs and those of the British army, inflict casualties on small parties of rebels, and further deplete the forage available to the rebels.[17]

Aedanus Burke, the state judge from the backcountry, described the change in the "temper of the people" because of the spirit of vengeance the British had "excited in the breasts of our Citizens"; the "very females talk as familiarly of sheding blood & destroying the tories as the men do." In turn, the "small tory parties who live in swamps & make horrid incursions on the peaceable settlements, [are] neither given nor receive quarter"; they "sally from their swamps, & destroy our people in cold blood, and when taken are killed in their turn." Robert Gray found that with the "swamps filled with loyalists, the rebels durst not sleep in their houses," and that Thomas Sumter used Catawba Indians to track them down and flush them from their hiding places. Few of the "outlyers" have been identified, but perhaps James Swinney, who had taken care of Cunningham's wounded after Hayes Station, could be used as an example. After an abortive attempt to reach Florida in 1777, Swinney had remained in hiding until the British took control of the backcountry. When they retreated to the coast, he once again found himself to be an "outlyer"; although he later reached Charlestown safely, he dropped from sight after that.[18]

Although the Whigs along the northern frontier of South Carolina had less trouble with "outlyers," their counterparts over the border were engaged in a civil war of their own. Cornwallis's march through North Carolina had .aroused the Tories to come forward only to be left unsupported when he moved into Virginia in the summer of 1781. Into the void left by his departure stepped young David Fanning, whose bold raids struck fear in the hearts of Whigs and briefly raised the flagging spirits of the loyalists in that state. Fanning, whose adventures in the South Carolina backcountry during the American Period have already been noted, raised a militia regiment and, encouraged by Major James Craig, the British commander at Wilmington, dashed to the capital at Hillsborough where he seized the rebel governor, Thomas Burke, and carried him to Charlestown. On other raids he seized and paroled local leaders, destroyed rebel property, and defeated small parties of militia. The evacuation of Wilmington deprived him of his base, but he and other North Carolina loyalists continued to receive help from their compatriots in the Little Pee Dee area.[19]

Although rebel commanders devoted their energies to tracking down the Tories who were hiding out, both General Greene and the returning state governor, John Rutledge, felt that offering amnesty to certain loyalists might separate them from their more inveterate compatriots and at the same time contribute enlistments to the state troops. Following the "glorious victory at Eutaw," Rutledge issued a proclamation on September 27, 1781, by which he offered to certain persons "free pardon and oblivion for such their offense of having borne arms with or [who] adhere to the enemy" if they would appear before a state militia brigade commander within thirty days and volunteer for six months service in the ranks. Upon satisfactory completion of this service their families would be permitted to return to their homes and to "hold and enjoy their property ... without molestation or interruption." Certain classes of persons were excepted from the terms of the proclamation; in broad outline, they were those who had left the state in the American Period and who had ignored earlier offers of pardon, or who had chosen exile after refusing the oath of abjuration; and others who since the fall of Charlestown had subscribed to congratulatory addresses to British commanders, held British civil or military commissions, or "whose conduct has been so infamous" that justice could not admit them to pardon.[20]

One result of Rutledge's policy could be foreseen: the deeply committed loyalists either had no interest in supporting the state or were among the classes excepted from its terms. The less committed, however, especially if they were frightened that rebel parties might hunt them down and offer no quarter, did begin to appear in some numbers at Sumter's camp near Orangeburg. When "outlying tories" crowded into his lines for safety, he could do nothing but recommend that they return to "their former habitations," although he feared that many would be "privately injured" if they did. In a four-day period in December over forty loyalists surrendered and others were expected daily. Even though the grace period set out by Rutledge had expired, Sumter continued to receive them pending further orders, reporting that the number of "women and children can't be conceived" who were in severe straits and could not "subsist much longer where they are." Early in January he reported that he had over 100 of the recently surrendered Tories in his command who had chosen their own officers and who were performing satisfactory service in a number of ways. In this manner, he was following Greene's instructions to "take off the Tories from the British interest" rather than to prolong the bloodletting by allowing his troops to commit indiscriminate acts of revenge on some for the misdeeds of others. Not all who had signed up were steadfast in their new allegiance, for about twenty went off with William Cunningham when he was operating in the neighborhood. On his part, Sumter continued to hunt down the "greatest offenders," killing and capturing a few and driving the others deeper into hiding.[21]

"Outlyers" also operated from the mountains and the "Indian Grounds" to which they had fled when Greene and Pickens had taken control of the backcountry. One reason that Cunningham and Williams had been successful in ravaging the countryside without retaliation was that Pickens was engaged in a brief but effective campaign against the Cherokees who had attacked several isolated settlements that autumn. Among those who received succor from Indians was another" Bloody Bill," William Bates, who led a party of Indians against Gowen's Fort on the upper Pacolet River in November 1781, and, after accepting the surrender of the families who had taken refuge there, allowed all to be massacred. The *Royal Gazette* announced the capture of the fort by a party of Indians and loyal militia, although there is no military record that Bates served the British or who his followers were. Pickens led two more retaliatory raids against the Cherokees in 1782, forcing them to sue for peace.[22]

As formal military campaigning grew less frequent, partisans reached agreements designed to end the civil conflict in two areas. The Marion-Gainey truce of 1781 in the Pee Dee worked fairly well until it was broken in the spring of 1782, each side charging the other with bad faith. When Fanning's raids through the Little Pee Dee caused the state governors of the Carolinas to plan a joint expedition to break loyalist resistance there, Marion renewed negotiations, and he and Gainey signed another agreement similar to that of 1781 except that Fanning and his men were exempt from its provisions. Gainey then resigned his British commission and, with some of his men, sought to obtain amnesty by enlisting for six months in the state troops. They were part of Marion's force that inflicted casualties on the South Carolina Royalists in September, and the truce lasted for the rest of the war. Gainey's action was not popular with some of his erstwhile followers, however, and threats against his life caused him to move into North Carolina after the war. Across the state, the activities of loyalist raiders prevented Whig families in the Salkehatchie area from planting their crops in the spring of 1782, so a two-month truce was worked out, which was soon broken when stronger state troops moved into the area. The evacuation of Savannah shortly thereafter deprived local loyalists of any support from that quarter, and they were forced either to join the rebels or to flee to the garrison in Charlestown.[23]

Notes

1. Sir Henry Clinton to Alexander Leslie, Dec. 1, 1781, Clinton Papers.
2. The Fenwicks had resided in England while young Edward and his brother Thomas received their education; Edward, Sr., who died in 1775, was a substantial planter and bred fine race horses on John 's Island. Young Edward married the daughter of John Smart, the Indian superintendent. "The Tattnall and Fenwick Families in South Carolina," *SCHGM* (1913), 3–19; William Harden to Marion, Apr. 18,1781, Gibbes, ed., *Documentary History*, III, 54; Clark, ed., *Loyalists*, I, 187–89.

3. Clark, ed., *Loyalists,* I, 171, 174–77. Legge's father, Edward, operated the Ashley Ferry and held land on the south side of that river just west of Charlestown; *South Carolina Gazette and Country Journal* (Charlestown), Jan. 23, 1770; *South Carolina and American General Gazette* (Charlestown), Feb. 20, 1777, Sept. 6, 1780; Deeds, Aug. 17,1771, W–3, 262–72 . John Lawrence, James Yarborough, and John Fanning raised troops of light horse that served for brief periods between September 1781 and February 1782, Clark, ed., *Loyalists,* I, 174–75, 178, 343. Thomas Commander, who owned land on Lynches Creek but kept a tavern at Moncks Corner before the war, formed an infantry company that served for seven months, until February 1782, ibid., 178–79.
4. Rawdon to Cornwallis, June 5, 1781, Gibbes, *Documentary History,* III, 90.
5. For Robinson and several other half-pay officers, see Clark, ed., *Loyalists,* I, 465; the extant muster rolls for the regiment during the war are in ibid., 1–48. Fraser married Ann Laughton Smith of Charlestown, Chesney, "Journal", 111–12; Wills, *XIX,* 275–76; *Royal Gazette* (Charlestown), Mar. 6, 1782; Clark, ed., *Loyalists,* 1, 36.
6. Enlistment figures for the Royalists are derived from comparisons for various periods in Clark, ed., *Loyalists,* I, 2–7, 12–16. 19–32, 34–38. For the outsiders, see "Colonel Jarvis, Loyalist," 43–55, and Joseph Allicocke to Christian Allicocke, June 21 , 1782, Continental Congress Papers, #51, 549–51, 621–22.
7. "Colonel Jarvis, Loyalist," 43, 47–55; *Royal South Carolina Gazette* (Charlestown), Sept. 12, 1782; Fraser to Leslie, Sept. 12, 1782. Leslie Letterbooks, #15641; Marion to Governor John Mathews, Aug. 30, 1782, SCHM (1916), 176–77; Clark, ed., *Loyalists,* I, 3–4, 13, 21, 30, 38–39.
8. Pearson held land on Bush River, Williams on a branch of Stevens Creek, and Young on a tributary of Tyger River, Plats, XI, 446; XX, 34; XXI, 474–75. See also *Canadian Claims,* 703; Loyalist Transcripts, LVII 439–44. The circumstances under which Pearson was promoted have not been revealed. Patrick Cunningham and some of his junior officers, Pearson included, were in Charlestown on June 1, 1781, while Ninety Six was under siege, but Cunningham was listed among the officers who left the backcountry with Cruger, apparently his last military service, Clark, ed., *Loyalists,* I, 253, 265.
9. Clark, ed., *Loyalists,* I, 162–65. Fisher did command a small contingent of Orangeburgers on James Island late in 1782, ibid., 214–18.
10. The number of militia is compiled from pay records printed in Clark, ed., *Loyalists,* I, 111–12, 125–26, 211, 224, 269–70, 297–99, 331–32, 339–40.
11. Colonel LeRoy Hammond to Greene, Dec. 2, 1781, Greene Papers, DUL.
12. Compiled from pay records in Clark, ed., *Loyalists,* I, 141–42, 214–18, 273–74, 288–89, 317–20, 336–37.
13. W.P. Rae, "Benjamin Thompson, 1753–1814," *DNB,* XIX, 605–8; *Royal Gazette,* Jan. 5, Mar. 2, 27, 1782.
14. McCrady, *S.C. in the Revolution, 1780–1783,* 628–31; for analysis of personnel in Cunningham's troop for pay periods in 1782, see Clark, ed., *Loyalists, I,* 224, 269–75; *Royal Gazette,* June 15, 1782.
15. *Royal Gazette,* Jan. 5, 1782; "Col. Jarvis, Loyalist," 50–55; "Marion's Report of the Affair at Wadboo," *SCHGM,* XVII (1916), 176–77.
16. McCrady, *S.C. in the Revolution, 1780–1783,* 640–46.
17. Pickens to Greene, Sept. 7, 1781, Greene Papers, CL (Waring photocopies, CUL); Sumter to Greene, Dec. 9, 1781, "Sumter-Greene Correspondence," 62.
18. Burke to Middleton, Jan. 5, May 14, 1782, Joseph W. Barnwell, ed., "Correspondence of the Hon. Arthur Middleton," *SCHGM* (1925), 192, 201; Robert Gray, "Observations," 201–21; Clark, ed., *Loyalists,* I, 218, 222. Swinney also claimed responsibility for having killed John Adam Treutlen, a former rebel governor of Georgia in the South Carolina backcountry in 1782.
19. Craig to Balfour, July 30, Nov. 22, 1781, CP, 30/11/6, 338, 401; dispatches to General Jethro Sumner from Samuel Chapman, July 1, William Loftin, July [?], John Armstrong, Nov. 25, 1781, and Joseph Rosser to Major Griffith, Feb. 28, 1782, Jethro Sumner Papers, SHC; and Thomas Burke to General Butler, Mar. 9, 1782, Preston Davie Coll., SHC.
20. Rutledge to Marion, Sept. 15, 1781, and undated, enclosing copy of the proclamation of Sept. 27, Gibbes, *Documentary History,* III , 162, 175–79.
21. Sumter to Greene, Dec. 13, 19, 22, and Greene to Sumter, Nov. 28, 1781, "Sumter-Greene Correspondence," 63–66, 69.
22. For Bates, see Draper, *King's Mountain,* 242; McCrady, *S.C. in the Revolution 1780–1783,* 477–80.
23. Marion to Greene, June 9, Fanning to Greene, June 25, and Leslie to Greene, June 30, 1782, Greene Papers-Correspondence, II, 219–20, 240, 249–51, LC (microfilm); Fanning, " Narrative," 36; Hugh F Rankin, *Francis Marion: The Swamp Fox* (New York, 1973), 280–87; *Royal Gazette,* May 18, June 8, 1782.

Chapter Fourteen

Displaced Persons and Pawns of War:
Loyalist Refugees and Black Slaves, 1781–1782

After their arrival in Charleston, they built themselves huts without the lines, which was called Rawdontown: many of these unfortunate women and children, who lived comfortable at their own homes near Camden, died for want, in those miserable huts.

—William Moultrie, 1802

All residents of Charlestown and vicinity, regardless of their political sentiments, suffered to some degree from shortages, high prices, abuse of their property by the military, and the other hardships of life in a beleaguered city, but for them there was at least the comfort of friends and familiar surroundings. The greatest sufferers, however, were the men, women, and children from the interior who from choice or necessity sought protection within the British lines.

Although the mild winter in their new surroundings might be something of a boon for people forced to live in the crude shelters available, refugees from the backcountry were unprepared for the toll taken by the steaming summers with their fevers and other maladies. Deaths and burials became a fact of everyday life as over 200 civilian refugees died during the period, nearly half of them children. Also, despite official assurances that British arms had suffered only a temporary setback, it must have become increasingly apparent to the refugee families in their makeshift quarters and the militiamen standing their dreary turns on guard that their chances of returning to their homes were vanishing. The news of Lord Cornwallis's surrender at Yorktown, the evacuation of Savannah in June 1782, and the persistent rumors that Britain was negotiating for peace all contributed to dash their hopes of resuming any kind of normal life in South Carolina. The obvious preparations to evacuate the city late in the year inevitably caused speculation about what disposition was to be made of them, further increasing their doubts and fears.

The refugees have left few personal accounts of their experiences, but British records provide occasional glimpses of them in the remaining months of the war.1

From the beginning of the war around Boston, British commanders had to deal with the large numbers of refugee loyalists driven into their occupied cities, and Sir Henry Clinton's experience with the situation around New York was fresh in his mind when Charlestown surrendered to him in 1780. Before returning to New York that summer he instructed Lord Cornwallis to "grant assistance to suffering loyalists through an Inspector of Refugees as practised in New York," and in July Commandant Patterson assigned the task to John Tunno, a loyalist merchant who had returned to the city with the Clinton expedition. Following his appointment, Tunno notified the public that he would receive applications from needy refugees at his office at 44 Bay Street, but there is no indication that his duties were onerous or that many refugees required aid while the British army controlled most of the state. After mid-1781 the plight of the refugees became a major problem for the commanding general and the commandant of the city.[2]

After Governor John Rutledge returned to the state he ordered district commanders to send the "wives and families" to join their loyalist men within the British lines as a simple matter of "justice" to the St. Augustine exiles "whose wives and families" were forced by the British authorities to go to Philadelphia to rejoin them. Early in the summer Nisbet Balfour advised Cornwallis that a serious "want of money" had developed, a condition caused primarily by the "sums paid for the distress'd refugees & militia," which with other needs had greatly increased "the expenditure of public money" beyond all expectations. After Alexander Leslie assumed command he, too, reported that the refugees were placing a heavy strain on "our resources, especially of provisions as these poor people come to us in the possession of every want." William Bull urged his superiors in England to "order a supply of money" to South Carolina to meet the increased cost of administering the province when the presence of Greene's army within six miles of Charlestown suggested that a siege was imminent and the high price of provisions "sold by country men" was draining the town of specie. Although the town did not come under siege, Leslie explained to Clinton that the "misery and helpless situation" of the militia "justifies our attention to them, tho perhaps, their services are not to be esteemed an equivalent."[3]

If the British were to maintain a following in South Carolina, it was essential that they try to sustain the faithful when the rebels were offering inducements to the less "obnoxious" loyalists to desert. Therefore, by every means available—raiding to collect cattle, foodstuffs, and slaves; cash allowances from the military chest; and some illicit trade with the rebels at which both sides winked—British and loyalist officers and administrators tried to meet the minimum needs of the "distressed" loyalists. Excluding men serving with the provincials or militia, as many as 1,000 persons from South Carolina may be classified as refugees: they comprised men too old and infirm to serve and former officers and men; the wives, widows, daughters, and other women related to loyalist men; and children of both sexes who were with one or both parents or who had been orphaned. Smaller numbers of refugees from Georgia and North Carolina added to the administrative and financial burden the British were incurring.[4]

The administration of the relief program was turned over to several militia regimental officers who were made inspectors of refugees for their own districts. While no longer in active service, these men apparently retained the confidence both of the refugees and of British officers like Nisbet Balfour who had recommended many of them for their original appointments in 1780. The largest group of refugees came from Ninety Six District, and three inspectors administered the program for them Thomas Fletchall of Fair Forest, an important opponent of the Provincial Congress in 1775; and Thomas Edghill and John Hamilton, who had served as conservators of the peace and second in command in the Long Cane and Stevens Creek militia regiments. The same function was performed for the refugees from Georgetown, Charlestown, and Cheraw districts by Colonel James Cassells, for Orangeburg District by Colonel John Fisher, and for Camden District by Colonel John Phillips. The actual distribution of provisions was handled at various times by about two dozen quartermasters, who were militia captains from the various districts. Inspectors were paid five shillings per day for this work and the quartermasters two. In addition, a refugee hospital was provided and its personnel received pay ranging from several shillings for the surgeon to sixpence per day for the nurses. The surgeon was Dr. Charles Fyffe of Georgetown, who since his arrival in 1748 had drawn substantial income from his practice, from the post of naval officer for his port, and from planting activities on lands his wife brought to their marriage. He was assisted by Dr. Nathaniel Bulline, a native of the province who had moved from Charlestown to Amelia Township in Orangeburg District before the war.[5]

Aid to the refugees took several forms: specific allowances paid periodically to certain classes; provisions or rations distributed as the need arose and supplies permitted; and the occasional payment of small sums to the most desperately needy among the families. Allowances were apportioned according to the military rank or prominence of the men, and to the size of the refugee family. Male refugees who held militia commissions were given their arrears of pay through May 1782, after which they received allowances as refugees unless they returned to active service. Thus refugees of the "first class," sixty men holding commission as captains or higher and thirteen of the more prominent civilians, received four shillings eightpence per day; a number of captains, lieutenants, and civilians of the "second class" received two shillings fourpence; and one shilling twopence was granted to those in the "third class," all of whom were civilians. Widows drew allowances commensurate with the status of their deceased husbands.[6]

It was possible for the militia officers who administered the aid to draw two incomes, as in the case of James Cassells who was paid five shillings as inspector and an allowance of four shillings eightpence as a refugee of the first class, or of Captain Hector Dickey who received pay as a quartermaster and an allowance as a second-class refugee. In contrast, Margaret Reynolds, a widow from Ninety Six and the sole support of three children, worked as a nurse in the hospital, but received no refugee allowance. There were, however, occasional special payments by the commandant to "distressed refugees," such as one in August 1782, in which nearly £600 was distributed to 800 people, 500 of them children, at the rate of $5.00 per adult and $2.00 per child. For Margaret Reynolds this special payment of $11.00 was more than she would have earned as a nurse in two months.[7]

The situation of Margaret Reynolds was unusual because she obtained employment, but it also reveals something of the problems faced by loyalist women in wartime South Carolina and, therefore, of all women of the time. The experiences of a few women have been printed since the war, the best known of which were Louisa Wells's *Journal,* which documented the difficulties faced by exiles in the American Period, and a view of life in occupied Charlestown by the spirited rebel Eliza Wilkinson. The recent emphasis on women's studies has directed attention to the roles and experiences of women in the Revolution. Mary Beth Norton has suggested, based on her research in the testimony of loyalist widows after the war, that most women knew little of the business affairs of their husbands and were bewildered by the responsibilities thrust upon them by the loss of their mates. The testimony of South Carolina loyalist women also supports that conclusion; but it should be noted that most of them were from the lowcountry and, before the evacuation of the province, that their principal adjustment was to widowhood. But refugee women from the interior had already made several adjustments before arriving in the lowcountry: some had already become widows because of military action or Whig vengeance; all had been driven from their homes and were striving to keep their families together in the face of disease and want in the refugee camps; and all were beset by doubts and fears of the future.[8]

The vast majority of the 352 women refugees who have been identified were or had been married, although some were spinsters or daughters of marriageable age. Virtually all of the 40 percent who were widows had lost their husbands before leaving the backcountry and were responsible for the support of children. These statistics do not reveal how omnipresent death or the threat of it was in the lives of these women. The classic case is that of Jean Henderson of the Long Cane settlement who had migrated from Ireland forty years before the war. After her son James was "murdered" while serving in Richard King's regiment, and her son-in-law Allen Hackett "hanged by the rebels," she with her husband Arthur, daughter Agnes Hackett, and two grandchildren had joined the hundreds from Ninety Six District who fled to the lowcountry. There Arthur and her son David, a militiaman under Colonel King, also died, and shortly thereafter Agnes succumbed to an undisclosed illness. Although she drew allowances for the grandchildren, Jean later testified in Nova Scotia that all of her family were dead.[9]

The Henderson case was an extreme illustration of the fact that sickness and death were matters of everyday life for the women refugees. Living husbands might still be lost in military action or to the same illnesses that prevailed in the crowded camps. Nothing points up the frequency of death better than the "coffin list," the record kept by carpenter James Donaldson to justify the charges he presented for making coffins for the refugees. Through September 1782 he was paid for making 180 coffins for the refugees, and other carpenters also produced a few.[10]

Half of those who died in the camps were under eighteen, most of them infants or in the early years of life. Many of Donaldson's entries do not denote age or sex, referring simply to a "child" or "an unknown person." Coffins were often issued to individuals, nearly always men, who apparently were handling burial arrangements out of family duty, friendship, or in some cases, because they were required to act as inspectors of refugees. In at least two instances—Colonel Edghill for "his son," and Colonel Phillips for "his daughter"—inspectors were also personally involved. If few families were unaffected by the passing of a relative, friend, or neighbor, some faced mourning more frequently than others. Martin Willard, a militiaman in Patrick Cunningham's regiment, buried his wife and two of his children within a period of three weeks; Alexander Wilson, his wife and two young children within seven; and Mrs. William Lettingham, her husband and a child within ten days. The proximity of dates of death in these and other cases suggests the likelihood of epidemics in the camps, although the causes of death are not revealed. Several elderly people also succumbed and the number of widows mounted. What is remarkable is that, considering the number of widows with small children who came in the exodus from the backcountry, there were not more orphans in the camps. There were a few, however, notably the seven children of the widower John Anderson, an Enoree River farmer and militiaman, who died and left them to the care of others. Apparently no institution was asked to care for the orphans, but a number of women, usually relatives or neighbors, assumed the responsibility. For example, the closest living relatives of Mary Conway, an orphan of about twelve, rallied to her support after her only brother was killed while serving with Dunlap's dragoons in 1781. Her aunt, Susannah Murray, herself a widow after her husband died of wounds received in a skirmish in the backcountry, and her uncle, Samuel

Hill, who had lost an arm in action, assumed the role of guardians for Mary as a refugee and, after the war, in Jamaica.[11]

Indeed, the phenomenon of the single parent was probably as prevalent among the loyal refugees of this time as at any time in South Carolina history prior to the Civil War. In one list of eighty-seven "distressed refugee" families from Ninety Six District, thirty-six widows and widowers were the sole support of an average of three children per family. For the refugee women the care of their numerous offspring must have occupied much of their time, and the high incidence of deaths among children indicates that nursing the sick must have been a normal part of that care. Childless and older women helped with the nursing and feeding, but the meager rations available must have taxed the ingenuity of cooks who had been accustomed to a diet at once more plentiful and varied. As if the dreary round of illness and death did not cause enough suffering for wives and mothers, their maternal duties did not cease because of the hardships they endured. While it is rare for the records to describe women as "big with child," as they did in one case, the proximity between the deaths of the infants and their mothers suggests that death in childbirth was at least as common in the refugee camps as in the general population at the time.

In spite of the presence of suffering and death, there were occasions for rejoicing and renewal for some of the refugees. In several instances widows accepted offers of marriage from loyalist men in the military service or among the refugees. Jane Downes, who had helped defend her home near Camden until the rebels killed her husband, married Colonel Zacharias Gibbs of the Spartan Regiment. Mary Mail of Cuffeetown Creek, left with five children when her husband died in the siege of Savannah, took Conrad Sheddie, a British soldier, as her second husband. Despite the hardships of refugee life, romance also blossomed among the young men and women, and Edward Jenkins, the rector of St. Michael's, Charlestown, performed weddings of daughters of the refugee families to militiamen or troopers of the South Carolina Royalists.[12]

Baptisms were also joyous occasions, and Jenkins performed that sacrament on numerous occasions for the children of refugees, some of whom were able later to return to their homes in the interior. That baptisms might be occasions of parental duty rather than joy is illustrated in the case of Rosannah Johnston, now the sole support of the five youngsters to whom Jenkins administered the sacrament.[13]

If but occasional glimpses are caught of the lives of the loyalist refugee women, there is even less evidence on their children. Some children, however, may have been better off in their unusual environment because they were able to take advantage of the opportunity for formal schooling. One John Bell, a farmer on Hard Labour Creek and a militiaman in Richard King's regiment whose educational attainments remain a mystery, conducted a school for refugee children during an eleven-month period through September 1782. The subjects Bell offered and the ages of the children are not revealed, but about fifty families sent 100 of their children to Bell during at least one of the four periods for which he was paid, and a few families had four or more children in attendance at one time or another. It is interesting that pupils of both sexes attended, with the boys being only slightly more numerous than the girls. Of further interest is the fact that parents were called upon to certify that Bell "taught school," apparently necessary before he could be paid from the refugee funds British authorities had made available and an indication that he must have been observed frequently by a committee of parents.[14]

There must have been lighter moments for the refugees, although we know little of them. The more prominent loyalist men probably participated in the frequent meetings of a General Committee of Loyalists of the Garrison in the summer of 1782 as they sought to obtain and discuss information about the possible evacuation of the province. In July the *Royal Gazette* noted the addresses of esteem tendered by that committee and the "officers of the Country Militia" to Nisbet Balfour as he prepared to turn command of the city over to Isaac Allen before departing for England via New York, sentiments which the colonel reciprocated in a gracious reply. A similar address of appreciation, perhaps more sincerely felt by the loyalists of Ninety Six who had served with him, was proffered to John Harris Cruger on the eve of his departure for New York in August.[15]

From time to time some of the refugees took the opportunity to return to the parts of the interior from which they had fled. In May twenty women, some with children and including four widows, declared that they were "going back to the country," and that they "renounced all future claim of support from the British government" Although the circumstances that induced these people to take this step are not clear, most apparently succeeded in resuming life in their former neighborhoods.[16]

Other refugees had become alienated from their families without any hope of reconciliation. Elizabeth Bowers, the daughter of German immigrants on Hard Labour Creek, had married into a family that disagreed with hers "about politicks." During the war her husband "turned her off," probably because she had warned a party of loyalists of a possible ambush rebels had set for them, and she returned to live with her parents. After Ninety Six was evacuated, her father was beaten up by rebels, but he and Elizabeth were rescued by loyalist raiders and taken within the British lines. As a refugee she helped to care for the orphans of a loyalist whose brother she later married after the death of her first husband. That other families were divided by "politicks" is suggested by the case of William Meek and his wife. After he had served as a wagonmaster for the British in the backcountry, they became refugees in the lowcountry and later in Canada, while her brothers and a sister remained in South Carolina.[17]

The burden of supporting the refugees fell primarily on the British "military chest," which was already hard pressed to pay the troops and prepare for a possible siege by the Americans. Conditions among the refugees were so desperate that refugee inspectors urged that pay due to militiamen who had deserted be turned over to "needy refugees and their families." These circumstances led to the promotion of a lottery in Charlestown "for the benefit of the REFUGEE POOR." This ambitious undertaking was designed to raise $36,000 from the sale of 6,000 tickets, and was managed by a board composed of British officers and royal officials. The proceeds were to be distributed in roughly equal proportions between the prizewinners and the "distressed refugees," but the scheme was not as well received as the promoters had hoped and the drawing was postponed several times before it was finally held on June 10. Although prizes of $500 apiece were won by a sister and a widow of officers in the South Carolina Royalists, the grand prize of $3,000 was never presented. Exactly how much was actually realized for refugee relief was never revealed, but about £1,200 was distributed to the refugees between the drawing and the evacuation of South Carolina.[18]

Altogether for this period, "refugee expenditures" by British authorities to South Carolinians exceeded £10,000, a sum that included direct allowances to individuals, provisions, building materials for the shacks in which many lived, services such as the hospital, the coffins, and Bell's school, and the cost of administering the program. The bulk of the allowances went directly to the refugees, but the practice of apportioning them according to military rank did little for those most in need. Seventy refugees of the first and second classes received a total of £2,900, while those of the third class and those classified as "distressed," over 600 in all, received about £1,200, barely 30 percent of the total distributed.[19]

One aspect of British policy that did not apply immediately to the loyalists, but for which some would suffer in the long run, was the disposition of the property of persons in rebellion, assuming, as always, that the province would be restored permanently to the Crown.

Among the arrangements Sir Henry Clinton made after he captured Charlestown was to appoint trustees for captured property to whom, after he left South Carolina, he occasionally referred claims for debts due from former rebels. Either Clinton failed to notify Cornwallis about the trustees, or the earl preferred to carry out his own policy; but this disagreement became one of the many, if in this case minor, points of contention in the controversy between the two officers that arose after the war.[20]

Cornwallis was faced with the problem of supplying his army from the grain and livestock of the province without stripping the countryside of the means of subsistence for the civil population. His problem was eased in the first months by supplies captured from the rebels, but a permanent source of food and forage for the army soon became necessary. For this purpose he turned to Charles Stedman, a Pennsylvania loyalist who was serving as a deputy commissary with the army, appointed him a commissary of captures, and charged him with procuring the supplies immediately available. By purchasing grain and cattle from loyalists or by seizing it from vacant rebel estates, and employing the slaves of rebels to do the work, Stedman accomplished his task.[21]

Stedman's activities took care of the army's immediate needs, and Cornwallis postponed action on a more permanent policy until after his victory at Camden. On September 16 he proclaimed from his headquarters in the Waxhaw area that the property of persons in rebellion or who had left the state to continue resistance was subject to seizure for the support of the army, and he named John Cruden, a loyalist merchant from Wilmington, North Carolina, to be "Commissioner for the Seizure, Superintendance, Care, Custody, and Management" of such property. Cruden was authorized to take an inventory of the real and personal property of certain designated estates; to give public notice in the press of all seizures and sales; and to manage or sell estates so as to earn maximum returns for the benefit of the service, always reserving one-sixth to one-fourth of the value of the property to the wives and children of the rebel owners. He was to maintain separate accounts for each estate, report semiannually, and receive a 5 percent commission for his services.[22]

Cruden planned for the sequestered estates to produce foodstuffs for the commissary, as well as such staples as tobacco and indigo that could be sold to supplement the resources of the paymaster of the British forces. He also expected to derive immediate returns from the sale of timber products as naval stores, building materials, and firewood for the garrison of Charlestown. Slaves belonging to rebels, like land and livestock, were considered to be public property for the support of the war effort, and they would perform the necessary labor. Brian Cape, a Charlestown merchant, was selected as Cruden's deputy.[23]

In November 1780 Cruden announced the seizure of the estates of twenty prominent rebels, and similar notices were published from time to time. In Charlestown he took over the warehouses of the rebel merchant Christopher Gadsden by "agreement with Mrs. Gadsden." Although his early efforts seemed to promise success, he soon had difficulties with Stedman over accounting for provisions furnished the commissary, and with other officers who simply took what they wanted. As he accumulated stocks of provisions and cattle, it became necessary to ask for militia to guard them.[24]

The slaves were a special problem for his estate managers, not because they were rebellious, but because they required constant supervision when out from under the discipline of their masters. Also, as a very valuable species of movable property, they had to be guarded by the militia to prevent rebel raiders from making off with them or suffering loyalists from taking them to compensate for their own losses. A conspicuous example was Colonel William Henry Mills who, plundered and driven from his property on the Pee Dee, had to be called to account by Nisbet Balfour for nearly "three hundred negroes he is carrying across the country pillaging and robbing every plantation he comes to." Mills's explanation was that Colonel James Wemyss had authorized him to keep 100 slaves to indemnify himself for his mills and other property the rebels had burned, and that he was bringing the rest to Cruden's department. Cruden estimated that at one time or another he had jurisdiction over as many as 5,000 slaves and employed 100 overseers.[25]

Greater difficulties were to come for Cruden's operation. Once Cornwallis left South Carolina the estates were much more vulnerable to rebel raiders, and after Eutaw Springs the retreat to the vicinity of Charlestown left most of the sequestered property outside the British lines. Except for a few estates all the nearby islands and the slaves removed from the interior, there was little rebel property left to manage. All the disruptions made it impossible for Cruden to render his accounts on time, but in September 1781 he reported to the Board of Police that the operations of the last twelve months had actually netted a loss. Nevertheless, the board allowed his claim of £6,854 as his commission on the transactions of his office and continued him in his post.[26]

Just how little control the British retained was revealed to the loyalists when the state government boldly convened its General Assembly in January 1782. Called by Governor John Rutledge after new elections had been held for members of the House of Representatives and of the Senate, it met at Jacksonborough, a village on the Edisto River, little more than thirty miles west of Charlestown. Rutledge opened the proceedings with a stirring address that reviewed the trials through which the state had passed during the British occupation and called for renewed efforts to raise and maintain the force necessary to expel the invaders.

Of more interest to the loyalists in Charlestown and the refugee camps, was his call for the confiscation of the property of those who had aided the British, an idea he had been contemplating for some time. In September 1781 he had asked Francis Marion to provide "an accurate alphabetical list of all persons having property within your Brigade," including those who held British commissions, who had "gone over" to the British or were "notorious and dangerous enemies" to America, and "British subjects residing abroad." In his proposal to the Jacksonborough legislature, Rutledge suggested that certain classes of persons were fit subjects for confiscation, categories that were very similar to the exceptions made in his offer of pardon to loyalists six months before. Over the next six weeks the General Assembly spent much time in considering the terms of such legislation and which individuals should suffer its penalties.[27]

As Jerome Nadelhaft has shown, the military situation at the time made the General Assembly at Jacksonborough unique among South Carolina legislatures of the eighteenth century because British control of the city and the nearby coastal islands made it impossible for many members chosen from those parishes to attend. Therefore, members from the interior and the more distant coastal parishes were in the unusual position of legislating a policy that in the matter of confiscation would fall with special force on the property of Charlestown loyalists and collaborators. The opportunity for military men to influence such legislation was especially notable in the Senate where a half-dozen or more active officers—Marion, Sumter, and William Harden are conspicuous examples—were able to exert influence in a body that rarely had more than half of its members in attendance. Perhaps, as Nadelhaft has suggested, revenge was the dominant motive among legislators at Jacksonborough, but at the very least they were intimately aware of the suffering that the war had brought to the interior and not overly sympathetic to the plight of the loyalists and their sympathizers in and near the city.[28]

The matter of confiscating loyalist property was first taken up in the House, which directed a small committee to "consider what estates in this Country are properly objects of Confiscation and Sequestration" and the purposes for which "profits arising from them" should be expended. The committee presented a "partial report" on January 23 after which the task was recommitted to an enlarged committee of one member from each parish and district. According to Judge Aedanus Burke, who thought that leading Tories should be banished from the state but did not favor widespread confiscation of the property of protectionists, the House committee during the course of its work had as many as 700 persons under consideration: "Everyone gives in a list of his own and the State's Enemies, and the Enquiry is not so much what he has done, as what estate he has." Most of the suggested names were rejected during debate, but after the bill was returned to committee another 240 names were presented. The House ultimately reduced the list to 118 names and sent it to the Senate. Nevertheless, the debate had revealed substantial differences of opinion among the members about the degree of culpability of persons under consideration, for on the same day a motion was approved to adopt the principle of amercement "for Persons whose conduct was not considered sufficiently criminal to merit confiscation." Those amerced would be required to pay a fine in lieu of forfeiting their estates or suffering banishment from the state.[29]

The smaller Senate debated the bill in Committee of the Whole and more than doubled the number of estates marked for confiscation. Altogether, 290 estates were grouped into the categories Rutledge had recommended, with one addition, persons who had "petitioned to be embodied as royal militia," and the bill was returned to the House. That body, deeply involved in determining how to meet its obligations to the Confederation and to maintain state troops in the field, added the names recommended by its committee and sent the bill back to the Senate.[30]

After further consideration, the Senate suggested the formation of a conference committee to reconcile differences between the versions passed by the two bodies; its report was submitted and passed by both houses on February 23. A conference committee also worked out disagreements over the amercement bill, and the two houses passed it on February 25. As a consequence of the consideration of the confiscation and amercement bills, a third measure to "pardon the persons therein described" was also passed.[31]

The confiscation law of February 26 declared in its preamble that, because the British had sequestered or wantonly destroyed property in the State and practiced cruelties against its citizens, the state could no longer protect the property of persons who had supported the Crown, and that it was "just and reasonable to apply the same towards alleviating and lessening the burdens and expenses of the war." The law specifically mentioned three statements by British officers in 1780 as grounds for confiscation: Clinton's proclamation of June 3, declaring forfeit the property of persons who subsequently took up arms against His Majesty; Rawdon's letter to Rugeley threatening physical punishment to militiamen who did not report deserters; and Cornwallis's order to Cruger to hang loyalist militiamen who took up arms for the rebels after the Battle of Camden. A bill of attainder, the act confiscated the real and personal property of 237 persons named on the six lists appended to the law. Persons on list number one were British subjects, but largely nonresidents, and those on list number six were "inveterate enemies"; those on lists two through five—congratulators of Clinton; petitioners for service in the royal militia; congratulators of Cornwallis; and those currently holding British commissions—were to suffer banishment from the state in addition to loss of property. "Commissioners of Forfeited Estates" were to administer the law, selling the property at auction, recording their transactions and turning over the proceeds to the state treasury. A certain number of the slaves sold (families were not to be separated) were to be reserved as bounties for persons enlisting in the state's Continental line, while others were to perform necessary work for the state. Of the persons named in the law, eighty-five had been contributed by the House, eighty by the Senate, and sixty-seven were added at one of the other stages in the process, probably when the House added names during its second consideration, or in conference committee. The Amercement Act affected forty-seven persons who had accepted British protection, although "bearing high and important trusts and commissions" from the state, or who had subscribed money to equip the South Carolina Royalists as cavalry; it fined them 12 percent of the appraised value of their estates. The Pardon Act required persons who had not met the terms of Rutledge's pardon proclamation of September 1781, but who had since performed military service for the state, to pay a fine of 10 percent in specie or in slaves.[32]

The Royal Gazette tried to keep abreast of the proceedings at Jacksonborough, first printing Rutledge's address, and later publishing the lists of persons named in the confiscation and amercement laws. It also announced a meeting of persons named in the act on March 22 at Strickland's Tavern in Charlestown. The proceedings of that meeting were not published, but it is likely that they were similar to those expressed by "Tory" in the Gazette, who suggested retaliation because rebel estates were "much larger than those of the tories."[33]

Alexander Leslie was aware that the rebel "sanguinary laws" could affect the steadfastness of loyalists and protectionists alike, noting that many, "being men with large estates and advanced in life, will…leave us and go to the Enemy," and he asked whether he should take measures to prevent the sales from being carried out. No such instructions came to him, but the seizure of slaves from rebel estates was one of the fruits of the cavalry raids that spring. The Commissioners of Forfeited Estates conducted the first sales that summer, auctioning land and personal property at Jacksonborough in May, at Pocotaligo in June, at Georgetown and again at Jacksonborough in August.[34]

To this point, little has been said about black people in South Carolina and then only as slaves performing useful labor or as objects of plunder between the contending military forces. Unfortunately, the records that relate to blacks at all reveal little about them as individuals or what the war meant to them. Yet the war had considerable impact on some blacks, changing their legal status and uprooting their families from scenes that had become familiar to them. It is one of the ironies of the Revolution in South Carolina that a struggle by white people to secure freedom from their oppressive imperial masters did little to bring the benefits of freedom to their chattels; instead, the oppressors were probably responsible for freeing as many slaves in South Carolina during the few years of the occupation as all of the kindly masters or committed northern abolitionists would do in the next three quarters of a century.

There were few free blacks in South Carolina before the war and those in bondage were concentrated in the parishes of the lowcountry, except for those in the Pee Dee and on the more prosperous backcountry plantations. Throughout most of the American Period, most slaves went about their usual tasks or performed public service on fortifications for their rebel masters. When the British undertook their southern campaign, however, blacks found themselves more directly involved as the tide of war ebbed and flowed. Augustine Prevost's campaign from Savannah to the gates of Charlestown in 1779 disrupted life on the plantations in his path, and some slaves returned to Georgia with his retreating troops. There they were joined by other South Carolina blacks whose services on the fortifications around Savannah were volunteered by British sympathizers. The *Royal Gazette* later carried a notice identifying the owners of a list of about 100 South Carolina "Negroes in the Engineering Department who had joined the army in Georgia" in 1779.[35]

Almost as soon as Sir Henry Clinton's army landed on the South Carolina coast in the winter of 1780 blacks began to drift into his lines, and they were soon put to work as laborers for the engineers, the commissary general, the quartermaster general, and the artillery. Immediately after the capitulation of Charlestown, so many other blacks sought employment that they had to be turned away until early in June when Clinton had found an opportunity to announce a policy that was designed to distinguish between the loyal slaveowners and those in rebellion. The army would return slaves to their loyalist owners provided they were not punished for their absence, and it was prepared to hire their slaves and reimburse them for those who died in service. The slaves of rebel owners, on the other hand, belonged to "the publick," and escaped slaves of nonloyalists who served the British faithfully were promised freedom at the end of the war. As will be seen, the distinctions set forth in the policy would become considerably less clear.[36]

Dr. James Clitherall, a Charlestown physician, Thomas Inglis, a merchant in the city, and Major Robert Ballingall of the Colleron militia were chosen commissioners of claims for slave property, and in the winter of 1781 they published lists of owners of about 500 slaves employed by various units of the army. Of the owners who can be identified, more were rebels than loyalists or protectionists. And John Cruden put much larger numbers of blacks to work on the rebel estates he managed under the sequestration policy.[37]

When Sir Guy Carleton, the last commander in chief, was preparing for the evacuation of New York in 1783, he ordered the registration of blacks in that city who planned to emigrate to other parts of the empire. Among them were 460 persons from South Carolina who had somehow made their way north during the war. The largest number had apparently accompanied Clinton when he returned after Charlestown surrendered but others had come with his earlier expedition in 1776 or joined during the operations in Georgia. Virtually all of the owners identified in this "Book of Negroes" were rebels, an indication of just how disruptive the war was to the slave system.[38]

The blacks who served in the British or loyalist armed forces are also difficult to identify. Several "mullatoes" were among the backcountrymen Richardson captured and sent to Charlestown in the winter of 1775–1776; a James Smart, a refugee, had been "wounded and disabled" while serving in Samuel Tynes's regiment in 1780; and one of William Cunningham's officers during the Saluda raids may have been black. A unit referred to several times as the "black pioneers" was formed in Georgia in 1779 and saw service in the southern campaign until it was sent to Jamaica in 1781, and late in the war some rebel sources also used the term "Black Dragoons" to refer to blacks they charged with marauding and plundering. Some blacks also served as artificers with the Royal Artillery, but whether they were actually serving in the army or were merely employed by it is not clear. The Earl of Dunmore, already notorious for his earlier suggestion as royal governor of Virginia that blacks be armed by the British, repeated the idea when he visited Charlestown in 1781. Although John Cruden enthusiastically endorsed Dunmore's plan, British commanders showed little interest in it.[39]

Once the British abandoned the backcountry, and especially after it became apparent that peace would be declared, blacks became valuable pawns in the contest between the two sides as local rebels tried to protect or recover their slave property, and the loyalists sought to compensate for their loss of other property by acquiring the slaves of their enemies. The contest began when the lowcountry loyalist exiles were not able to recover all their slave property on their return to the province after Charlestown fell; rebel slaveholders became aggrieved after John Cruden seized their slaves to work on the sequestered estates; and the Jacksonborough General Assembly responded by confiscating the property of certain loyalists. Although the state had the last word in retaliation, by 1782 a great many rebel slaves were within the British lines or within striking distance of British raiding parties.

Once the Jacksonborough confiscation legislation was made public, Alexander Leslie, apparently under great pressure from loyalist leaders, ordered Major Thomas Fraser of the South Carolina Royalists to pursue rebel raiders "who have taken away the Negroes of the loyalists from their plantations in St. Thomas Parish." That he had more in mind than mere retaliation for a particular raid was made clear in Fraser's instructions: "his principal business" was to collect "all the slaves who belong to those, in arms against the British government" so that the rebels and their blacks would understand that his mission was undertaken "in consequence of the enemy seizing and confiscating the property of the loyalists"; further, slaves of rebels would understand that they and their families would be protected "by the English government should they behave with fidelity during the course of the war", Leslie instructed Fraser not to take the slaves of rebels indiscriminately "unless you are well informed that the slaves of Loyalists are seized by order of the rebell

Government," but he was to give notice widely that blacks were encouraged to make their way to the British lines. Fraser carried out his mission with zest, returning with 150 slaves, three times the number taken by the rebels; thus, the *Royal Gazette* announced triumphantly, the rebels had discovered "that their estates, not those of the loyalists, have been confiscated by the Assembly at Jacksonborough." Leslie followed this by asking Clinton's instructions in response to a request by loyalists that blacks be armed for service with the British, and he also appointed a commission of officers and leading loyalists to examine the status of blacks who had been serving the British and thus would be "obnoxious" to their former rebel masters. When the state government actually conducted sales of loyalist estates during the summer, including that of Colonel Elias Ball of Wambaw, the *Royal Gazette* announced that "a party of our Dragoons...went over to St. Thomas's Parish to assist that gentleman in removing his Negroes to a place of security."[40]

Although slave property was an important bone of contention between the rebels and the loyalists, because of their value blacks were generally considered to be desirable plunder by some on both sides. Governor Rutledge had to warn Marion to guard against sea captains "with a commission or Letter of Marque from Congress" who seized slaves from loyalist plantations; such property, Rutledge emphasized, belonged to the state. And General Leslie had to order Brigadier General O'Hara to send ashore a number of slaves that his officers had carried on board transports that were about to sail for St. Lucia.[41]

Thus, when Leslie and the loyalists received word that South Carolina was to be evacuated by the British, large numbers of slaves belonging to rebels, to loyalists, or to protectionists were under British jurisdiction. The state government was determined not to be despoiled of the fruits of victory, and individual rebels were desperate to recover their slaves so that they could renew planting operations; on the other side, the British had made promises to loyal subjects and to individual slaves who had served faithfully, and Alexander Leslie was determined to carry them out. Only in the last case would the slaves themselves receive any consideration, and then only briefly, but the stage was set fat one of the major controversies during the evacuation of the State and after the war.

Notes

1. The principal source for the loyal refugees in and near Charlestown in the last eighteen months of the war is T50/1/3. For the convenience of the reader, citations from the applicable T50/1/3 records will be made from Clark, ed., *Loyalists*, I, where possible.
2. Clinton to Cornwallis, June 3, 1780, CP, 30/11/61, 7; *Royal South Carolina Gazette* (Charlestown), July 6, 1780; Loyalist Transcripts, LVII, 418–38; Rawdon to Alexander Swart, July 25, 1781, *The Remembrancer, Or, Imperial Repository of Public Events,* 1781 (London, 1781), XV, 8.
3. Rutledge to Marion, Sept. 3, 1781, Gibbes, *Documentary History,* III, 134: Balfour to Cornwallis, June 7, 1781, CP, 30/11/6, 190; to Clinton, Oct. 2, 1781, Leslie Letterbooks, #15529; Bull to Hillsborough, Nov. 11, 1781, S.C. Records in P.R.O., XXXVI, 137; H.M.C., *Report,* II, 388.
4. The total is composed of 90 men, 211 women, and 51 children; the adults are usually listed by name, although the children rarely are. Sample entries in these records of allowances paid are " Brown, John, with wife and five children," and "Rosannah Johnson (widow)," Clark, ed., *Loyalists,* I, 145, 181, 491–531.
5. Clark, ed., *Loyalists,* I, 515–23, 506–8, and for the hospital, ibid., 535–44; for Fyffe, see Loyalist Transcripts, LV, 428–47, and for Bulline, *Canadian Claims,* 180.
6. Clark, ed., *Loyalists,* I, 491–504.
7. Ibid., 493, 502, 505, 507, 518, 534–35.
8. Wells, *Journal;* Caroline Gilman, ed., *Letters of Eliza Wilkinson* (New York, 1969 [orig. publ. New York, 1839]): Mary Beth Norton, "Eighteenth Century Women in Peace and War: The Case of the Loyalists,"

WMQ (1976), 386–409, and "What an Alarming Crisis Is This," in *The Southern Experience in the American Revolution*, ed. Jeffrey J. Crow and Larry E. Tise (Chapel Hill, N.C., 1978), 203–34.
9. *Canadian Claims*, 143; Clark ed., *Loyalists*, I, 285, 288, 292–94; Barnwell, ed., "Exiles," 43.
10. T50/1/5; see Clark, ed., *Loyalists*, I, 545–50.
11. Loyalist Transcripts, LIV, 593–97, and LV, 570–73; Clark, ed., *Loyalists*, I, 296, 517.
12. *Royal Gazette* (Charlestown), June 8, 1782; *Canadian Claims*, 158; Edward Jenkins Papers, *SCHS*.
13. Jenkins Papers, SCHS.
14. Clark, ed., *Loyalists*, I, 485–89.
15. *Royal Gazette* for June and July 1782, particularly July 24 and Aug. 14.
16. Clark, ed., *Loyalists*, I, 515. A Jane Miller, her husband Samuel, and their three children are among those listed here as returning to their home in Cheraw District; in December, however, a Samuel Miller and four others are among those who sought refuge in East Florida, Refugees to East Florida.
17. Loyalist Claims, XXVI, 58–63, 71–74; *Canadian Claims*, 183.
18. *Royal Gazette*, Feb. 2, June 1, 5, and 22, 1782; total compiled from figures in T50/1/3, many of which may also be found in Clark, ed., *Loyalists*, I, 491–532.
19. T50/1/3, and Clark, ed., *Loyalists*, I, 491–552.
20. Clinton, *American Rebellion*, 179; petition of Greenwood & Higginson, et al., to the King in Council, July 28, 1780, forwarded by Clinton to Trustees of Captured Property, Charlestown, Jan. 2, 1781, and James Moncrief, et al, Trustees, to Clinton, Dec. 29, 1780, and Clinton to Sir James Wright, May 29, 1780, H.M.C., *Report*, II, 130, 165, 231, 226. That a sequestration program of sorts was already being implemented before Cornwallis turned to the problem is evident in Evan McLaurin to Balfour, Aug. 2, 23, 1780, McLaurin Papers, NYPL.
21. Franklin and Mary Wickwire, *Cornwallis: The American Adventure* (Boston, 1970), 141–42; Cornwallis to Turnbull, June 16, suggesting that he "give permission to the militia to do what they please with the plantations abandoned by the Rebels," harvesting the crops and turning "them to their own use," or occasionally, "if it is more convenient now and then to destroy one"; otherwise, property the troops did not need should be turned over to the commissary, to McArthur, June 18, 1780, CP 30/11/77, II, 15.
22. *South Carolina and American General Gazette* (Charlestown), Oct. 14, 1780; CP, 30/11/7, 22–28.
23. Cruden to Captain McKinnon, Feb. 2, 1781, CP, 30/11/7, 9; CEP, for Cape; Loyalist Transcripts, LIV, 6–18, for statement of James Alexander, a loyalist militia captain, who was assigned to guard and "work off a quantity of tar" on the rebel Governor John Rutledge's plantation.
24. *South Carolina and American General Gazette*, Nov. 22, 1780. For Cruden's report on the progress of the program in the first months, see his "Narrative and Observations," accompanying his accounts, September 1781, CP, 30/11/7, 38.
25. Balfour to Cornwallis, Nov. 17, 1780, CP, 30/11/4, 152, and Cruden to Balfour, May 28, 1781, CP, 30/11/7, 9.
26. "Narrative and Observations," CP, 30/11/7, 32, 36–37; Wickwire, *Cornwallis: The American Adventure*, 239–40. See R Arthur Bowler, *Logistics and the Failure of the British Army, in America* (Princeton, N.J., 1975),88–91, for the conclusion that rebel owners of estates may have benefited more from improvements Cruden made in their property than the British army did from the supplies and services it was furnished.
27. Rutledge to Marion, Sept. 27, 1781, Gibbes, *Documentary History*, III, 134–35,175–79; Rutledge's address is printed in *House Journal, 1782*, 9–13, and the progress of the confiscation legislation is followed in it and in *Senate Journal, 1782*.
28. Jerome Nadelhaft, *The Disorders of War: The Revolution in South Carolina* (Orono, Me., 1981), 74–75, 84.
29. Burke to Middleton, Jan. 25, 1782, Joseph W. Barnwell, ed., "Correspondence of the Hon. Arthur Middleton," *SCHGM* (1925), 192–93.
30. *Senate Journal, 1782*, 74–79; *House Journal, 1782*, 93, 99, 106–7.
31. *Senate Journal, 1782*, 124–25, 132–33, 126, 142; *House Journal, 1782*, 106, 110, 119–20.
32. *Statutes at Large*, IV, 516–23; VI, 629–35.
33. *Royal Gazette*, Feb. 23, Mar. 20, 27, 1782; the laws were published in England in *Remembrancer*, XIV, 140–43; XV, 47–49.
34. Leslie to Clinton, Mar. [?], 1782, H.M.C., *Report*, II, 438; "Sales of Sundry Land &c. by the Commissioners of Forfeited Estates," 1782, CEP; *Royal Gazette*, July 6, 1782.
35. *Royal Gazette*, Mar. 3, l781.
36. Benjamin Quarles, *The Negro in the American Revolution* (Chapel Hill, N.C., 1961), 137–38.
37. *Royal Gazette*, Mar. 10, 1781.

38. Book of Negroes Registered and Certified after Having Been Inspected by the Commissioners Appointed by His Excellency Sir Guy Carleton, K.B., General & and Commander in Chief, on Board Sundry T'sports in which they were to Embark, Previous to the Time of Sailing from the Port of New York between 23 April and 31st May, 1783, both days in included. BHP, LV, #10427.
39. Gibbes, ed., *Documentary History,* I, 249–53; Clark, ed., *Loyalists,* I, 151, 520; Charles H. Stewart, comp., *The Service of British Regiments in Canada and North America: A Resume* (Ottawa, 1964), 419; a complaint about "Black Dragoons" is in Bee to Governor John Mathews, Dec. 9, 1782, Thomas Bee Papers, SCL; *Royal Gazette,* Mar. 14, 1781; Quarles, *Negro in the American Revolution,* 150–51.
40. Leslie to Fraser, Mar. 27, 1782, and draft of a "Commission appointed to examine the situation of Negroes in the Forces or Public Departments who have served because of promises by Proclamations, etc.," n.d. [l782], Leslie Letterbooks, #15667, 15675; Leslie to Clinton, Mar. 30, 1782, H.M.C., *Report,* II ,435; *Royal Gazette,* Mar. 30, July 9, 1782.
41. Rutledge to Marion, Oct. 12, 1781, Gibbes, *Documentary History,* III, 188–89.

Part IV

THE LOYALIST EXPERIENCE AFTER THE WAR

British authorities began to plan to evacuate South Carolina in the summer of 1782, and before the end of that year regular troops, provincials, and a large number of loyalist civilians and slaves had withdrawn from the state.

The loyalists scattered to several destinations, either to make a fresh start in other parts of the empire or to reestablish themselves in Great Britain. Their experiences varied, and some moved several times before establishing themselves permanently. The British government furnished transportation to the loyalists and granted them lands in Canada and the West Indies, and it sought to indemnify those who had suffered loss of property and income because of their loyalty.

Some loyalists and protectionists were able to remain in or return to South Carolina, and during the 1780s they obtained relief from the confiscation laws. Although such relief measures were not universally popular and private vengeance was taken against a few of the more violent loyalists, a measure of reconciliation was achieved by the end of the decade.

Chapter 15

British Evacuation of South Carolina

The Tories are turning arrant Rebels, and Bob Williams, Wells, Alexr. Inglis & the rest of that crew, say they are. They have no fears upon them, they rely on their own innocence & our Justice, for they know not what they have done to be afraid of.

—Aedanus Burke, January 1782

Eventually the North ministry in England lost the confidence of the House of Commons and was replaced in the winter of 1782 by one committed to make peace with the Americans. As the year progressed General Leslie was ordered to prepare for the evacuation of the southern ports still in British hands. By late summer preliminary arrangements were under way to evacuate South Carolina altogether, and between then and the end of the year many thousands of loyalists, their slaves, and British, German, and provincial troops left the state.

Once it became generally known in British-occupied South Carolina that Lord Cornwallis had surrendered, rumors began to circulate among the loyalist troops and refugees that Britain was planning to end the war and that loyal subjects might be abandoned to the wrath of the rebels. British authorities and loyalist leaders tried their best to dispel such fears. "Carolina Loyalist" in the *Royal Gazette* pointed out that loyal sentiment was much stronger in the Carolinas and Georgia than in Virginia and that the garrisons of Savannah and Charlestown were more than a match for American forces. Some leaders among the refugees declared that they were prepared to arm 1,200 men to attack the Americans, but as a North Carolina officer complained privately, Leslie apparently had no authority to do more than conduct raids at a time when his army should be taking advantage of the dwindling numbers among Greene's ragged troops.[1]

Throughout the winter of 1781–82 the rumors seemed to be no more than that, but with the approach of spring there were signs that changes were indeed under way. When Leslie received orders to send 2,000 troops to Jamaica, Balfour and other officers protested that "as the inhabitants of Charlestown...are mostly of doubtful principles, many desirous to make their peace with the country," local people would take such a reassignment as a preliminary to evacuating the province. Leslie replied to Clinton that he could spare only 1,000 men, but he warned Brigadier General Alured Clarke at Savannah to prepare plans for evacuating that city, "taking all possible care not to give suspicion of so alarming an intention." In March public notice was given that an agent was prepared to talk with "Refugees who are desirous of going to East Florida to settle there, agreeable to the encouragement contained in Governor Tonyn's proclamation," another indication of impending change.[2]

Every vessel brought disquieting intelligence from New York. Clinton had responded to an inquiry from the Board of American Loyalists in March by assuring them that no "garrison in which Loyalists are joined with the King's troops, should be surrendered on any terms which might discriminate" between them. But when Sir Guy Carleton reached New York from Britain as Clinton's replacement, he returned a gracious but noncommittal response to a stirring address of welcome that had emphasized the union rather than the splintering of the empire. In Charlestown, the editor of the *Royal Gazette* took notice of the rumors of peace, and pointed out that the Earl of Shelburne, who had urged in the House of Lords that independence be granted, was the head of the new ministry.[3]

While these rumors mounted, plans were being laid for the evacuation of all the southern garrisons. Carleton informed Leslie late in May to expect a fleet of transports within a few days for the evacuation of Savannah and St. Augustine; he ordered that the troops and supplies, and all the loyalists who wished to leave, should be removed; that all assistance should be given to rebel authorities for an orderly transfer; and that there should be no destruction of fortifications or property by departing troops. But Leslie's efforts to carry out the order brought sharp protests from Governors Wright and Tonyn and the loyalists in Savannah who were disturbed by the prospect that the British would give up St. Augustine as well as Savannah, a position also supported by Charlestown loyalists. Leslie countermanded the order, a conclusion Carleton himself had reached because there was not enough shipping available to evacuate both towns.[4]

The evacuation of Georgia was completed in July. Agreements were reached between the British and American commanders for a peaceful transfer of authority, and to permit British merchants who traded with Great Britain to remain in Savannah until they could dispose of their inventories and export local "produce to the amount of their said goods & merchandise." Savannah was evacuated on the 11th, "leaving the works and the town perfect," but many refugee families remained on Tybee Island at the mouth of the Savannah River where "many of the loyalists died." Most of the survivors ultimately made their way to East Florida overland or in sundry small craft, or sailed to Jamaica, and to those places they took about 5,000 slaves. The troops sailed for New York accompanied by the royal officials and some of the more prominent loyalists.[5]

The New York fleet from Savannah arrived off the bar of Charlestown on July 27, lingered long enough to take on Nisbet Balfour, John Harris Cruger, and other officers, and resumed its northward voyage in a few days. The presence of the fleet and the tales brought by some of the Georgia refugees who landed at Charlestown brought home to South Carolina's loyalists as nothing else could the difficulties they could expect to face in the months ahead. By then, at least some of the committed loyalists must have reached the conclusion that Carleton was expressing privately to Leslie, namely, that the "evacuation is not a matter of choice but of deplorable necessity in consequence of an unsuccessful war."[6]

Still Leslie delayed making any public announcement that would confirm the rumors that the province would be abandoned to the rebels. Even as the fleet from Savannah lay outside the harbor, he received a petition of sixty-five "loyal inhabitants" of the city urging him, because Admiral George Rodney had won a great victory over the French fleet in the Caribbean, to countermand the order to evacuate Georgia. And Leslie reported to Carleton late in June that although rumors were circulating " from the Northward of our intend'd evacuation, the people in town don't much believe it," and he, "knowing the jealousy of the people," had not given official notice that the province was to be abandoned. But as the truth about the evacuation of Georgia became known, particularly the "miseries that the loyal inhabitants of Georgia have already experienced," as the *Royal Gazette* put it, Leslie could put off an announcement no longer.[7]

The *Royal Gazette* of August 7 confirmed the worst fears of the loyalists, carrying Leslie's notice informing the "inhabitants" that "a Convoy will be ordered, and every possible assistance given to convey to Augustine such of them, who, from the expected withdrawal of the King's troops from this town, may desire to remove with their families and effects to the Province of East-Florida." Those who wished to take advantage of the opportunity were asked to register at the office of the quartermaster general, and to designate the specific property they wished to carry with them. Those wishing to go to other places were asked to register those intentions, and inhabitants who preferred to "make their peace" with the state government were encouraged to do so.[8]

The loyalists had many private worries about adjusting to the evacuation, but in public expressions to royal officials their leaders were most concerned with the status of their property, particularly in slaves. Leslie noted immediately that loyalists named in the rebel confiscation law expected some compensation from the sequestration fund for their losses, and when the General Committee of Loyalists asked permission to send Charles Ogilvie and Gideon Dupont, Jr., as agents to explain their plight to Carleton, Leslie acceded warmly. In the memorial these emissaries presented to Carleton, however, their first concern was that the evacuation of Charlestown be postponed so that refugees might avoid winter weather at sea, have more time for the collection of debts and an orderly removal of property, or to "make such terms" with the state as would permit them to stay. Only then did they request what was especially on the minds of slaveholders, that the evacuees be permitted to take sequestered slaves with them in order to indemnify themselves for other property and the uncollected debts they would be forced to leave behind.[9]

The question of slave property had several dimensions and Leslie sought instructions from Carleton on how to handle the problem. To allow loyalists and British officers to take sequestered slaves was not the simple solution to that problem that it seemed; although the confiscation law exempted debts owed British merchants and marriage settlements from its provisions, the state authorities now threatened to ignore those exemptions if slaves of rebels were carried off at the evacuation. The state's threat was very real to some loyalists who petitioned Leslie in September to issue "peremptory orders" to prevent persons from carrying off blacks whom they did not own, and that compensation be paid for slaves whose rebel masters might consider them to be "obnoxious" and exact retribution for their service to the British. These issues were further complicated by the promises of freedom made by British officers to blacks for faithful service. These competing pressures from both sides made it desirable to reach agreement on the slave property issue. Arrangements were made for Intendant Alexander Wright, and Attorney General James Johnston, as Leslie's representatives, and Edward Rutledge and Benjamin Guerard for the new state governor, John Mathews, to meet at a neutral site early in October.[10]

At their first meeting Wright and Johnston proposed that all American property within the British lines be returned except such "domestics as had rendered themselves obnoxious," and that in return Governor Mathews should suspend enforcement of the confiscation law and seek its repeal at the next session of the legislature. The state's negotiators said they had no power to agree to suspend an act of the General Assembly and pointed out that the confiscation law currently did not apply to debts due British merchants. After further instructions, the negotiators agreed on October 10 that, where possible, slaves would be returned to rebel owners except those considered obnoxious or who had received specific promises of freedom; that persons named in the confiscation act and British merchants would be permitted the same right to sue in the state courts for the recovery of debts as citizens of the state; and that returned slaves would not be punished or departing loyalists insulted. The state's commissioners were allowed to search some of the ships loading for St. Augustine, but of the 136 slaves found who should have been returned, only seventy-three had actually been delivered when Leslie suddenly suspended the agreement because the Americans seized three soldiers near the city gates. One of the conditions of the agreement was that the British would pay for slaves promised their freedom; without positive assurance from Carleton on the matter of compensation and with the ships ready to sail, Leslie may have found it impossible to keep both the agreement with the State and his pledge to the loyalists and simply found a pretext to suspend the former.[11]

Several other agreements between the two sides were carried out. For some months the British had sought to buy rice and other foodstuffs for the use of the garrison, but when Greene had refused to accommodate them, they resorted to raiding the countryside. In time Greene's troops became short of certain supplies available to the British through the ports, particularly such items as "salt, rum, blankets and hospital stores," and the Americans agreed to exchange provisions for these items. Leslie also gave merchants in the city permission to negotiate with the state, and Governor Mathews agreed to offer them protection for six months after the evacuation "with a right to sell or barter their goods and collect their debts freely during that time," although they could not sue in the courts to collect debts due them without permission of the General Assembly. And late in October the two armies worked out a comprehensive prisoner exchange agreement.[12]

These issues and agreements affected some of the loyalists, but many of them still did not know whether they could "make their peace" with the rebels, and they sought to persuade relatives and neighbors to support their efforts. Henry Rugeley had accepted a commission for West Indian service in Lord Montagu's regiment but had not joined it. Still in South Carolina in the spring of 1782, he resigned his commission and determined "to live amongst my friends and acquaintances in & about Camden" because his orphaned niece Betsy wished to return to that area. When he tried to escort her to Camden, however, General Greene refused to permit him to pass through the lines, and Rugeley turned to the prominent Camden rebel John Chesnut for help to arrange the sale of certain property to support her. When Rugeley made a second attempt to go to Camden in September, he was stopped again because he was named in the Confiscation Act. By early October Rugeley was in a quandary about whether to go in the fleet that was preparing to sail for Jamaica, fearing that if Leslie allowed the British "to carry away every Negro,...it would not in that case be prudent to stay." He preferred to remain in South Carolina if the confiscation law could be suspended, "Provided always...that my feelings are not to be hurt by any conversation after I have got absolution," but he would need assurances that he would not be molested because Lord Montagu was still urging him to report to his regiment in Jamaica. Rugeley's situation is unusually well documented; fragmentary evidence on other loyalists, and especially the protectionists, indicates that they were very active in seeking the intercession of friends and connections to permit them to stay.[13]

Through the columns of the city's two newspapers loyalist merchants and professional men announced that they intended to sail to Europe at an early opportunity, and they naturally urged their customers to settle their accounts. William Charles Wells notified the public in August that he would suspend publication of the *Royal Gazette* in order to settle his "private affairs," but he assured his readers that he would provide them with any good news that came before "that direful event shall happen, the Dread of which now fills every loyal Breast with Terror and Dismay." The *Royal South Carolina Gazette* expressed similar sentiments and both papers ceased publication before the end of September.[14]

The evacuation of South Carolina occurred in two well-defined stages rather than in the one that Carleton had originally planned. The evacuation of Georgia demonstrated to Alexander Leslie that much more shipping would be necessary to carry away the loyalists and their property than had originally been anticipated. Despite its decision to end the war, the ministry in England had made no unusual efforts to provide additional transportation beyond that necessary to redeploy troops and equipment to Britain and other parts of the empire. Thus the needs of the loyalists could be met only in succession; that is, ships that had carried Georgians and their property to Jamaica and St. Augustine were ordered to rendezvous at Charlestown for its evacuation, but some vessels from St. Augustine arrived with troops bound for New York. Therefore, over two months passed from the sailing of the first convoys from Charlestown in October until the second stage was completed, employing many of the same vessels, in December.[15]

By mid-August over 4,200 loyalists had been registered as planning to leave South Carolina, including nearly 2,500 women and children. Nearly 7,200 blacks were to accompany them, and it was estimated that about 25,000 tons of shipping would be needed to carry these people and their effects. Their principal destinations were East Florida and Jamaica, while others chose to go to Great Britain or Nova Scotia. The provincial regiments from the Carolinas and Georgia were to be sent to East Florida, and those serving in the active militia units were paid for the remainder of 1782 before they embarked for their destinations.[16]

Over a month passed before enough transports were available for those who wished to go to East Florida, and embarkation plans were changed several times before refugees could be taken on board. At the end of September Leslie wrote Tonyn to expect "in a few days...to see a fleet off your Bar full of Refugees, and Negroes, &c.," although the convoy did not actually clear Charlestown until mid-October. Among the passengers embarking were the South Carolina Royalists, whose party consisted of 242 officers and men, fifty-two women and children, and thirty-one servants. Most of the families leaving apparently did not own slaves, but some slaveholders like Gabriel Capers, a protectionist from Christ Church Parish, who took sixty-two, and Patrick Cunningham and Colonel James Cassells who took over twenty apiece, contributed to the large number of blacks carried to East Florida. Leslie sent "provisions" for six months for 1,000 whites and 2,000 blacks.[17]

The experience of Colonel David Fanning illustrates the difficulties the refugees faced. Once aboard the *New Blessing,* he waited eight days before she sailed; the voyage took three, and his vessel lay offshore for eight more before he could land. The bar off the harbor of St. Augustine was treacherous, and several vessels ran aground and were broken up by the waves, causing much loss of property although most of the passengers were saved. The Florida fleet divided when it neared its destination because many of the passengers preferred to settle in the valley of the St. John's River and had asked to be landed there.[18]

Enough shipping was also available to send a small fleet to Nova Scotia, and it cleared for Halifax late in October with the army's heavy ordnance and stores and about 500 refugees aboard. Colonel Samuel Campbell of the North Carolina militia was put in charge of the refugees, who were from both Carolinas and included over fifty blacks. Leslie wrote the commandant at Halifax to expect them, that they had been provided with clothing and the militiamen paid, but that he hoped supplies for them could be available at Halifax.[19]

Although a substantial number of loyalists and blacks were relocated by the Florida and Halifax convoys in October, transportation had to be found for others who wished or felt compelled to leave South Carolina as well as the bulk of the British, German, and provincial military personnel who were to be redeployed or separated from the service. Not until December had enough vessels returned from earlier voyages or been supplied from other places to complete the evacuation.

For the time being, at least, Henry Rugeley's dilemma had been resolved. He would embark for Jamaica, he wrote John Chesnut early in December, but he hoped that, when the General Assembly convened, his friends would "do everything in their power" to remove his name from the confiscation law. Already indebted to Chesnut for arranging to take care of his niece, Rugeley now introduced the new Mrs. Rugeley, who was coming to Camden, and asked that the income received from the labor of the slaves sent earlier be given to support her and Betsy until he was allowed to return or could send for them.[20]

Altogether, an armada of 126 vessels had been concentrated at Charlestown and there divided into groups intended for five destinations. Bound for the island of St. Lucia, the smallest fleet carried about 200 Black Pioneers whom Leslie had organized from among the free blacks too "obnoxious" to remain in Carolina; Rugeley joined over 1,200 loyalists and 2,600 blacks in the fleet of twenty vessels for Jamaica; and eight ships were to take another contingent of loyalists and blacks to St. Augustine. The largest number of vessels was set aside to carry the garrison of British, German and provincial troops and large quantities of stores to New York, while twenty ships were to take royal officials, and a number of officers and loyalists to England. The last British troops left the city on December 14 without incident, arrangements having been made between Leslie and Brigadier General Anthony Wayne that the British would not harm the city if they were not molested during their withdrawal. Not until December 18 did the last vessel cross the bar and join the other ships as they dispersed for their destinations. The vessels bound to the northeast sailed together for two days before those destined for England departed.[21]

General Archibald Campbell, the royal governor of Jamaica who had been instrumental in the conquest of Georgia barely four years earlier, had been notified to expect the arrival of large numbers of southern loyalists and their slaves for resettlement in his plantation province. Among the prominent loyalists who embarked in the Jamaica convoy were John Rose, Colonel James Cary, and Colonel Thomas Fletchall. Rose transported 171 slaves to the island, and Cary and Fletchall brought smaller numbers in hopes of employing them in producing staples. Most of the vessels reached Jamaica in January 1783.[22]

The second and smaller exodus to East Florida also included a number of blacks, among them over 200 who accompanied the senior Elias Ball and his family. William

Curtis, who had settled in Charlestown during the occupation, had no slaves to bring but did "pull down" his recently constructed house and loaded it on board for use in St. Augustine. His enterprise was not rewarded, for most of his materials were lost when his vessel capsized on the bar off the town. John Champneys, the merchant who had suffered so many misadventures after his first exodus from Charlestown in 1778, had remarried during the occupation; once again he left his wife behind as he boarded a vessel in the Florida fleet.[23]

For the royal officials and many of the loyalists sailing in the fleet for England this was also a second exile, an experience they probably had not expected to repeat. One would give a great deal to know William Bull's thoughts as the aging lieutenant governor wrote his report to Colonial Secretary Thomas Townshend upon landing at Torbay early in 1783. After describing the fleets and their destinations, and listing the officials who had sailed with him, he expressed his pleasure at the care Alexander Leslie had taken to see that Charlestown suffered no damage as the troops were departing. Revealing little of his own feelings, he showed his sympathy for the "many gentlemen and merchants who were in such a predicament in regard to their lives & property by the laws & declarations of the State of Carolina, that they dared not remain, "as well as the" poor Refugee loyalists who are destitute of every resource & even hope of gaining maintenance, either in Florida or Jamaica." He estimated "the total number of these unhappy men & their families white and black who have evacuated that valuable province" at over 9,000, a figure that conforms closely to the best estimates made by contemporaries and recent scholarship.[24]

Notes

1. Burke to Middleton, Jan. 25, 1782, Joseph W. Barnwell, ed., "Correspondence of the Han. Arthur Middleton," *SCHGM*, XXVI (1925), 191. The most comprehensive recent study of the British evacuation of the southern provinces is Eldon Jones, "British Withdrawal," particularly 262–78, for Charlestown; it is especially thorough on the details of shipping, numbers who left, and the negotiations between the contending forces prior to the departure of the British. George S. McCowen, Jr., *British Occupation of Charlestown* (Columbia, S.C., 1970), 131–50, is also useful. Except as noted, the framework of the present discussion is based upon these two works.
2. A Board of General Officers to Clinton, Apr. 15, and Leslie to Clarke, Apr. 28, 1782, Leslie Letterbooks, #15574, 15582.
3. *Royal Gazette* (Charlestown), Mar. 23, Apr. 4, May 29, June 22, 1782.
4. Carleton to Leslie, May 23, Wright to Carleton, May 30, Memorial of Upper and Commons House of Assembly of Georgia to Leslie, June 16, Leslie to Carleton, June 11, Address of Loyalists of North and South Carolina to Carleton, June 5, Memorial from Loyal Inhabitants of South Carolina to Leslie, June 12, Wright to Carleton, July 6, 1782, H.M.C., *Report*, II, 494–95, 505–6, 512, 520, 524, 527; III, 11; John Simpson to Thomas Townshend, June 19, 1782, Georgia Miscellaneous Coll., DUL; Jones, "British Withdrawal," 267.
5. Jones, "British Withdrawal," 267–69; Anthony Wayne to Greene, July 12, 1782, Rodman MSS., NCAH; Anthony Stokes, A *Narrative of the Official Conduct of Anthony Stokes* (London, 1784), 90–107.
6. *Royal South Carolina Gazette* (Charlestown), July 9, Aug. 13, 1782; *Royal Gazette* (New York), Aug. 14, 28; Carleton to Leslie, July 15, and Leslie to Carleton, July 19, 1782, H.M.C., *Report*, III, 19–20, 28–29.
7. Petition of Loyal Inhabitants of Charlestown, n.d., BHP, #10036; Leslie to Carleton, June 27, 1782, H.M.C., *Report*, II, 543–44; *Royal Gazette* (Charlestown), July 27, 1782.
8. *Royal Gazette* (Charlestown), Aug. 8, 1782; Leslie to Carleton, Aug. 2, 1782, Leslie Letterbooks, #15623; Greene to Benjamin Lincoln, Aug. 13, 1782, Greene Papers, NYPL.
9. Leslie to Carleton, Aug. 10, 1782, H.M.C., *Report*, III, 63; Memorial of Charles Ogilvie and Gideon Dupont, Jr., to Carleton, n.d., Chesney, "Journal," 116–17.

10. Memorial of Loyal Inhabitants of South Carolina to Leslie, Sept. 9, 1782, BHP, #10008; Jones, "British Withdrawal," 273–75.
11. Quarles, *Negro in the American Revolution* (Chapel Hill, N.C., 1961), 164–67; Leslie to Carleton, Oct. 3, 18, 1782, Leslie Letterbooks, #15564, 15569; Rutledge to Mathews, Oct. 4, 1782, "Letters to General Greene and Others," *SCHGM*, XVII (1916), 11–13; Moultrie, *Memoirs of the American Revolution*, 2 vols. (New York, 1968 [orig. publ. New York, 1802]), II, 341–51; *Canadian Claims*, 1244; Loyalist Transcripts, LIV, 551–92; Alexander R. Stoesen, "The British Occupation of Charleston, 1780–1782," *SCHM*, LXIII (1962), 81–82; Jones, *"British Withdrawal,"* 274–76; Jerome Nadelhaft, *Disorders of War: The Revolution in South Carolina* (Orono, Me., 1981), 88–89.
12. H.M.C., *Report*, III, 373–74; Johnson, *Traditions & Reminiscences*, 389; Articles of Agreement for the Release and Exchange of Prisoners of War...,23rd of October, 1782, Emmet Coll., NYPL.
13. Rugeley to John Chesnut, Apr. 21, Sept. [?], Oct. 9, 1782, Greene Papers, CL.
14. *Royal South Carolina Gazette*, Aug. 13, Sept. 12, 1782; *Royal Gazette* (Charlestown), Aug. 7, Sept. 28, 1782.
15. David Syrett, *Shipping and the American War, 1775–1783* (London, 1970), 238.
16. BHP, Aug. 31, 1782, #10316; Leslie to Carleton, H.M.C., *Report*, III, 64; Embarkation Return of the Troops under Major General Alexander Leslie, Oct. 30, 1782, Earl of Shelburne Papers, CL.
17. Leslie to Tonyn, Sept. 30, Oct. 9, 1782, Leslie Letterbooks, #15561, 15657; Jones, "British Withdrawal," 264–66; Refugees to East Florida, 812; Siebert, *Loyalists in East Florida*, II, 133–36; CEP; *Royal South Carolina Gazette*, Sept. 10, 1782; *Royal Gazette*, Sept. 28, 1782; Return of South Carolina Royalists, Nov. 1, 1782, East Florida, Officers Present, BHP, #20329; Carleton to Leslie, Sept. 10, 1782, H.M.C., *Report*, III, 112.
18. Fanning, "Narrative," 28–29.
19. Leslie to Major General Patterson, Oct. 22, 1782, Leslie Letterbooks, #15661 ; Number of Loyalists Leaving Charlestown for Halifax, Oct. 20, 1782, H.M.C., *Report*, III, 179.
20. Rugeley to Chesnut, Dec. 12, 1782, Greene Papers, CL
21. Jones, "British Withdrawal," 278–79; Greene to the President of the Continental Congress, Dec. 19, 1782, Joseph W. Barnwell, ed., "The Evacuation of Charlestown," *SCHGM* (1910), 8–10.
22. List of Transports Appointed to Receive the Garrison of Charlestown, Jan. 3, 1783, Shelburne Papers, CL; Loyalist Transcripts, LIII, 273–306.
23. Refugees to East Florida, 811; Loyalist Transcripts, LV, 373–96; LVI, 627.
24. Bull to Townshend, Jan. 19, 1783, C.O.5/176, 216–19. The source of Bull's information on the numbers evacuating is not certain. The figures most frequently cited are those in "Return of People Embarked from South Carolina and Georgia, 13th and 14th December 1782," *Charleston Yearbook, 1883* (Charleston, S.C., 1883), 416, in which the total numbers departing from Charlestown for various places are 3,794 whites and 5,333 blacks, but these include North Carolinians sailing from Charlestown to various destinations.

Chapter Sixteen

DISPERSAL OF THE LOYALISTS

I have taken a furnished house at Brumton Row No. 17 very near to Mr. John Savage who has bin very kind to us...his Brother Jerry is near us & Mr. John Rose has shown me many marks of Friendship ... Mr. Gaillard and several other American friends is quite near.

—Elias Ball of Wambaw, September 1784

The families who left South Carolina in 1782 because they preferred not to live under the state government or feared that they and their property could not remain there in safety sought refuge in four places outside the United States. The largest number went to East Florida only to learn shortly after landing that the province had been ceded to Spain in the peace settlement ending the war. However much they had wished to leave an independent South Carolina, most did not wish to live under Spanish jurisdiction and moved again. All but a very few of the other exiles from South Carolina went directly to Jamaica or maritime Canada or to Great Britain. Some of the exiles to East Florida moved on to one of these three destinations, while some others followed Georgia loyalists to the nearby Bahamas.

A large, if undetermined, number returned openly or inconspicuously to South Carolina, and others slipped quietly into nearby states or the open areas beyond the mountains. The loyalists by their very numbers had an important impact wherever they settled in the old British empire, while some individuals who had demonstrated qualities of leadership during the war assumed similar roles in their new communities. British-born loyalists who returned to the home islands tended to be readily absorbed in the large and stable population, usually in the counties from which they had originally migrated; bur the native Americans who came to Britain found the adjustment to be more difficult.

The British government launched an extensive program after the war to allow loyalists partial compensation for their lost property and income in America, and many of the exiles made the long journey to Britain to press their claims before returning to their new residences in the empire. Although some of the refugees from South Carolina settled down in their new homes, others wandered restlessly from one part of the empire to another during the 1780s.

East Florida had seemed to offer the refugees several possibilities. For committed loyalists it was a relatively short move to a part of America that was physically similar to parts of South Carolina, and a few of the diehards may have hoped that it might again be a base for recovering the southern provinces. For protectionists and some loyalists, its proximity to South Carolina offered the chance to be in position to return to their homes if the state government removed their disabilities.

Before the loyalists and slaves from Georgia and the Carolinas arrived in East Florida in the latter half of 1782, the population of that province had numbered approximately 1,000 whites and 3,000 slaves. The influx of refugees and their chattels raised the estimated population of the province to over 17,000 souls by 1783 and, despite the best efforts of General Leslie and other officers to send provisions with their refugees, placed a heavy burden on the resources of the tiny province. Of the more than 13,000 newcomers, over 8,000, including nearly 5,000 slaves, had come from "Carolina." The first fleet from Charlestown in October 1782 had brought about 900 provincials and some civilians; the second, in December, landed almost 4,600 whites and blacks; and about 1,800 persons, mostly slaves, had come in private vessels or overland early in 1783. Virtually all of the blacks and a substantial majority of the whites who came from "Carolina" were South Carolinians.[1]

The several thousand loyalists who emigrated to East Florida on the evacuation of South Carolina included people from both the backcountry and the lowcountry, and from every economic level and family status. Great planters like Elias Ball of Wambaw and John Gaillard brought hundreds of slaves, backcountry planters like Patrick Cunningham were also slaveowners and brought smaller numbers, but most of the immigrants held no slaves or, at most, only a single servant or small family. Blacks themselves are largely anonymous in the records, although a very few who were free men are listed. The names of about sixty widows and single women appear on General Leslie's emigration lists because they had assumed responsibility for children, other relations, or a few servants, but most women and children are unidentified. All occupations were represented among the men-farmers and planters, artisans, merchants and professional men.[2]

The South Carolina loyalists settled in three principal areas. The smallest group took up lands along the northern border of the province on or near the St. Mary's River or on Amelia Island near its mouth. A familiar name among these settlers was Henry O'Neall, the Little River loyalist, who began to farm about three miles from the mouth of the St. Mary's.[3]

Many of the loyal refugees preferred the valley of the St. John's River, a stream that flowed north through the peninsula until it turned and emptied into the Atlantic between the St. Mary's and St. Augustine. The entrance to the harbor at the mouth of the St. John's was less dangerous for oceangoing vessels than that at St. Augustine, and some slave-manned estates had been established along its banks during the British Period. This area appeared to promise the South Carolinians the opportunity to practice a form of agriculture with which they were familiar, and slaveowners among the newcomers soon obtained grants from the province and began to prepare the ground for planting. As early as the fall of 1781, Colonel John Harrison of the South Carolina Rangers had sent David Drennan's family and fourteen slaves to begin planting operations for him in East Florida. Drennan obtained a grant for Harrison on the St. John's and cleared ground for a crop before Harrison arrived a year later, after which the Drennans settled on Amelia Island. Colonel James Cassells of Georgetown and the Charlestown merchant Gabriel Capers joined forces in a planting venture on rented lands, where they employed their combined workforce of over eighty slaves. The physician 187 was among the more than sixty loyalists and their families from South Carolina who tried to make a new start along the river or in the small community of Hesterstown.[4]

During its British period, East Florida's long-established capital town of St. Augustine had developed close commercial ties with Charlestown, and many of the South Carolinians settled there in hopes of reestablishing their mercantile and professional careers. The sudden influx of southern loyalists greatly expanded all economic activity, and buildings were hastily thrown up and nearby lands cleared in a booming atmosphere of speculation and rising prices. Prominent among the newcomers from South Carolina was William Charles Wells who began to publish the *East Florida Gazette* on the presses he had brought from Charlestown.[5]

The South Carolina Royalists, along with the provincials from North Carolina and Georgia, now composed the garrison of East Florida, having replaced the regular British and German troops, who had been moved to New York. Consisting of six companies that mustered just under 200 officers and men in the spring of 1783, the Royalists did routine duty in and around Sr. Augustine or were scattered on various assignments in other settlements or provincial forts.[6]

England was still technically at war with Spain, and in the spring of 1783 a South Carolina loyalist conceived and led a daring expedition against the Bahama Islands, which the Spanish had captured from the English in 1782. The younger Andrew Deveaux of Beaufort, who had been active in that area as second in command of Lechemere's militia regiment, had, with the aid of that experienced Tory raider David Fanning, assembled volunteers and private vessels in East Florida for an attempt to retake the Bahamas. The expedition first sailed to Harbour Island where more men were recruited, among them a number of blacks; Deveaux then captured a fort on the island of New Providence and, after convincing the Spanish governor that he faced overwhelming force, received the surrender of troops more than double their own numbers. Perhaps the Spanish governor gave in so easily because he had learned that the island was to be returned to England in the peace settlement between the two countries, but the exploit was generally good for the morale of loyalists in East Florida.[7]

Shortly after the refugees from Charlestown landed, they were greeted by new rumors that England had agreed to cede the Floridas to Spain in the peace treaty between the two countries. When the rumors were verified by the official announcement of the cession, most of the refugees were left with only the choice between moving to a strange part of the empire, or the risk of an unfavorable reception if they returned to South Carolina.

As it turned out, the necessity for a hasty decision on these alternatives was not as great as it had first appeared to be. Governor Tonyn officially revealed the terms of the preliminary treaty of peace for East Florida in April 1783, urged the inhabitants to settle their affairs, and promised that shipping would be available to carry them and their property to new destinations—a familiar refrain to southern loyalists. Not until the definitive treaty was signed that September did its clause requiring the transfer and evacuation to take place within eighteen months become effective, and Tonyn's superiors ordered him to remain in the province until its evacuation was completed. Because of various delays, an extension of time was granted and Tonyn did not actually depart from St. Mary's until November 1785, although the new Spanish governor, Vicente Zespedes, accepted delivery of the fort at St. Augustine in July 1784. The transfer of the province to Spain and the extended period required to terminate British influence there had both good and bad effects on British subjects, and the refugees from South Carolina shared in them.[8]

The announcement that East Florida had been ceded to Spain caused a near mutiny among provincial troops who feared that they would be transferred to other parts of the empire without their consent. After a few of the ringleaders were arrested, the men were promised that they could obtain discharges in East Florida. The promise of land grants in Nova Scotia appealed to some of the provincials, who agreed to accept discharges after they were transported to that province, and each of the three southern provincial regiments was reorganized for that purpose. Sixty-four members of the South Carolina Royalists agreed to these terms; they departed, accompanied by families and servants in some cases, for Halifax under the command of Captain George Dawkins in the fall of 1783.[9]

The discharge of the provincial regiments exacerbated lawlessness along the Florida-Georgia frontier. Outlying settlements in the southern backcountry had long been plagued by gangs of outlaws, and the war had made conditions worse as the lawless elements became involved in the civil strife between Whigs and Tories. Among the most famous of these "banditti" was Daniel McGirt, whose followers had become the scourge of the Georgia frontier during the war and continued their activities in the Floridas after hostilities had ceased. Frightened by the discharge of the provincial regiments and the increased boldness of McGirt and others, property holders along the St. John's River petitioned the governor to take action to protect them. Tonyn responded by organizing two troops of mounted militia, and he gave the command of one of them to Colonel William Young, the Tyger River militia officer who had led some of the raids in lowcountry South Carolina in 1782. Young's troop consisted of nearly fifty volunteers, principally from South Carolina.[10]

Although Daniel McGirt had a long-standing reputation as a gang leader, several South Carolina loyalists were also charged with pillaging the East Florida settlements. Best known was William Cunningham, but Colonel Baily Cheney, the John Linders, father and son, of Purrysburg, and Stephen Mayfield of Brown's Creek in Ninety Six District were also directly implicated in the frontier raiding. William Young's troop had several brushes with them and succeeded in capturing McGirt in 1783, but Governor Tonyn wished to show leniency at the end of his regime and did not prosecute. Tonyn offered the services of Young's troop to the Spanish, but Zespedes wanted to begin his regime quietly and offered to provide the outlaws with safe conduct to other provinces if they would surrender themselves. The Linders and Cheney accepted the offer and obtained passes to go to Tensaw above Mobile in West Florida, but the others continued their depredations. Tonyn was suspected of using Young's men primarily to guard his own extensive plantations, and there were charges that Young was more interested in plundering than in pacifying the frontier.[11]

Zespedes finally cracked down on bandit activities after Cunningham, Mayfield, and Daniel Cargill were implicated in looting silver and other valuables from houses at St. John's Bluff. They and McGirt were arrested and shipped off to the viceroy in Havana, who banned them from all Spanish territory. McGirt and Cunningham slipped back into Florida once more, but were seized again and transported to New Providence. in the St. Mary's area, where Governor Tonyn and other officials lived until they left the province for good, violence frequently flared up because of bandit raids or disputes over title to land and slaves. Henry O'Neall, the local magistrate, complained that Tonyn would do nothing to protect loyalists like himself who planned to remain under Spanish jurisdiction.[12]

Another issue that stirred trouble during the period before Spain took control of the province was the ownership of slaves brought into East Florida from the southern provinces. Almost as soon as the refugees reached Florida, the state of South Carolina sent an agent to arrange for the recovery of the property of its citizens taken away by the departing loyalists, and Governor Tonyn also sent an agent to Charlestown to represent the loyalists. Dr. James Clitherall, a Charlestown physician listed in the Confiscation Act who had served on the commission on slave property during the British occupation, had come to East Florida as surgeon to the South Carolina Royalists. Allied by marriage to the influential Thomas Loughton Smith family, he immediately began to try to recover the property of South Carolina slaveowners. Clitherall and John Cruden, the commissioner of sequestered property under the British, urged Tonyn to cooperate with their efforts to recover slaves improperly taken from the Carolinas. Once Tonyn knew that his province would be ceded to Spain, he refused to cooperate, declaring that he would hold such slaves until the southern state legislatures repealed their confiscation laws. It was Clitherall's opinion that Tonyn hoped to profit from the seizure of the slaves.[13]

South Carolina's loyalists responded in almost every conceivable way to the transfer of East Florida to Spanish jurisdiction, although few chose to remain there. The British government provided transportation to all parts of the empire for those displaced by the transfer. In addition to the lands promised the provincials who agreed to go to Nova Scotia, the British government encouraged loyalists to migrate to the Bahamas by promising to turn ungranted lands there over to them free of charge. Public officials and others sailed to Great Britain, and some of the slaveholders moved on to Jamaica. It was at this point that the largest number of loyalists and protectionists openly or surreptitiously returned to South Carolina.

The British government later agreed to compensate loyalists who chose to leave the Floridas for losses incurred because of the cession to Spain, and a familiar figure to many lowcountry South Carolina loyalists, Colonel Nisbet Balfour, was one of the two commissioners assigned to the task of hearing and reporting on their claims.

Governor Zespedes ordered that a census be taken of the British subjects present, seeking information from them on their place of birth, location in the province, and whether they preferred to "retire" from his province or to remain under Spanish jurisdiction. These and other sources throw some light on the sacrifices that loyalists and protectionists incurred in settling and leaving East Florida, and the problems they faced in their choice of new homes. Patrick Cunningham, who had employed his twenty-nine slaves in preparing lumber from live-oak timber, was able to return to South Carolina after its legislature removed him from the confiscation list and amerced him in 1784. One of his company commanders, Captain William Payne of Rayburn's Creek, was also reunited with his family but only in Sunbury, Georgia, after friends had helped them to reach that place. The Paynes apparently did not return to South Carolina. The Proctor brothers of Cunningham's regiment came to East Florida on the evacuation of Charlestown and served in Young's mounted militia, but Philip and his wife and child returned to settle in the Dutch Fork, while Edward, a bachelor, chose to move to an undisclosed destination. Before departing, William Hendricks, another of Patrick Cunningham's captains, registered with magistrate Henry O'Neall at St. Mary's a power of attorney over his South Carolina property to his wife and Colonel Thomas Brandon, the state militia commander of his district. James Sloan and his mother, the surviving members of the Long Cane family nearly wiped out in the backcountry civil war, also moved on. Colonel Daniel Plummer of Fair Forest, who had been left for dead on Kings Mountain, apparently felt that it would be useless to return to his property and arranged to sell it to a relative before he left. Colonel William Young moved to Dominica where he found good use for his military talents in helping to suppress an uprising of blacks on the island. After William Charles Wells returned to England in 1783, his brother John came out to move the family press to Nassau where he began to publish the *Bahama Gazette*.[15]

Colonel James Cassells, who had cleared and planted land along the St. John's River in partnership with Gabriel Capers, planned to take his thirty slaves to the Bahamas to begin planting operations there. To his surprise, the blacks refused to go, declaring that they would take to the woods if he did not arrange for them to return to South Carolina. He granted their wish, taking them through the inland navigation in order to sell them to a "Mr. Johnson." It is one of the many ironies of the loyalist experience that his slaves were thus able to return to more familiar surroundings, but, despite strong support from his former neighbors, he could not because his petition for relief from the Confiscation Act was rejected by the General Assembly. Capers, on the other hand, was amerced and did return to the state. Captain John Gaillard and Colonel Elias Ball of Wambaw, both natives of South Carolina, also sought relief from the Confiscation Act, but the legislature did not accept their pleas, and they sailed for England. John Morgridge, the former customs official who had had so many stirring adventures during his earlier exile from South Carolina, simply sailed for England at the first opportunity and settled in Chelsea.[16]

These are some of the means used by South Carolina's loyalists to end their brief residence in East Florida, a pause before they moved on to other parts of the empire or returned to South Carolina. The official charged with keeping records on the people leaving the province because of its cession to Spain estimated that just under 10,000 people departed. The largest group, 3,247 (of whom over 2,200 were black), went to the Bahamas; over 3,000 went to "the States of America," including nearly 2,600 blacks; and the remainder were scattered among other parts of the empire—principally (about 900) to Nova Scotia, mostly provincials and their families, largely white; and to Jamaica, also about 900, mostly black. Tonyn reported that "more than four thousand, have passed into the interior parts of America among the mountains; and that at least three thousand have gone into the American states."[17]

To the southern loyalists who left East Florida, the nearby Bahama Islands seemed to be the most attractive destination among the alternatives open to them within the empire. Although land rights and governmental powers in islands remained with the descendants of the original proprietors, the British government had promised that the loyalists could have first chance at the ungranted lands there. An officer sent from East Florida to investigate conditions in the islands gave a mixed report, saying that, although much of the terrain was rocky, there was probably enough soil suitable to produce cotton and perhaps other commercial crops. The population of the archipelago in 1783 numbered barely 4,000 souls, two thirds of whom lived on the island of New Providence, with the rest scattered over six other islands. Their economy was based on a few export crops, and the income derived from the salvage of ships wrecked on their treacherous reefs and, in wartime, from privateering. The Spanish captured the islands in May 1782, shortly after Colonel William Henry Mills, the Cheraw loyalist, abandoned South Carolina and brought his slaves to New Providence to resume planting. Mills was one of a small group of refugees from the southern provinces who arrived in the Bahamas during the war, a trickle that became a veritable flood after hostilities ended.[18]

The influx of loyalists trebled the population of the islands in five years, with blacks accounting for over two-thirds of the total. As a result, much new land was taken up and devoted to plantation agriculture in which some planters from the southern provinces experienced early success in the production of cotton of the sea-island variety. The rush of new settlers created demands that led to high prices and a wave of prosperity in the middle 1780s, but a pest infestation and the limited amount of arable soil restricted the expansion of cotton production. The economy of the islands soon settled into an expanded version of what had existed before the loyalists came. The newcomers concentrated on New Providence, whose population more than doubled in three years. The traveler Johann Schoepf noted that Nassau was jammed with Americans who had come from "the States of Georgia and South Carolina, as of the royal party, and were expecting here the result of their trials or a permission to return." Those interested in commercial agriculture took up lands on Exuma, Abaco, and Cat Island, several of the "out islands" that had been sparsely settled until this time. Some of the loyalists resented what they claimed was a lack of concern for them by the old inhabitants who controlled the political and economic life, but the granting of representation in the General Assembly to the newer settlements, and the purchase by the Crown of proprietary rights in the islands acted to reduce tensions, and the quarrel subsided.[19]

The Bahamas were in Spanish hands when Charlestown was evacuated, and no transports with troops or refugees went directly to the islands. Therefore the first southern refugees to arrive in the islands from East Florida found young Andrew Deveaux occupying the governor's palace until British officials could assume formal control. They were soon joined by refugees from the evacuation of New York, including a number of West Florida residents interned since the conquest of that province by the Spanish in 1781, and who, with the encouragement of Sir Guy Carleton, had hoped to find in the Bahamas the kind of lifestyle they had been forced to leave. Exactly how many of the immigrants were from South Carolina is not certain, but they did include some very familiar names.

John Wells's *Bahama Gazette* began to appear in 1784, and he soon used its columns to support the charges of the loyalists that Governor John Maxwell was indifferent to their needs. Once this early controversy died down, the paper settled into the usual pattern of the provincial press and appeared regularly until after Wells's death in 1799. His uncle, "Dr. John;" who accompanied him there, sought to return to South Carolina in the early 1790s, but the legislature apparently did not act on his petition. Dr. Hugh Rose, after several unsuccessful attempts to return to South Carolina, left East Florida for the Bahamas, journeyed to England to present his claim, and returned to New Providence. Several prominent backcountry loyalists settled in the Bahamas. Richard Pearis and his family settled on Great Abaco from whence he filed claim for substantial property losses, receiving a handsome award of £5,624 and an annual military allowance of £70 until his death after 1800. General Robert Cunningham went to Nova Scotia from East Florida and from there to England to present his claim before the Royal Commission. There he was joined by his cousin William, and the two men filed claims for property in South Carolina and in East Florida, then sailed for the Bahamas. Robert settled on New Providence, was awarded £1,080 on his

South Carolina claim and received half-pay as a brigadier general until his death in 1813. Little is known of William after he returned to the Bahamas, although his South Carolina claim was dismissed as fraudulent and he received a very small award for his Florida property. Major Christopher Nealey brought his family to New Providence, traveled alone to Halifax to file his claim, and then returned to settle his family on Great Abaco.[20]

Except for John Wells, the South Carolinians in the Bahamas generally did not occupy very important positions in the political and commercial life of the islands. Wells and Robert Cunningham lived out their days on New Providence, but others drifted back to the mainland or to England. The five sons of Joseph Curry, the Charlestown merchant and partner with Evan McLaurin in the Congaree store, came to the Bahamas after the war and married into "Conch," or old-settler, families. Some of their descendants and other Bahamians were pioneer developers of Key West to which they moved in the 1830s.[21]

The great majority of the South Carolina loyalists who chose to migrate to Jamaica after the war went in the great convoy from Charlestown that reached Port Royal in mid-January 1783, although a few others, notably Moses Kirkland, had arrived earlier in the fleet from Savannah. The British administrators, Governor Archibald Campbell and the former commandant at Savannah, Brigadier General, now Lieutenant Governor, Alured Clarke, were sympathetic to their plight. Among the benefits available to the newcomers were land grants, and exemption from parochial taxes and from the import duties on the slaves they brought with them.[22]

The Jamaican economy was based on the production of sugar and other tropical products, and nearly 90 percent of its people in the 1780s were slaves. It was this characteristic that made the island attractive to the slaveowners among the refugees, who hoped to recoup their losses by resuming planting operations. Almost immediately they petitioned the Crown to grant in Jamaica the bounty on the production of indigo that they had enjoyed in South Carolina and Georgia before the war.[23]

We know very little about the mass of the refugees who went to Jamaica from Carolina, but those who have been identified ranged from the wealthy ship builder John Rose to small and middling backcountry farmers and militia officers and some Charlestown artisans. Robert Frogg, the tailor, had "pulled down" the house he had built on leased land in Charlestown and brought it with him. The cabinetmaker John Fisher settled in Kingston where he followed his trade for ten years or more, and William Hanscomb, a coachmaker, returned to that place, having spent several months there during his first exile from Charlestown in 1779.[24]

A planting venture started by the Camden loyalist James Cary and his South Carolina partner provides a well-documented example of the difficulties the refugees faced in their efforts to get a new start. The partners had a falling out and divided the property, but Cary continued to try to produce sugar with his share until, £4,200 in debt to local agents of London bankers, he left the island in 1786 to present his case for compensation before representatives of the Royal Commission then hearing claims in Nova Scotia. He never did return to Jamaica, finally turning over his land and slaves in 1790 to satisfy his creditors in the island. We do not know how capable a manager Cary was, although he had successfully run estates in South Carolina, or what effect the quarrel with his partner had, but conditions in Jamaica were not ideal for the newcomers during these years. Business leaders resented both the concessions made to the wealthier refugees and the burdens assumed by the island's government in taking care of the destitute among them. Wedded to a sugar economy at a time when demand for that staple was declining in Britain, the planters preferred to cling to old ways, petitioning Parliament fruitlessly to allow them to trade with the United States rather than to face the island 's need to be more self-sufficient. Thus new planters like Cary merely added to the local competition but were not efficient enough to profit in the declining market. And if this were not enough, Jamaica suffered extensive damage from hurricanes in three consecutive years in the mid-1780s.[25]

We do not know how the mass of the Carolina refugees fared in Jamaica in the years immediately following their arrival. Some of the small farmers may have survived by raising cattle and foodstuffs to supply the plantations, and perhaps the artisans in the towns did reasonably well; of those who, like James Cary, traveled to present their claims, some did not return to the island. Henry Rugeley did go back to South Carolina, but Colonel Joseph Robinson stayed in Jamaica for just one year before moving to the new province of New Brunswick in maritime Canada where he prospered. And death took its toll among the refugees, Moses Kirkland dying on a voyage to England in 1787 and Thomas Fletchall, the most prominent of the early backcountry loyalists, succumbing shortly thereafter.[26]

The Maritime Provinces of Canada became a refuge for many American loyalists after the war, and the refugees from South Carolina went there directly after the evacuation of Charlestown or later by way of East Florida. Although the total number of South Carolina refugees settling in Nova Scotia was probably smaller than those migrating to the Bahamas or Jamaica, their movements are easier to trace because they were better recorded at the time.

Exactly what directed recent residents of the relatively mild Carolina piedmont toward the windswept shores of Nova Scotia is not clear, but two possible reasons suggest themselves. Some of the loyalist families who chose to go north instead of toward the tropics were German immigrants who, thwarted in their efforts to settle in Nova Scotia in the 1760s, had been compensated with lands along Hard Labour Creek. It is another of the ironies of the loyalist story that, because of their loyalty to the British King, Christian Sing, John Adam Bowers, and other Germans were finally able to settle in Nova Scotia two decades later. Most of the people who chose to go to Canada from East Florida were backcountrymen whose origins lay in the British Isles or in the interior of the southern provinces. Some of these loyalists had already served in Florida during the war and did not relish returning, while others disliked its climate or had no interest in plantation agriculture.[27]

South Carolinians made up a substantial part of the group that sailed from Charlestown to Nova Scotia in November 1782. John Sanderson, a Long Cane refugee who landed at Halifax with this first party, made his way across the peninsula to the vicinity of Newport just above Windsor at the head of navigation where the Avon River flowed into the Bay of Fundy. Although warned to expect hordes of refugees, officials in Nova Scotia were apparently not prepared to grant full title to the lands promised, and for eighteen months Sanderson lived near Newport until "he got his land" about seven miles above that settlement. While he and the others labored to establish themselves on the bounty grants they obtained in 1784, they brought supplies in by water and through the woods on their backs until "the new settlers made a sort of road." More than twenty families and as many single men from South Carolina became a part of a community that was appropriately named Rawdon.[21]

Other South Carolinians who came directly from Charlestown to Halifax late in 1782 tended to go to one of three other areas. Abraham Fritz, Conrad Mark, and Daniel Migler, other Germans who came to South Carolina instead of Nova Scotia in the 1760s, settled near Shelburne on rivers that flowed into the Atlantic at some distance southwest of Halifax. South Carolinians made up just a few of the thousands of loyalist refugees whites largely from the New England and Middle Atlantic states, and blacks largely from the south who had congregated in New York during the war—who tried to make new homes near Shelburne. Christian Sing and several other Germans chose to move to Ship Harbour on one of the many coastal inlets east of Halifax, while Henry Sideman settled at Jeddore nearby. The third group, apparently composed of younger families, proved to be more venturesome than the others. Under the leadership of Colonel John Hamilton, who had served as second in command of the Stevens Creek militia regiment, they agreed to take their lands in the broad valley of the Saint John's River across the Bay of Fundy. After they had wintered at Halifax, Hamilton went to New York early in the next spring and obtained from Sir Guy Carleton the promise of a year's provisions for about 350 men, women, and children, including twenty-four black "servants." Before the supplies arrived, a number of these families set out for their new homes, settling along the streams that converge near the port of Saint John, although several moved as far inland as the vicinity of Fredericton and Moncton. This area of the mainland became part of the new province of New Brunswick in 1784.[29]

Most of the South Carolinians who came directly from Charlestown to Halifax had lived in the Stevens Creek and Long Cane valleys in Ninety Six District. They had much in common-their origins as Irish or German immigrants, their neighborhoods, war service and sufferings as loyalists, and Colonel Hamilton's leadership-and they seem to have been among the more stable settlers who came to the Maritime Provinces from South Carolina. Although they did settle in different places, some, such as the Fralicks and the Snells, the Fritzes and the Marks, were related by marriage; others had taken responsibility for children whose families had been broken by the war—Reuben Lively for the two younger sons of the late Thomas Thornton, and George Snell for his younger brothers—until they were eligible for their own grants.[30]

George Dawkins and some of the South Carolina Royalists had agreed to take their discharges in Nova Scotia, and his group landed at Halifax from East Florida in November 1783. It was probably the next spring before they could sail eastward along the Atlantic coast for perhaps 150 miles to a long inlet known as Country Harbour. There they held a final muster in June 1784, before claiming their land grants on the eastern shore around Stormont near where the other southern provincial regiments also were to settle. Eight of the sixty-four men were accompanied by wives and children, and the four officers had twelve servants with them. Nineteen other men chose land in New Brunswick and with their dependents, about sixty persons in all, moved over to that province late in 1784. Late in the same year the transport *Argo* arrived at Halifax from East Florida with its refugee passengers, many of them South Carolinians, in various stages of destitution. After receiving provisions and warrants for lands, they settled on Chedabucto Bay in extreme eastern Nova Scotia in 1785.[31]

Several prominent Carolina loyalists ultimately settled in the Maritime Provinces. Colonel Zacharias Gibbs visited Jamaica after leaving East Florida, and then settled in the Rawdon community. The loyalist raider David Fanning came to New Brunswick in 1784, settled in Kings County, and became a respected magistrate and member of its legislature. In the following year Colonel Joseph Robinson, after spending two years in East Florida and Jamaica, came to New Brunswick where he settled on the Kennebecacie River northeast of Saint John.[32]

The backcountry refugees who came to the maritime provinces seem to have been among the more steadfast loyalists from South Carolina. Included among their number were men who had participated in the original outbreak in 1775, and joined the British army in Georgia or Florida before the fall of Charlestown, and some had served at Kings Mountain and in the siege of Ninety Six.

The Royal Commission in London sent two of its members, Colonel Thomas Dundas and Jeremy Pemberton, a barrister, out to Canada in 1785 to hear the claims of the loyalists there, and they held sessions at Halifax and Saint John early in their visit. Seventy South Carolina loyalists then residing in Nova Scotia and New Brunswick filed claims in 1786 along with several others who had come from the West Indies for that purpose.[33]

The testimony of the South Carolina claimants and witnesses reveals the traumatic effects of the war and subsequent exile on their families. Young George Anderson, a militiaman who was the senior member of his family after the death of his parents and older brother, had brought his youngest sister with him but had left five of his other siblings in the States. Lieutenant Joel Hudson of the Royalists had survived his parents and brought five of his brothers and sisters with him to Nova Scotia, leaving a married sister and two brothers in South Carolina and Georgia: David Dunsmore's five children were still in Carolina in 1786; in contrast, George Snell's brothers were with him at Rawdon but two of his sisters had gone to New Brunswick with their husbands. William Meek's wife, the daughter of a loyalist who died in Charlestown, was the only one of her family to leave South Carolina, while both George Weaver and George Shobert had left parents and siblings in Ninety Six District.[34]

South Carolinians from the Bahamas and Jamaica came to present their claims before the commissioners and then returned to the islands. Colonel James Cary came from Jamaica and appeared before Pemberton in the spring of 1786; however, the documents Cary presented were not satisfactory, and, after waiting through most of the summer for passage, he and his wife sailed for England to present his case to the full commission. Several of the more prominent South Carolina loyalists in the Maritime Provinces preferred to file their claims in England, among them Zacharias Gibbs and Colonel John Hamilton. The latter continued his help to men who served with him, filing claims in London for James Moffatt and Nathaniel Wilson who could not afford to make the trip.[35]

After completing their business in Halifax, Commissioners Dundas and Pemberton "visited all the different settlements in Nova Scoria" and found many communities "thriving," although there was much evidence of "rum and idle habits," and that many of the older inhabitants were hostile toward the loyalists. Jealousy played a smaller part in New Brunswick, where the loyalists far outnumbered the earlier settlers, and the royal commissioners found the "half-pay provincial officers" there to be "valuable settlers," who lived well and were busy improving their lands. On the other hand, in many places commerce did not seem to prosper, and they found that "tradesmen" were "starving here or gone to the States."[36]

The evidence for the movement of southern white loyalists into the Maritime Provinces is adequate, but there is little documentation for the thousands of blacks who were shipped to Nova Scotia and New Brunswick after the peace. The ships that brought southern loyalists also carried some blacks, usually classed as "servants," as in the case of the dozen who came with George Dawkins and his officers, but a much larger group of blacks from the southern states had been congregating around British-occupied New York during the war. In preparation for the evacuation of that last garrison town, British authorities encouraged loyalists, blacks as well as whites, to migrate to Atlantic Canada, and thus a large number of those listed in Sir Guy Carleton's "Book of Negroes" did settle there. Some came as slaves to whites, but most in Nova Scotia were considered to be free and, therefore, entitled to land grants as loyalists. Although small numbers of black settlers were scattered through many parts of both provinces, the greatest concentrations were located at Birchtown near Shelburne, at Preston near Halifax, and at Tracadie in Sydney County. The men are denoted as "Negro" in the land records and as recipients of tracts ranging from one to twenty, and occasionally to forty, acres, grants generally much smaller than those made to white families. Although much of the land granted to loyalists was of mediocre quality, the areas where blacks settled were often even less arable. Where blacks were concentrated in large numbers, they tended to be segregated from white communities.

Although some blacks were able to subsist on their lands, many others gave up and drifted into a kind of peonage on the fringes of the white settlements. Their willingness to work for lower wages aroused jealousy on the part of white workers, especially in areas where economic conditions declined during the 1780s.[37]

Leaders of the blacks in Nova Scotia were able to interest English abolitionists in their plight, and early in the 1790s nearly 1,200 sailed for Africa where they settled in Sierra Leone. Among them were Boston and Violet King, two of the few South Carolina black loyalists to be identified: after serving the British in South Carolina they had come on a British warship to New York after Charlestown was evacuated, and then to Birchtown. After a conversion experience, Boston King became a preacher and teacher in the new African colony.[38]

Nor did all go well with the white loyalists who settled in Nova Scotia and New Brunswick, and as the years passed people began to drift away from the sites of their original grants. Despite the efforts of government to make the best use of the aid available, a provost marshal 's report in 1785 mentions "abuses that have been committed in the issue of the Bounty of Government at Chedabucto," especially in the vicinity of Country Harbour where " many of the Carolina Loyalists had already abandoned their farms, but their rations continued to be drawn by their comrades." When William Meek and two others administered the assessment for taxes in the Township of Rawdon in 1791, less than half of the families that came from Charlestown in 1783 were represented on the roll. Among the missing were the families of the brothers John and William Bryson, both of whom had returned to Laurens County, South Carolina, but there are few clues to the whereabouts of most of the departed. Even the destination of a prominent man like Zacharias Gibbs was not revealed when he gave public notice in 1791 that his two farms at Rawdon were for sale because he planned to leave in the spring. To his neighbors he left free of rent for five years the "handsome small church [built] at his private expense," and he donated two acres as a site on which another could be constructed. Two well-known loyalists in New Brunswick also moved, but for different reasons. Joseph Robinson was honored by an appointment as lieutenant governor of Prince Edward Island and moved to Charlottetown. David Fanning, expelled from the New Brunswick legislature on a morals charge in the early 1800s, took refuge across the Bay of Fundy in Digby where he continued to protest his innocence until his death in 1825. Correspondence related to the Fanning matter reveals that Colonel John Hamilton, who had devoted much of his time to the welfare of his fellow South Carolinians in New Brunswick, sold his property and returned to the United States.[39]

But others among this generation of loyalist refugees from South Carolina remained on the lands acquired shortly after their arrival. George Dawkins and some of his officers were still listed on the Country Harbour assessor's roll in 1791, and familiar South Carolina loyalist surnames still appear in modern telephone directories for that community. And equally familiar surnames on grave markers near Rawdon attest to the continued residence of these immigrants and their descendants near the original grants to their families.[40]

Great Britain was a major destination for the refugee loyalists from South Carolina, either because their origins lay in the home islands, or because they could serve as a temporary residence while they took care of business affairs or laid plans to settle in another part of the empire. A few had come in the last year of the war to be followed by a substantial number shortly after the evacuation of Charlestown, and a smaller but fairly steady stream during the middle 1780s.

Irish Protestants from the interior of South Carolina formed the first distinct group to seek refuge in Britain shortly before and after the evacuation of Charlestown. These people had taken up lands in Camden District along Jackson's Creek or just north of the town of Camden barely ten years before the outbreak of hostilities. Conspicuous among this group was Colonel John Phillips, who had settled near the town of Winnsboro in 1770, and later distinguished himself as the commander of the Jackson's Creek militia regiment. Having lost two sons and a brother during the fighting and abandoned his property to the rebels, Phillips brought his wife and eight other children to Charlestown after Camden was evacuated, and then returned with them to northern Ireland in 1783. Alexander Chesney and several other Irishmen had preceded him in 1782, and as many as thirty others followed after the peace. Except to come to London to support their claims before the Royal Commission, these men all resumed life in the northern counties. Chesney, James Miller (one of Phillips's captains), and Major John Robinson of Little Lynches Creek obtained appointments in the customs service in County Antrim and Robert McKeown kept a "small store" in Down Patrick. The most prominent Irishman, Chief Justice Thomas Knox Gordon, and his family also returned to Ireland after he presented his claim.[41]

A larger group of Crown officers and lowcountry merchants and professional men accompanied William Bull in the large convoy that sailed for England after the evacuation of Charlestown. These families initially took lodgings in London while their claims were being processed, and some of the more affluent or better connected among them settled permanently in the city. Most in this group were British-born and had family and business ties in England, although in some instances more than thirty years had passed since they had migrated to South Carolina. Virtually all of these people were listed in the state's confiscation law and included three classes who, because they were individually "obnoxious" or because of their property, were the particular targets of that legislation-placement, members of the Scottish community, and persons who had taken a conspicuous part for the British during the occupation. But there were also a few natives of America among these people to whom England was a "strange country," and, they hoped, a temporary residence. And at least two free black men from the Carolina lowcountry came to England during this period to file their claims.[42]

Following the evacuation of East Florida, a smaller wave of loyalists who were unable or unwilling to negotiate a return to South Carolina reached Britain. And through the mid-1780s a small but steady stream of loyalists came to England from other parts of the empire, usually in order to make personal appearances before the Royal Commission. Among this latter group, in addition to individuals like the Cunningham cousins, were several families for whom England was but one stopping-place as they sought a better location or more support for their claims. The James Carys, who had come to South Carolina by way of North Carolina and Virginia, arrived in England in 1786 after living in Jamaica and visiting Nova Scotia. Among many other examples were the Georgetown schoolmaster John Wilson, who had come to England when Charlestown was evacuated, was then turned away when he tried to rejoin his family in South Carolina under the terms of the treaty of peace, and then wandered from Philadelphia to New York to Jamaica before reaching England once again in 1786; John Mills, organist at St. Philip's, who traveled to London by way of East Florida and the Bahamas; and Daniel DeWalt of Cannon's Creek in the Dutch Fork, who had served with the South Carolina Royalists in East Florida during the American Period, had suffered a second exile to East Florida after the evacuation of Charlestown, and then journeyed to Jamaica before arriving in England in 1786.[43]

Reference has frequently been made to the work of the five-man commission established by Parliament in 1783 to examine evidence of the losses and suffering incurred by the loyalists in America. The commissioners sought information about procedure and rules of evidence from loyalists who had recently arrived in the kingdom, particularly from the Board of Agents of the American Loyalists on which William Bull and former royal governor Thomas Boone represented South Carolina, and on property and currency values in the several states from such individual loyalists as the former attorney general, James Simpson. The commission then agreed to consider only losses incurred as a direct result of loyalty, in effect ruling out claims for losses incurred because of the war itself; and it adopted rules that required claimants to prove their loyalty. The commission's authority was extended several times, and several of its members took evidence in America before its final report was submitted in 1789. Altogether, the commission heard claims amounting to over £8,000,000, and it awarded something over £3,000,000; South Carolina loyalists received 321 awards, second only to the number granted from New York. Many loyalists were also granted temporary allowances pending decisions on their claims, and many officers who had military service during the war applied for military pensions.[44]

The claims were presented in the form of memorials to the commission from individual loyalists in which they set out their services, their "suffering," and a table of the losses incurred because of their loyalty. When called before the commission to testify in their own behalf, claimants also presented witnesses who could confirm their services and evaluate their property. South Carolina militia officers of higher rank received the support of Lord Cornwallis and Lord Rawdon, usually in writing, and of who on a number of occasions testified in person; Cornwallis also supported civilians who held important positions during the occupation. But supporting claims was not the only type of assistance sought from the earl, who wrote early in 1784 of being "plagued to death and impoverished by starving Loyalists," and complained six months later that "I am as usual pestered to death every morning by wretched starving Loyalists." Claimants who were of lesser rank obtained substantiation of their claims from local officers, neighbors, and persons of similar status, and there was a good bit of testifying for each other. The usual pattern is illustrated by the case of Colonel John Phillips whose claim was warmly supported by Balfour, by Alexander Chesney (a relative by marriage who could describe his property), and by James Miller, one of his company commanders; in turn, Phillips, Miller, and Zacharias Gibbs testified for Chesney; and Miller was supported by Phillips, Chesney, and a neighbor, Samuel McKee. All of these men except Gibbs had migrated from Ireland within five years of the outbreak of the "troubles," and had returned to or were en route to Ireland. The commissioners questioned claimants closely, showing particular interest in when they had joined the British, whether they had taken oaths to or served with the Americans, and if their property had been confiscated or seized. In a few cases such questioning elicited testimony less than completely favorable to the claimant. John Hopton, who had returned to South Carolina during the war and had actually served in the state Senate, was quizzed at some length about his loyalty, and Balfour declared "the real truth to be that he was guided by his interest in the part he took." Witnesses made such statements about Thomas Phepoe as that, although loyal, "the Americans did not consider him as hostile," and "if his interest had been out of the way his wishes were for Gt. Britain." Robert Cunningham refused to acknowledge that a certificate he had purportedly signed for Andrew Moore was in his handwriting, and both he and Margaret Reynolds declared that to their knowledge Moore owned no property.[45]

Eventually the claimants were notified of their awards, and they received their compensation in two stages, a preliminary payment of 30 to 40 percent in cash, and the balance later in the 1780s. James Cary employed Alexander Shaw, a North Carolinian who had moved to England before the war, to act as agent in handling his claim and pension application and also drew upon him for small loans until official decisions were made. The modest pension Cary received was retroactive to 1783, and that sum and the first installment on his award from the commission enabled him and his wife to pay off some debts incurred in Jamaica. The balance of his award came in the form of interest-bearing debentures, and the income from them and the pension enabled them to live in modest comfort.[46]

The South Carolina refugees in England were of two groups, those who had no intention of returning to America, and those who hoped to do so. Once they had completed their business with government, those who were British-born and planned to remain settled down in or near their places of origin in northern Ireland, Scotland, or England. For those who were natives of America or who had long resided there, however, other choices had to be made.

Colonel Elias Ball of Wambaw, after being refused permission to return to South Carolina from East Florida, had come with his wife to London where they took a furnished house in Knightsbridge near which other Carolinians lived. Although they liked London and the presence of these friends, the Balls found living expenses to be high, and in 1785 they moved to Bristol from which place he awaited action on his claim. The Carys also found London to be expensive, and they moved to Bath and then to Bristol. Harry Michie, a Scottish merchant, remained in London and took a position "in the India house."[47]

About a dozen widows made their way to England after Charlestown was evacuated and sought compensation from the commissioners. Catherine Creighton joined her husband in Jamaica shortly before he died, and Governor Campbell provided her with funds to go to England. After her husband died in England, Mary Anne Gibbes sought compensation for their Charlestown house that had been destroyed while occupied by the Commissary General. Eleanor Lester, in her seventies and widowed many years before, had run a "grogshop for sailors" in Charlestown after migrating from Ireland. She obtained an allowance of £20 from the Treasury while awaiting action on her claim. Barbara Mergath, whose husband had baked bread for the British army, came to England after his death and supported her two children on a Treasury allowance and by taking in washing, and Mary Miller, an American who had married and buried her English husband during the war, was also supporting two small children on a Treasury allowance. Margaret Reynolds, whom we have seen as a nurse in the refugee hospital in Charlestown, brought her "three fatherless children" to London where she lived on an allowance and sought compensation for the property they had left on Long Cane Creek. Isabella McLaurin, who was able to obtain testimony from Colonel Alexander Innes and numerous other statements certifying the service of her husband, Evan, obtained an allowance of £40 to support her children. Although deprived of the support of their mates and forced to leave their homes and property some of these widows seem to have developed a degree of self-reliance that was perhaps unusual for the time, while others pleaded ignorance of their husbands' business affairs.[48]

Some of the loyalists who came to England began shortly after the treaty of peace to inquire about the possibilities of returning to South Carolina. The elder Robert Williams, a resident of South Carolina for forty years, after landing at Torbay in 1783 was shocked to find in the treaty of peace "no provision made for the return of persons in my situation to their connexions"; and Williams pleaded with an old friend in South Carolina, Rawlins Lowndes, to keep him abreast of the actions of the legislature so that he might be reunited with his family. Loyalists like John Rose and Elias Ball, who had already failed in an attempt to return from East Florida, continued to press their friends to get their names dropped from the confiscation law; and many others petitioned the General Assembly for relief during the 1780s. Neither Ball nor Rose was successful, but a law passed by the General Assembly in 1784 replaced confiscation and banishment with amercement for a large group, some of whom like Paul Hamilton, William Ancrum, and John Gaillard had held offices or commissions under the British and were in London at the time preparing to file or testify before the claims commission.[49]

There were other ways of maintaining business contact with South Carolina. Several loyalist merchants now in England resumed partnerships with protectionists or rebels who had remained in the state. John Tunno, inspector of loyal refugees during the occupation and John Rose's son-in-law, "set up" as a merchant in London in partnership with his brother Adam in Charlestown, and similar arrangements were continued between Plowden Weston in Charlestown and Charles Atkins after the latter came to London.[50]

Powers of attorney were extended to people in South Carolina to sell or manage property on behalf of exiles in Britain, and exiles frequently named executors on both sides of the Atlantic. Indeed, the few surviving wills of the exiles in Britain reveal their continuing ties with South Carolina. William Bull left his property in America to relatives, his law books to Robert Williams in London, and named Williams and John Hopton in England and Rawlins Lowndes, Nathaniel Russell, and Christopher Gadsden in South Carolina as his executors. In similar fashion, Paul Hamilton left his property in America to nephews, made bequests to Robert Williams and Thomas Harper in London, and named Williams and the Reverend Alexander Hewatt in London and Alexander Chisholm in Charlestown as executors of his estate.[51]

While the bonds established over many years remained strong, it is clear that most of the loyalists exiled to the British Isles from South Carolina did not wish to return or yielded to the inevitable and made the best of their new lives. Most had resided in South Carolina for fifteen years or less before seeking refuge in Britain, and the turmoil, waste of time and energy in getting established, and personal loss of loved ones and property that characterized their experience during the "troubles" must have left them with little to be sentimental about except when reminiscing in old age. In the extreme case of Alexander Chesney, who lived for sixty years after returning to Ireland, the South Carolina years—though full of excitement and suffering—were but a tiny proportion of a long life.[52]

The adjustment must have been most difficult for natives and longtime residents of America, especially those of advanced age, yet once their claims were settled and their affairs put in some semblance of order they may have found the cosmopolitan atmosphere of British communities more agreeable than they had feared. The older men had but a few years to live. John Savage reported that William Bull, although afflicted with "the stone," was in his eighties, "cheerful, his memory & understanding clear and good." Bull died in 1791, and Savage himself succumbed at eighty-nine, three years later. White Outerbridge, who had served in one of James Oglethorpe's independent companies nearly fifty years before, was not so fortunate, now being subject, according to James Simpson, to "giddiness in his head...in the Nature of Epileptic Fits." Robert Williamson, who had kept a spirits and grocery shop in Charlestown, went for a walk and was pulled out of the New River near Sadlers Wells two days later. One refugee literally did go home again. After James Cary died in 1794, his widow accepted the invitation of relatives to return to live with them in her native Virginia. When she died in 1804, she left her modest savings in Bank of England stock, derived largely from the compensation to her husband as a loyalist, to her nieces and nephews.[53]

Notes

1. Siebert, *Loyalists in East Florida*, is basic to the subject, valuable both for his narrative, in vol. I, and for the Florida loyalist claims filed in England and the biographical sketches in vol. II. His population and migration estimates in vol. I, 129–32, are the best in print and, except as noted, I have followed them. See also Tonyn to Shelburne, Nov. 14, and to Townshend, Dec. 24, 1782, and May 15, 1783, C.O.5/560, 235, 252, 292.
2. These conclusions are drawn from Refugees to East Florida; individual claims in Loyalist Transcripts; and from Governor Vicente Zespedes's census of British subjects, Spanish Census, 1784. I am grateful to Professor David Chesnutt of the University of South Carolina for calling this last and very valuable source to my attention. It should be noted that the Spanish census was taken long after many South Carolina loyalists had left East Florida, and it therefore has limited value as a record of the total number who departed.

3. Spanish Census, 1784.
4. Ibid.; Charles L. Mowat, *East Florida as a. British Province, 1763–1784* (Gainesville, Fla., 1943), 136–38; Siebert, *Loyalists in East Florida,* II, 105–8, 133–36, 140–44.
5. Siebert, *Loyalists in East Florida,* I, 132–35; Mowat, *East Florida,* 138.
6. Clark, ed., *Loyalists,* I, 6–7, 16–17, 22–23, 29, 32–33, 45–46; CP, 30/11/560, 247–48.
7. McArthur to Leslie, May 31, 1783, CP, 30/11/560, n.p.; Siebert, *Loyalists in East Florida,* I, 145–47.
8. Mowat, *East Florida,* 142–47; Siebert, *Loyalists in East Florida,* I, 161–66.
9. C.O.5/560/247–48; Clark, ed., *Loyalists,* I, 17–19; Siebert, *Loyalists in East Florida,* I, 142.
10. Lockey, *East Florida, 1783–1785,* 14–16; Spanish Census, 1784: Loyalist Transcripts, LVII, 439–49.
11. Young to Tonyn, July 10, 1784, Petition of Linder and McGirt, Aug. 4, 1784, Lockey, *East Florida,* 346–47; J. Leitch Wright, *Florida in the American Revolution* (Gainesville. Fla., 1975), 138, 169.
12. Petition of Inhabitants to Zespedes, Jan. 25, Zespedes to Galvez, Feb. 9, and Bernard Troncoso to Zespedes, Nov. 7. 1785, and Zespedes to Troncoso, Jan. 7, 1786, O'Neall to Carlos Howard, Apr. 17, and July 3,1785, Lockey, *East Florida,* 456–58, 470–71, 529–30, 737, 537–39, 543.
13. Chesney, "Journal," 111–12; Siebert, *Loyalists in East Florida,* I, 123; II, 351; Wright, *Florida in the American Revolution,* 136–37; George C. Rogers, Jr., *Evolution of a Federalist: William Loughton Smith of Charleston* (Columbia, S.C., 1962), 120.
14. Few loyalists from South Carolina had acquired enough property in East Florida to make it worthwhile to file claims with the commission.
15. *House Journals, 1783–1784,*552; Loyalist Transcripts, LVII, 402–17, 439–49; Spanish Census, 1784; *Census, 1790, S.C.,* 80; Refugees to East Florida, 816, 817; Union County, S.C., Court of Common Pleas and General Sessions, *Minutes, 1785–1791* (WPA Transcript), 3; Union County, S.C., Register of Mesne Conveyance, *Deeds,* A, 142–44 (WPA Transcript): Union County, S.C., *Record Book, I–II,1785–1800,*203 (WPA Transcript). Siebert, citing William Brown, the commissioner for evacuation of East Florida, lists 462 whites and 2,561 blacks as leaving for "the States of America," *Loyalists in East Florida,* I, 208.
16. Siebert, *Loyalists in East Florida,* II, 15–18, 35–37, 133–36; George C. Rogers, Jr., *History of Georgetown County, South Carolina* (Columbia, S.C. 1970), 126; *House Journals, 1783–1784,* 552; Refugees to East Florida, 811–13, 816; Loyalist Transcripts, LV, 87–106, 556–69.
17. Brown's report is printed in Siebert, *Loyalists in East Florida,* I, 208, and Lockey, *East Florida,* 11 ; see Tonyn to Lord Sydney, Apr. 4,]785, Lockey, *East Florida,* 499.
18. Thelma Peters "The Loyalist Migration from East Florida to the Bahama Islands" *Florida Historical Quarterly* (1961), 127–29; Loyalist Transcripts, LVII, 80–117.
19. Michael Craton, *A History of the Bahamas* (London, 1962), 162–72; Johann David Schoepf, *Travels in the Confederation,[1783–1784]* (New York, 1968 [orig. publ. Erlangen, 1788]), 264.
20. Loyalist Transcripts, LIII , 356–94; LIV, 317–26, 459–68; LVI, 201–20, 407–16; *Canadian Claims,* 169, 727; CEP, SCAH.
21. Thelma Peters, "The American Loyalists in the Bahama Islands: Who They Were" *Florida Historical Quarterly* (1962), 227–28.
22. Campbell to Thomas Townshend, Apr. 5, 1783, C.O.137/83/II (microfilm, LC); Siebert, *Loyalists in East Florida,* 1, 202–3.
23. Edward Brathwaite, *The Development of Creole Society in Jamaica, 1770–1820* (London, 1971), 152; Campbell to Lord North, Aug. 1, 1783, C.O.137/83/III.
24. Loyalist Transcripts, LIII, 272–306; LVI , 378–97,423–27; LVII, 249–59.
25. R.S. Lambert, "A Loyalist Odyssey, James and Mary Cary in Exile, 1783–1804," *SCHM* (1978), 174–75, 179; *Canadian Claims,* 187, 646; Brathwaite, *Creole Society,* 83–85.
26. Chesney, "Journal," 105–8; *Canadian Claims,* 799.
27. Loyalist Transcripts, XXVI, 71–74; *Canadian Claims,* 674.
28. H.M.C., *Report,* III, 179; grants in Marion Gilroy, comp., *Loyalists and Land Settlement in Nova Scotia* (Halifax, 1937), 43–54, 60–61.
29. *Canadian Claims,* 679; Return of the Loyalists from South Carolina Settled near Windsor, Old Townships & Loyalist Settlements, 1784, #63. PANS; Gilroy, *Land Settlement,* 119–44; *Canadian Claims,* 62, 63, 127, 265, 525, 674; Frederick McKenzie to Governor John Parr, Mar. 3, 1783, H .M.C., *Report, III ,* 381–82: Memorial of David Bleakney and Christopher Rubart [Rubert], Jan. 20, 1785, Ganong MSS, Box 20, NBM.
30. Loyalists Settled near Windsor, PANS; *Canadian Claims,* 63, 157, 170, 175, 276, 525, 692.
31. Clark, *Loyalists,* 1, 176–78; *Canadian Claims,* 33; Edward Winslow to Ward Chipman, Jan. 7, 1784, and "Return of the Total Numbers of the Men, Women, and Children of the Disbanded Corps and Loyalists on

the River St. John," in W.O. Raymond, ed., *Winslow Papers* (Saint John, New Brunswick, 1901), 161, 244; A List of the Loyal Refugees on Board the *Argo*, Transport from East Florida Gone to Chedabucto, Gideon White Papers, III, #228, PANS.
32. *Canadian Claims*, 703, 799; Loyalists Settled near Windsor, PANS.
33. See Loyalist Claims, XXXII, 227–385, for awards to South Carolinians. Claims, in sterling, ranged from a high of £2,368 for George Dawkins to a low of £69 for Hannah Lamb, a widow; Dawkins received the highest award, £964, and Lamb, the lowest, £10. The average among the seventy claims submitted was £420, and the average award, £139, or about one-third. The claims of southern loyalists heard in the Maritime Provinces of Canada, who were primarily backcountrymen of modest means, were more representative of the South Carolina loyalist population than those presented in England.
34. *Canadian Claims*, 34, 156, 170, 171, 183,675,677, 849.
35. Lambert, "A Loyalist Odyssey," 174; Loyalist Claims, XXVI, 420; Loyalist Transcripts, LII, 227–58; LIII, 127–46,487–98.
36. Thomas Dundas to Cornwallis, Dec. 28, 1786, *Correspondence of Charles, First Marquis Cornwallis*, ed. Charles Ross, 3 vols. (2d ed., London, 1859), 1, 291.
37. This discussion is taken from Carole Watterson Troxler, *The Loyalist Experience in North Carolina* (Raleigh, N.C., 1976), 49–54; Ellen Gibson Wilson, *The Loyal Blacks* (New York, 1976), 41–67,81–131 ; and Robin W. Winks, *The Blacks in Canada: A History* (New Haven, Conn., 1971), 29–60.
38. Benjamin Quarles, *Negro in the American Revolution* (Chapel Hill, N.C., 1961), 177–81; and Wilson, *Loyal Blacks*, 177–238; Phyllis R. Blakely, "Boston King: A Black Loyalist,' I in *Eleven Exiles: Accounts of Loyalists in the American Revolution*, ed. P. R. Blakely and John N. Grant (Toronto, 1982), 265–88.
39. Assessment upon His Majesty's Subjects in the Township of Rawdon...[1791], and Assessment Made... of Country Harbour...1791, Poll Tax, 1791–97, PANS: "Robinson, Lt. Col. Joseph, Memoir of," Rare Book Room, McLennan Library, McGill University, Montreal; *Royal Gazette and Nova Scotia Advertiser* (Halifax), Feb. 15, 1791. For the Fanning affair, see Fanning to Jonathan Odell, Feb. 9, and C. Allison to J. Howe, June 2, 1801, Fanning Family Papers, NBM; A. W. Savary's introduction to Fanning, "Narrative," *Canadian Magazine* (1907); tombstone, Trinity Anglican Church Cemetery, Digby, Nova Scoria.
40. Assessment Rawdon, 1791, PANS.
41. Loyalist Transcripts, LII, 267–90, 314–27, 399–411; LIV, 479–86; LVI, 417–42: Chesney, "Journal," 29–30.
42. Loyalist Transcripts, LIII, 166–77, 257–61.
43. Loyalist Transcripts, LVI, 213–20, 314–22; LVII, 311–17.
44. The best discussion of the work of the commission, and the awarding of allowances and pensions, is Mary Beth Norton, *British-Americans: The Loyalist Exiles in England*, 1774–1789 (Cambridge, Mass., 1972), 185–222, 224–34, especially 209–12 , for South Carolina. For Simpson's report, see "Arbitrations of Claims for Compensation from Losses and Damages Resulting from Lawful Impediments to the Recovery of Pre-War Debts," in *International Adjudications, Modem Series*, ed. John Bassett Moore (New York, 1931), III, 445–53.
45. Cornwallis to Alexander Ross, Jan. 24, June 13, 1784, Charles Ross, ed., *Cornwallis Correspondence*, I, 163, 177, Loyalist Transcripts, LII, 267–327; LIV, 509–30; LV, 133–41; H.M.C., *Report*, 1245.
46. Lambert, "A Loyalist Odyssey," I 77–78; Norton, *British-Americans*, 209–10.
47. Ball to Elias Ball, Jr., Sept. 19, 1784, Apr. 29, Sept. 27, 1785, Ball Family Papers, SCL; Lambert, "A Loyalist Odyssey," 176, 178; Loyalist Transcripts, LV, 575–85.
48. Loyalist Transcripts, LII, 83–89, 258–66; LIII, 320–32; LIV, 340–51, 491–96; LV, 246–51, 476–83, 539–47. Gibbes's claim was rejected because, although she was deemed to be loyal, a witness testified that her husband preferred the Americans, Egerton, *Royal Commission*, 14.
49. Williams to Rawlins Lowndes, Feb. 13, 1783, William Lowndes Papers, SHC; Ball to Elias Ball, Jr., Sept. 19. 1784, Ball Family Papers, SCL; Loyalist Transcripts, LIII, 272–306.
50. Loyalist Transcripts, LV, 457–75; LVII, 418–38.
51. Wills, XXIV, 984–86; XXVII, 804–7.
52. Chesney, "Journal."
53. Savage to Rawlins Lowndes, Dec. 31, 1790, William Lowndes Papers, SHC; Loyalist Transcripts, LIV, 173–83; LVII, 118–23; Lambert, "A Loyalist Odyssey," 181.

Chapter Seventeen

Retribution and Reconciliation:
The Loyalists in Postwar South Carolina

James Cook, the carpenter... is now charged with promoting a petition to Col. Balfour prohibiting all those that were prisoners of war & had not taken protection from following their trades...his name was taken off the Confiscation &Banishment Act,...Next morning he was hanged in effigy, carted through the town, & Burnt at Gadsden's Wharf

—John Lewis Gervais, April 1784

After the British evacuated South Carolina, a great many persons who had served the king more or less willingly during the war remained in the state or returned to it in the postwar years. These were people who had in some way come to terms with the state government or were anxious to do so. An examination of the treatment accorded former loyalists and protectionists by the State and its citizens reveals that, despite the bitterness engendered by the long war, a degree of reconciliation between former enemies was achieved in the 1780's.

When the South Carolina General Assembly met in January 1783, it was flooded with petitions for relief from the confiscation or amercement laws. The petitions were presented by persons who had remained in the state, usually protectionists, or by wives or other relatives and neighbors of men who had left. The petitions of Henry Rugeley, then in Jamaica, Patrick Cunningham from East Florida, offered by "inhabitants" of their neighborhoods, and Brian Cape, offered by his wife, Mary, and several presented by Christopher Gadsden were among the many submitted to the House of Representatives on January 22. Petitioners usually pleaded that they had joined the British from necessity: Philip Porcher of St. Stephen's Parish, "from an anxiety of his Own Welfare, and to escape the artifices of designing men," had accepted a commission; it was with "unfeigned grief" that Gilbert Chalmers, a Charlestown artisan, found himself named in the confiscation law for "Signing an Address to Sir Henry Clinton"; and the elderly mariner Thomas Buckle had received a British pardon because his name had been signed by his son to the address to Clinton, an act that had shielded the elder Buckle from Nisbet Balfour's wrath after the commandant learned of his early success in bringing gunpowder to the state government. The merchant John Deas, who was listed in the Amercement Act, served as an attorney for several petitioners who had been forced to leave during the British evacuation.[1]

Many petitioners were able to present witnesses to substantiate their claims for relief. John Wigfall who had commanded a loyalist militia regiment before resigning his commission in 1781, presented five witnesses who testified to his "abhorrence" at British destruction of property around Georgetown, and that "he was much hurt in his mind by taking a Commission & that if he could have the least assurance that his life would not be taken" he would have come out of the British lines. Colonel John Winn declared Henry Rugeley to be a "humane man" who had "tendered him every act of friendship when he was a prisoner"; witnesses for Henry Peronneau, who had spent much of the war in England, testified that he had expressed warm sentiments toward the American cause in correspondence with them. Not all the testimony presented was favorable to the petitioners; Francis Marion declared that James Gordon, a lieutenant colonel under James Cassells in Georgetown District, had acted "in conjunction to keep the Little Peedee men in arms against us," and several men pointed out that James Rugge had petitioned the commandant "to prevent every person from following their employment without taking protection, which was carried into effect." Yet most of the testimony was favorable to the petitioners, who were variously described as "warm & zealous" in sentiment toward the American cause, or who, as in one instance, had "discharged his duty with fidelity" before the British came. Another petitioner who had signed the congratulatory address to Lord Cornwallis developed an "anxiety of mind on that account" that threatened his life, and during his illness he expressed "great sorrow" at having taken such a step.[2]

Altogether, 137 cases were examined during the first session of the General Assembly in 1783. In most instances, the House committees recommended that petitioners be removed from the Confiscation Act and that their property be amerced 12 percent. For example, they declared that John Walters Gibbes "appears to be a Character beneath the attention or Resentment of this House; his turn for Buffoonery seems to have been a principal inducement for his being taken notice of by the British officers to whom he was attached no longer than whilst they remained Masters of the Town." Indeed, the offenses of many petitioners were considered to be minor: others like David Bruce—"by printing the Pamphlet entitled *Common Sense* had rendered himself very obnoxious to the British" —had contributed such conspicuous service to the American cause that their errors during the occupation could be forgiven. The pleas of others were flatly rejected, the merchant William Burt not having "assigned sufficient reasons in extenuation of his past conduct,...having during the residence of the British...shewn himself uniformly [sic] attached to their measures," and Robert and Patrick Cunningham were declared to be "inveterate enemies" to American independence. The property of those whose petitions had been rejected was subject to sale by the confiscation commissioners during that summer. Some petitioners did not appear and their cases were postponed. Because of the press of business, the House and Senate formed a Free Conference Committee to reconcile differences in their versions of a relief measure, but no agreement could be reached and no persons were actually dropped from the confiscation law during either of the sessions held in 1783.[3]

In March a second Confiscation Act extended the penalties of the original law to persons reported by militia regimental commanders to have left the state with the British. But the General Assembly did refine the original confiscation legislation by suspending sales of property of persons whose petitions for relief were pending before the legislature, and by providing further safeguards for widows and heirs. Purchasers who did not pay cash for confiscated property were required to mortgage it to the state so that it could be resold if the terms of the sale were not met.[4]

Hearings on the Amercement Act of 1782 were also conducted in the winter of 1783. The persons named therein were protectionists who had done little more than take the British oath or sign a congratulatory address. Although the prominence of some like Daniel Horry, Colonel Charles Pinckney, and John Deas had perhaps set a poor example, these men had rarely held office or taken any conspicuous part for the British; indeed, as testimony revealed, they had often provided valuable information or been helpful to distressed Americans during the occupation. Although the reaction to the requests of the petitioners was usually favorable, formal action on them was also postponed until the following year.[5]

Loyalists and protectionists who had fled overseas, anxious to learn how the peace treaty might affect them, inquired of influential friends whether it would be worthwhile to try to return to recover their property and resume their lives in South Carolina. Henry Laurens, who remained in England to restore his health after his release from the Tower of London, was asked by several South Carolinians about their prospects for returning to the state. Aaron Loocock, a Charlestown merchant who had moved his family to England in 1780 after signing an .address to Cornwallis, left them there while he came to New York to await favorable news. Laurens tried to reassure Mrs. Loocock that her husband would be cordially received when he returned to South Carolina. Laurens also gave advice to others on how to secure relief from the confiscation law, and he recommended attorneys to handle their affairs until they learned whether they could return. To the governor of South Carolina he expressed the hope that young Edward Fenwick, who, despite having held a British militia commission, was "descended from ancestors whose memories are highly respectable," would be "acquitted in the judgment of his Country and become a valuable citizen" of the state.[6]

Correspondents in Carolina also reported to friends abroad on the fate of relatives who had remained in the state. Young Philip Porcher in England received word that his "worthy father and family" had remained on their Santee estate until he was called to testify before the General Assembly in January, but that, unlike others, his father had not been "confined in the Provost." Because his father had a "great many Powerful Friends from his Universal Good Character," committees had reported favorably on his case, but the legislature had hastily adjourned before taking final action.[7]

Despite the apparently moderate temper of the legislature, many residents of Charlestown resented the presence of so many people who had given comfort to the British during the occupation, whether loyalists, protectionists, or the "British merchants" who remained to settle their affairs under the agreement worked out with Governor Mathews. Daniel Stevens, the high sheriff of Charlestown District, was ordered to arrest those listed in the confiscation law who had remained in the state after the British departed, and he complied by casting "about 126 persons" altogether in the "Provost." In spite of this action, the presence of so many recent enemies in and near Charlestown had infuriated elements in the city who were prepared to take matters into their own hands. Members of the artisan community, so conspicuous in the anti-British agitation before independence, had found a new leader in Commodore Alexander Gillon, the commander of the state's navy. With the support of merchants who resented the presence of and competition from the "British merchants," Gillon formed the Marine Anti-Britannic Society, which almost immediately began to agitate in the press and in the streets against the "aristocrats" and the British elements they were protecting. The unrest increased that summer after the General

Assembly adjourned when a number of loyalists sought to reenter the state.[8]

Dr. Peter Spence, who came from East Florida under a flag of truce in April, had the captain land him quietly on the Stono River. Spence was arrested on orders of the Privy Council and, despite General Greene's protest over the violation of the flag of truce, was ordered to leave. He sailed for England in June. When John Tunno, John Scott, Alexander Inglis, and Dr. Hugh Rose returned from East Florida in June, they were refused permission to land, as enemies of the state, and retreated to Savannah. Despite Henry Laurens's optimistic forecast, Aaron Loocock's reception was anything but cordial when he reached the city, and he was quickly "confined in the Provost." His petition demanding that he be "liberated" was turned down by a majority of the Privy Council who recommended that he "be sent away as the law directs." In July a crowd seized and "pumped" several persons "obnoxious to the state," causing Governor Guerard to threaten prosecution if such disorders continued.[9]

Amid this turmoil young Dr. William Charles Wells returned from St. Augustine under a flag of truce in order to collect debts due his family, and was promptly arrested and put in jail. Through the aid of John Harleston, who was himself on the amercement List, and others, Wells secured space in editor John Miller's newspaper to protest his imprisonment and conditions in the jail, and that his small trunk had been taken. He also explained why he had left South Carolina in 1775 and again in 1782 and declared that "If indeed to wish well to my Country...be a crime, I cheerfully plead guilty to the charge." This notice drew a rejoinder from Sheriff Stevens, who said that Wells had been arrested on a writ of trover sworn out by Samuel Prioleau for an unpaid debt; and he went on to say that Wells had been granted the unusual privilege of a room in the jailer's quarters and freedom of the grounds, favorable treatment that had been protested by the public, but which Wells subsequently denied receiving. The Harlestons received many threats because of their kindnesses to Wells; one night a mob appeared at their home while John was away, but his wife defied them and they went off. After spending three months in jail, Wells was released and returned to St. Augustine.[10]

The full force of Gillon's protest movement reached its peak in midsummer when a general meeting on July 21 declared that both the presence of persons who had acted against America and the agreement with the British merchants, were "real grievances," and urged the General Assembly not to give greater indulgence to such persons than required by the preliminary articles of peace. David Ramsay noted that' 'A spirit has gone forth among the lower class of people to drive away certain persons whom they are pleased to call Tories," and that "a few firebrands" had seized "supposed tories & maltreated them" to pressure them into leaving the state. Such "anarchy" caused him to wonder whether "mankind are capable of enjoying the blessings of freedom" without such "extravagances," a sentiment echoed by "A Patriot," who declared that "good men" should not be excluded merely "because they have belonged to Great Britain."[11]

During the summer of 1783 auctions of confiscated property were held at several places in the interior. Sheriff William Moore of Ninety Six District tolled off more than fifty tracts to forty different buyers early in July. The lands had belonged either to prominent Tory leaders like Thomas Fletchall, Moses Kirkland, and Patrick Cunningham, and some of their officers, or to lowcountry speculators like former Governor Montagu, John Savage, and Charles Atkins. Buyers favored the lands of the prominent loyalists, but most speculators' tracts did not sell, probably because they were undeveloped. Several of the unsold tracts were purchased at a supplementary auction in December. The lands of the loyalist militia colonels James Cary and Robert English and the Charleston merchant Archibald Brown sold quickly at Camden District sales in June, while at Georgetown in August a variety of lands, livestock, and personal property, including Dr. Charles Fyffe's "elegant sulkey," attracted a number of buyers.[12]

When the General Assembly met the following winter, the Free Conference Committee resumed its task of dealing with the many petitions still pending, and during February and March 1784 it made a series of recommendations. Once again, witnesses appeared and depositions were presented in support of, and occasionally in opposition to, the person under investigation. Although most cases required relatively little discussion, a few were particularly controversial; and the questions posed of the accused and their witnesses reveal what conduct during the occupation was thought to have been reprehensible, and what part, if any, the accused took in such actions. The detailed testimony taken in the case of John Gaillard is especially useful in showing how one prominent lowcountry planter reacted after the fall of Charlestown.

Gaillard, of St. James Santee Parish, and his brother Theodore, a Charlestown merchant, had accepted commissions in the Berkeley-Craven County loyalist militia regiment commanded by Theodore's brother-in-law, Colonel Elias Ball of Wambaw. One of the many South Carolina refugees who reached London in 1783, John Gaillard was preparing to give evidence to support Elias Ball's claim before the Royal Commission, when he apparently received word that his wife's petition seeking repeal of his banishment from South Carolina was to be considered in Charlestown. He presented himself before the Conference Committee on February 14, 1784, where "a paper containing heavy accusations" against him was presented. First, he was charged with having, as a British officer, "levied contributions on his neighbours," an accusation quickly refuted by the protectionist Philip Porcher. More serious was the charge that " he took a commission & oblig'd the people to take ye Oath of Allegiance or to be sent to ye prevost." Gaillard admitted taking the commission, but claimed that he did it at the request of some of his neighbors; he also admitted administering the oath but denied threatening to imprison anyone who refused to take it, a position generally supported by testimony and depositions from others. One Benjamin Walker accused Gaillard of arming slaves and with complicity in burning a neighbor's house, but Gaillard's witnesses also absolved him of responsibility for these acts. Perhaps most serious was the charge that as a militia officer he had escorted men who refused the British oath to Charlestown, where Nisbet Balfour had them shipped off to St. Augustine as dangerous rebels. Although the duty of escorting prisoners to Charlestown had been thrust upon him, witnesses declared that the "order for ye men marching originated from Col. Ball &.not from Mr. Gaillard." Gaillard's answers and the numerous statements of witnesses made a favorable impression on the committee, and it recommended that his estate be restored and amerced 12 percent, and that his banishment be revoked. His brother Theodore, whose original petition for relief had been drawn up on board the *Carolina Packet* in the harbor, was less extensively questioned and obtained the same verdict from the committee a few days later. The committee refused to recommend that relief be granted to Colonel Elias Ball of Wambaw, the apparent instigator of the order to escort the prisoners; however, it did recommend that his son and second in command at the time, Elias Ball of Comingtee, be relieved.[13]

One witness against Colonel John Wigfall "produced papers to prove his tyranny," but this testimony was refuted by others who commended Wigfall's "indulgence' in handling personal situations, suggesting that he was "an imprudent man but no ways dangerous," and that, "except for threatening letters" he had received, he really would have preferred to "lay down his commission & go out" of the British Lines. In fact, "humane" was the word used by a parade of witnesses to describe their treatment at the hands of Wigfall and others under investigation. Altogether in that session the General Assembly removed 122 persons from the confiscation law, relieving thirty of all future penalties, amercing the estates of sixty-two at 12 percent, and amercing and disqualifying thirty others from voting or holding office for seven years. In addition, forty-seven persons were dropped from the Amercement Act.[14]

After the General Assembly adjourned in 1784, there were sporadic incidents of violence against a few persons who had been removed from the confiscation and amercement laws. This time, however, those harassed had the law on their side. When a public notice appeared that warned certain persons to leave the state in ten days or face the consequences, Governor Guerard on the advice of the Privy Council offered a reward for the apprehension of those responsible for the notice. James Cook, a carpenter accused of asking British authorities during the occupation not to permit mechanics who refused the British oath to practice their trades, was among those amerced by the General Assembly, although a petition from eighty-nine persons demanded that he receive the full penalties of the confiscation law. In June, after a crowd had hanged Cook in effigy, they appeared at his house and demanded that he show himself. Learning that he was not present, the crowd insulted his family and threatened to hang him in person before going off. The next day Governor Guerard summoned several witnesses before the Privy Council to give their versions of the incident, then ordered the attorney general to prosecute a member of the mob who had been identified.[15]

James Donavan, an exiled tanner who tried to return to settle some business affairs in 1783, identified Alexander Gillon and Henry Peronneau, Jr., as leaders of a "Hint Club" who had sent him a warning that he would be wise to leave. In taking a leading part in harassing former Tories and protectionists, Gillon may have been motivated as much by a concern for personal gain as for the public welfare; among the persons whose property had been restored by the sweeping action of the legislature in 1784 were John Savage, Theodore Gaillard, and the cabinetmaker John Fisher, who among them owned five parcels of city property purchased by Gillon at the confiscation sales. And perhaps young Peronneau's zeal for hounding former Tories was an effort to compensate for the sins of his relatives who were living in England: his father, Henry, formerly joint public treasurer of the Province, and his uncle Robert, a physician; his aunt, Ann, who had married the Reverend Robert Cooper, successively rector of St. Michael's and St. Phillip's; and his aunt, Elizabeth, the wife of Dr. Alexander Garden.[16]

Among the protectionists affected by this harassment was Rawlins Lowndes, the former state president who had been relieved of amercement by the legislature in 1784. In 1785 Lowndes sued William Clay Snipes for implying that Lowndes had been a traitor to the state, and at the trial he was able to call on Henry Laurens to speak in his behalf In turn, Lowndes provided Laurens with an account of his conduct after Charlestown fell to be shown to men whose opinion he valued. Lowndes won his suit, but another of his witnesses, Colonel Maurice Simons, also a rebel who had taken protection during the occupation, was killed by Snipes in a duel. Lowndes returned to the practice of law, and later served in the convention called to ratify the new Federal Constitution, where he took a leading part against its adoption. The protectionist Daniel Horry was less fortunate; relieved of his amercement, he fell on hard times and then died in 1786. His widow, Harriott, sister of the rebel leaders Charles Cotesworth and Thomas Pinckney, tried to comfort her absent son by reminding him that his own "good conduct" had fulfilled his duty to his father's memory.[17]

With occasional exceptions, lowcountry people removed from the confiscation law were natives or residents of long standing in South Carolina who, after supporting or at least acquiescing in independence, found themselves vulnerable after the fall of Charlestown. To protect families and property, they did cooperate with the British in various ways. All accepted at least "nominal" protection, a descriptive term that appeared frequently in the testimony; others, however, by accepting commissions in the militia or positions of responsibility in Charlestown, had more seriously compromised their allegiance to the state. In deciding what punishment these various actions warranted, the Jacksonborough General Assembly had permitted the "nominal" protectionists to remain by paying an amercement, but a much larger group of men who had collaborated more directly with the foe were banished and their property was forfeited to the state.

Several factors aided the more serious offenders to secure relief from the penalties of the confiscation laws. Of great importance was the fact that the "nominal" protectionists who were amerced by the Jacksonborough General Assembly got to remain in the state after the evacuation; thus men like Rawlins Lowndes and Philip Porcher were in a position to be helpful to friends abroad, and John Harleston had at some risk befriended William Charles Wells and Aaron Loocock when they returned from exile. Others like young Edward Fenwick were able to enlist the support of powerful figures in the state. Both Henry Laurens and General Nathanael Greene vouched for him, the latter because Fenwick had furnished the Americans with valuable information on British troop strength and movements. Fenwick was removed from the confiscation law in 1785. Especially important to the more vulnerable collaborators was the network of relationships by blood and marriage that characterized lowcountry society. John Deas, a protectionist listed in the Amercement Act, obtained relief at the same time that his son-in-law, Archibald Brown, who had held a British commission and signed the address to Sir Henry Clinton, was amerced. Alexander Inglis, son-in-law of David Deas, was amerced at the same time; Inglis did experience difficulty in paying his fine, and after his death in a duel with his wife's cousin in 1791, his widow sought relief from the fine for her children. That Dr. James Clitherall was removed from the confiscation law was due as much to his marriage into the powerful Smith family as to his work in trying to recover the slaves of rebels in East Florida. It would be an exaggeration to claim too much for family ties in these matters: blood was only so thick, as Elias Ball of Wambaw and others found when they sought to return. And the Deas family and in-laws certainly were exceptions to the rule that members of the prewar Scottish community rarely were permitted, or did not seek, to resume residence in the state.[18]

There were fewer appeals from the confiscation and amercement laws in sessions of the General Assembly during the remainder of the 1780s. In 1787 the auditor general reported that eighty-seven names—persons whose appeals had been rejected or who had not sought relief—remained "on the confiscation law," but an attempt to repeal the act was defeated by a substantial margin in the House of Representatives. Thus, although petitions to repeal amercements or to postpone payments due on them continued to occupy the General Assembly's attention, by 1787 nearly two-thirds of those named in the confiscation law had earned the right to resume residence in the state. In the years that followed, a few others, such as the merchants John Champneys and William Greenwood, received permission to return and settle in Charleston (as it was known after 1783), and in 1796 Edward Jenkins returned as co-rector of St. Michael's. A few families whose rights were restored did not take advantage of it, but most did resume residence in the state.[19]

By removing persons from the confiscation law, the legislature necessarily became concerned in issues arising from the restoration of confiscated property to its owners. During the hard times that befell the state in the postwar years, purchasers of confiscated property had difficulty in meeting the terms of sale, and some lands reverted to control of the commissioners who put them up for sale again in 1786. Likewise, amerced persons experienced trouble in keeping up with their payments to the state, and many petitioned for extension of time, remission of interest, or relief altogether. So much property had been restored to its owners as a result of the extensive relief measures enacted in 1784, however, that legislators in succeeding years were reluctant to give up the potential state income represented by the fines due the state. Wives or widows of banished persons petitioned, usually with success, for the recovery of their husbands' property, but generally persons under amercement were not excused from their obligations.[20]

That the ties of friendship persisted between families who remained in the state and those who had taken refuge abroad is occasionally revealed in surviving correspondence and in the wills of the deceased. John Deas provided that mourning rings should go to such exiles in England as Robert Wells, Robert Philp, and Dr. Alexander Garden, and the elder Henry Peronneau made Garden, Robert William Powell, John Hopton, and John Savage, all of London, and Rawlins Lowndes of South Carolina, his executors.[21]

When the traveler Francisco de Miranda visited South Carolina after the war, he remarked on the number of widows in Charleston, a phenomenon he learned was even more widespread in Ninety Six District where the war between the Whigs and Tories had been so bitter. That bitterness had forced large numbers of loyalists to leave their homes when the British garrisons were withdrawn from the interior and ultimately to go into exile. What is less well understood is that many persons who had supported the British before and during the occupation were able to resume some kind of normal life in the interior after the war.[22]

There was a good deal of marauding in the back settlements by "outlyers" after the war, and the state supported a troop of rangers to bring the bandits to justice. There were frequent reports that William Cunningham was involved in the pillaging, and Governor Guerard offered rewards for the apprehension of Cunningham, William Lee, and others for "murders, robberies, and other offenses" in 1783, and Governor William Moultrie also proclaimed Lee, Jesse Gray, Augustine Hobbs, and Edward Turner to be outlaws in 1785. Several of those named had been associated with Cunningham during his 1781 raid and in East Florida after the war, but there is no clear evidence that he was directly involved in plundering the Carolina frontier after he went to East Florida in 1782.²³

Certain loyalists who tried to return to their former neighborhoods after the war did receive rough treatment from Whigs with long memories. One man who ventured to return to Ninety Six District was "taken up" by a justice of the peace on the ground that he had committed acts so "barbarous" during the war that the subsequent peace treaty could not apply to him. This was Mathew Love, who was prosecuted by the state's attorney for participating in the slaughter at Hayes Station during William Cunningham's foray into the valley of the Saluda in 1781. Love was indeed with Cunningham on that occasion and, after suffering wounds, was left in the care of sympathizers. According to Judge Aedanus Burke, who presided at Love's trial in the circuit court at Ninety Six, survivors of the affair at Hayes Station testified that Love was "a principal actor in this tragical business," who had "traversed the ground" among the bodies of "his former neighbours and old acquaintances," and with his sword had dispatched any who were still breathing. But Burke had "overruled the prosecution," holding that the treaty did apply and that Love's "conscience, his feelings alone, stood responsible for what was alleged." He then accepted a defense motion to discharge the accused man. Because Love's case was the last in that term, and "all seemed reconciled" to the decision, Burke adjourned court until the next term and returned to his "lodgings." Shortly thereafter, "A party of men, as respectable for good character and services in the war…composed of the fathers, sons, brothers and friends" of the victims at Hayes Station quietly seized Love. They "put him on horseback," and, proceeding by a circuitous route so as not to embarrass the judge, escorted him to the edge of a wood. There a rope was passed over a tree limb and "tied around his neck" and he was told to "prepare to die." Despite Love's protests that he was being killed without trial, "the horse, drawn from under him, left him suspended till he expired."²⁴

Other Tories who tried to return to the interior after the war met violent ends. Shortly after the evacuation of Charleston, when the country between the Broad and Saluda rivers was "much invested with outlyers Tories Robers Murderers & Plunderers," a militia patrol captured Robert Gilliam of Mudlick Creek and two other men who had been present "at the Murdring [of] Major Duggan his brother & several other good men"; tried by court martial, they were "Condem'd & Hung, which in a Great Measure restor'd peace & safety to that Quarter." The other "Bloody Bill," William Bates, in jail on a charge of horse-stealing after the war, was killed by one Motley who broke into the jail and shot Bates in revenge for killing members of his family in the massacre at Gowen's Fort. In faraway Nova Scotia it was reported that former Tories who had tried to return to Fishing Creek in the upper part of Camden District had been killed or run out of the area. And James Collins remembered that while he tended their horses, his older companions had routed former loyalists from their homes, which they then set afire.²⁵

These spectacular acts of vengeance for the real or alleged crimes of backcountry loyalists during the war are exceptions to the general truth that there was real accommodation among former enemies in the years after peace came. Judge Burke looked upon Love's summary execution as exceptional, noting that many "plunderers and other mischievous people, who had taken part with the enemy, now set down among them without molestation," nor did former rebels seek revenge "against any man who acted like a soldier, and fought them, or killed their friends in fair open action." Collins, too, indicated that later in his life he saw "many" men whom he had helped evict from their property who had settled down to become good citizens. And there are bits and pieces of evidence that indicate clearly that many former loyalists were able to return to the interior of the state, often to the very places where they had resided before the war.[26]

The process of reconciliation in Camden District was in some ways similar to that achieved in the lowcountry. During the ten months that Cornwallis and Rawdon held the town of Camden, a number of local people had made their peace with the British by taking protection or accepting commissions in the militia. When Rawdon gave up the town in 1781, many fled to the lowcountry to escape the vengeance of the returning Whigs. But once the British had left the state for good, family connections and ties with the lowcountry were reasserted to enable some of the more prominent protectionists to return to the area.

Of particular interest here is the mercantile connection between the Charlestown firm of William Ancrum, Lambert Lance, and Aaron Loocock, all of whom had taken protection, and their Camden factors Joseph and Eli Kershaw and John Chesnut, who had supported the state until Chesnut returned to British allegiance in October 1780. Perhaps Joseph Kershaw's presence in the Jacksonborough General Assembly was helpful to Chesnut whose name is not mentioned in the proceedings of that body; if so, Kershaw was less successful with the Charlestown partners, for Lance was named in the amercement law and the others in the Confiscation Act. In 1784, however, Ancrum was amerced and Loocock and Lance were relieved of all penalties. John Adamson, who had taken a lieutenant's commission in Henry Rugeley's regiment, was protected by Joseph Kershaw and Chesnut from Whig vengeance after Rawdon evacuated Camden; but he was named in the Confiscation Act and went to Jamaica after the war. Adamson was amerced in 1784 but barred from holding office for seven years. While in Jamaica, he attempted to recover slaves belonging to Joseph Kershaw and others whom the loyalist Colonel James Cary had taken with him when Charlestown was evacuated. Adamson's brother-in-law was Joshua English who had performed secret service for Cary and the British and later may have held a commission in William Ballentine's regiment. Adamson was also related by marriage to Colonel Robert English, who had commanded a loyalist militia regiment after Camden was abandoned. Robert English was banished and died in exile, but because Joshua's part was less conspicuous, he escaped any penalties and resided in the district until his death fifteen years after the war.[27]

Henry Rugeley had tried unsuccessfully to remain in South Carolina in 1782, finally sailing in the convoy for Jamaica. Whether John Chesnut's influence was crucial is not certain, but Rugeley was taken from the confiscation law, amerced, and disqualified from political activity in 1784. He did seek limited compensation from the Royal Commission in London for certain property destroyed during the occupation, but he did not pursue the matter because he was permitted to return to South Carolina later in the 1780s. Although his substantial property was no longer subject to confiscation, Rugeley was responsible for heavy obligations incurred in partnership with his late brother, Rowland, and others; indeed, it is possible that his return was made easier so that his many creditors might salvage something from his property. In any case, he entered into an agreement in 1790 by which most of his lands, twenty-eight parcels in all, and the substantial uncollected debts due his firm were put into a trust administered by Charles Cotesworth Pinckney and another lawyer for the benefit of creditors.[28]

Not all former loyalists who returned to Camden District managed to avoid the consequences of their wartime acts. William and Benjamin Rees, who had served as captains in Samuel Tynes's ill-fated regiment recruited from the High Hills of Santee, became refugees in the lowcountry after Rawdon abandoned Camden, and William had gone to East Florida after Charlestown was evacuated. Both men were named in the confiscation law but, because a number of their neighbors petitioned the legislature in their behalf, they were amerced in 1784. Apparently some of their neighbors felt less charitable toward them, for when William returned to his district he received threats at High Hills Tavern and later fifty lashes at the hands of a party of men. All of this might have been only of local notice had one "IMcK" not rejoiced at Rees's punishment in a letter to a Charleston newspaper. Ambrose Gayle and several men from the High Hills responded, identifying IMck as one James McCormick who had sought favor with the British and had even offered to help Rees capture Gayle and the others. Although they implied that Rees's punishment was deserved, Gayle and his colleagues declared that those protected by law should not be molested further. William Rees did settle in the district, although his brother did not return.[29]

In Ninety Six District, which had contained the largest concentration of loyalists in the state, and where the civil war had aroused so much bitterness, many men who had served the British were able to return after the war. Indeed, so many men had resisted the blandishments of the Provincial Congress in 1775 and later served in the loyal militia that some parts of the district might have suffered real depopulation had efforts not been made to allow the less objectionable Tories to return.

The process of reconciliation could be rather involved, as the experience of the widower Alexander Cheves illustrates. Cheves fled his home on a branch of the Savannah River after Ninety Six was evacuated, leaving his infant son with a brother. He returned to Scotland and remarried. After the Crown turned down his application for a military allowance, he returned to South Carolina in 1785, reclaimed his son, and opened a shop on King Street in Charleston. His son, Langdon Cheves, who later had a distinguished political and financial career in the state and was president of the Second Bank of the United States, achieved this distinction in spite of his father's Toryism. A more conspicuous former resident of the district, General Andrew Williamson, apparently made no effort to return to his home on Hard Labour Creek. Although included in the Confiscation Act by the Jacksonborough General Assembly, he had communicated useful information on the British garrison to General Greene; none of his extensive properties were advertised or sold by the confiscation commissioners, and in 1784 he was quietly amerced and disqualified. He died in 1786, apparently on the plantation in St. Paul's Parish where he lived during the occupation. He left an estate valued at nearly £2,500.[30]

Both young Cheves and General Williamson preferred to settle in the lowcountry rather than to incur the hostility of former neighbors in the Long Cane or Stevens Creek areas of Ninety Six District, but a number of loyalists returned to the Lower District in the fork of the Broad and Saluda rivers after the war. Daniel Clary, who had commanded the loyalist regiment in this district, must have reached an accommodation with rebel leaders before the British evacuated Charlestown. Although banished by the Jacksonborough General Assembly, he apparently did not leave the state; amerced and disqualified from political activity in 1784, he settled once more in what became Newberry County. More than 130 men who had served the British in some capacity are named in the 1790 census for Newberry County, forming nearly a tenth of those listed. Included among them was Daniel DeWalt who had wandered to England and several places in America before returning. Of eight neighbors in the area who signed a letter of good character for one of their number many years later, four had confirmed loyalist backgrounds. In 1786 managers of an election in that district reported that among "several candidates and Voters" present were "Three persons who distinguished themselves in His Britannic Majesty's Cause in the late War and from the great number of disaffected persons in this district were like to carry their Election." Thereupon the Whigs present "wrested" the ballot box from the managers and destroyed the votes.[31]

But the largest concentration of confirmed British supporters residing in Ninety Six District in the 1780s was in the Little River District in the newly formed Laurens County where the Cunningham family had exerted a great deal of influence in 1775. Of the four brothers, only General Robert Cunningham was exiled permanently; Patrick was amerced in 1784 and returned from East Florida in the following year; John, who had served as a paymaster for the British, apparently did not leave the state but was amerced; and David apparently suffered no penalties at all. Not only did the three brothers resume residence in the state after the war, but the evidence suggests that Patrick's influence may have helped to pacify the region.

It is certain that a number of the men in Patrick's Little River Regiment who went to East Florida when Charlestown was evacuated returned to settle in or near their homes. Virtually none of his captains returned to the district, but over half the enlisted men in his regiment did so. Moreover, those who returned included several of the "powder" men of 1775 and a few who had served with William Cunningham, although most of the latter left the state for good. In addition, among Patrick's immediate neighbors who were listed with him in the confiscation law and were amerced with him, was the Hugh Brown who had been accused of serving with the Cherokees in 1776.[32]

Indeed, the presence of so many of Patrick's men in their home district after the war suggests that the process of reconciliation was well under way long before the British finally left the state. Many of his men must have made their peace with the rebels, either by coming out from the refugee camps to serve with the state in the last months of the war, or because their families had remained on good terms with rebel neighbors. On the last point, it is interesting to note that of the 167 families represented in the Little River Regiment, over 100 had only one member each who actually served, suggesting that other family members were neutral or leaned toward the rebel side. In some cases family divisions of this nature caused lasting bitterness, but for families that did not feel strongly toward either side, it may have been considered politic to be represented in the local loyalist militia unit by at least one son. These can be but inferences in the absence of more concrete evidence, but it is suggestive that some loyalists thought that the Cunninghams had shown a lack of zeal in 1780. And it will be recalled that, except for the detachment that served with Patrick Ferguson that summer, the Little River Regiment does not seem to have been engaged during the year the British held Ninety Six.[33]

Patrick's personal influence and the family's good reputation in the district undoubtedly aided the process of reconciliation. He paid off his amercement and seems to have prospered during the late 1780s. The Commissioners of Forfeited Estates restored three of his tracts in the interior and a house he and his brother John owned in Charleston, and he acquired an additional 1,800 acres from the state in 1786. He even collected a claim for hiring a team and wagon to the state in 1779, bought up several claims against the state to help hard-pressed friends and neighbors, and was given power of attorney to act for a former neighbor living in Nova Scotia. By 1790 he owned forty-six slaves, and after his disabilities were removed he was elected to the South Carolina House of Representatives. Although fulsome eulogies of prominent men were not unusual for the day, the notice of his death at fifty-three in 1796 "at his plantation...truly lamented by a large circle of acquaintances" clearly indicated that the political sins of this very early and prominent loyalist had been forgiven.[34]

Notes

1. Several hundred such petitions were presented at this session alone, *House Journals, 1783–1784*, 706–17; *Biographical Directory of the South Carolina House of Representatives*, ed. Walter B. Edgar (3 vols. to date (Columbia, S.C., 1974) III, 178–79.
2. Examination of Persons on the Confiscation Bill, 1783, CEP.
3. *House Journals, 1783–1784*, 209, 216–22, 259n, 260, 276–78.
4. W. Robert Higgins, "A Financial History of the American Revolution in South Carolina," Ph.D. dissertation (Duke University, 1970), 188–95.
5. On the Amercement [1783], CEP
6. Laurens to Mrs. Loocock, Mar. 7, to the Reverend Archibald Simpson, Mar. 20, to the Governor of South Carolina, and to Fenwick, July 20, and to Mrs. Ann Burn, Aug. 8, 1783, Laurens Papers (microfilm). Laurens had been captured at sea while en route to join the American peace commission in Paris.
7. Stephen Mazyck to Porcher, June 14, 1783, *SCHGM*, XXXVIII (1937), 11–15.
8. Richard Walsh, *Charleston's Sons of Liberty: A Study of the Artisans, 1763–1789* (Columbia, S.C., 1959), 113–17; "Autobiography of Daniel Stevens, 1746–1835," *SCHM*, LVIII (1957), 16.
9. Loyalist Transcripts, LV, 170–87; *Privy Council Journals, 1783–1789*, Apr. 9, May 28, 1783, 15–22, 62; Stephen Mazyck to Philip Porcher, June 14, 1783, *SCHGM*, XXXVIII (1937), 11–15; George C. Rogers, Jr., *Evolution of a Federalist: William Loughton Smith of Charleston* (Columbia, S.C., 1962), 101–2; *South Carolina Gazette: and General Advertiser* (Charleston), July 15, 1783.
10. *South Carolina Gazette and General Advertiser*, July 8, 15, 30, 1783; Wells, *Journal*, 100–103. Prioleau may have sought the writ over a sequestered slave child Wells had purchased and then manumitted just before leaving for East Florida in 1782, Miscellaneous Records, TT, 202, *SCAH*.
11. *Gazette of the State of South Carolina* (Charleston), July 23, 1783; Ramsay to Benjamin Rush, July 11, 1783, *David Ramsay, 1749–1815, Selections from His Writings*, ed. Robert L. Brunhouse, American Philosophical Society, *Transactions*, New Ser., LV, Part 4 (1965), 65; *South Carolina Gazette and General Advertiser*, Aug. 15, 1783.
12. Sales...of Forfeited Lands...at William Moore Esqr., Ninety Six District, the 8th Day July 1783, Sales...of Forfeited Lands...in Ninety Six District the 8th Decemr. 1783, Sales...of Forfeited Lands...at Mrs. Wilsons the 30th Day June 1783, Public Auction, Sales of Lands &c. at Charleston the 1st November 1786, all in Sale of Land at Public Auction in CEP.
13. Conference Committee Minutes, 1784, SCAH; "Autobiography of Daniel Stevens, 1746–1835," 10; *House Journals, 1783–1784*, 23, 27, 41n, 99, 164, 180, 399; John Lewis Gervais to Laurens, Apr. 15, 1784, Laurens Papers (microfilm).
14. Conference Committee Minutes, 1784; *House Journals, 1783–1784*, 551–52, 617n, 630; *Statures at Large*, VI, 633–35.
15. *Privy Council Journals, 1783–1789*, 101, 117; John Lewis Gervais to Laurens, Apr. 15, 1784, Laurens Papers (microfilm).
16. Loyalist Transcripts, LII, 568–98; LVII, 478–93; Commissioners of Forfeited Estates Papers, SCHS; *Canadian Claims*, 1201–6; Wills, XX, 115–17; XXII, 112–14.
17. Carl J. Vipperman, *The Rise of Rawlins Lowndes* (Columbia, S.C., 1978), 236: Ramsay to Benjamin Lin-

coln, Jan. 29, 1788, *David Ramsay*, ed. Brunhouse, 118; Harriott Horry to Mr. [Edward] Jenkins, Mar. [?], 1786, and to her son, Feb, 6, 1786, Harriott Horry Letterbook, St. Julien Ravenel Childs Papers, SCHS.
18. Laurens, July 10, 1783, and Greene, Feb. 5, 1785, to Governor Guerard, CEP; Wills, XXIV, 852–54; "Marriage and Death Notices in the City Gazette," *SCHGM*, XXI (1920), 77–78; Rogers, *Evolution of a Federalist*, 120, 121.
19. *State Gazette of South Carolina* (Charleston), June 18, 1787; CEP; *Directory and Revenue System for 1790* (Charleston, 1790); George W. Williams, *St. Michael's, Charleston, 1751–1951* (Columbia, S.C., 1951), 312–13; Loyalist Transcripts, LV, 548–58.
20. State of Amercements Put in My Hands, June 20, 1792, Forfeited Estates, Attorney General, SCAH.
21. Wills, *XXII*, 112–14; XXIII, 722–25.
22. Francisco de Miranda, *The New Democracy in America*, ed. John S. Ezell (Norman, Okla., 1963), 224.
23. *South Carolina Gazette and General Advertiser*, Apr. 5, 1783; *Gazette of the State of South Carolina*, Mar. 14, 1785; Lyman C. Draper, *King's Mountain and Its Heroes* (New York, 1929 [n.p., 1891]), 340, says that Hobbs was one of those hanged at Gilbertown after Kings Mountain.
24. Burke to Governor Benjamin Guerard, Dec. 14, 1784, Aedanus Burke MSS., SCL; Clark, ed., *Loyalists*, I, 270.
25. *House Journals, 1783–1784*, 474–75; Johnson, *Traditions and Reminiscences*, 429; *Nova Scotia Gazette* (Halifax), June 6, 1784; [James P. Collins], *A Revolutionary Soldier* (New York, 1979 [orig. publ. Clinton, La., 1859]), 66–67.
26. Burke to Guerard, Dec. 14, 1784, Burke MSS., SCL; [Collins], *A Revolutionary Soldier*, 67.
27. Rogers, *Evolution of a Federalist*, 101; P.R.O. *457/520/40*; *Statutes at Large*, VI, 633–35; Edward Boykin to Lyman C. Draper, Oct. 1, 1872, Sumter Papers, VV, 17, 227, Draper Coll.; "Descendants of Joshua English," Elizabeth Doby English Papers, SCL; *Judicial Cases Concerning Slavery and the Negro*, ed. Helen T. Catterall, (Washington, D.C., 1926–37), II, 272. The Joshua English mentioned here was presumably of a later generation than the earlier settler of that name, above p.00.
28. Loyalist Transcripts, LVII, 379–401; Indenture of Henry Rugeley, Miscellaneous Records, CCC, 37–56 (microfilm, reels 1991–93), SCAH. The schedules included with the trust agreement show that the firm dealt primarily with settlers living near Camden, but also as far away as Ninety Six and parts of North Carolina.
29. *Gazette of the State of South Carolina* Apr. 29, Sept. 13, 1784. *Census, 1790, SC.* 17; Refugees to East Florida; *Statures at Large* VI, 635. McCormick had taken an early part for the Americans, while the Reeses apparently had not.
30. Archie Vernon Huff, *Langdon Cheves of South Carolina* (Columbia, S.C., 1977), 1–14. An Anglican missionary who tried to make contact with his congregation on Cuffeetown Creek in 1782 reported from the Congaree area that his German loyalist parishioners had paused to make a crop in the Dutch Fork among the "Palatines" before risking a return to their homes where much hostility was reported to exist toward them, Samuel F. Lucius to Dr. William Morice, Secretary of the Society for the Propagation of the Gospel, Oct. 30, 1783, SPG, II, Miscellaneous Unbound *MSS.* (South Carolina), LC; Williamson to Nathanael Greene, June 24, Dec. 22, 1783, Greene Papers, DUL; Charleston Inventories, B, 12–14, 528, SCAH; *Statutes at Large*, VI, 635. Williamson was convinced that he had acted honorably and that Andrew Pickens was among those raising "much clamour against me" because he feared that Williamson, if relieved, would once again be his superior.
31. *Census 1790, S.C.*, 76–80; *Statutes at Large*, VI, 635; the account of the election is in Jerome Nadelhaft, *Disorders of War: The Revolution in South Carolina* (Orono, Me., 1981), 214. T he letter of good character for John Wilhelm Stein, Feb. 14, 1801, intended to support his belated claim for compensation from the Crown for his l oyal service twenty years earlier, was kindly shown to me by Mrs. Ann-Joy Griffith, Greenville, S.C.
32. This analysis is drawn from the biographical files of men listed in the Little River Regiment in 1780–81, Clark, ed., *Loyalists*, I, 253–68.
33. Ibid.
34. Commissioners of Locations North of the Saluda, Greenville County Plat Book B, 378, 386, SCAH: Accounts Audited, AA1951, 3414, 3415, 3416; *Census, 1790, S.C.*, 72; Laurens County Court Minutes, Book D, 83, SCAH; "Marriage and Death Notices from the City Gazette," *SCHGM*, XXIII (1922), 106. Later generations of upcountry South Carolinians were deeply proud of the heroic deeds of their Revolutionary forebears and were less forgiving of Patrick's family for having supported the British cause. His son Robert had felt the sting of criticism of the part taken by the Cunninghams, a name stained by the

misdeeds of "Bloody Bill." When in 1845 a piece on "Major William Cunningham of South Carolina" appeared as an appendix to the published letters of a Massachusetts loyalist, it drew a scathing review in the *Southern Literary Messenger* from South Carolina's novelist-historian William Gilmore Simms; what Simms did not know was that Ann Pamela, Patrick's semi-invalid granddaughter, had submitted the offensive article based on materials gathered by her father. Other Cunningham descendants sought to defend the family's reputation by securing character references from descendants of Whig families, including Senator John C. Calhoun; while their friend Benjamin F Perry mollified the younger Cunninghams and drew praise from Simms by publishing an article that delineated the character and motives of the committed Cunninghams and carefully distinguished them from their violent cousin. Ann Pamela subsequently turned her talents to organizing the movement to rescue George Washington's Mount Vernon estate from ruin and to preserve it as a national shrine. I am grateful to my colleague Ernest Lander who, during his research in Calhoun's correspondence for his *The Calhoun Family and Thomas Green Clemson* (Columbia, S.C., 1983), first called my attention to the efforts by Cunningham descendants to defend the family's reputation; and to David Moltke-Hansen for permitting me to see his "Why History Mattered: The Background of Ann Pamela Cunningham's Interest in the Preservation of Mount Vernon" before it appeared in *Furman Studies*, New Ser, XXVI, 34–42. For Ann Pamela's article, see George A. Ward, ed., *Journal and Letters of the Late Samuel Curwen...A Loyalist Refugee in England during the American Revolution* (New York, 1845), 618–48. The efforts to settle the ensuing controversy may be followed in Simms to James A. Hammond, Jan. 25, Simms to Perry, Mar. 10, to Hammond, Mar. 29, and May 20, 1847, in *The Letters of William Gilmore Simms*, ed. Mary C. Simms Oliphant, 5 vols. (Columbia, S.C., 1952–56), II, 260, 281–82, 317–18; Calhoun to John Cunningham, Nov. 25, 1846, Papers of John C. Calhoun, CUL; and Benjamin F Perry, "Revolutionary History of S. Carolina," *Southern Quarterly Review* (1847),481–85. For Ann Pamela's subsequent career, see Moltke-Hansen, "Why History Mattered," 39–40; and Elswyth Thane, *Mount Vernon Is Ours* (New York, 1966).

Conclusion

Perhaps as many as one-fifth of South Carolina's free population in 1775 became loyalists during the American Revolution-that is, they performed one or more acts that opposed the movement for independence or that supported British authority against the state government during the war. In addition, a smaller proportion, the protectionists, resumed British allegiance after the capitulation of Charlestown in 1780, but did little more to give overt aid to the British.

This generalization is flawed by two facts: that some of the loyalists and most of the protectionists at one time or another performed acts—military service, payment of taxes, furnished supplies, or loaned money—that supported independence and the state government; and that families were divided. The Revolution in South Carolina was a long struggle in which the fortunes of the two sides ebbed and flowed, and it was literally possible for individuals to be confronted with a choice of allegiance three or four times.

The loyalists in the interior tended to be relatively recent immigrants who had moved into South Carolina after the Cherokee War, from northern Ireland or Germany, or from other colonies, particularly Virginia. The number of foreign and American loyalists with north Irish backgrounds suggests that caution should be exercised before accepting a simple "Scotch-Irish" explanation of backcountry support for independence; it seems more likely that their relative newness to the areas in which they settled contributed to their indifference or hostility to the aggressive designs of the Provincial Congress in 1775. Loyalists were clearly in a minority in the coastal areas of the province and their greatest strength lay among a large number of Scots business and professional men and among recently arrived artisans and merchants with close ties to Great Britain.

There were two high points of loyalist strength in the period. In 1775 large numbers of back countrymen turned out to oppose the organizing efforts of the Provincial Congress, but this movement was crushed and its leaders jailed or forced into exile. The failure of a British force to take Charlestown and a successful expedition sent by the congress against the Cherokees in the summer of 1776 permitted the rebels to establish a new state government; it also left British sympathizers isolated, and some fled into exile in the Floridas and Great Britain, while many others did the minimum required to remain quietly at home under the state government. Despite its failure, the uprising of 1775 in the backcountry had a very important effect on British strategy for prosecuting the war. Grasping at straws after France took the American side, the North ministry accepted the idea that a minimum commitment of British resources might salvage some of Britain's colonies because of reportedly strong loyal sentiment in the southern backcountry.

British commitment to this strategy brought about the second high point of loyalism, in 1780, when thousands of South Carolinians joined the militia or provincials and acknowledged allegiance to the Crown. Despite the apparent collapse of American arms and the state government and a splendid victory at Camden, it seems in retrospect that British success was more apparent than real.

Given the British goal of recovering all the southern provinces while maintaining the major base at New York, British resources in troops and materiel soon proved to be inadequate to the task. British commanders were alternately heavy-handed or frustrated as they sought to deal with what they saw as a mercurial attitude toward allegiance among people in the Carolinas. But had British commitment been greater and leadership wiser, it probably could not have compensated for the weakness of the foundation on which Britain's strategy rested; it is clear that the loyalists were neither as numerous nor as steadfast as expected. As a result of these deficiencies, British and loyalist arms could not control the countryside, and within a year they were confined to the vicinity of Charlestown. But their presence and policies ignited a civil war that caused much suffering and many deaths on both sides.

Robert Calhoon's assessment that "despite their fighting ability and numbers, the loyalists in the South possessed only fragments of social purpose and political capacity," certainly applies to South Carolina's Tories. It should be added that South Carolina loyalists left little literary evidence that would inform us of their reasons for supporting the British effort to suppress the rebellion.[1]

The British government ultimately agreed to evacuate the southern provinces and to grant independence, and large numbers of loyalists left South Carolina for Britain or its possessions. The exodus represented a net loss of 9,000 or 10,000 people, roughly 5 percent of the state's prewar population, and included slightly more blacks than whites. The postwar location of 40 percent of the free people who left is unknown, however, and suggests that they went over the mountains or into remote parts of other States to begin their lives anew. If so, neighboring and later states may have gained population at South Carolina's expense. The British presence did, however, result in freedom for thousands of black slaves, although those who were taken to the Bahamas or Jamaica were not in that generation to realize the benefits of that policy.

Many loyalists remained and others returned from exile to resume residence in South Carolina. The state government achieved mixed results from its attempt to aid its depleted treasury and punish the loyalists by confiscating their property; some revenue was realized, but the property of many was restored and their punishment reduced to the payment of a fine. By the end of the 1780s a degree of reconciliation had taken place between loyalist residents and the state and its citizens.

Note

1. Robert F. Calhoon, *Loyalists in Revolutionary America, 1760–1781* (New York, 1973), 499.

BIBLIOGRAPHY

Essay on Methods and Sources

Nineteenth-century American studies of the War for Independence, with the notable exception of Lorenzo Sabine, *Biographical Sketches of Loyalists of the American Revolution with an Historical Essay* (Port Washington, N.Y., 1966 [orig. publ. Boston, 1864]), tended to concentrate on the Whig, or American, side of that ideological and military conflict and to treat the pro-British population merely as deviants from the norm of the natural development of American nationhood. After 1900 more attention was paid to the loyalists in their own right: first by Claude H. Van Tyne, *The Loyalists in the American Revolution* (New York, 1902); then in monographs on such individual states as North Carolina, Virginia, New York, and Massachusetts; while other scholars analyzed the careers of conspicuous leaders like Thomas Hutchinson and Joseph Galloway. Since World War II, and especially during the commemoration of the bicentennial of the Revolution, a wide range of sources, particularly British, have become more readily available in print and in microcopy. In addition, a cooperative effort of scholars in Britain, Canada, and the United States, "A Bibliography of Loyalist Source Material in the United States," ed. Herbert Leventhal and James E. Mooney, American Antiquarian Society, *Proceedings*, LXXXV, Parts 1, 2 (1975); LXXXVI, Part 1 (1976); XC, Parts 1, 2 (1980), has located and described much source material in the United States; more recently, materials in British and Canadian repositories have been combined with those in the United States, as A *Bibliography of Loyalist Source Material in the United States, Canada, and Great Britain*, ed. Gregory Palmer (Westport, Conn., 1982). The most comprehensive distillation of this fresh material into a major analysis of loyalism is Robert M. Calhoon, *The Loyalists in Revolutionary America, 1760–1781* (New York, 1973).

In preparing to undertake this study, it seemed that two fundamental questions that all loyalist studies have tried to deal with would need to be addressed for South Carolina: (1) motivation—why certain individuals and groups supported the British cause; and (2) numbers—the proportion of South Carolina's population in the 1770s who were identified with that cause. It would also be desirable to know how much the loyalists contributed to the British war effort in South Carolina through military service and other means; how many suffered and died, or became exiles, because of their identification with or attachment to the British cause; and to what degree those who had supported the British were able to remain in the state.

In order to confront the central questions of motivation and numbers, it seemed essential to identify as many individual loyalists as possible; to go beyond those persons who (1) were singled out in the state's confiscation laws, *Statutes at Large*, IV, 516–23, and VI, 629–35; or (2) whom the British government had acknowledged in their claims for compensation after the war, Loyalist Claims, Loyalist Transcripts, and *Canadian Claims;* or (3) who kept one of the rare diaries or memoirs of their experiences. From as wide a range of sources as possible, it seemed to be necessary to create a "list" of all those persons who performed acts that their contemporaries, British or American, considered to be "loyal" or pro-British. Then, employing the methods of the biographer and genealogist, these persons, herein referred to as "the List," could be traced through the records to construct profiles of a great many individuals, the better to reach conclusions about loyalism in general.

British records provided three very large groups of persons for the List: those who served in the loyal militia during the war, found in T50/1, Miscellaneous, I–VI, recently printed as Clark, ed., *Loyalists,* I, 111–344; those who took the oath of allegiance to the Crown after Charlestown surrendered in 1780, CP, 30/11/107, P.R.O., microfilm, LC; and those on the muster rolls of the provincial regiments, the South Carolina Royalists, Rangers, and Dragoons, LMR, printed in Clark, ed., *Loyalists,* I, 1–48, 87–110. In addition to those whose property was confiscated by the state after the war, or who claimed compensation from the Crown, there are shorter but important sources of loyalist names:

Signers of the Counter-Association, 1775, Simms Coll.
Men in Confinement for "fighting in arms against this state," Apr. 10, 1779, at General Williamson's camp opposite Augusta, Matthew Singleton Papers, SCL.
Proclamation of Governor John Rutledge, Nov. 8, *South Carolina and American General Gazette,* Nov. 24, 1779.
Petition of Fifty-one "Unhappy Wives," Feb. 5, 1780, *House Journals, 1776–1780,* 274–75, 279–80.
"Massacred," Fletchall, "Address."
Refugees to East Florida.
Petition of Loyal Inhabitants of Charlestown, n.d. [1782], BHP, #10036.
Barnwell, ed., "Exiles."
Spanish Census, 1784.

In addition, a number of smaller lists and individual references in British and American records were consulted. Except for widows and scattered references to females in private correspondence, the very nature of the records available assured that the List would consist predominantly of males; likewise, the difficulty of identifying persons listed only by single names ("Tom" or "Sarah") in the few extant lists of South Carolina blacks who served the British meant that whites would predominate in the final list. As all these groups of names were compared, it soon became apparent that persons whose only "loyal" act was to take an oath of allegiance to the Crown could not be considered loyalists on that basis alone, and they were dropped from that category and considered only under the term "protectionists." As it finally emerged, the List included some 5,500 to 6,000 white and a very few black men, and about 700 white women, mostly widows, who could be said to have performed loyal acts, either directly or by association, during the war.

Records available in South Carolina and elsewhere for the period 1760–90 were then searched for references to individuals on the List, particularly for the date and place of their birth or from which they migrated, their occupations, their property holdings, military and civilian service on either or both sides, and residence and status after the war.

When this material had been gathered for individuals on the List, an attempt was made to subject it to quantitative analysis in the hope that a profile of "typical" loyalists might emerge. It quickly became apparent, however, that the data that the records revealed about these people was such that although detailed information was available for some persons, and a small amount for a good many more, for the rest virtually no information was available beyond the mere fact of a loyal act (one enlistment in the loyalist militia was the most frequent example of this). Further, the identity of individuals was not always clearly revealed by this type of analysis—the duplication of the common Anglo-Saxon names of the period, especially in a day when middle names or initials were rarely used (six John Davises, for example, apparently performed loyal acts) was confusing: and it was often necessary to make judgments in the absence of precise information. (E.g., Did the John Davis in the Fair Forest militia regiment actually live in that part of South Carolina?) Nevertheless, this method was worthwhile because it identified more clearly and assembled a great deal more information on the kinds of people who performed loyal acts than had been known before.

Sources that proved to be especially valuable for analyzing certain categories of information about individuals on the List are:

Place and date of birth:
Loyalist Transcripts; *Canadian Claims;* Spanish Census, 1784.

Place of origin:
Council Journal, 1664–1774, SCAH; printed for certain years in Janie Revill, comp., *A Compilation of the Original Lists of Protestant Immigrants to South Carolina, 1763–1773* (Columbia, S.C., 1939); Loyalist Transcripts.

Military service:
(1) with the British-T50/1/1–5, for the loyal militia; LMR, for provincial service with the South Carolina Royalists and the South Carolina Rangers, and for a few enlistments in other units that fought in the state; (2) with the Americans-Accounts Audited. British pay records generally furnish more detailed information about loyalist militia service than is to be found for state service in Accounts Audited.

Real property and location within the province and state:
Plats, 1731–75; ICHA, 1765–75; Colonial Grant Books, 1766–75, Series 3A; Wills, 1732–84; *Senate Journals, 1782–90;* Miscellaneous Records, 1763–92, MM–ZZ; Charleston County Deeds (for the entire province); and a mass of records of the counties created in 1785, including deeds, wills, and those of the Commissioners of Locations South of the Saluda (with Abbeville County), and North of the Saluda (with Greenville County), all in SCAH: *Charlestown Directory for 1782,* and *Charleston Directory for 1785* (Charleston, S.C., 1951); *Directory and Revenue System for 1790* (Charleston, S.C., 1790). See also Loyalist Transcripts and *Canadian Claims.*

Personal property:
Miscellaneous Records (above), the inventories filed with Wills in Charleston and the counties (above); Loyalist Transcripts and *Canadian Claims.*

Movements and locations during and after the war:
Records of Payments to Refugees in South Carolina and East Florida, from T50/1/3, P.R.O., now conveniently printed in Clark, ed., *Loyalists,* I, 491–543*; South Carolina Gazette and Country Journal; South Carolina and American General Gazette* (Charlestown); and *Gazette of the State of South Carolina* (Charlestown) for announcements of departures of loyalists who refused the oath of abjuration in 1778; *Royal Gazette* (Charlestown), and *Royal South Carolina Gazette* (Charlestown) for departures in 1782; Refugees to East Florida; Spanish Census, 1784; Siebert, *Loyalists in E. Fla.,* II *;* Marion Gilroy, comp., *Loyalists and Land Settlement in Nova Scotia* (Halifax, 1937); Loyalist Transcripts, and *Canadian Claims;* Census, 1790, S.C.

This method also provided less than ideal answers to the question of the proportion of the South Carolina population who were loyalists. In the first place, the very nature of the war in South Carolina—where persons were forced to make choices between British and American authority as many as three times—suggests that many men served on both sides during the struggle (British pay records do furnish more precise information about enlistment periods and units served in than do claims for back pay filed with the state after the war). Second, it is not always clear how many people the individuals on the List represent. Measurements of colonial American population before the day of regular censuses usually employed the technique of counting taxpayers as heads of households, then extrapolated from that by a multiple of four or five to derive an estimate of total population. But the List is derived largely from militia records, which clearly show that, although many families contributed only one member, many others were represented by a father and one or more sons, or by two or more brothers: thus it would be more difficult to use a fixed multiple than if all families were represented by a head of household.

Yet, if the List as a means of estimating the proportion of loyalists lacks precision, it is worth comparing with the suggestions by two scholars who in recent years have grappled with the subject of the overall proportion of loyalists in Revolutionary America. In *The King's Friends: The Composition and Motives of the American Loyalist Claimants* (Providence, R.I., 1966), Wallace Brown analyzed the chums that loyalists filed with the Royal Commission after the war to find out more about the kinds of people who supported the Crown. In the course of his investigation, he concluded that South Carolina, based upon its estimated population, had a larger proportion of claimants than any states but Georgia and New York; that generally "Loyalism was a distinctly urban and seaboard phenomenon," although the proportion residing in and around Charleston was smaller than that in coastal areas in a number of other states; but he did recognize that there were "minor rural concentrations" of loyalists in the interior of South Carolina.

Although Brown tries to avoid generalizing about loyalism purely on the basis of the claimants, analysis of the List indicates that, for South Carolina, the claimants are not representative of the loyalist part of the population; for, despite the importance of Charlestown as a seat of government and the commercial and cultural center of the colony and the fact that a number of tidewater loyalists filed claims and went into exile, the evidence of the List indicates that the large majority of loyalists were to be found in interior rural areas. On this point, I would generally agree with the conclusions drawn by Eugene R. Fingerhut, "Uses and Abuses of the Loyalists' Claims: A Critique of Quantitative Analysis," *WMQ (1968)* 245–258, that, when applied to South Carolina, generalizing from the claims about the residence of loyalists tends to "overemphasize the commercial, professional, and officeholding eastern loyalists." Yet the personal experiences of loyalists and the property data in the claims are vital to the study of loyalism; beyond that, the claims provide one of the few substantial bodies of data about how people in the interior of South Carolina lived in the late eighteenth century.

Paul Smith has made careful use of the numbers of men who served in British provincial regiments in "The American Loyalists: Notes on Their Organization and Numerical Strength," *WMQ* (1968), 259–77, to conclude that loyalists composed perhaps 20 percent of the white population in the thirteen revolting colonies. After determining that about 15 percent of the persons named in Lorenzo Sabine's *Biographical Sketches* had seen provincial service, he applied that measure to all loyalists, then used the 1:4 multiple per family to conclude that there may have been as many as 500,000 loyalists. His analysis provides what is probably as satisfactory an estimate as can be derived by any other means.

But when arbitrarily applied to a specific geographical area, which Smith certainly did not intend, provincial service as an indicator of loyalist strength is less than satisfactory for South Carolina. If anything, South Carolina's loyalists were under-represented in Sabine, and the South Carolina Royalists is the only regiment included in Smith's calculations. Generally, service in a provincial regiment should indicate a greater degree of commitment to the British cause than service in the loyal militia, yet that is not necessarily so for South Carolina. Many men who enlisted in the Royalists in exile in Florida and Georgia did not continue to serve after the British conquered South Carolina, being replaced by new enlistees during and after 1780. The militia enlistments followed a similar pattern as many recruits did not reenlist after their first hitch in 1780, but because the total numbers enrolling in the militia are from two to three times greater than those joining the Royalists, it is probable that in South Carolina actual enlistments in the Royalists (and John Harrison's Rangers) plus enlistments in the militia might provide a closer approximation of real loyalist strength. The danger in using the militia enlistments as an indicator, however, is that there is clear evidence that a number of militiamen served on both sides during the war, whereas that happened much less frequently among provincials.

The use of a multiple like 1:4 to estimate a population is perhaps reasonable when the sample is drawn from heads of households or taxables, but the fact that more than one male from an existing household enlisted in a military unit suggests that such a multiple is likely to be less accurate when based upon military service. A random sample of men serving in the South Carolina loyalist militia and provincial regiments indicates that multiple-enlistment families were nearly 25 percent of all families providing an enlistment. If that measure is applied to reduce the 3,900 men who enlisted in loyalist units by one-fourth, application of the 1:4 multiple means that there were about 12,000 persons in families furnishing one or more members for military service with the British. When to that total are added those men identified as loyalists for other than military service, approximately 900, and the 1:4 factor is applied to them, a grand total of between 15,000 and 16,000 loyalists can be derived, which is about 22 percent of the 70,000 estimated as white population of South Carolina, slightly larger than Smith's estimate for all the colonies.

Other Sources Consulted

Manuscripts

William L. Clements Library, Ann Arbor, Mich.
    Sir Henry Clinton Papers
    Nathanael Greene Papers
    Earl of Shelburne Papers
    Wedderburn Papers
Clemson University Library, Clemson, S.C.
    John C. Calhoun Papers
    Andrew Pickens Letters (Waring photocopies from Greene Papers, CL)
Colonial Williamsburg, Inc., Williamsburg, Va.
    BHP
Book of Negroes Registered and Certified by the Commissioners
    Appointed by Sir Guy Carleron. 1783, LV, #10427
Manuscripts Division, Library of Congress, Washington, D.C.
    British Museum. Additional Manuscripts (transcripts)
    Force Transcripts-South Carolina, 1780–82

Nathanael Greene Papers (microfilm)
Society for the Propagation of the Gospel, Miscellaneous Unbound Manuscripts
McLennan Library, McGill University, Montreal
    "'Robinson, Lt. Col. Joseph, Memoir of" (1797)
New Brunswick Museum, Saint John
    Ganong Manuscripts
    Fanning Family Papers
    Beverly Robinson Papers
        "Anchony Allaire Orderly Book and Diary, 1780–1795"
Manuscripts Division, New York Public Library
    Bancroft Collection
    John Bowie Papers
    Chalmers Collection
        Georgia
        Robert Gray, "Observations"
        South Carolina
    Emmet Collection
        Gordon Lester Ford Papers
        Alexander Leslie Letterbooks
        Evan McLaurin Papers
        South Carolina Miscellany
North Carolina Department of Archives and History, Raleigh
    James Cary Papers
    English Records
        Colonial Office Papers, 1682–1782
    Horatio Gates Letterbook (microfilm, NYPL)
    Military Collection, War of the Revolution
    Rodman Manuscripts
    Salisbury District, Superior Court Miscellaneous Papers
Perkins Library, Duke University, Durham, N.C.
    Georgia Miscellaneous Collection
    Nathanael Greene Papers
    Journal of Enos Reeves
Public Archives of Nova Scoria, Halifax
    Old Townships and Loyalist Settlements
    Poll Tax, 1791–97
    Gideon White Papers
South Carolina Department of Archives and History, Columbia
    Diary of John Boudinot, 1780 (copy, Thorne Boudinot Coll., Princeton University Library)
    Confiscated Estates Papers
    Constitutional Papers
        Articles of Association in the District East of the Wateree, 1775
    James Cook, *A Map of the Province of South Carolina.* (London, 1773)
    Court of Common Pleas: Judgment Rolls, 1703–90
    General Assembly, Petitions, 1782–1862
    B. Romans, *A General Map of the Southern British Colonies in America*... (London, 1776)
South Carolina Historical Society, Charleston
    Correspondence of Elias Ball, 1763–1800
    John Bennett Collection
    John Chesnut Papers
    Mrs. St. Julien Ravenel Childs Papers
    Forfeited Estates Papers
    Edward Jenkins Papers
    Henry Laurens Papers
    Mrs. Charles Pinckney Letters, 1775–82
    St. Andrew's Society Papers

David Saylor Receipt Book, 1784–87
South Caroliniana Library, Columbia
    Ball Family Papers
    Thomas Bee Papers
    Aedanus Burke Papers
    Elizabeth Doby English Papers
    Nathanael Greene Papers
    Henry Laurens Papers (microfilm)
    Matthew Singleton Papers
    Andrew Williamson Militia Reports, 1778–79
Southern Historical Collection, Chapel Hill, N.C.
    Preston Davie Collection
    William Lowndes Papers
    Josiah Smith Letterbook, 1771–84
    Jethro Sumter Papers
State Historical Society of Wisconsin, Madison
    Lyman C. Draper Collection
        Thomas Sumter Papers

Newspapers

Bahama Gazette (Nassau)
The East Florida Gazette: Facsimiles of the Extant Issues of the First Florida Newspaper, Printed at St. Augustine, Florida, in 1783... (Evanston, Ill., 1942)
Gazette of the State of South Carolina (Charleston), 1783–85
Nova Scotia Gazette and Weekly Chronicle (Halifax), 1783–89
Royal Gazette (New York), 1779–83
Royal Gazette and Nova Scotia Advertiser (Halifax), 1789–1800
Royal Georgia Gazette (Savannah), 1779–82
South Carolina Gazette and General Advertiser (Charleston), 1783–84

Printed Primary Sources

Bartram, William, *The Travels of William Bartram*, ed. Mark Van Doren (New York, 1928).
[Bentham, James], "Regimental Book of Captain James Bentham, 1778–1780," *SCHGM*, LIII (1952), 13–18, 101–12, 161–71, 230–40.
Brown, Tarleton, *Memoirs of Tarleton Brown, A Captain in the Revolutionary Army* (Barnwell, S.C., 1894).
[Brown, Thomas], "A Loyalist View of the Drayton-Tennent-Hart Mission to the Upcountry," ed. James H. O'Donnell, *SCHM*, XLVII 1(1966), 15–28.
Budka, Metchie J. B., ed., *Autograph Letters of Thaddeus Kosciuszko in the American Revolution* (Chicago, 1977).
[Burke, Aedanus], "Aedanus Burke to Arthur Middleton, July 6, 1782," *SCHGM*, XXVI (1925), 203–6.
—. Cassius, *An Address to the Freemen of the State of South Carolina* (Charleston, S.C., 1783).
The Case of the Inhabitants of East-Florida,... (St. Augustine, Fla., 1784).
Chalkley, Lyman, *Chronicles of the Scotch-Irish Settlement in Virginia: Extracted from the Records of Augusta County, 3 vols.* (Baltimore, Md., 1965).
[Champneys, John], *An Account of the Sufferings and Persecution of John Champneys, A Native of Charlestown, South Carolina,...* (London, 1778).
[Collins, James], *A Revolutionary Soldier* (New York, 1979 [orig. publ. Clinton, La., 1859]).
[Cornwallis, Charles], *Correspondence of Charles First Marquis Cornwallis*, ed. Charles Ross, 3 vols. (2nd ed.; London, 1859).
[Council of Safety], "Journal of the Second Council of Safety," SCHS, *Colls.*, III (Charleston, S.C., 1859).
—. "Papers of the First Council of Safety of the Revolutionary Party in South Carolina, June-November, 1775," *SCHGM*, I–III (January 1900–July 1902).
Crary, Catherine S., ed., *The Price of Loyalty: Tory Writings from the Revolutionary Era* (New York, 1973).
Cruden, John, *An Address to the Loyal part of the British Empire and the Friends of Monarchy Throughout the Globe*

(London, 1785).
[Curwen, Samuel], *Journal and Letters of Samuel Curwen*, ed. George Atkinson Ward (3d ed.; New York, 1845).
Dalrymple, Sir John, *The Address of the People of Great Britain to the Inhabitants of America* (London, 1775), reprinted Peter Force, *American Archives*, 4th Set., 6 vols. (Washington, D.C., 1837–46), I, 1413–31.
de Miranda, Francisco, *The New Democracy in America*, ed. John S. Ezell (Norman, Okla. 1963).
Documents Relating to Indian Affairs, 1754–1765, ed. W. McDowell (Columbia, S.C., 1970).
[Drayton, William Henry], *Letters of Freeman, Etc.: Essays on the Nonimportation Movement in South Carolina*, ed. Robert M. Weir (Columbia, S.C., 1977).
[Elliott, Bernard], "Diary of Captain Bernard Elliott, "City of Charleston, *Yearbook*, 1899 (Charleston, S.C., 1899).
[Ferguson, Patrick], "An Officer Out of His Time: Correspondence of Major Patrick Ferguson, 1779–1780," ed. Hugh F. Rankin in Howard H. Peckham, ed., *Sources of American Independence: Selected Manuscripts from the Collections of the William L. Clements Library*, 2 vols. (Chicago, 1978), II, 287–98.
Force, Peter, comp., *American Archives*, 4th Ser., 6 vols. (Washington, D.C., 1837–1846).
Fries, Adelaide L., ed., *The Records of the Moravians in North Carolina*, 8 vols. (Raleigh, N.C., 1922–54).
[Gadsden, Christopher], *The Writings of Christopher Gadsden*, ed. Richard Walsh (Columbia, S.C., 1966).
[Gervais, Lewis], "Letters of John Lewis Gervais to Henry Laurens, 1777–1778," ed. Raymond Starr, *SCHM*, LXVI (1965), 15–37.
[Grimke, John F], "Journal of the Campaign to the Southward," *SCHGM*, XII (1911), 60–69, 118–34, 190–206.
——. "Order Book of John Faucheraud Grimke, August, 1778 to May, 1780," *SCHGM*, XII–XVI (1912–15), passim.
Henry, Robert, and David Vance, *Narrative of the Battle of Cowan's Ford,... and Narrative of the Battle of King's Mountain* (Greensboro, N.C., 1891).
Hewat, Alexander, *An Historical Account of the Rise and Progress of the Colonies of South Carolina and Georgia* (Spartanburg S.C., 1962 [orig. publ. London, 1779]).
Higgins, W. Robert, comp., "Charles Town Merchants and Factors Dealing in the External Negro Trade, 1735–1775," *SCHM*, LXV (1964), 205–17.
[Hill, William], *Col. William Hill's Memoirs of the Revolution*, ed. A. S. Salley (Columbia, S.C., 1921).
"Historical Notes," *SCHGM*, VIII (1907), 222–23.
Holcomb, Brent, comp., *Ninety Six District, South Carolina: Journal of the Court of Ordinary, 1781–1786* (Easley, S.C., 1978).
——. camp., *Probate Records of South Carolina*, 2 vols. (Easley, S.C., 1978).
Hough, Franklin B., ed., *The Siege of Charleston by the British Fleet and Army under the Command of Admiral Arbuthnot and Sir Henry Clinton.* (Spartanburg, S.C., 1975 [orig. publ. Albany, N.Y., 1867]).
——. ed., *The Siege of Savannah* (2d. ed.; Spartanburg, S.C., 1975 [orig. publ. Albany, N.Y., 1866]).
[Innes, Alexander], "Charles Town Loyalism in 1775: The Secret Reports of Alexander Innes," ed. Bradley D. Bargar, *SCHM*, LXIII (1962), 125–36.
Johnson, William, *Sketches of the Life and Correspondence of Nathanael Greene,... in the War of the Revolution*, 2 vols. (Charleston, S.C., 1822).
Jones, Alice Hanson, ed., *American Colonial Wealth: Documents and Methods*, vol. III (New York, 1977).
Jones, Charles Colcock, ed., *The Siege of Savannah by Count d'Estaing, 1779* (2d ed.; New York, 1968).
[Kinloch, Francis], "Letters of Francis Kinloch to Thomas Boone, 1782–1788," ed. Felix Gilbert, *JSH*, VIII (1942), 103–5.
[Kirkland, Moses], "A Backcountry Loyalist Plan to Retake Georgia and the Carolinas," ed. Randall L. Miller, *SCHM*, LXXV (1974), 207–14.
[Leigh, Egerton], *The Nature of Colony Constitutions: Two Pamphlets on the Wilkes Fund Controversy in South Carolina by Sir Egerton Leigh and Arthur Lee*, ed. Jack P. Greene (Columbia, S.C., 1970).
McKenzie, Roderick, *Strictures on Lieut. Col. Tarleton's History* (London, 1787).
[Manigault, Ann], "Extracts from the Journal of Mrs. Ann Manigault, 1754–1781," *SCHGM*, XX (1919), 57–63, 128–41, 204–12, 256–59; XXI (1920), 10–23, 59–72, 112–20.
[Manigault, Gabriel], "Papers of Gabriel Manigault, 1771–1784," *SCHM*, LXIV (1963), 1–12.
[Marion, Francis], "General Marion's Report of the Affair at Wadboo," ed. John Bennett, *SCHGM*, XVII (1916), 176–77.
——. "Marion-Gadsden Correspondence," ed. John Bennett, *SCHGM*, XLI (1940), 48–60.
"Marriage and Death Notices in the City Gazette," *SCHGM*, XXI (1920), 77–78.

[Mazyck, Stephen], "Stephen Mazyck to Peter Porcher," *SCHGM*, XXXVIII (1937), 11–15.
[Middleton, Arthur], "Correspondence of the Hon. Arthur Middleton," ed. Joseph W. Barnwell, *SCHGM*, XXVI (1925), 183–213.
Milling, Chapman J., ed., *Colonial South Carolina: Two Contemporary Descriptions by Governor James Glen and Doctor George Milligen-Johnston* (Columbia, S.C., 1951).
Moultrie, William, *Memoirs of the American Revolution*, 2 vols. (New York, 1902).
Mouzon, Henry, et al., *An Accurate Map of North and South Carolina, with Their Indian Frontiers.* (1775), in W. P. Cumming, *North Carolina in Maps* (Raleigh, N.C. 1966), Plate V.
Paltsits, Victor H., ed., "The Siege of Charleston, 1780," in *Yearbook of the City of Charleston, 1897* (Charleston, S.C., 1898), 342–425.
Peckham, Howard H., ed., *The Toll of Independence: Engagements & Battle Casualties of the American Revolution* (Chicago, 1974).
[Pinckney, Thomas], "Letters of Thomas Pinckney, 1775–1780," ed. Jack L. Cross, *SCHM*, LVIII (1957), 19–35, 67–83, 145–62, 224–42.
[Provincial Congress], *Extracts from the Journals of the Provincial Congresses of South Carolina, 1775–1776*, ed. W. Edwin Hemphill and Wylma Wates (Columbia, S.C., 1960).
[Ramsay, David], *David Ramsay, 1749–1815: Selections from His Writings*, ed. Robert L. Brunhouse, American Philosophical Society, *Transactions*, New Ser., LV, Part 4 (1965).
Raymond, W.O., ed., "Roll of Officers of the British American or Loyalist Corps, Compiled from the Original Muster Rolls and Arranged Alphabetically, A.D. 1775–1783," New Brunswick Historical Society, *Collections*, No.5 (1904), 224–72.
"Return of People Embarked from South Carolina and Georgia, 13th and 14th December 1782,"*Charleston Yearbook*, 1883 (Charleston, S.C., 1883), 416.
"Revolutionary Letters," *SCHGM*, XXXVIII (1937), 75–80.
[Rutledge, John], "Letters of John Rutledge," ed. Joseph w. Barnwell, *SCHGM*, XVII (1916), 131–46; XVIII (1917), 42–49, 59–69, 131–42, 155–67.
Salley, A. S., ed., *Minutes of the Vestry of St. Matthew's Parish , S.C., 1767–1838* (Columbia, S.C., 1939).
—. ed., *An Order Book of the Third Regiment, South Carolina Line, Continental Establishment, Dec. 3, 1776–Mar 2, 1777* (Columbia, S.C., 1942).
—. *Stub Entries to Indents Issued in Payment of Claims against South Carolina Growing Out of the Revolution* (Columbia, S.C., 1910– 27).
—. and D. H. Smith, eds., *Register of St. Philip's Parish, Charleston, S.C., 1754– 1810* (Charleston, S.C., 1927*)*.
Schenck, David, *North Carolina, 1780– 1781* (Spartanburg, S.C., 1967 [orig. publ., Raleigh, N.C., 1880]).
Schoepf, Johann David, *Travels in the Confederation [1783– 1784]* (New York, 1968 [orig. publ. Erlangen, 1788]).
[Shelby, Isaac], " King's Mountain: Letters of Isaac Shelby," ed. J.G. de Roulhac Hamilton, *JSH*, IV (1938), 367– 77.
[Simms, William Gilmore), *The Letters of William Gilmore Simms*, ed. Mary C. Simms Oliphant, 5 vols. (Columbia, S.C., 1952– 56).
[Simpson, James], "Arbitrations of Claims for Compensation from Losses and Damages Resulting from Lawful Impediments to the Recovery of Pre-War Debts," in *International Adjudications, Modern Series*, ed. John Bassett Moore (New York, 1931), 445– 53.
—. "James Simpson's Reports on the Carolina Loyalists, 1779–1780," ed. Alan S. Brown, *JSH*, XXI (1955), 511–l9.
Smyth, J.F.D., *A Tour in the United States of America*, 2 vols. (London, 1784).
Stedman, C[harles], *The History of the Origin, Progress, and Termination of the American War*, 2 vols. (New York, 1969 [orig. publ. London, 1794]).
Stevens, Benjamin F., *Facsimiles in European Archives Related to America 1775–1783*, 25 vols. (Wilmington, Del., 1970).
[Stevens, Daniel], "Autobiography of Daniel Stevens, 1746–1835," *SCHM*, LVIII (1957), 1–18.
[Stokes, Anthony], *A Narrative of the Official Conduct of Anthony Stokes* (London, 1784).
Stoney, Samuel G., ed., "The Great Fire of 1778 as Seen through Contemporary Letters," SCHM (1963), 23–26.
[Stuart, Henry], "Deputy Supt. Mr. Henry Stuart's Account of His Proceedings with the Cherokee Indians about Going against the Whites," in *Colonial Records of North Carolina*, ed. William L. Saunders, 26 vols. (Goldsboro, N.C., 1886–1907), X, 763–85.

Tarleton, Banastre, *A History of the Campaigns of 1780 and 1781 in the Southern Provinces of North America* (London, 1787).
[Tennent, William], "The Writings of the Reverend William Tennent, 1740–1777," ed. Newton B. Jones, *SCHM*, LXI (1969), 189–209.
Uhlendorf, Bernard A., ed., *The Siege of Charleston with an Account of the Province of South Carolina: Diaries and Letters of Hessian Officers from the Von Junkenn Papers in the William L. Clements Library* (Ann Arbor, Mich., 1938).
Webber, Mabel L., comp., "Register of St. Andrew's Parish, Berkeley County, South Carolina, 1719–1774," *SCHGM*, XII–XV (1911–14), passim.
—. comp., "Parish Register of St. James Santee, 1758–1788," *SCHGM*, XV–XVII (1914–16), passim.
Wells's Register and Almanac for 1775 (Charlestown, S.C., 1775).
[Wilkinson, Eliza], *Letters of Eliza Wilkinson*, ed. Caroline Gilman (New York, 1969 [orig. publ. New York, 1839]).
[Winn, Richard], "General Richard Winn's Notes, 1780," ed. Samuel C. Williams, *SCHGM*, XLIII (1942), 201–12; XLIV (1943), 1–10.
[Winslow, Edward], *Winslow Papers*, ed. W. O. Raymond (Saint John, New Brunswick, 1901).
Woodmason, Charles, *The Carolina Backcountry on the Eve of the Revolution*, ed. Richard J. Hooker (Chapel Hill, N.C., 1953).

Printed Secondary Sources

Alden, John Richard, "John Stuart Accuses William Bull," *WMQ*, 3d Ser., II (1945), 315–20.
—. *John Stuart and the Southern Colonial Frontier: A Study of Indian Relations, War, Trade, and Land Problems in the Southern Wilderness, 1754–1775* (New York, 1966 [orig. publ. Ann Arbor, Mich., 1944]).
—. *The South in the American Revolution, 1775–1783* (Baton Rouge, La., 1957)
"American Loyalists," *Southern Quarterly Review* (Charleston, S.C.), IV (1843), 97–156
Andreano, Ralph L., and Herbert D. Werner, "Charleston Loyalists: A Statistical Note," *SCHM*, LX (1959), 164–68.
Baker, George F.R., "Francis Rawdon Hastings," *DNB*, V, 117–22.
Bargar, Bradley D., *Royal South Carolina, 1719–1763* (Columbia, S.C, 1970).
Barnwell, Joseph W., "The Evacuation of Charleston," *SCHGM*, XI (1910), 1–26.
Barnwell, Robert W., "Migration of Loyalists from South Carolina," SCHA, *Proceedings* (1937), 34–42.
Barrow, Thomas C., *Trade and Empire: The British Customs Service in Colonial America, 1660–1775* (Cambridge, Mass., 1967).
Bass, Robert D., "A Forgotten Loyalist Regiment: The South Carolina Rangers," SCHA, *Proceedings* (1977), 64–71.
—. *The Green Dragoon: The Lives of Banastre Tarleton and Mary Robinson* (New York, 1957).
—. "The Last Campaign of Major Patrick Ferguson," SCHA, *Proceedings* (1968), 16–28.
—. *Ninety Six: The Struggle for the South Carolina Backcountry* (Lexington, S.C., 1978).
Bellot, H. H., "The Leighs of South Carolina," Royal Historical Society, *Transactions* (1956), 161–87.
Bennett, John, "Historical Notes," *SCHGM*, XVIII (1917), 97–99.
Bennett, Susan S., "The Cheves Family of South Carolina," *SCHGM (1934)*, 79–87.
Berkeley, Edmund, and Dorothy Smith Berkeley, *Dr. Alexander Garden of Charles Town* (Chapel Hill, N.C., 1969).
"Blake of South Carolina," *SCHGM*, II (1900), 153–66.
Blakely, Phyllis R, "Boston King: A Black Loyalist," in *Eleven Exiles: Accounts of Loyalists of the American Revolution*, ed. P. R. Blakely and John N. Grant (Toronto, 1982), 265–88.
Boddie, William Willis, *History of Williamsburg [County, 1705–1923]* (Columbia, S.C., 1923).
Bowden, David K., *The Execution of Isaac Hayne* (Lexington, S.C., 1977).
Bowler, R. Arthur, *Logistics and the Failure of the British Army in America, 1775–1783* (Princeton, N.J., 1975).
Brathewaite, Edward, *The Development of Creole Society in Jamaica, 1770–1820* (London, 1971).
Bridenbaugh, Carl, *Myths and Realities: Societies of the Colonial South* (Baton Rouge, La., 1952).
Brigham, Clarence S., comp., *History and Bibliography of American Newspapers, 1690–1820*, 2 vols. (Worcester, Mass., 1947).
Brown, Richard Maxwell, *The South Carolina Regulators* (Cambridge, Mass., 1963).

Brown, Wallace, *The Good Americans: The Loyalists in the American Revolution* (New York, 1969).
—. "Loyalists and Non–Participants," in *The American Revolution: A Heritage of Change,* ed. John Parker and Carol Urness (Minneapolis, Minn., 1975).
—. "The Loyalists in the West Indies, 1783–1834,"*Red, White and True Blue: The Loyalists in the Revolution,* ed. Esmond Wright (New York, 1976) 73–98.
"The Bull Family of South Carolina," *SCHGM,* I (1899), 76–90.
Calhoon, Robert M., and Robert M. Weir, "The Scandalous History of Sir Egerton Leigh," *WMQ,* XXVI (1969), 47–74.
Cann, Marvin L., "Prelude to War: The First Battle of Ninety Six, November 19–21, 1775," *SCHM,* LXXVI (1975), 205–14.
—. "War in the Backcountry: The Siege of Ninety Six. May 22–June 19, 1781," *SCHM* LXXII (1971), 1–14.
Cashin, Edward J., and Heard Robertson, *Augusta & the American Revolution: Events in the Georgia Back Country,* 1773–1783 (Augusta, Ga., 1975).
Clowse, Converse D., *Economic Beginnings in Colonial South Carolina, 1670–1730* (Columbia, S.C., 1971).
Cole, David, "A Brief Outline of the South Carolina Colonial Militia System," SCHA, *Proceedings* (1954), 14–23.
Coleman, Kenneth, *The American Revolution in Georgia, 1775–1789* (Athens, Ga., 1958).
Cook, Harvey T., *Rambles in the Pee Dee Basin, South Carolina* (Columbia, S.C.,1926).
Corkran, David H., *The Carolina Indian Frontier* (Columbia, S.C., 1970).
—. *The Cherokee Frontier: Conflict and Survival, 1740–1762* (Norman, Okla., 1962).
Crane, Verner W., *The Southern Frontier, 1670–1732* (Ann Arbor, Mich., 1932).
Craton, Michael, *A History of the Bahamas* (London, 1963).
Crouse, Maurice A. "Cautious Rebellion: South Carolina's Opposition to the Stamp Act," *SCHM,* LXXIII (1972), 59–71.
Curtis, Edward E., *The Organization of the British Army in the American Revolution* (East Ardsley, England, 1972 [orig. publ. New Haven, Conn., 1926]).
Dabney, William M., and Marion Dargan, *William Henry Drayton and the American Revolution* (Albuquerque, N.M., 1962).
Dalcho, Frederick, *An Historical Account of the Protestant Episcopal Church in South Carolina* (New York, 1972 [orig. publ., 1820]).
Davis, Robert Scott, Jr., "The Loyalist Trials at Ninety Six in 1779," *SCHM,* LXXX (1979) 172–81.
—. and Kenneth H. Thomas, Jr., *Kettle Creek: Battle of the Cane Brakes* (Atlanta, Ga., 1974).
Deas, Anne S., *Recollections of the Ball Family of South Carolina and the Comingtee Plantation* (Summerville, S.C., 1909).
DeMond, Robert O., *The Loyalists of North Carolina during the Revolution* (Hamden, Conn., 1965 [orig. publ. Durham, N.C, 1940]).
Easterby, J. Harold, *The History of the St. Andrew's Society of Charleston, South Carolina* (Charleston, S.C, 1929).
Edgar, Walter, ed., *Biographical Directory of the South Carolina House of Representatives,* 4 vols. to date (Columbia, S.C., 1974–).
Ferguson, Clyde, "Carolina and Georgia Patriot and Loyalist Militia in Action, 1778–1783," in *The Southern Experience in the American Revolution,* ed. Jeffrey J. Crow and Larry E. Tise (Chapel Hill, N.C., 1978), 174–99.
—. "Functions of the Partisan-Militia in the South during the American Revolution: An Interpretation," in *The Revolutionary War in the South,* ed. W. Robert Higgins (Durham, N.C, 1979), 239–58.
Ferguson, James, *Two Scottish Soldiers* (Aberdeen, Scotland, 1888).
Gee, Wilson, *The Gist Family of South Carolina and Its Maryland Antecedents* (Charlottesville, Va., 1934).
Gould, Christopher, "Robert Wells, Colonial Charleston Printer," *SCHM,* LXXIX (1978), 23–49.
Green, Edwin L., *A History of Richland County [1732–1805]* (Columbia, S.C, 1932).
Greene, Evarts B., and Virginia D. Harrington, *American Population before the Federal Census of 1790* (Gloucester, Mass., 1966 [orig. publ. New York, 1932]).
Greene, Jack P., "Bridge to Revolution: The Wilkes Fund Controversy in South Carolina, 1769–1775," *JSH,* XXIX (1963), 19–52.
—. "The Gadsden Election Controversy and the Revolutionary Movement in South Carolina," *MVHR,* XLVI (1959), 469–92.
—. "'A Posture of Hostility': A Reconsideration of Some Aspects of the Origins of the American Revolution,"

AAS, *Proceedings*, LXXXVII, Part I (1977), 27–68.
———. *Quest for Power: The Lower Houses of Assembly in the Southern Royal Colonies, 1689–1776* (Chapel Hill, N.C, 1963).
———. "'Slavery or Independence': Some Reflections on the Relationship among Liberty, Black Bondage, and Equality in Revolutionary South Carolina," *SCHM,* LXXX (1979), 193–214.
Gregg, Alexander, *History of the Old Cheraws...From about A.D. 1730 to 1810...* (2d ed.; Columbia, S.C, 1905).
Gregorie, Anne K , *History of Sumter County, South Carolina* (Sumter, S.C., 1954).
———. *Thomas Sumter* (Columbia, S.C., 1931).
Gruber, Ira D., "Britain's Southern Strategy," in *The Revolutionary War in the South,* ed. W. Robert Higgins (Durham, N.C., 1979), 205–38.
Hamer, Philip M., "John Stuart's Indian Policy during the Early Months of the American Revolution," *MVHR,* XVII (1930), 351–66.
Hart, Harriet Cunningham, *History of the County of Guysborough, Nova Scotia* (Belleville, Ont., 1975).
Haynes Robert v., *The Natchez District and the American Revolution* (Jackson, Miss., 1976).
Higginbotham, Don, "American Historians and the Military History of the American Revolution," *AHR,* LXIX (1964), 18–34.
———. "The American Militia: A Traditional Institution with Revolutionary Responsibilities," in *Reconsiderations on the Revolutionary War,* ed. Higginbotham (Westport, Conn., 1978), 83–103.
Hoffman, Ronald, "The 'Disaffected' in the Revolutionary South," in *The American Revolution: Explorations in the History of American Radicalism,* ed. Alfred P. Young (DeKalb, Ill., 1976), 273–318.
Howe, Jonas, "Major Ferguson's Riflemen: The American Volunteers," *Acadiensis,* VI (1906), 237–46.
Huff, Archie Vernon, *Langdon Cheves of South Carolina* (Columbia, S.C., 1977).
Johnson, Cecil, *British West Florida, 1763–1783* (New Haven, Conn., 1942).
———. "Expansion in British West Florida, 1770–1779," *MVHR,* XX (1933), 481–96.
Johnson, Elmer D., "Alexander Hewat: South Carolina's First Historian," *JSH,* XX (1954), 50–62.
Jones, Lewis P., *The South Carolina Civil War of 1775* (Lexington, S.C., 1975).
Katcher, Philip R N., comp., *Encyclopedia of British, Provincial, and German Army Units, 1775–1783* (Harrisburg, Pa., 1973).
Kirkland, Thomas J., and Robert M. Kennedy, *Historic Camden, Part I: Colonial and Revolutionary,* 2 vols. (Columbia, S.C., 1905).
Kyte, George W., "British Invasion of South Carolina in 1780,"*Historian* ,XIV (1952), 149–72
———. "General Greene's Plans for the Capture of Charleston, 1781–1783," *SCHM,* LII (1961), 96–106.
Labaree, Leonard, "The Nature of Loyalism," *AAS, Proceedings,* LIV (1944), 15–58.
Lambert, Robert S., "A Loyalist Odyssey: James and Mary Cary in Exile, 1783–1804, " *SCHM,* LXXIX (1978), 167–81.
Landrum, J.B.O., *Colonial and Revolutionary History of Upper South Carolina* (Spartanburg, S.C., 1971 [orig. publ. Greenville, S.C., 1897]).
Levett, Ella P., "Loyalism in Charleston, 1761–1784," SCHA, *Proceedings* (1936), 3–17.
Lynah, James, "James Lynah: A Surgeon of the Revolution" *SCHGM,* LX (1939), 87–90.
McCowen, George S., Jr., *The British Occupation of Charleston, 1780–1782* (Columbia, S.C., 1970).
———. "The Charles Town Board of Police, 1780–1782: A Study in Civil Administration under Military Occupation," SCHA, *Proceedings* (1964), 25–42.
McCrady, Edward, *History of South Carolina in the Revolution, 1780–1783* (New York, 1902).
———. *History of South Carolina under the Royal Government, 1719–1776* (New York, 1899).
McMurtrie, Douglas C., *The Beginnings of Printing in Florida* (Hattiesburg, Miss., 1944).
Mackesy, Piers, *The War for America, 1775–1783* (Cambridge, Mass., 1965).
Maier, Pauline, "The Charleston Mob and the Evolution of Popular Politics in Revolutionary South Carolina, 1765–1784," *Perspectives in American History,* IV (1970), 73–96.
———. "Popular Uprisings and Civil Authority in Eighteenth-Century America," *WMQ,* 3d Ser., XXVII (1970), 3–35.
Meats, Stephen, "Artist or Historian: William Gilmore Simms and the Revolutionary South," in *Eighteenth Century Florida and the Revolutionary South,* ed. Samuel Proctor (Gainesville, Fla., 1978), 94–109.
Meriwether, Robert Lee, *The Expansion of South Carolina, 1729–1765* (Kingsport, Tenn., 1940).
Meroney, Geraldine M., "William Bull's First Exile from South Carolina, 1777–1781*,*" *SCHM,* LXXX (1979), 91–104.
"Middleton [Family] of South Carolina, *SCHGM,* I (1900), 228–62.

Moltke-Hansen, David, " Why History Mattered: The Background of Ann Pamela Cunningham's Interest in the Preservation of Mount Vernon," *Furman Studies,* New Ser., XXVI (1980) 34–42.

Moore, M[aurice] A[ugustus], Sr., *The Life of Gen. Edward Lacey with a List of Battles and Skirmishes in South Carolina during the Revolutionary War* (Spartanburg, S.C., 1859).

Mowat, Charles L., *East Florida as a British Province, 1763–1784* (Gainesville, Fla., 1943).

Nadelhaft, Jerome, *The Disorders of War: The Revolution in South Carolina* (Orono, Me., 1981).

Norton, Mary Beth, *The British Americans: The Loyalist Exiles in England 1774–1789* (Cambridge, Mass., 1972).

—. "Eighteenth Century American Women in Peace and War: The Case of the Loyalists," *WMQ,* 3d Ser., XXXIII (1976), 386–409.

—. "The Fate of Some Black Loyalists of the American Revolution," *Journal of Negro History* LVIII (1973), 402–26.

—. "The Loyalist Critique of the Revolution," *The Development of a Revolutionary Mentality: Papers Presented at the First Library of Congress Symposium on the American Revolution,* 1972 (Washington, D.C., 1972), 127–48.

—. "What an Alarming Crisis Is This," in *The Southern Experience in the American Revolution,* ed. Jeffrey J. Crow and Larry E. Tise (Chapel Hill, N.C., 1978) 203–34.

O'Donnell, James H., *The Southern Indians in the American Revolution* (Knoxville, Tenn., 1973).

Olson, Gary, "Loyalists and the American Revolution: Thomas Brown and the South Carolina Backcountry, 1775–1776," *SCHM,* LXVIII (1967), 201–19; LXIX (1968), 44–56.

—. "Thomas Brown, the East Florida Rangers, and the Defense of East Florida," in *Eighteenth Century Florida and the Revolutionary South,* ed. Samuel Proctor (Gainesville, Fla., 1978), 15–28.

O'Neall, John Belton, *Biographical Sketches of the Bench and Bar of South Carolina,* 2 vols. (Charleston, S.C., 1859).

Perry, Benjamin F., "Revolutionary History of S[outh] Carolina," *Southern Quarterly Review,* II (1847), 468–85.

Peters, Thelma, "The American Loyalists in the Bahamas: Who They Were," *Florida Historical Quarterly,* XL (1962), 226–240

—. "The Loyalist Migration from East Florida to the Bahama Islands," *Florida Historical Quarterly,* XL (1961), 123–144.

Pope, Thomas H., *The History of Newberry County, South Carolina,* 2 vols. (Columbia, S.C., 1973), vol. I.

Pugh, Robert C., "The Revolutionary Militia in the Southern Campaign, 1780–1781," *WMQ,* 3d Ser., XIV (1957), 154–75.

Quarles, Benjamin F., *The Negro in the American Revolution* (Chapel Hill, N.C., 1961).

Rae, W.P., "Benjamin Thompson, 1753–1814," *DNB,* XIX, 605–8.

Ramsay, David, *History of the Revolution of South Carolina from a British Province to an Independent State,* 2 vols. (Trenton, N.J., 1785).

—. *The History of South Carolina, from Its First Settlement in 1670, to the Year 1808,* 2 vols. (Charleston, S.C., 1809).

Ramsey, Robert W., *Carolina Cradle: The Settlement of the Northwest Carolina Frontier, 1747–1762* (Chapel Hill, N.C., 1964).

Rankin, Hugh F., "Charles Lord Cornwallis: A Study in Frustration," in *George Washington's Opponents,* ed. George A. Billias (New York, 1969), 193–232.

—. "Cowpens: Prelude to Yorktown," *NCHR.,* XXXI (1954), 336–69.

—. *Francis Marion: The Swamp Fox* (New York, 1973).

Rawlyk, George A., "The Guysborough Negroes: A Study in Isolation," *Dalhousie Review,* XLVIII (1968), 24–36.

Reynolds, Emily B., and Joan Reynolds Faunt, comps., *Biographical Directory of the Senate of South Carolina, 1776–1964* (Columbia, S.C., 1964).

Robertson, Heard, "The Second British Occupation of Augusta, 1780–1781," *GHQ,* LVIII (1974), 430–42.

Robson, Eric, "The Expedition to the Southern Colonies, 1775–1776," *English Historical Review,* LXVI (1951), 535–60.

Rogers, George C., Jr., "Aedanus Burke, Nathanael Greene, Anthony Wayne, and the British Merchants of Charleston," *SCHM,* LXVII (1966), 75–83.

—. *Charleston in the Age of the Pinckneys* (Norman, Okla., 1969).

—. *Evolution of a Federalist: William Loughton Smith of Charleston* (Columbia, S.C., 1962), particularly 97–111.

—. *The History of Georgetown County, South Carolina* (Columbia, S.C., 1970).

Royster, Charles, *A Revolutionary People at War: The Continental Army and American Character, 1775–1783* (Chapel Hill, N.C., 1979).

Ryan, Frank W., Jr., "The Role of South Carolina in the First Continental Congress," *SCHM*, LX (1959), 147–53.
Salley, A. S., *The History of Orangeburg County, South Carolina from Its First Settlement to the Close of the Revolutionary War* (Orangeburg, S.C., 1898).
Sellers, Leila, *Charleston Business on the Eve of the American Revolution* (Chapel Hill, N.C., 1934).
Shy, John, "The American Revolution: The Military Conflict Considered as a Revolutionary War," in *Essays on the American Revolution*, ed. Stephen G. Kurtz and James H. Hutson (Chapel Hill, N.C., 1973), 121–56.
—. "American Society and Its War for Independence," in *Reconsiderations of the American Revolution*, ed. Don Higginbotham (Westport, Conn., 1978), 72–82.
—. "British Strategy for Pacifying the Southern Colonies, 1778–1781," in *The Southern Experience in the American Revolution*, ed. Jeffrey J. Crow and Larry E. Tise (Chapel Hill, N.C., 1978), 155–73.
—. A New Look at Colonial Militia," *WMQ*, 3d Ser., XX (1963), 175–85.
Siebert, Wilbur H., "The Legacy of the American Revolution to the British West Indies and Bahamas: A Chapter Out of the History of the American Loyalists," Ohio State University, *Bulletin*, XVII, no. 27 (1913).
—. "The Loyalists in West Florida and the Natchez District," *MVHR*, II (1915), 465–83.
[Simms, William Gilmore], "Biographical Sketch of the Career of Major William Cunningham of South Carolina," *Southern and Western Literary Messenger*, XII (1846), 513–24, 577–86.
—. "Civil Warfare in the Carolinas and Georgia during the Revolution," *Southern and Western Literary Messenger*, XII (1846), 257–65, 320–36, 385–400.
Sirmans, M. Eugene, *Colonial South Carolina: A Political History. 1663–1763* (Chapel Hill, N.C, 1966).
—. "The South Carolina Royal Council, 1720–1763, "*WMQ*, 3d Ser., XVIII (1961), 373–92.
Smith, D. E. Huger, "An Account of the Tatnall and Fenwick Families, in South Carolina," *SCHGM*, XIV (1913), 1–19.
Smith, Henry A. M., "The Ashley River: Its Seats and Settlements," *SCHGM*, XX (1919), 3–51, 75–122.
—. "Goose Creek," *SCHGM*, XXIX (1928), 1–25.
—. "The Upper Ashley; and the Mutations of Families," *SCHGM*, XX, (1919) 151–98.
Smith, Paul H., *Loyalists and Redcoats* (Chapel Hill, N.C, 1964).
Smith, W. Roy, *South Carolina as a Royal Province, 1719–1776* (New York, 1903).
Sosin, Jack M., "The Use of Indians in the War of the American Revolution: A Re-Assessment of Responsibility; ' *Canadian Historical Review*, XLVI (1965), 101–2l.
Starr, J. Barton, *Tories, Dons, and Rebels* (Gainesville, Fla., 1976).
Stephens, Henry M., "Nisbet Balfour," *DNB*, 1, 976–77.
Stewart, Charles H., *The Service of British Regiments in Canada and North America: A Resume* (Ottawa, 1964).
Stoesen, Alexander R., "British Occupation of Charleston, 1780–1782," *SCHM*, LXIII (1962), 71–82.
Syrett, David, *Shipping and the American War, 1775–1783* (London, 1970).
Thane, Elswyth, *Mount Vernon Is Ours* (New York, 1966).
"The Thomas Pinckney Family of South Carolina," *SCHGM*, XXXIX (1938), 15–35.
Townshend, Leah, *South Carolina Baptists, 1670–1805* (Florence, S.C., 1935).
Troxler, Carole Watterson, *The Loyalist Experience in North Carolina* (Raleigh, N.C., 1976).
Ubbelhode, Carl, *The Vice Admiralty Courts and the American Revolution* (Chapel Hill, N.C, 1960).
Upton, L. F S., "The Claims: The Mission of John Anstey," in *Red, White and True Blue*, ed. Esmond Wright (New York , 1976), 135–47.
Ver Steeg, Clarence L., *Origins of a Southern Mosaic: Studies of Early Carolina and Georgia* (Athens, Ga., 1975).
Vipperman, Carl J., *The Rise of Rawlins Lowndes* (Columbia, S.C., 1978).
Wallace, David D., *The History of South Carolina*, 4 vols. (New York, 1934).
Walsh, Richard, *Charleston's Sons of Liberty: A Study of the Artisans, 1763–1789* (Columbia, S.C, 1959).
Ward, Christopher, *War of the Revolution*, 2 vols. (New York, 1952).
Waring, Alice Noble, *The Fighting Elder: Andrew Pickens, 1739–1817* (Columbia, S.C., 1962).
Waring, Joseph I., *A History of Medicine in South Carolina*, 3 vols. (Columbia, S.C., 1964).
Watterson, John S., "The Ordeal of Governor Burke," *NCHR.*, XLVIII (1971), 95–117.
Webber, Mabel L., comp., "Early Generations of the Seabrook Family," *SCHGM*, XVII (1916), 14–25, 58–72,
—. "South Carolina Loyalists," *SCHGM*, XIV (1913), 36–43.
Weigley, Russell F., *The Partisan War: The South Carolina Campaign of 1780–1782* (Columbia, S.C., 1970).
Weir, Robert M., *Colonial South Carolina: A History*, (Millwood, N.Y., 1983).
—. "'The Harmony We Are famous For': An Interpretation of Pre-Revolutionary South Carolina Politics," *WMQ*, XXVI (1969), 473–501.

—. *"A Most Important Epocha": The Coming of the Revolution in South Carolina* (Columbia, S.C., 1970).
Weller, Jac, "The Irregular War in the South," *Military Affairs*, XXI (1957), 119–31.
Wells, Robert V., *The Population of the British Colonies in America before 1776: A Survey of Census Data* (Princeton, N.J., 1975).
Wickwire, Franklin, and Mary Wickwire, *Cornwallis: The American Adventure* (Boston, 1970).
Willcox, William B., *Portrait of a General: Sir Henry Clinton in the War for Independence* (New York, 1964).
Williams, George, *St. Michael's, Charleston, 1751–1951* (Columbia, S.C., 1951).
Wilson, Ellen Gibson, *The Loyal Blacks* (New York, 1976).
Winks, Robin W., *The Blacks in Canada* (New Haven, Conn., 1971).
Wood, Gordon S., "Rhetoric and Reality in the American Revolution," *WMQ*, 3d Ser., XXIII (1966), 3–32.
Wood, Peter, *Black Majority: Negroes in South Carolina From 1670 to the Stono Rebellion* (New York, 1974).
—. "'Taking Care: of Business,' in Revolutionary South Carolina: Republicanism and the Slave Society," in *The Southern Experience in the American Revolution*, ed. Jeffrey J. Crow and Larry E. Tise (Chapel Hill, N.C., 1978), 268–93.
Woody, Robert H., "Christopher Gadsden and the Stamp Act," SCHA, *Proceedings*, IX (1939), 3–12.
Wright, Esmond, ed., *A Tug of Loyalties: Anglo-American Relations, 1765–1785* (London, 1975).
Wright, J. Leitch, *Florida and the American Revolution* (Gainesville, Fla., 1975).
Wyatt, Frederick, and William B. Willcox, "Sir Henry Clinton: A Psychological Exploration in History," *WMQ*, 3d Ser., XVI (1959), 3–26.

Dissertations

Bulger, William T., Jr., "The British Expedition to Charleston, 1779–1780" (University of Michigan, 1957).
Ferguson, Clyde R., "General Andrew Pickens" (Duke University, 1960).
Higgins, W. Robert, "A Financial History of the Revolution in South Carolina" (Duke University, 1970).
Klein, Rachel, "The Rise of the Planters in the South Carolina Backcountry, 1767–1808" (Yale University, 1979).
Knepper, David Morton, "The Political Structure of Colonial South Carolina, 1743–1776" (University of Virginia, 1971).
Peters, Thelma, "The American Loyalists and the Plantation Period in the Bahama Islands" (University of Florida, 1960).
Smith, Paul, "American Loyalists in British Military Policy, 1775–1781" (University of Michigan, 1962).

INDEX

Unless otherwise noted, all place names refer to South Carolina and all personal names to South Carolinians. Military officers are British or loyalist unless (State), (rebel), or (Continental) precedes the title; the rank given is the highest attained during the war.

Adamson, John 214
Address of the People of Great Britain to the Inhabitants of America 26
Aedanus Burke 158, 170, 178, 213, 218, 228
Alexander, Robert 9–10
Allaire, Lt. Anthony 64, 101, 103
Allen, Lt. Col. Isaac, of New Jersey 70, 116, 123, 167
  commandant of Charlestown 70, 167
Allicocke, Lt. Charles 155
Allison's Creek 90
Altamaha River, Georgia 49
Amelia Island, East Florida 187
Amelia Township 1, 164
Amercement Act, 1782. *See* Property confiscation programs, state
American rights movement, backcountry opposition to 18–20, 25–31
American Volunteers 69, 71, 97, 99, 100, 233. *See also* Ferguson, Maj. Patrick
Ancrum, William 201, 214
Anderson, George 20, 196
Anderson, John, Irish immigrant 9
Anderson, John, widower, Enoree River 165
André, Major John 146
Arbuthnot, Admiral Marriott 64, 68, 71. *See* Clinton, Sir Henry
Argo, an exile vessel 195
Arness Ford, Catawba River 100
Ashe, (State) Brig. Gen. John, of North Carolina, 60
Atkins, Charles 134, 201, 208
Atrocities. *See* Civil War
Augusta, Georgia
  British occupation and evacuation of
    1779 58–59
    rebel attack on, Aug., 1780 74, 96
    siege and surrender of, 1781 122–123
Avon River, Nova Scotia 194

Backcountry
  early settlement of 1–2
  efforts to conciliate 22–24
  expansion of, after 1761 9–10
  grievances of, Woodmason 10–11.
    See also Circuit Court Act, 1769; Woodmanson, Charles
Bahama Gazette 191–192
Balfour, Lt. Col. Nisbet, of the Twenty-third Regiment 63, 70–72, 94, 108–109, 114, 120, 131, 138, 150–151, 163, 167, 169, 205, 209
  and Hayne execution 146
  commandant of Charlestown 69
  conducts march to interior 73–79
  departs for England 179
  postwar aid to loyalists 190, 199
Ball, Col. Elias, Sr., of Wambaw 80, 174, 183, 186, 187, 191, 200, 201, 209, 211
Ballentine: Col. William 150, 156, 157, 214
Ballingall, Col. Robert 85, 155, 172
Ball, Lt. Col. Elias, Jr., of Comingtee 80, 85, 209
"Banditti" 53, 82, 149
  in East Florida 189. *See also* "Outlyers"; "Scopholites"
Barbados 2
Baron, Dr. Alexander 134
Bates, William ("Bloody Bill") 160, 213
Beattie's Mill 143

Beaufort 4, 9, 17, 43, 45, 46, 61, 85, 133, 188
Beaverdam Creek 33, 78
Begbie, James 133
Begbie, William 18
Bell, John 166
Bethebara, North Carolina 103
Biggerstaff's Plantation, North Carolina 102
Birchtown, Nova Scotia 197
Black River 79, 82, 93, 111
Blacks
  as pawns in civil war 169–174
  as property, issue at evacuation 180–181
  as slaves 3–5, 8, 169, 172
  as soldiers 33, 64, 188
  British policy toward 172–174
  destinations at evacuation 182–183
  use as labor 169, 172. *See also* Exiles, loyalist, Bahamas, East Florida, Jamaica, Nova Scotia
Board of American Loyalists 178
Board of Police. *See* Charlestown, British occupation of
Board of Trade 12
Boone, (royal) Gov. Thomas 9, 12, 199
Boston, Mass., reaction to coercive measures against 15–16
Bowers, John Adam 10, 194
Bowers, Mrs. Elizabeth 167
Bowman, Jacob 30, 52
Boyd, Colonel [James] 57–58, 63 n. 11
Bradley, Lt. Samuel 144
Brandon, Charles 103
Brandon, Col. Thomas 78, 190
Bratton, Col. Wm 91
Bridenbaugh, Carl 8, 20
Brier Creek, Georgia, Battle of. *See* Ashe, John
Brisbane, James 41, 134
British policy toward rebels; *See* Loyalty and allegiance, British
British strategy for recovery of her southern colonies 55–57, 66–67

assessed 126–128
British (Tarleton's) Legion, Provincial Regiment 69, 71, 90–91, 120
Broad River 1–2, 9, 23–24, 26, 60, 80, 94, 100, 119
Brown, Archibald 209, 211
Brown, Capt. Hugh 36–37, 216
Brown, Lt. Col. Thomas, of Georgia 25, 114–115, 127
  joins Nonassociators in the backcountry 25–28
  to East Florida, 1776 28, 34
Brown, Richard Maxwell 6, 18, 20
Bruce, David 52, 206
Bryan, Col. Samuel, North Carolina Militia 90, 93
Bryson, John 197
Bryson, William 197
Buckle, Thomas, Sr. 205
Buford, (Continental) Col. Abraham, of Virginia 70
Bull, Lt. Gov. William 1, 10, 13, 16, 146, 151, 163
  and evacuation of Charlestown 184
  death 202
  in England 45
  pardons Regulators 11
  refuses state oath, departs for England, 1777 15
  returns to South Carolina, 1781 132, 134
  settles in England 198–199, 201
Bullock's Creek 26
Bull, Stephen 42
Burgoyne, Maj. Gen. John, defeat at Saratoga 46, 55
Burke Court House 103
Burke, Judge Aedanus 158, 170, 178, 213, 218, 228
Burke, (State) Gov. Thomas, of North Carolina 159, 161
Burt, William 206
Bush River 33, 124
Butler, James 148
Butler, (State) Capt. William 157

Index 239

Caldwell, Capt. John 30
Calhoun, Patrick 149
Calhoun, Sen. John C. 219 n. 34
Camden 83–85, 92, 120
  British evacuation of 122
  British occupation of 80
  loyalist garrison of 121–122
Camden, Battle of 67, 89, 92–93, 97, 124, 171
Camden Militia (Rugeley's) Regiment 83, 117, 214
Cameron, Alexander, Deputy Supt. of Indian Affairs 19, 26, 29–30, 36, 38–39, 57, 135
Campbell, Capt. Alexander 158
Campbell, Capt. Archibald, of the South Carolina Royalists 158
Campbell, Col. Samuel, of North Carolina 183
Campbell, Gov. Lord William 21, 24, 28, 63, 156
Campbell, Lt. Col Archibald 46, 57–60
  Gov. of Jamaica 183, 193, 201
Campbell, (State) Col. Wm., of Virginia 100
Cane Creek 99, 148
Cape, Brian 168, 205
Cape Fear River, North Carolina 93
Capers, Gabriel 182, 187, 191
Cargill, Ens. Daniel 156, 189
Carleton, Lt. Gen. Sir Guy 192, 195
  appointed commander in chief 172, 180
  plans for evacuating South Carolina 179, 181–182
  register of blacks in New York City 172
Carsan, James 19, 41
Carsan, William 19
Cary, Col. James 84, 92, 208, 214
  commands militia regiment 84
  death 202
  travels as an exile 183, 193–194, 196, 199–200
Cary, Mary 202
Cassells, Col. James 4, 45, 163, 164, 182, 187, 206
  captured 91–92
  commands Georgetown regiment 85
  to East Florida 182, 191
Catawba Indians 158
Catawba River 2, 83, 91, 93
Cat Island, Bahamas 192
Chalmers, Gilbert 205
Champneys, John 41, 52, 134
  returns to South Carolina 212
Charlestown
  affluence of 8–9
  American rights movement in 12–15
  British attack on, 1776 34–35
  British evacuation of, 1782 178–185
  British occupation of 132–139
  British siege and capture of 62, 66
  chamber of commerce 15
  commandants of 69, 70, 137, 162, 167
  early development of 1–4
  economic and social classes in 3, 8–9
  fire, 1778 43
  loyalists and protectionists in 132–134, 137
  postwar unrest in 207–208
Charlestown Gazette 135
Charlestown Militia (Powell's) Regiment 134
Charlotte, North Carolina 83–84, 90, 93–94, 100, 104, 117, 119
Charlottetown, Prince Edward Island 197
Chedabucto Bay 195, 197
Chelsea, England 191
Cheney, Lt. Col. Baily 38
  Commands militia regiment 156
  in East Florida 189
Cheney's Militia Regiment 157
Cheraw District 23, 41, 82, 83, 85, 156, 163
Cheraw Hill 82, 90, 91, 93, 119
Cheraw Militia (Mills's) Regiment 83, 85, 91, 93
Cherokee Indians 2, 7, 10, 17, 19, 22, 26, 29–30, 35–37, 39–40, 46,

49–51, 57, 76, 127, 141, 147, 160, 216, 220
Cherokee Treaty, 1777 37
Cherokee War 2, 4, 7, 8, 9, 10, 11, 12, 17, 33, 220
Chesney, Lt. Alexander 50, 118
  and Cowpens 129 n. 16
  at Kings Mountain 101, 103
  returns to Ireland 198, 200, 202
Chesnut, John 181, 183, 214
Cheves, Alexander 10, 50
  returns to South Carolina 215
Cheves, Langdon 215
Chisholm, Alexander 202
Chisholm, John 10, 20
Circuit Court Act, 1769 11
Civil War, 198–215
Clarke, Brig. Gen. Alured 178, 193
Clarke, (State) Col. Elijah, of Georgia 94, 96, 99, 115, 121, 123
Clary, Col. Daniel, commands militia regiment 78, 112, 150, 215
Cleveland, (State) Col. Benjamin, of Virginia, 100, 103
Clinton, Lt. Gen. Sir Henry 48, 70–71, 108, 168
  address to 67, 211
  and Admiral Marriott Arbuthnot as commissioners to make peace 67
  and Lord Cornwallis 67–68
  appoints Cornwallis to southern command 68
  captures Charlestown, 1780 62
  commander in chief in America 50
  fails to take Charlestown, 1776 34
  loyalty program 66–71
  plans for occupation 168
  policy toward refugees 162–163
Clitherall, Dr. James 172
  returns to South Carolina 211
  to East Florida 190
Cloud's Creek 148, 149, 151, 157
Coffell, Joseph 11
"Coffin list" 165
Coffin, Major John, of Massachusetts 155, 158
Colleton County Militia (Ballingall's) Regiment 85, 155
Collins, James 105, 213
Commander, Thomas 161
Commissary of Captures (British). *See* Property confiscation
Commissioners of Claims for Slave Property (British) 134, 172
Commission of Depreciated Currency (British), 134, 138
Commission of Enquiry into the Losses and Services of American Loyalists 214
  in Great Britain: awards 199–201
  in Nova Scotia 196
  procedure and evidence 199–200
Committees of observation and inspection (rebel) 15, 23–24
Commons House of Assembly 3, 5, 7, 12
Confiscation Act, 1782. *See* Property confiscation
Congaree River 1, 116
Congaree-Wateree Militia (Cary's) Regiment 84
Constitution of 1776 (State), 34
Constitution of 1778 (State) 43
Continental Armies in South Carolina. *See* Military operations, Continental; Military units, Continental
Continental Association 15, 17, 23
Continental Congress, First 15
  Second 15
Conway, Mary, orphan 165
Conway, William 152 n. 5
Cooke, George 134
Cook, Hugh 103
Cook, James 205, 210
Cooper, Joseph 143
Cooper, the Reverend Robert 9, 17, 210
Cornwallis, Lt. Gen. Charles, Earl of 76, 96, 100, 115, 116–117, 119, 154, 162, 168, 171, 178, 199, 214
  address to 67

and close subordinates 68–70, 72
appointed to southern command 68
loyalty program of 70–71
plans to move into North Carolina 97
policy toward parole violations 93–104
surrenders at Yorktown, Virginia 162
view of loyalists 90, 111
view of militia and provincials 104, 108–110
Cotton, Col. John,
   commands Stevens Creek Militia Regiment 78
Council of Safety 15
"Counter-Association" 24
Country Harbour, Nova Scotia 195, 197, 198
Country Ideology 5
Cowpens 100
Cowpens, Battle of 70, 119
Craig, Maj. James 159
Craven and Berkeley 80
Creek Indians 56
Creighton, Catherine 200
Creighton, Thomas 133
Creighton, Wm. 44
Cross Creek, North Carolina 79, 93, 120
Crouch, Charles 135
Cruden, John 168, 172, 173, 190
Cruger, Lt. Col. John Harris, of New York 70, 103, 104, 114, 171
   and local rebel leaders 95–96, 114–116
   commands at Ninety Six 94
   leadership in siege of Ninety Six 123–124
   leaves South Carolina 179
   relieves Augusta, Georgia, 1780 96
   view of loyalists 108–109, 111. See also Andrew Pickens; Andrew Williamson
Cuffeetown Creek 49, 60, 78, 101, 166, 218
Cunningham, Ann Pamela (granddaughter of Patrick) 219
Cunningham, Brig. Gen. Robert of Saluda River 24, 36–37, 38 n. 9, 49, 52, 74, 78, 216
   commands all Ninety Six loyal militia 109–110
   elected to South Carolina Senate 52
   Nonassociator leader, arrested, jailed 28, 31
   settles in Bahamas 192
Cunningham, Capt. Robert (son of Patrick) 115
Cunningham, David 147
Cunningham, Lt. Col. Patrick, of Little River (of the Saluda) 24–25, 33, 109, 161, 206, 208
   captures powder 30–31
   commands loyalist militia regiment 78
   jailed 31
   leader of Nonassociators 27
   returns to South Carolina 216–217, 218–219 n. 34
   to East Florida 187
Cunningham, Maj. William ("Bloody Bill") 156, 157, 212, 218–219 n. 34
   commands loyal militia regiment, raids in Saluda valley 147–149, 156
   settles in Bahamas 192
   to East Florida 189
Cunningham's, Loyal Militia Regiment 148–149, 156
Curry (Currie), Joseph 10, 19, 38, 193
Curtis, William 183

Dawkins, Capt. George, of the South Carolina Royalists 74, 155, 158
   settles in Nova Scotia 195, 198, 203 n. 33
   to East Florida 189
Deas, David 211
Deas, John 205, 207, 211, 212
decided to send Kirkland 27
DeKalb, Baron 91
Delancey's Brigade, New York provincial unit 70, 71, 123
de Miranda, Francisco 212
de Peyster 97, 99, 100–101, 105 n. 6

D'Estaing, Adm. Charles, Comte 61–62
Deveaux Family, of Beaufort 4, 85
Deveaux, Maj. Andrew, Jr. 61, 188, 192
DeWalt, Daniel 199, 216
Dick, Walter 44
Dickey, Capt. Hector 164

Digby, Nova Scotia 198, 204
Dominica, British Island of. *See* Exiles, loyalist
Donaldson, James 165
Donavan, James 210
Donnahoe, John 151
Dorchester 26, 44, 147
Downes, Major Wm. 143
Downes, Mrs. Jane 166
Dragoons, loyalist 112, 125, 144 n. 3. *See* Military operations, loyalist
Draper, Lyman C. 101
Drayton, John 14
Drayton-Tennent Mission 25–27, 50
Drayton, William Henry 14, 25, 30, 32, 78, 127
Drennan, David 187
Dundas, Col. Thomas 196, 204
Dunlap, Maj. James 112, 116, 121, 143
Dunmore, Earl of 173
Dunsmore, David 196
Dupont, Gideon, Jr. 134, 180
Dutch Fork. *See* Broad-Saluda Fork
Dutch Fork Militia (Clary's) Regiment 78, 156

East Florida
  British Province of, American invasion of, 1778 49
  cession to Spain 188–190
  compensation to loyalists for losses in 190
  lawlessness in 188–189
  refuge for southern loyalists, 1776-1780 46–51. *See also* South Carolina Royalists; Brown, Thomas; *East Florida Gazette*; East Florida Rangers; Tonyn, Gov. Patrick

East Florida Gazette 188
Edghill, Lt. Col. Thomas 163, 165
Edisto River 1, 169
Ellison, Thomas 149
English, Col. Robert 156, 208, 214
English, Joshua, the elder 2
English, Joshua, the younger 214
Enoree River 10, 23, 26, 31, 33, 34, 50, 60, 95, 104, 108, 165
Eutaw Springs, Battle of 126
Exiles, loyalist, from South Carolina
  1777-1778 42–45, 48–51
  1782 183
  blacks 179, 182–183, 188–190, 193, 195, 196, 199
  to Dominica 191
  to East Florida 48–50, 178, 180, 182, 186–191
  to Great Britain 42–45, 198–202
  to Jamaica 165, 183, 193–194
  to New Brunswick 194–198
  to Nova Scotia 182, 192, 194–198
  to St. Lucia 183
  to the Bahama Islands 188, 190–193
  West Florida 51–52
  women 44, 187, 200
Exuma Island, Bahamas 192

Fair Forest Creek 23, 33, 58
Fair Forest Militia (Plummer's) Regiment 78, 101, 103, 224
Fanning, Col. David 36, 40 n. 42, 49–50
  raids into North Carolina 159–160
  settles in New Brunswick 196
  to East Florida 182–183, 188
  to Nova Scotia 197
Fanning, John 60, 160 n. 3
Farquharson, Dr. John 18, 44
Fenwick, Capt. Edward 18, 125, 154, 160 n. 21, 207, 211
Ferguson, Maj. Patrick of the American Volunteers 69, 70, 76–79, 95, 97, 216
  death of 101

defeat at Kings Mountain 99–101
First Camden Militia (English's) Regiment 156
First Provincial Congress 22
Fisher, Col. John of Orangeburg 73–74, 156, 163
Fisher, John of Charlestown, cabinetmaker 193, 210
Fletchall, Lt. Col. Thomas 23, 31, 79, 163, 208
  negotiates for Nonassociators 28
  to Jamaica 183, 194
Floyd., Col. Matthew 85
Forfeited Estates, Commissioners of (State). *See* Property Confiscation and Sequestration (State)
Fort Balfour 125
Fort Barrington 49
Fort Charlotte 24–25, 27–28, 147
Fort Granby 120
Fort Johnson 42
Fort McIntosh 48
Fort Motte 120, 122, 143, 150
Fort Rutledge 74, 75
Fort Watson 120, 122
France 2, 7, 12, 43, 46, 55–56, 108, 220
Fraser (Frazer). Dr. James 18, 45
Fraser (Frazer), Maj. Thomas, of the South Carolina Royalists 109, 120, 146, 155, 158, 173
Fritz, Abraham 195
Frogg, Robert 193
Fulker, Lt. George 143, 150–151
Fundy Bay of 194–195, 197
Fyffe, Dr. Charles 163, 209

Gadsden, Christopher 12, 16, 139, 168, 201, 205
Gaillard, Capt. John 186–187, 187, 191, 201, 209
Gainey Maj. Micajah, of Little Pee Dee River 121, 126, 147
Garden, Dr. Alexander 18, 45, 210, 212
Gates, (Continental) Maj. Gen. Horatio 91, 139, 146

Gayle, Ambrose 215
Gazette of the State of South Carolina 135
General Assembly, meets at Jacksonborough 149, 169, 173, 211
Georgetown, as colonial port 4
  British occupation of 80, 85, 92, 120, 121, 125
  evacuation of 126
Georgetown Militia (Cassell's) Regiment 85
Georgia, British Province of
  evacuation of 179
  occupation of 57–59. *See also* Military operations, British, Continental
Germain, Lord George 55
Germans, settle in South Carolina 1, 10, 25–26
  loyalists return to homes 218
  loyalists settle in Nova Scotia 194–195
Gibbes, John Walters 206
Gibbes, Mary Anne 201
Gibbs, Lt. Col. Zacharias 58–60, 118, 150–151, 156, 166, 200
  commands loyalist militia regiment 78
  Kings Mountain 101–102, 104
  sentenced to hang 59
  settles in Nova Scotia 195–197
Giessendanner, John 1
Gilbertown, North Carolina 97, 99–100, 102, 112, 121, 142–143
Gilliam, Robert 213
Gillon, (State) Commodore Alexander 207, 208, 210
Gist, Wm. 50, 103
Gordon, Chief Justice Thomas Knox 9, 42, 46, 198
Gowen's Fort 160, 213
Granville County Militia (Lechemere's) Regiment 85, 125, 188
Gray (Grey), Col Robert 83, 86, 91–93, 109, 146, 158
Gray, Jesse 212
Great Abaco Island, Bahamas 192
Great Britain. *See* Exiles, loyalist, Great Britain

Great Cane Brake, Battle of 31
Greene, (Continental) Maj. Gen. Nathanael 126, 181, 211, 215
  appointed to command southern army 117
  efforts to recruit loyalists 159
  observations on the civil war 143
  retreats into North Carolina 119–120
  returns, campaigns in South Carolina 121–125
Greenwood & Higginson 45
Greenwood, William 212
Gregory, Benjamin 49
Grimke, Lt. Col. John F. 145
Groundwater, Andrew 46
Groundwater, John 151
Gruber, Ira 55
Guerard, (State) Gov. Benjamin 180, 208, 210, 212
Guilford Court House, North Carolina, Battle of 120

Habersham, Maj. James, of Georgia 145
Hackett, Agnes 165
Hackett, Allen 165
Halifax, Nova Scotia 183, 189, 193, 194, 195, 197
Hall, Aquilla 59
Hamilton, Lt. Col. John 163, 195, 196, 198
Hamilton, Lt. Col. John, of Royal North Carolina Regiment 90
Hamilton, Paul 45, 61, 201
Hammond, (State) Lt. Col. LeRoy 74, 142, 149
Hammond, (State) Maj. Samuel 75, 115, 128
Hampton, (State) Col. Henry 144
Hampton, (State) Col. Wade 74, 116, 143
Hanscomb, William 64 n. 20, 193
Harbour Island, Bahamas 188
Harcombe, Thomas 44
Harden, (State) Col. William 125, 160, 170

Hard Labour Creek 1, 10, 166–167, 194, 215
Harleston, John, protectionist 208, 211
Harper, Thomas 202
Harrison, Capt. Robert 82
Harrison, Capt. Samuel 82
Harrison, Maj. John 60
  commands South Carolina Rangers 82, 155, 187
Hart, the Reverend Oliver 25
Hayes, (State) Col. Joseph 148
Hayes Station 148, 149, 151, 158, 213
Hayne, (State) Col. Isaac 141, 145, 150, 155
Head, Sir Edmund 44
Helms, Capt. William 156
Henderson, Arthur 165
Henderson, David 165
Henderson, James 165
Henderson, Mrs. Jean 165
Hendricks, Capt. William 190
Henry, Robert 102
Hest, William 44
Hewatt, the Reverend Alexander 9, 18, 202
Heyward, Thomas 59
High Hills of Santee 92, 120
High Hills of Santee (Tynes's) Regiment 83, 112, 173, 214
Hill, Samuel, refugee 152 n. 5, 165
Hillsborough, North Carolina 9, 159
Hill's Ironworks 90, 142
Hill, (State) Col. William 90
Hobbs, Augustine 212
Hobkirk's Hill, Battle of 121–122, 143, 155
Holmes, David 51
Hood, Capt. John 148, 156
Hope, an exile vessel 44
Hopton, John 133, 134, 137, 200, 201, 212
Horry, Harriott 211
Horry, (State) Col. Peter 126
Horry, (State) Maj. Daniel, protectionist 133, 157, 211

Howe, (Continental) Brig. Gen. Robert 49, 57
Howe, Sir William 55
Huck, Capt. Christian 90, 108, 142
Hudson, Lt. Joel 196
Hudson's Ferry, Georgia 59
Hutchins, Anthony 51

Imrie, John, shipbuilder 18, 35
Indian Line 2, 12, 26, 29, 35
Inglis, AJexander 208, 211
Inglis, Thomas 44, 172
Innes, Col. Alexander, of the South Carolina Royalists 51, 74, 90, 95, 107, 108, 138, 201, 229
Irving, Thomas 42

Jacksonborough 18, 149, 169, 170–171, 173–174, 211, 214–215
Jackson, John 143
Jackson's Creek 9, 26, 45
Jackson's Creek Militia (Phillips's) Regiment 84, 155-156, 198
Jamaica, British Province of. *See* Exiles, loyalist.
Jarvis, Lt. Stephen of Connecticut 155
Jeddore, Nova Scotia 195
Jenkins, the Reverend Edward 166, 212
John's Island 18, 62
Johnson, Dr. Uzal 102
Johnston, James 180
Johnston, Rosannah 166
Jones, Lewis 24

Kennebecacie River, New Brunswick 196
Kershaw, Eli 214
Kershaw, Joseph 2, 25, 214
Kettle Creek, Georgia, Battle of 63, 78
Kincaid, George 44
King, Boston 197
King, Lt. Col. Richard 76, 95, 101, 114–115, 123, 125, 143, 165–166
Kings County, Nova Scotia 196
Kingsley, Zephaniah 15, 45, 133, 134

Kings Mountain, Bartle of
 casualties from 102
 maneuvering prior to 99–100
 significance of 105 n. 6
 treatment of loyalist prisoners after 102–103
Kingstree 93
King, Violet 197
Kirkland, Lt. Col. Moses, early backcountry settler 1, 24, 104, 156, 208
 commands loyalist militia regiment 78–79
 joins Nonassociators 27
 mission to Gov. Campbell 27–28
 plan for recovering southern provinces 48, 57–58
 rivalry with Robert Cunningham, resigns commission 110–111
 settles in Jamaica 193
Kirkland's Militia Regiment 109–110
Klein, Rachel 10, 18

Lamb, Hannah 203 n. 33
Lance, Lambert 214
Larimer, Capt. David 101
Laurens, (Continental) Col. John 158
Laurens, Henry 13, 27, 45, 135–136, 158, 207–208, 210–211, 217 n. 6
Lawrence, John 160 n. 3
Lawson's Fork (of Pacolet River) 26
Lechemere, Lt. Col. Nicholas 85, 125
Lee, (Continental) Lt. Col. Henry 122–124
Lee, William 212
Legge, Capt. Benjamin Smith 155
Leigh , Sir Egerton 9, 13, 16, 134
Lenud's Ferry 80
Leslie, Lt. Gen. Alexander 112, 154, 187
 and question of slave property 171, 173–174
 lands with reinforcements 117
 presides over the evacuation of South Carolina 178, 182–184
Lester, Eleanor 201
Lettingham, Mrs. William 165

Lincoln, (Continental) Maj. Gen. Benjamin 60, 62, 65
Lincolnton, North Carolina 90
Linder, John, Jr. 189
Linder, John, Sr. 189
Lindley, James 59
Lindley's Fort 36
Lindsay, Robert 15
Lisle, (State) Col. John 91
Little Pee Dee (Gainey's) Regiment 121
Little Pee Dee River area, loyalists in 92–93, 121
Little River Militia (Patrick Cunningham's) Regiment 78, 156, 165, 216
Little River Militia (Pearson's) Regiment 156
Little River, of the Saluda, district of 27, 33, 60
  elections in 52
Little Saluda River 148
Lively, Reuben 195
Livingston, Capt. Martin 155
Lochaber 19
London, England, exiles in 44, 200–202
Long Cane Creek settlements 2, 9–10, 27, 114–116
Long Cane Militia (King's) Regiment 76, 95, 101, 114, 163, 165–166
  at siege of Ninety Six 123
  defections in 116, 119
Long, Capt. Richard 156
Loocock, Aaron, protectionist 132, 207–208, 211, 214
Love, Mathew 213
Lowcountry, prewar economic and social conditions in 2–5, 8
Lowndes, Rawlins 201
  protectionist 133, 210–211, 212
  (State) President 43
Loyalists, North Carolina
  at Kings Mountain 100–101
  premature uprising of, 1780 90. *See also* Fanning, Col. David; North Carolina Volunteers; Royal North Carolina Regiment
Loyalists, South Carolina
  British policy toward 76
  characteristics of 16–20, 220
  in occupied Charlestown 133–134, 137
  leadership of 118
  number of 39, 67, 75, 118, 126–127, 220–221, 224–226
  reconciliation of (with state) 207–209, 210, 214, 215–217
  treatment of (by rebels) 37, 41–44, 59, 212–213, 214–215
  trials of 36, 59. *See also* Civil war; Exiles, loyalist; Military operations, loyalist; Military units, loyalist; Nonassociators; Property confiscation (State); Protectionists; Refugees, loyalist
Loyalty and allegiance programs to promote
  British 46, 59–60, 68, 72, 74–75, 90–93, 103, 116, 118–119, 127, 144–145, 171
  State 35, 37, 41–46, 59, 62, 125, 158–159
"Lucullus" 150
Lynch, Thomas 13
Lyttleton, Henry (Royal) Gov. 5

Mail, Mary 166
Maitland, Lt. Col. John 61
Manson, Daniel 18, 44
Marine Anti-Britannic Society 207
Marion-Gainey truce, of 1781 121, 126, 147
  of 1782 160
Marion, (State) Brig. Gen. Francis 80, 82–83, 92, 111, 121–122, 125, 146, 154, 169, 206
Maritime Provinces in Canada. *See* New Brunswick; Nova Scotia
Mark, Conrad 195
Marr's Bluff 11
"Massacred" list. *See* Civil war

Mathews, John (State) Gov. 59, 180, 181, 207
Maxwell, Gov. John, Bahama Islands 192
Mayfield, Stephen 189
Mayson, (rebel) Maj. James 23–24, 27, 31, 110
McArthur, Maj. Archibald, 71st Regiment 82, 90–91, 100, 146
McCall, (State) Maj. James, of Georgia 115
McCord's Ferry 120
McCormick, James 215
McCowen, George 138
McCrady, Edward 72 n. 7, 144
McDowell, (State) Col. Charles, of North Carolina 99
McGirt, Daniel 189
McKee, Samuel 200
McKenzie, John 15
McKeown, James 45
McKeown, Robert 45, 198
McLaurin, Isabella 201
McLaurin, Maj. Evan 10, 20, 25, 96, 108, 110, 151, 193
  early Nonassociator 30
  in South Carolina Royalists 58
  to East Florida 48
McWhorter, James 143
Meanwhile, Cornwallis had been waiting 119–120
Meek, Wm., 167, 196–197
Merchants. *See* Professions and occupations
Mergath, Barbara 201
Michie, Harry 41, 200
Middleton, Arthur, protectionist 133
Migler, Daniel 195
Military operations
  British 57–59, 61–62, 73–76, 79–80, 86, 92–94, 119–120, 121–122, 124, 126, 157
  Continental 49, 60–61, 61, 91, 92, 117, 119–120, 123–124, 126
  loyalist 57, 62, 99–102, 121–122, 124, 147–149, 157–158, 160

Military units, South Carolina loyalist, militia. *See* Camden (Rugeley's), Charlesttown (Powell's), Cheney's, Cheraw (Mills's), Colleton (Ballingall's), Congaree-Wateree (Cary's), Craven and Berkeley (Ball's), William Cunningham's, Dutch Fork (Clary's), Fair Forest (Plummer's), First Camden (English's), Georgetown (Cassells's), Granville (Lechemere's), High Hills of Santee (Tynes's), Jackson's Creek (Phillips's), Kirkland's; Little Pee Dee (Gainey's), Little River (Patrick Cunningham's), Little River (Pearson's), Long Cane (King's), Orangeburg (Fisher's), Rocky Mount (Floyd's), Second Camden (Ballentine's), Stevens Creek (Cotton's), Sparton (Gibbs's), Williams's, Young's; South Carolina Provincials. *See* South Carolina Royalists, South Carolina Rangers; other provincials. *See* American Volunteers, British Legion, Delancey's, East Florida Rangers, King's American, New Jersey Volunteers, New York Volunteers, North Carolina Volunteers, Royal North Carolina Regiment, Volunteers of Ireland
Militia, South Carolina: loyalist 70, 71, 76–79, 82–85, 95, 104, 109–110, 114–116, 118, 155–157, 164
  State 23, 37 n. 3, 49. *See also* Military operations, loyalist; Military units, loyalist militia
Miller, James 198, 200
Miller, John 208
Miller, Mary 201
Mills, Col. Ambrose, of North Carolina 90, 91, 112
  hanged 102, 142
Mills, John 199
Mills, Lt. Col. William Henry, of Cheraw

District 83, 92, 118, 125, 169, 191
Moffatt, James 196
Moncks Corner 73, 86, 120, 122, 124–125, 155
Montagu, (royal) Gov. Lord Charles 11, 181, 208
  recruits Continental prisoners 145, 181
Moore, Andrew 200
Moore, Daniel 13
Moore, Isham 111–112
Moore, (State) Sheriff William 208
Morgan, (Continental) Maj. Gen. Daniel 116–117, 119
Morgridge, John 191
Moultrie, (Continental) Brig. Gen. William 60, 145, 162, 212
Murphy, John 49
Murray, Mrs. Susannah, refugee 165
Murray's Ferry 80, 92
Musgrove's Mill, Battle of 95–96, 108

Nadelhaft, Jerome 170
Nassau, New Providence, Bahamas 191, 192
Nealey, Maj. Christopher 59, 60, 193
Nelson's Ferry 10, 20, 120, 122
New Acquisition, District of 23, 24
New Blessing, an exile vessel 182
New Brunswick, Canadian province of. *See* Exiles, loyalist
New Jersey Volunteers, Loyalist Provincial regiment 70, 71, 102, 103, 123
Newport, Nova Scotia 194
New Providence, Bahamas 188, 189, 191, 192, 193
New York City
  loyalist exiles sail for 183
  slaves in 173
New York Volunteers, Loyalist Provincial Regiment 70, 71, 84, 94, 103, 109, 155
Ninety Six District
  British occupation of 75–79
  loyalist exodus from 124–125
  struggle for control of 23–32
Ninety Six, Treaty of
  Nov. 22, 1775 31
  Sept. 16, 1775 28
  28
Ninety Six, Village of 24
  American siege of, 1781 123, 129
  British evacuation of 124–125
  British occupation of 75, 85
  destruction in 126
  fortification of 95
  Rawdon's relief of 124
  rebel raids on 115–116
Nonassociators 25–28, 30–31, 33–36, 39, 50, 127
Nonimportation agreements 14
North Carolina Volunteers loyalist provincial regiment 71
Northern frontier, characteristics of 79–80
Northern Ireland 2, 10, 76, 84, 198, 200, 220
North, Frederick Lord, Ministry of 22, 66, 111
Norton, Mary Beth 164
Nova Scotia, British province of. *See* Exiles, loyalist

Oaths of loyalty. *See* Loyalty and allegiance
Ogilvie, Charles 180
O'Hara, Brig. Gen. Charles 174
Olson, Gary 31
O'Neall, Henry, early Little River Nonassociator 30, 52, 74
  settles in East Florida 187, 189, 190
Orangeburg District
  British occupation of 73–74
  retreat from 122
Orangeburg Militia (Fisher's) Regiment 73, 156
Orangeburg, town of 1, 74, 147, 159
  surrender of 122
Outerbridge, White 202
"Outlyers" 158, 160, 212

Pacolet River 26, 103, 160
Pardon Act, 1782 (State). *See* Property confiscation
Parker, Adm. Sir Peter 34, 45
Parker, Capt. William 156
Parker's Ferry Gazette 157–158
Parliament, of Great Britain 5, 7, 13, 14, 15, 17, 26, 56, 150, 194, 199
Patterson, Brig. Gen. James 69, 137, 138, 162
Payne, Capt. William 190
Pearis, Capt. Richard 29, 30, 39 n. 33, 57
  becomes Nonassociator 30–31
  recruits loyalists in backcountry 49
  settles in Bahamas 192
  takes surrender of rebels in backcountry 74–75
  to West Florida, East Florida 51
Pearis, Capt. Robert 155
Pearson, Lt. Col. Thomas 156, 161 n. 8
Pee Dee River 2, 11, 93, 119, 146
Pemberton, Jeremy 196
Pensacola, West Florida 27, 36, 48, 49, 51
Peronneau, Henry, Jr. 210
Peronneau, Henry. Sr. 42, 134, 206, 210, 212
Peronneau, Robert 210
Perry, Benjamin Frankin 219 n. 34
Petitions
  to General Lincoln 67
  to the Crown and British officers 45, 67
  to the state 37, 62
Phepoe, Thomas 46
  protectionist 133
  to England 200
Philadelphia, Pennsylvania 7, 15, 27, 55, 56, 69, 107, 135, 139, 163, 199
Phillips, Col. John 85, 118, 124, 150, 151
  commands militia regiment 84
  in relief of Ninety Six 156

  Irish immigrant 9
  refugee 163, 165
  returns to Ireland 198, 200
Philp, Robert 134, 212
Pickens, (State) Brig. Gen. Andrew 27, 38 n. 9, 58, 60, 76, 95, 96, 103, 110, 119, 121, 124
  at sieges of Augusta, Georgia and Ninety Six 123–125, 218 n. 30
  efforts to convert 114–116
  gives up parole 116, 117
  surrender of 75, 87 n. 8
Pinckney, Charles Cotesworth 214
Pinckney, Col. Charles, protectionist 133, 207
Pinckney, Thomas 157, 211
Pinetree Hill. *See* Camden
Placemen 5, 13, 16, 42
Plummer, Maj. Daniel 94, 100, 102, 103, 150
  at Kings Mountain 101, 151
  commands militia regiment 78
  to East Florida 190
Pocotaligo 171
Porcher, Philip, Jr. 207
Porcher, Philip, Sr., protectionist 205, 207, 209, 211, 217
Postell, Capt. John 144
"Powder" Men 34, 35, 52, 74, 216
Powder, seizure of, 1775 30, 38 n. 8
Powell, Robert William 133, 138, 212
  commands Charlestown Militia regiment 134
Powell, Thomas 14
Press, loyalist 3, 17, 135–136, 140 n. 12. *See also Bahama Gazette*; *East Florida Gazette*; *Royal Gazette*; *Royal South Carolina Gazette*; *South Carolina and American General Gazette*
Prevost, Brig. Gen. Augustine 41, 48, 50, 56, 57, 60, 61, 172
Prevost, Col. James Mark 51, 59, 60
Prince of Wales American (Provincial) Regiment 71

Prioleau, Samuel 208
Prisoners of war, treatment of 102–105, 142
  exchanges of 145, 180
Privy Council of South Carolina 34, 207–208, 210
Proclamation of June 3, 1780. *See* Loyalty and Allegiance programs, British
Proctor, Edward 190
Proctor, Philip 190
Professions and occupations in South Carolina 2–3, 4–5, 8–9, 12, 17, 134
Property Confiscation and Sequestration
  British 168–169, 172, 175 n. 26
  State 67, 169, 170–171, 205–206, 209–212
Protectionists 182, 209, 211, 214
Providence, an exile vessel 44
Provincial Congress, of South Carolina 15, 23
Provincial troops, loyalist 50, 107–108, 109. *See also* East Florida Rangers; South Carolina Rangers; South Carolina Royalists; Military units, provincial, other

Quaker Meadows, North Carolina 100, 103
Quakers 2, 9, 45, 84, 133
Quarter House 144, 158
Quartermasters. *See* Refugees, loyalist

Ramsay, Dr. David 149, 208
Rawdon, Col. Francis Lord 69, 70, 71, 72, 80, 82, 87, 88, 90, 91, 93, 94, 97, 104, 105, 109, 111, 112, 113, 116, 117, 120, 121, 123, 125, 129, 130, 142, 143, 144, 146, 152, 155, 156, 161, 171, 174, 199, 204, 215, 231
  and Isaac Hayne 150
  at Hobkirk's Hill 122
  commands at Camden 84
  evacuates Camden 122, 128
  postwar aid to loyalists 214
  relieves siege of Ninety Six 124
Rawdon, Nova Scotia, loyalist settlement in 194, 196, 197, 198
Rayburn's Creek 35, 36, 50, 58, 59, 190
Ray, Robert 44
Rebecca, an exile vessel 44
Reedy River 31, 33, 36, 52, 148
Rees, Benjamin 214–215
Rees, David, "powder man" 75
Rees, Wm., 214–215
Refugees, loyalist, 1781-1782
  British aid to 162, 163–164, 167, 174 n. 4
  camp conditions 165–166
  evacuation of backcountry 1781 122, 124
  in vicinity of Charlestown 162, 163
  return to homes 167, 175 n. 16
  women 164–166, 167
Regulators 11, 18–19, 20, 39
Reluctant rebels. *See* Protectionists
Reluctant tories. *See* Protectionists
Reynolds, Mrs. Margaret 164, 200, 201
Rhem, Capt. Joseph 155
Richardson, Col. Richard 25, 78
  commands expedition to crush Nonassociators, 1775 31–37
Richbourg, Henry 112
Richmond, Duke of 150
Robertson, James 135
Robinson, Lt. Col. Joseph 22, 33, 150–151
  commands South Carolina Royalists 51
  early Nonassociator 24, 26–27, 31, 36
  resigns commission 109
  to East Florida 34, 48
  to Jamaica 194
  to New Brunswick 194, 196
  to Prince Edward Island 197
Robinson, Maj. John 198
Rocky Mount 85, 90, 91, 92, 94
Rocky Mount Militia (Floyd's) Regiment 84

defection of 91
Rogers, Thomas 36
Rose, Alexander 137
Rose, Dr. Hugh 18, 187, 192, 208
Rose, H.M.S., British naval vessel 44
Rose, John 3, 18, 186
   settles in England 201
   to Jamaica 183, 193
Ross, Capt. Alexander 70
Roupell, George 13
Rowand, Robert 3, 41, 44
Row, Capt. Samuel 73, 143
Royal Commission. *See* Commission of Enquiry into the Losses and Services of American loyalists
Royal Council 5, 9, 12, 14, 15
Royal Gazette 147–148, 151, 158, 160, 167, 171, 172, 173, 174, 178, 179, 180
   established 136
   publication suspended 182
   publicizes rebel atrocities 144, 150
Royal North Carolina (Provincial) Regiment 90
Royal officials
   return of, 1780-1781 134
Royal South Carolina Gazette
   established, 1780 135
   publication suspended 182
Rugeley, Lt. Col. Henry 84, 116, 145, 156, 205, 206
   as example of loyalist leadership 118
   commands militia regiment 83
   returns to South Carolina 194, 214
   seeks to remain in the state 181, 183, 214
   surrenders 117
   to Jamaica 183, 214
Rugeley, Rowland 83, 214
Rugeley's Mill, surrender of 117
Rugge, James 206
Russell, Nathaniel 201
Rutherford, (State) Brig. Gen. Griffith, of North Carolina 37
Rutledge, Edward 180

Rutledge, John, (State) 13, 35, 37, 41, 50, 55, 62, 102, 103, 174 n. 23
   confiscation policy of 169, 170
   Gov. 59, 80, 103
   offers amnesty 159
   order evicting loyalist families 149
   President, resigns 34, 43. *See also* Loyalty and allegiance (State)

Saint John, New Brunswick 195, 196
Saint John River, New Brunswick 195
Saint John's River, East Florida 187, 189, 191
Salisbury, North Carolina 30, 93, 104
Salley, Capt. John 73
Saluda River 1, 2, 11, 24, 25, 29, 31, 33, 49, 60, 74, 147, 157
Sanderson, John 194
Santee River 4, 20, 61, 73
Saratoga, Battle of 46, 55, 56, 60
Satilla River, Georgia 48
Saunders, Capt. John 144, 145
Savage, Edward 9, 35, 134
Savage, John 186, 202, 208, 210, 212
Savannah, Georgia 60–62
   British capture and occupation of, 1778-1782 56–57, 96, 123
   evacuation of 160, 162
   siege of, by French and Americans, 1779 61
Saxe-Gotha Township 1, 25
Schoepf, Johann 192
Scopholites 33, 53 n. 31, 39 n. 40
Scotch-Irish 2, 78, 84, 220. *See also* Northern Ireland
Scottish community, lowcountry 17–18, 211
Scott, John 208
Second Camden Militia (Ballentine's) Regiment 156
"Second Revolution" 89–90
Senate of South Carolina 170–171
Seneca River 74
Shaw, Alexander 200
Sheddie, Conrad 166

Shelburne, Earl of 179
Shelburne, Nova Scotia, loyalist settlements in 195, 197
Shelby, (State) Col. Isaac, of North Carolina 100, 102
Ship Harbour, Nova Scotia, loyalist settlements in 195
Shobert, George 196
Sideman, Henry 195
Sierra Leone. *See* Exiles, loyalist, Nova Scotia
Simms, William Gilmore 219 n. 34
Simons, Col. Maurice 210
Simpson, James, royal attorney general 44, 67, 136
  departs for England 35
  heads Board of Police 134, 138
  returns 74, 133
  to England 199, 202
Sing, Christian 10, 194
Skottowe, Thomas 9, 134
Smart, James 173
Smith, Levi 143
Smith, Paul 225
Smith, Thomas Loughton family 190, 211
Snell, George 195, 196
Snipes, William Clay 210
"Snow Campaign," 1775 31–32
South Carolina and American General Gazette 3, 135–136
South Carolina, British evacuation of 178–180, 182–183. *See also* Exiles, loyalist
South Carolina, British occupation of 67–87, 132–139
South Carolina, British Province of
  backcountry settlement 1–2, 9–11
  immigration to 9, 10
  lowcounrry economic and social groups 1–4, 8–9
  population, 1775 12
  relations with Great Britain 12–13
South Carolina Gazette 8, 14, 17
South Carolina (Harrison's) Rangers, loyalist provincial regiment 82, 85, 92, 121, 154, 187
  absorbed in South Carolina Royalists 155
South Carolina Royalists, loyalist provincial regiment 73, 74, 94, 95, 96, 120, 166, 167, 173
  campaigns in Georgia 57–58
  campaigns in South Carolina 62, 95, 120, 122, 158, 160
  casualties in 158, 160
  discharges in Nova Scotia 189, 197
  furlough and discharge of veterans, 1780 74
  organized in East Florida, 1778 50
  to East Florida, 1782 189
Sparrow Swamp 82
Spartan Militia (Gibbs's) Regiment 101, 156, 166
  at Kings Mountain 94
Spence, Dr. Peter 18, 207
Spurgin, John 58, 63 n. 13
Stamp Act, reaction to 13
St. Andrew's Society, Charlestown 18
St. Augustine's
  East Florida loyalist exiles to 182–183
  rebel leaders exiled to 131
Stedman, Maj. Charles 90, 116, 168
Steedham, Adam 143
Stevens Creek 1, 10, 33, 60, 78, 156, 163, 195, 215
Stevens Creek Militia (Cotton's) Regiment 102, 156, 163, 195
Stevenson, Lt. William 103
Stevens, Sheriff Daniel 207
Stewart, Col. Alexander 126
St. James Santee Parish 209
St. Lucia, British Island of 174. *See* Exiles, loyalist
St. Mark's Parish 10
St. Mary's River, East Florida 187
St. Michael's Parish, Charlestown 9, 17, 166, 210, 212
Stono Ferry, Battle of 61
Stormont, Nova Scotia 195

Index 253

St. Philip's Parish, Charlestown 17, 199, 210
St. Stephens Parish 4, 205
Stuart, Henry 36
Stuart, John, royal Supt. of Indian Affairs for the Southern Department 17, 19, 22, 27, 29, 36, 46, 56, 75
    to East Florida 51
Sumter, (State) Brig. Gen. Thomas 80, 89, 91, 92, 95, 96, 110, 115, 116, 120, 121, 122, 124, 125, 126, 143, 148, 149, 158
    efforts to enlist loyalists 159, 170
Swinney, Capt. James 158, 161 n. 18

Tamar, H.M.S. 27, 28
Tarleton, Lt. Col. Banastre 69, 70, 71, 80, 82, 84, 86, 89, 92, 94, 95, 97, 100, 103, 104, 110, 119, 120, 127, 141, 142, 146, 147, 150, 154
Taylor, Lt. John 103
Tea Act, 1773 15, 45
Thicketty Creek 26, 119
Thomas, Col. John 28, 37
Thompson, Benjamin 157
Thomson's House 120
Thomson, (State) Col. William 23, 73
Thornton, Thomas 195
Timothy, Peter 17, 135
Tonyn, (British) Gov. Patrick, of East Florida 28, 41, 48, 50, 51, 56, 63, 178, 179, 182, 188, 189, 190, 191
Torbay, England 184, 201
Townshend, Thomas 184
Tracadie, Nova Scotia 197
Treutlen, Gov. John Adam, of Georgia 161 n. 18,
Tryon County, North Carolina 90, 97, 99, 100
Tunno, Adam 201
Tunno, John, merchant 18, 35, 41, 133, 162, 201, 208
Turnbull, Lt. Col. George, of New York Volunteers 70, 84, 91, 109
Turner, Edward 212
Tweed, William 46
Tyger River 33, 36, 78, 189
Tynes, Maj. Samuel 118, 156
    commands militia regiment 83
    resigns 111

Valk, Jacob, protectionist 133
Volunteers of Ireland, loyalist provincial regiment 69, 71, 84, 121

Waccamaw River 2, 4
Walker, Benjamin 209
Washington, (Continental) Col. William 116, 117, 119, 146
Wateree River 2, 79, 84
Watson, Col. John 121, 122, 144
Waugh, Lt. David 144
Waxhaw area 2, 83, 84, 90, 120, 168
Wayne, (Continental) Brig. Gen. Anthony 183
Weaver, George 196
Weir, James 133
Weir, Robert 5
Wells, Dr. Wm. Charles, son of Robert 136, 182, 191, 211. *See also East Florida Gazette*
    attempts to return to South Carolina 208
    to East Florida 188
Wells, John, Jr., son of Robert 17, 135
    becomes loyalist 135, 135–136, 140 n. 12
    to the Bahamas 191, 192–193
Wells, Louisa Susannah, daughter of Robert 21, 135, 164
    description of voyage as an exile 44
Wells, Robert 3, 8, 17, 18, 136, 212
    departs for England 135
    establishes *South Carolina and American General Gazette* 3
Wemyss, Maj. James, of 63rd Regiment 82, 85, 89, 169
West Florida, British province of. *See*

Exiles, loyalist
Weston, Plowden 201
"White Indians" 35, 49
Whitley, Moses 48
Wigfall, Lt. Col. John 205, 209, 210
Wilkes Fund controversy 14–15
Wilkinson, Edward 29, 30, 36
Wilkinson, Eliza 164
Willard, Martin 165
Williams, Col. Hezekiah 148–149, 156–157, 161 n. 8
  Williams's Militia Regiment 148, 156, 157
Williamson, Robert 202
Williamson, (State) Brig. Gen. Andrew 1, 27, 29, 31, 35, 36, 49, 50, 59, 75, 96
  British efforts to convert 114–116
  kidnapped and released 146, 155
  relieved of penalties 215
  surrender of 75, 87 n. 8
  takes protection 96
Williams, Robert, Sr. 3, 133, 134, 201, 202
Williams's Fort 116
Williams, (State) Col. James 52
Wilmington, North Carolina, British base 120, 126, 146, 147
Wilson, Alexander 165
Wilson, Capt. Robert 103
Wilson, John 199
Wilson, Nathaniel 196
Windsor, Nova Scotia 194
Winnsboro 84
Winn, (State) Col. John 206
Woodmason, the Reverend Charles 10
Wragg, William 4, 5, 13
  death in exile 42
Wright, Alexander 133, 134, 138, 180
Wright, Gov. Sir James, of Georgia 96, 179
Wright, Major James, Jr., of Georgia 96

Yarborough, James 160
York, Capt. John 36, 40 n. 51, 49, 50

Yorktown, Virginia, Cornwallis's surrender at 104
Young, Lt. Col. William
  commands militia regiment 156, 189
  in postwar East Florida 190
  to Dominica 191
Young's Regiment, raids of, 157, 189

Zespedes, Vicente (Spanish) Gov. of East Florida 188, 189, 190

www.ingramcontent.com/pod-product-compliance
Lightning Source LLC
Chambersburg PA
CBHW022004220426
43663CB00007B/951